Sold on Language

How Advertisers Talk to You and What This Says About You

Julie Sedivy
Greg Carlson

WILEY-BLACKWELL

A John Wiley & Sons, Ltd., Publication

This edition first published 2011
© 2011 John Wiley & Sons Ltd.

Wiley-Blackwell is an imprint of John Wiley & Sons, formed by the merger of Wiley's global Scientific, Technical, and Medical business with Blackwell Publishing.

Registered Office
John Wiley & Sons Ltd, The Atrium, Southern Gate, Chichester, West Sussex, PO19 8SQ, UK

Editorial Offices
The Atrium, Southern Gate, Chichester, West Sussex, PO19 8SQ, UK
9600 Garsington Road, Oxford, OX4 2DQ, UK
350 Main Street, Malden, MA 02148-5020, USA

For details of our global editorial offices, for customer services, and for information about how to apply for permission to reuse the copyright material in this book please see our website at www.wiley.com/wiley-blackwell.

The right of Julie Sedivy and Greg Carlson to be identified as the authors of this work has been asserted in accordance with the UK Copyright, Designs and Patents Act 1988.

Library of Congress Cataloging-in-Publication Data

Sedivy, Julie.
    Sold on language : how advertisers talk to you and what this says about you / Julie Sedivy, Greg Carlson.
        p. cm.
    Includes bibliographical references and index.
    ISBN 978-0-470-68309-5 (pbk.)
    1. Advertising–Language. 2. Advertising. I. Carlson, Greg N., 1948- II. Title.
    HF5821.S446 2011
    659.101'4–dc22

                                                                            2010035847

A catalogue record for this book is available from the British Library.

Set in 10/12 pt, Minion Regular by Thomson Digital, Noida, India
Printed and bound in Singapore by Fabulous Printers Pte Ltd

3   2012

For my parents, Vera and Ladislav, who understood better than most the power of choice.
—JS

To sons Matthew and Geoffrey, in fondest hopes for their world.
—GC

Contents

About the Authors   ix

Preface   xi

1   The Power of Choice   1

2   The Unconscious Consumer   15

3   The Attentional Arms Race   59

4   We Know What You're Thinking   97

5   Why Ads Don't Say What They Mean
    (Or Mean What They Say)   123

6   Acting Out   157

7   Divide and Conquer   193

8   The Politics of Choice   245

Sources   291

Index   307

About the Authors

Julie Sedivy was formerly an Associate Professor at Brown University, and is now an Adjunct Associate Professor at the University of Calgary. She has taught Linguistics and Cognitive Science for the past 15 years, and has authored and co-authored several dozen articles on language and the mind. She currently lives and writes in Calgary, and climbs nearby rocks.

Greg Carlson is Professor of Linguistics, Philosophy, and Brain and Cognitive Sciences at the University of Rochester. He has authored or co-authored more than a hundred articles on natural language semantics and psycholinguistics. He is the author of *Reference to Kinds in English* and is co-editor of *The Generic Book* with F.J. Pelletier. Professor Carlson is a former editor of the journal *Linguistics and Philosophy* and is currently editor of *Language*, the journal of the Linguistic Society of America.

Preface

This book is what happens when a couple of language scientists start talking about ads. In our case, the seeds for this book were sown more than 15 years ago. It went like this: The first author (Julie Sedivy) was working on a PhD in Linguistics with the second author (Greg Carlson). Now, the thing about language is that once you start getting analytical about it, you can't stop. So research meetings would often trail off into discussions about language and meaning in everyday life. Since everyday life happens to be saturated by advertising, it became a natural target for all this analytical excess. Eventually, we decided we'd gathered enough material that we should put it to some good use, so we developed a class on the topic. Nature took its course, Julie graduated and took a job elsewhere, but both of us continued to teach the class at our home institutions. In fact, over time, the ideas grew to preoccupy us more and more, and as we continued thinking about them, took on a seriousness that went far beyond their origins as interesting diversions.

As our original observations about advertising have rolled on through the years, they've picked up a great deal of material from fields that are outside of our immediate areas of research. They've also picked up many insights and examples from students over time, a number of whom write to us years after taking the class with just one more example of an ad that reminded them of something they learned in that long-ago language and advertising course. These students have shown us that teaching is the art of serendipity. Each of us has had the experience of finding out that something we intended as only the most casual of remarks, or the stray example, changes what some student thought to the point of changing their lives in some important way. It is experiences like these that propelled us to take the step from the comfortable activity of teaching to the torturous activity of writing a book. You never know where that stray remark will land.

A note on pronouns: Being linguists, we had lengthy discussions as to what "author voice" to use. For aesthetic reasons, we settled on the first person singular form "*I*," even though two of us stand behind the pronoun. Just think of the referent as your favorite amalgamation of a short jazz-loving, rock-climbing, Canadian/American female of Czech descent and a six-foot-five Midwesterner with Scandinavian roots who occasionally goes deer-hunting but has only ever hit one with his pick-up truck. The result will no doubt be more interesting than either one of us.

As always, thanks are in order. First and foremost we'd like to thank and formally apologize to those people who put up with us in the final (truly torturous) stages of writing this book. Gratitude to Craig Chambers, Kate Sedivy-Haley, and Ian Graham for reading sections of this book, sometimes at points when they were still unreadable. An especially warm thanks to writers Brad Somer, Nancy Hayes, Elena Aitken, and Leanne Shirtliffe for helping us make the step from academic English into English English in the writing of this book.

1

The Power of Choice

A trillion dollars is, as they say, a lot of money. A lot. Here's what you do. You take a house, yours will do fine, and remove all the furniture, rugs, dinnerware, everything. Once everything is cleared out, pack the house full of sand. Floor to ceiling. Make sure you open the closet and cabinet doors. Don't forget the medicine chest. Every inch. Now, sharpen your tweezers and start counting the grains of sand, one at a time, until you have counted every grain of sand in the house. Let's just ignore the fact it would take you maybe three or four thousand years at 24 hours a day, more if you wanted to sleep, eat, have a life, etc. Done with your house? Good! Now persuade your neighbors to move all their belongings out, and pack their house with sand and count all of those grains. You're not done yet. Go to the next house, then the next, and do the same for three more down the street. You're finally done—you have now counted a trillion grains of sand, and if you received one dollar for every grain you counted, you'd be the world's first (and oldest) trillionaire.

Your bank account now would hold as much money as is spent each year worldwide on advertising and marketing. Actually, the amount spent is a "little" more, a few hundred billion dollars more, but let's not sweat the details. Roughly 40% of this figure is in the United States. The companies typically with the largest advertising budgets, Procter & Gamble, Verizon Wireless, General Motors, Johnson & Johnson, etc., each spend in the ballpark of two billion annually on advertising. Two billion is nothing to sneeze at. If you had this money and invested it unimaginatively, you could retire on an income of maybe $100 million per year and buy that fleet of helicopters you've always dreamed of. Come to think of it, if P&G didn't advertise at all for a year, the execs there could just keep that two billion, invest it, and grab that extra 100 mil for themselves to split with their golf buddies (and since they wouldn't invest it unimaginatively, probably a lot more).

But companies typically choose not to keep the money for themselves. That money spent is, like most other company expenditures, an investment. It's expected to yield returns. If your company spends $10 000 on advertising your new juice squeezer, you expect to get in return more than $10 000 in profits coming

Sold on Language: How Advertisers Talk to You and What This Says About You. By Julie Sedivy and Greg Carlson
© 2011 John Wiley & Sons Ltd.

from increased juice squeezer sales. Like investing in new plants to produce truck transmissions, or new machinery to put the toothpaste in the tube, the expectation is return on investment—you spend the money in order to make even more money. And the annual worldwide investment of a trillion dollars plus change is expected to yield more than that in profits.

Looked at this way, advertising is responsible for a great deal of economic prosperity. Just consider momentarily what might happen if all advertising suddenly disappeared. Let's not dwell on the unemployed advertising executives forced to retire early to their condos, but look at the potential broader effects. We know several things for certain. You'd have to pay a lot more for your suddenly much thinner newspapers and magazines, and doubtless many would go out of business. You'd also have to pay a lot to watch television (though you'd have an extra 15–20 minutes per hour of actual programming to watch instead of commercials). Sales of existing products would plummet, and new products would be few and far between. With far more than a trillion dollars in decreased profits, unemployment would soar, tax revenues would dry up, and investment would lag. A worldwide depression would set in, one we would never recover from—except by reintroducing advertising. From this view, the presence of advertising is not merely a sign of prosperity—it's a major cause of it. Raise a glass to Madison Avenue.

Salvation Through Advertising

But some people go even further than this in singing the praises of advertising. The greatest cheerleader for the ad industry may well have been none other than a long-ago president of the United States. It was the Roaring Twenties, a time of unprecedented economic growth and optimism in America. The stock market was booming, with no end in sight—at least for the time being. Reigning over this euphoria was President Calvin Coolidge from Vermont, nicknamed "Silent Cal" for his sparing use of Yankee words. But in 1926, addressing a group of admen at their annual convention, Cal was far from silent. He got downright lyrical about the unparalleled virtues of the advertising industry:

> *Advertising ministers to the spiritual side of trade. It is a great power that has been entrusted to your keeping which charges you with the highest responsibility of inspiring and ennobling the commercial world. It is all part of the greater work of the regeneration and redemption of mankind.*

This is religious language full force. It might appear somewhat out of place in our era. After all, he's talking about the very people who brought us Ronald McDonald, the Jolly Green Giant, and the Pillsbury Doughboy. Hardly religious iconography. But Coolidge saw in advertising's fruits the salvation of mankind:

The uncivilized make little progress because they have few desires. The inhabitants of our country are stimulated to new wants in all directions. In order to satisfy their constantly increasing desires, they necessarily expand their productive power. They create more wealth because it is only by that method that they can satisfy their wants. It is this constantly enlarging circle that represents the progress of civilization. If we proceed under the present system, there would appear to be little reason to doubt that we can maintain all of these high standards in wages, in output and in consumption indefinitely.

Coolidge was very clear that advertisers do much more than just cater to people's existing wants and needs. Advertising is *regenerative* because it creates entirely new wants and desires, ones that would never visit our neurons were it not for advertising. And, this creation of new wants is a good thing as it civilizes and enriches everyone. It is the engine of progress. Unlike the Buddhists' Nirvana which results from the absence of desire, the capitalist's Nirvana is achieved by reveling in want and desire, by fully embracing it.

Coolidge's glittering remarks contain some perfectly valid points, leaving aside for a moment the gathering clouds of the Great Depression, or the fact that eventually, we would need to colonize nearby planets in order to continue this endless regenerative trajectory. But as Coolidge continued his speech, he went on to say a few things that would make even the less cynical among us squirm a bit. Advertisers, it would seem, belong on the same pedestal as that first-grade teacher who taught you to sound out your words, or that college professor who enflamed a simmering intellectual passion:

When we stop to consider the part in which advertising plays in the life of production and trade, we see that basically it is that of education.

Coolidge's key assumption about how consumers and advertisers related to each other was that the whole thing was all about the transmission of information; the advertiser provided it, and the consumer evaluated and considered it. Teachers (advertisers) would act out of a sense of responsibility to their students (consumers), and students (consumers) would act out of trust. With this bond firmly in place, positive business practices would flourish. Because they served as the pipelines of information between companies and consumers—and who wants to serve as a pipeline for sewage?—advertising would apply gentle pressure on the business world, giving more room to its angels than its demons:

My conception of what advertising agencies want is a business world in which standards are so high that it will only be necessary for them to tell the truth about it. It will never be possible to create a permanent desire for things that do not have permanent worth. It is my belief that more and more of our country is conforming to these principles.

History has a way of making all predictions seem either prescient or clueless, and Coolidge's over-the-top jubilation about the economic situation of the time now seems badly off the mark. It's also hard to buy into the idealistic and sentimental portrayal of advertisers as conduits of truthful and useful information to a receptive, discerning, thoughtful public.

The problem is that the notion of advertising as education only limps along for a block or two before tripping over some fundamentally flawed assumptions.

"Education" as we know it these days brings to mind things like seminars, instructional videos, NOVA television series, news articles, books, informational websites, and so on. But using such educational materials has a very different feel than our typical interactions with advertising. Think about tuning in to an educational program about emperor penguins, for example. Imagine what a "documentary" on emperor penguins might be like if it were presented in the format of a typical television commercial:

> *Panning shot of the frozen wind-blown wasteland of Antarctica.*
> *Cut to shot of the sea by the ice shelf.*
> > **Sound: "plop"**
> *Cut to another shot of water by the ice shelf: nothing.*
> > **Sound: "plop, plop"**
> *Cut to still another shot of the sea on an ice shelf: still nothing.*
> > **Sounds: "plop, plop … plop plop plop … plop plop …"**
> *Cut to shot of a flock of Emperor penguins diving into the sea, each one making a "plopping" sound when they hit the water.*
> *Cut to one "tobogganing" into the water on its belly.*
> **Voice-over: Emperor penguins. Hundreds of them.**
> *Cut to shot of penguins swimming underwater gracefully (graceful music here).*
> **Voice-over: Emperor penguins, ballet artists in the water…**
> *Cut to shot of penguin waddling across the ice (bouncy simple music here).*
> **Voice-over: …but out of the water, they walk like Charlie Chaplin…**
> **Voice-over: Emperor penguins: In Antarctica and at selected zoos and**
> **aquariums.**
> *Cut to close-up of penguin apparently laughing and clapping its flippers.*

To watch something that went on and on like this for even half an hour would feel really strange. Yeah, penguins are cute, but what else did you learn? The "educational" aspect of modern ads obviously doesn't measure up to the content we see in media broadcasts that everyone agrees are truly educational.

Conflict of Interest

Why is it that your typical TV commercial is so different from a documentary program? The differences stem from this single essential fact: advertising is a form of persuasion. This means that from square one, your goals and interests are often very different from those of the advertiser. Let's say your goal is to buy the best dishwashing machine you can afford. I don't have to be the first to break it to you that this is not the main concern of an advertising copywriter for Maytag. He's unlikely to suffer a single pang of failure upon finding out that, by buying the washer in his beautifully-crafted ad, you've passed up a wiser purchase. If you really want to read something that's written with your best interests in mind, you pick up a copy of *Consumer Reports*, you don't go flipping through *Good Housekeeping* to find that Maytag ad you saw last week. When you do read the ad, you take it for granted that any comparisons it makes to the competition are not necessarily "fair and balanced."

You're well aware that the whole point of ads is to try to get you to align your *perception* of your own interests with the interests of the company doing the advertising. But when you watch a documentary, your goals in watching it are already aligned just about exactly with the communication goals of the people who made the program. You watch mainly to learn something about penguins (and to be entertained); the goal of the program's creators is mainly to teach you something about penguins (and to entertain you). There's a reason why documentaries aren't required to remind you, "*You are watching an educational program. Its content has been approved by the National Geographic Society.*" A message to that effect wouldn't cause you to suddenly revise how you view that footage about emperor penguin dads hatching baby chicks on their feet. You wouldn't suspect the program of being thinly-veiled penguin propaganda. On the other hand, ads *are* legally required to be readily identifiable as such, because the mindset you bring to persuasive communication is very different.

It seems to take small children some time to learn that persuasive messages are different from ones that provide helpful information, which is one reason some people have raised concerns about advertising aimed at kids (and some places, such as Quebec and the UK have outright forbidden ads targeted at children younger than 13).[1] It was, therefore, a point of parental pride when I watched the following interaction between my then five-year-old daughter and her young friend who was visiting for breakfast and coveting her cereal.

> **Friend:** You should try _my_ cereal. It's much better than _your_ cereal. Here. Let's trade.
> **Daughter** (barely looking up from the bowl): Naaah. That's just advertising.

Interestingly, the skill of persuasion-detection appears earlier in kids who have older siblings (and, I would guess, friends who attempt manipulation). Seems that there are learning benefits to being thrown into social interactions in which there are flagrant conflicts of interest.

---

[1] The prohibition in the UK, though, had more to do with the impact of advertising on childhood obesity than with general concern about kids' critical abilities.

Looking back at Coolidge's speech, he seems to be assuming that the goals of advertisers and consumers are more or less synced up. It's easy to see how, given this rosy view, you might reach the same conclusion Coolidge did, and have faith that advertising would exert a noble pressure on the business world for higher standards. If advertising is basically a mutually beneficial transmission of information, the best ad will be the one that is able to transmit the most glowing information about the product. This depends on there being positive things about the product to transmit, which puts pressure on companies to make good products.

But the collision of interests makes persuasion quite a bit different from not just things like teaching math, but almost anything else you might do with language, such as reciting a poem, gossiping, news reporting, helping someone fix their car, or taking a medical history.

It turns out that persuasion isn't the only act of communication in which the goals of the hearer and speaker are out of sync. There are other times when the interests of the speaker may veer off from those of the hearer.

For example, consider this excerpt from a news article about Russia's lackluster performance in the 2010 Winter Olympics:

> *Russia suffered its worst ever Olympic performance, coming 11th in the medal table with just three golds. Mr. Medvedev said that the trainers and coaches who had prepared Russian athletes for the Vancouver games 'should take the brave decision and submit their resignations,' he said. 'If they cannot do it, we will help them,' Mr. Medvedev added.*

It's doubtful that the ensuing resignation of trainers and coaches could truly be deemed to be due to an act of *persuasion* (even though it might euphemistically be called that). It doesn't count as persuasion unless the persuadee has some choice in the matter in the first place; absent that, he's been coerced, or commanded, not persuaded.

Some other examples of nonpersuasion: a boss tells an employee to write a tedious report, a parent orders a resistant child to unplug himself from his videogame and play outside, a professor instructs perspiring students to turn in their exam papers. In these cases, the speaker's goal—as in persuasion—is also to affect the hearer's actions, and it doesn't much matter whether this is what the hearer *really* wants in the first place. But the hearer does as he's told because he accepts that the speaker has authority over his actions (or at least some of them) simply by speaking. This is part of the implicit ground rules.

Things get more complex—and more interesting—when the hearer hasn't abdicated control over his actions. To successfully persuade, the speaker has to do more than simply utter some words under the cloak of authority. She has to change not just the hearer's actions, but also the internal state that leads to those actions. She has to impact the hearer's *choice*. These two elements—potential misalignment of goals, and the power of choice—set persuasion apart from all other types of communication, and run through every aspect of our interactions with advertising.

So, there's no persuasion without choice. And the instant there's choice, the door is flung wide open for persuasion.

The Downside of Choice

It would be fun to put Calvin Coolidge in a time machine so that he could see for himself the glorious result of that upward spiral of stimulated wants and expanded production. I'd like to assign psychologist Barry Schwartz, author of *The Paradox of Choice*, as his tour guide. A stroll through Barry's neighborhood grocery store would reveal the following:

285 varieties of cookies (including 21 chocolate chip varieties)
13 "sports drinks"
65 "box drinks" for kids
85 other flavors and brands of juices
15 flavors of bottled water
80 different kinds and permutations of pain relievers
29 different chicken soups
120 pasta sauces
175 salad dressings
15 extra-virgin olive oils
275 varieties of cereal
175 types of tea bags

And the local electronics store offers up:

45 different car stereo speakers, with 50 different speaker sets
42 different computers, most customizable in various ways
27 printers
110 televisions
50 DVD players
20 video cameras
85 telephones (not counting cell phones)
and enough components to combine into 6,512,000 differently-configured stereo systems.

It's hard to imagine that in the 1960s and 1970s, when factories were spewing out battalions of the same model of car or television set, people actually worried that the age of mass production and mass consumption would usher in the *end* of choice. There was much fretting by cultural commentators that the technology of mass standardization would turn all consumers into uniform, undifferentiated, robotic automatons who would all drive the same vehicles, serve the same TV dinners, read the same magazines, and watch the same shows. The sun was about to set on the age of the individual.

What bunk, wrote Alvin Toffler, author of *Future Shock*. His book, published in 1970, correctly predicted that technological advances in production would bring about a super-industrial age in which it would soon be possible to produce a jaw-dropping *variety* of products very cheaply. Rather than being on the threshold of the death of choice, society was on the brink of overchoice. Toffler was much less worried about there being too little of it, and far more worried about there being too much.

Living as we do in a culture that worships choice, it might be hard to lose sleep at night over the idea of too much choice. After all, a time-traveling Coolidge might go slightly and temporarily catatonic in the face of all these purchasing decisions, but once he got over the culture shock, he'd surely adapt and revel in the multitude of consumer possibilities.

But some psychologists these days think that when it comes to the impact of choice on well-being, more choice is often less happiness. For instance, Barry Schwartz, who's been kind enough to take the time-traveling Coolidge shopping, can provide a litany of reasons why too much choice diminishes happiness. For one, the process of making decisions is actually not all that enjoyable. People often experience stress when they have to decide, and in many cases will jump at the chance to avoid the whole hassle. Too much choice can even induce buyer-paralysis; in one study, when researchers allowed people to sample different varieties of jams in a grocery store, 30% of customers made a purchase when they were offered six samples. But when facing down a dizzying 24 options, only 3% bought anything at all. And nowadays, consumer products are often marketed and perceived by consumers as not just useful or desirable *things*, but as tools for expressing who you are. This raises the stakes—a bad purchase doesn't just saddle you with a lousy product, it can leave you stuck with a crummy identity as well. Do you buy the plain yellow French's mustard, the honey mustard, or the Dijon made with white wine and tarragon for your guests? And what does it all say about *you*?

Moreover, the more choices you have, the greater the opportunity for regretting all the things you could have chosen but didn't. The pain of regret can be so sharp that people are often happier with situations in which they've had little choice, which may explain why arranged marriages can be surprisingly successful. And all the time and energy you spend on navigating your way through a sea of choices in life—choosing the right school for junior, updating your wardrobe, figuring out what health plan is best for you, deciding how to invest your retirement savings—may take you away from the things that truly make people happy in life: cultivating friendships and spending quality time with family and loved ones.

There are many reasons to think choice might be overrated.

But for Alvin Toffler, the consequences of too much choice went beyond just the stresses and anxieties that come with making a zillion decisions, large and small, on a daily basis. He hinted that beyond a certain point, too much freedom would lead to unfreedom.

He may have had a point. When pollster Louis Harris asked people in 1966 whether they agreed with the statement "What I think doesn't matter anymore," 36% agreed. In 1986, with the super-industrial age in full swing, 60% agreed.

To see how too much choice can eventually lead to a loss of control, imagine yourself in the greatest possible position of power—suppose you're a benevolent dictator with unchallenged control over the nation you govern. The ultimate choice over any important matter of policy lies in your hands alone. But this also sets you up as the nation's biggest persuasion target. There will be lots of people seeking to influence you for a number of reasons that may or may not be consistent with your own goals. These interactions will come in many guises. In some interactions, you'll still able to maintain a good deal of control over the decision-making process and its outcome. For example, you'll hold meetings with trusted consultants whose advice you'll seek out. You'll set these up at a special time when you're not distracted by other things, and you'll decide who to invite. You'll tell them what you're hoping to accomplish, and they'll come prepared to make a reasoned case with detailed information to present to you. You'll understand that they may have their own interests and they might argue passionately for one solution over another, and you take this into account. Because they really want to impact your choice, they in turn will put pressure on others to be able to deliver on promises they'd like to be able to make to you.

This is the kind of scenario that Coolidge had in mind for consumers, a situation in which the consumer's power to choose and the advertiser's desire to influence yield the greatest good for the greatest number. But this idealized set of conditions happens in only a pretty narrow set of consumer situations. Shopping for a dishwasher is probably not a bad example. You've identified certain features as important to you: You need something that will fit in a specific space in your kitchen, and you really want it to be quiet. You're on a tight budget, so it has to be pretty inexpensive and reliable. You don't care if it can wash pots and pans, as you normally do these by hand anyway. Armed with a checklist of your needs, you set about finding out which model of dishwasher best fits them. You read spec sheets and talk to salespeople about the features of the dishwashers. You expect that the information provided to you is accurate, and you can check it against consumer reports, so you can easily hold the salespeople accountable for what they tell you.

But consumers and powerful leaders alike are targets of persuasion whether it's invited or not. As our fearless leader, you'll be bombarded on all sides by attempts to get you to make certain decisions. Some of these will be overtly aggressive, with implicit or explicit threats of terrible things happening if you don't choose some course of action. But many of these will be covert and manipulative. Some may zero in on your desire to be flattered and admired by people you care about. Some may work by sowing seeds of distrust in you towards other people who might have influence over you. Some may be so subtle and carefully concealed that you won't even recognize them as attempts to influence you at all. You'll simply encounter a set of circumstances that seems to lead to a single obvious solution. You'll believe that it was entirely your own conclusion, reached entirely through your own judgment. In order to truly maintain control, rather than a self-delusion of control, you'll have to be very alert to all of these sources of influence. You'll also really need to understand your own vulnerabilities and possible weaknesses that might expose you to being manipulated against your will.

Likewise, as a consumer, advertising comes at you whether you want it or not, and whether or not you have the time, mental energy or interest to really process the information it contains. Advertising interrupts the TV shows or radio programs you *have* chosen to tune in to. It's peppered throughout the articles you're trying to read. It pops up on your computer screen with attention-grabbing animations. It floods your physical and virtual mailboxes. It interrupts your dinner through perky telemarketers' phone calls. It has to compete with other advertising, or with other information that you may or may not want to attend to at the moment.

So, the problem of too much choice is not just that there are too may decisions to make. It's that as consumer choice escalates, it sets off an arms-race-style chain of consequences. By holding the power of choice in your fist, you become a target for persuasion. Because of the endless profusion of your choices, there's ferocious competition to influence your decisions. Modern communication technology makes it easy for advertisers to fill every nook and cranny of your life with ads. You get blasted with more information than you can sift through in any thoughtful or deliberate manner, so you try to screen much of it out. In order to penetrate this screen, advertisers become more and more savvy at getting through. They develop techniques to bypass your attentional defenses with ever harder-to-ignore ads, or by placing ads in new, unexpected places. Ads proliferate. They get more compressed. Denied an appointment with your deliberate attention, they start to rely less on facts and arguments, and more on gut-level feelings that can be stirred up even when you're not paying that much attention. More and more persuasive messages are covert, affecting you outside the sphere of your conscious, rational decision to exercise your powers of judgment. Advertising comes to work more and more on the edges of your awareness.

At what stage does your power of choice bring you down a path to the point where you're less and less able to actually be the true agent of this power, like a puppet dictator whose strings are pulled from backstage?

The Illusion of Choice

It's worth asking: What does it mean to choose? Some fuzziness arises. When in 1997, 39 members of the Heaven's Gate cult drank poison and wrapped their heads in plastic bags so that they could be beamed up to a higher plane of existence, it was hard not to see them as victims of their charismatic leader, Marshall Applewhite.

And yet, they left behind videotapes in which they grinned with joy as they described how they were about to advance "beyond human." Several members of the sect posted "Earth exit statements" on the Heaven's Gate website (which was still up as of 2010, by the way). One statement, by a member who took on the name of "Glnody" reads:

> First let me explain that our Older Members have upon numerous occasions given us each the task of carefully examining and deciding if we are absolutely sure that Ti and Do [Applewhite and his partner leader] are indeed from the Next Level and that we want to continue on in this classroom. The door out of this classroom has always been wide open. Those who have decided to leave have never been asked to reconsider or coerced to stay in any way. We never expressed animosity at their leaving but instead sent them off with hugs and best wishes, wanting only the best for them.

Like many cult members, the Heaven's Gate group fervently believed they were acting of their own free will. How do we know they were not? Why can't we take their insistence at face value?

Though little is known about the inner workings of the Heaven's Gate cult itself, nowadays, psychologists who study cult behavior can usually point to a number of specific persuasion methods and group dynamics that can lead people to extreme behavior they might never agree to in a different environment. These methods tend not to be that different in kind from run-of-the-mill techniques that might be used by your typical gifted salesman. They're just applied much more aggressively and systematically so that members experience total immersion in the persuasive environment. All of which suggests that persuasion and coercion—and choice and nonchoice—can begin to shade into each other.[2]

What's striking about many cult members, though, is that they themselves are usually blind as to why they're making the choices they are. They can't acknowledge that there are extreme aspects of the group environment—insulation from alternative messages, intense social approval or disapproval by the group, a shedding of individual identity to be replaced by a group identity—that are playing havoc with their thinking. When experts try to deprogram these victims, they focus a lot of effort on getting them to understand how such external factors affected their decisions. Once the victim is able to do this, the "choice" to belong to the cult often evaporates.

---

[2] Sometimes this shading poses very subtle legal challenges. In 2004, a Massachusetts court acquitted a mother who acted under the "leading" of a fellow sect member, and starved her child by feeding him nothing but breast milk. Being pregnant, she failed to produce enough milk, and the child died. The defense case was built on arguments that the mother had lost the capacity for free choice, as she was being brainwashed by the cult. Demonstrating the shades of gray inherent in such a ruling, her husband was convicted and sentenced to life in prison, as the court deemed that his ability to choose was not compromised to the same degree.

So a good test of what it means to make a real choice might be whether the choice would be the same or different depending on whether you're aware of exactly how and why it was made.

Having some *awareness* of the things that are causing your internal state seems important. So is being able to have some control over them. When both of these are missing, you have the sense that your power of choice is seriously undermined, even when the ultimate decision to act rests in your hands.

To bring us back from the realm of cults and into the world of commerce here's a hypothetical news story for you: let's say the beef industry has developed a tasteless and odorless chemical that causes intense cravings for red meat. The industry cuts a deal with Pepsi, and pays to have this chemical dissolved in Pepsi's products. The practice is, strictly speaking legal, as the chemical has been proven to be completely harmless, and is listed under its scientific name in the list of ingredients, along with all the flavorings and additives. Anyone is free to look up the properties of this chemical on the Internet, and decide not to drink Pepsi, should they be inspired to research the ingredients. Chances are, though, that if this practice were discovered, it would result in a public outcry and legislators would scramble to regulate the use of such substances. There's something about this that makes us feel that choice is violated.

This scenario sounds like science fiction. More science than fiction, though. Everyday science tells us that it's entirely possible to understand and alter internal states in targeted ways, here and now. For example, in 2005, neuroscientist Michael Kosfeld and his colleagues at the University of Zurich had subjects sniff a nasal spray containing oxytocin. This is the hormone that plays a starring role in enhancing bonding behavior – mothers who have just given birth or are nursing are awash in it, and having an orgasm causes it to spike nicely. The Zurich team had their subjects play an investment "game"—with real money at stake— in which "investor" participants chose how much money to entrust to "trustee" partici-pants, who then freely decided how much of the invested money they would return to the investor. Subjects who'd been given a squirt of oxytocin risked more money than those who'd inhaled a placebo. The oxytocin seemed to specifically home in on the investor's willingness to trust the other participant. It wasn't that it just made the subjects more willing to take risks. To rule this out, the researchers ran a comparison study in which the investors' return was determined purely randomly, rather than by human participants. If oxytocin affected risk-taking, rather than trust, it should make the oxytocin-sniffing subjects invest more money, but it didn't.

Studies like this always attract the attention of the mainstream media, as this one did, and invite speculations about possible sinister abuses of this knowledge. Nightmarish speculations ensue: imagine politicians misting the crowd with oxytocin at political rallies. Imagine banks piping in oxytocin during clients' meetings with financial advisors. Surely, the public needs to be protected from such possible assaults on individual freedom.

Hang on, say the neuroscientists. What's missing from this dystopian speculation is the fact that oxytocin is *already* likely being manipulated in all kinds of ways by marketers and politicians and the like. It's a chemical produced by the brain. All kinds of things can cause it to be released, including *information* we take in subconsciously or consciously that leads us to size up someone's trustworthiness. A sales person chit-chatting about your cute kids, and using your first name. The firmness of a canvasser's handshake. The fact that a political candidate uses the same regional accent you do. The connotations that slogans evoke. The uproar over the oxytocin study ignores the fact that brain science's greatest discovery over the past couple of decades has been this: our brains are shaped by more than just our DNA, or the drugs we ingest. They're also shaped by our *experiences*, and by the information we take in. As neuroscientist Antonio Damasio wrote in a commentary about the Zurich hormone study, "current marketing techniques—for political and other products—may well exert their effects through the natural release of molecules such as oxytocin in response to well-crafted stimuli. Civic alarm at the prospect of such abuses should have started long before this study."

In fact, the trajectory of advertising in the super-industrial age, in which more and more ads fight for smaller and smaller slivers of your attention, shifts the balance steadily towards the use of techniques that affect our brains without our awareness. It's important to realize that all this isn't part of some grand conspiracy in which malevolent corporations and ad agencies purposely set out to deceive and control you. It comes from a dynamic pattern of communicative moves and countermoves in which both consumers and advertisers try to preserve their own often conflicting interests. It can arise in any situation where someone has a choice that others want to influence.

Philosophers as far back in time as Plato were aware of this connection (though Plato certainly didn't couch it in terms of brain chemistry), and flagged it as a troublesome side effect of the freedom of choice in a political democracy. In his classic essay "The rhetoric of democracy," author Daniel Boorstin writes:

> One of the tendencies of democracy, which Plato and the other antidemocrats warned against a long time ago, was the danger that rhetoric would displace or at least overshadow epistemology; that is, the temptation to allow the problem of persuasion to overshadow the problem of knowledge. Democratic societies tend to become more concerned with what people believe than with what is true, to become more concerned with credibility than truth. All these problems are accentuated in a large-scale democracy like ours, which possesses all the apparatus of modern industry. And the problems are accentuated still further by universal literacy, by instantaneous communication, and by the daily plague of words and images.

Plato, as you'll see in Chapter 8, had some rather creative and radical solutions to this conundrum, all involving a dramatic reduction of choice for the general population. This kind of strategy doesn't fly too readily in most Western societies, but the problem remains: what to do when apparent choice is not necessarily true choice? There's some grappling to be done.

Not to push the cult analogy too far, but for the average consumer, much of the cognitive action that happens in the face of persuasion falls below a threshold of awareness. We rarely truly understand exactly how and why we respond to advertising. The analogy has its limits—brilliant or subtle advertising may move us, but it doesn't usually reduce us to cult-like followers. It rarely has the power to make us do something we weren't kind of inclined to do anyway, and if it ever caused someone to become fully detached from a sense of right and wrong, there was surely a pre-existing psychiatric condition. But it works at the margins of our actions, and, like the hormonal nasal spray, it often works in parts of our brains that are hidden to us.

Just as deprogramming can sometimes restore choice to cult members, having a clearer sense of how our minds work when advertisers talk to us can only bolster our own power for choice. Stringent regulation isn't the answer—how on earth could you regulate how someone dresses, or the emotional content of the words they use, or whether they call you by your first name? But scientific understanding of the processes that underlie persuasive language—while still primitive in many ways—does offer a starting point for awareness. In knowing our own minds a bit better, we just may put ourselves into a better position to choose how we choose.

2

The Unconscious Consumer

According to Sigmund Freud, the founder of psychoanalysis, we live in constant danger of having our unconscious memories and longings grab us by the throat and lead us down a path of irrational choices. Even worse, these lurking drives can shape our decisions even while we fool ourselves into thinking that we are rationally sizing up the piles of pros and cons we've meticulously gathered. By throwing a glaring spotlight onto the unconscious, Freud reshaped the study of the mind. Not all modern psychologists buy his theories about penis envy and little boys wanting to marry their mothers. But they do agree that a lot of the machinery that drives the decisions we make or even the way we process information lies outside of our conscious control or awareness. Freud probed these hidden motivators by having people lie on a couch and relate their dreams and memories. Today, scientists of the mind probe them with clever experimental tasks in labs and use expensive devices to measure the gaze patterns of eyes, and the electrical activity and blood flow in the brain. All this technological proliferation just emphasizes how elusive our own minds are to us.

"Torches of Freedom"

The implications of Freud's ideas for persuasion were immediately snatched up by none other than his nephew, Edward Bernays. It's hard to imagine these two men as related. Freud was a thoughtful, articulate, scholarly man in the traditional European mold. American culture left a bad taste in his mouth. His American nephew was a brash entrepreneur who not only embraced the ideals of consumerism and capitalism, but did a great deal to advance them. Just as Freud can be seen as one of the great innovators in the field of psychology, Bernays played a founding role in the field of public relations as

Sold on Language: How Advertisers Talk to You and What This Says About You. By Julie Sedivy and Greg Carlson
© 2011 John Wiley & Sons Ltd.

we know it today. He did so by borrowing many of his uncle's ideas and applying them to the practice of persuasion—and then returned the favor by promoting his uncle's books, helping Freud achieve the stature he enjoyed in America.

At the time, much of advertising tried to persuade by appealing to the intellect, enumerating good reasons to buy a product. Bernays was fascinated by the possibility that persuasion could work best by cutting a wide loop around the rational intellect and drilling straight into the mother lode of those unconscious desires his uncle Sigi talked about. He began what would turn out to be some of the most defining experiments in persuasion.

Bernays understood that to sell a product, a company could do much more than promise to satisfy a need or desire for that product—it could promise consumers that they could use the product to satisfy a *deeper* need. Sometimes he created such a link by exploiting symbolism and attitudes that were already present. For example, in 1929, Bernays was consulting for Lucky Strikes cigarettes. The company had recognized that wads of money could be made by inducing women to smoke—only problem was, there was a pesky social taboo against females smoking in public, seriously cutting into potential sales. Bernays made tracks to a local psychoanalyst, who informed him that women equated cigarettes with masculine power, and that for some, cigarettes could be seen as "torches of freedom". Bernays had his angle. He snagged a list of 30 debutantes from a friend at *Vogue* magazine, and sent each of them the following telegram, signed by his secretary:

IN THE INTERESTS OF EQUALITY OF THE SEXES AND TO FIGHT ANOTHER SEX TABOO I AND OTHER YOUNG WOMEN WILL LIGHT ANOTHER TORCH OF FREEDOM BY SMOKING CIGARETTES WHILE STROLLING ON FIFTH AVENUE EASTER SUNDAY. WE ARE DOING THIS TO COMBAT THE SILLY PREJUDICE THAT THE CIGARETTE IS SUITABLE FOR THE HOME, THE RESTAURANT, THE TAXICAB, THE THEATER LOBBY BUT NEVER NO NEVER FOR THE SIDEWALK. WOMEN SMOKERS AND THEIR ESCORTS WILL STROLL FROM FORTY-EIGHT STREET TO FIFTY-FOURTH STREET ON FIFTH AVENUE BETWEEN ELEVEN-THIRTY AND ONE O'CLOCK.

An ad with similar wording, signed by a prominent feminist, also urged women to participate in this "protest". The recruitment efforts picked up 10 willing debutantes. Bernays was ready, having alerted the papers. The next day, their front pages reported on this parade of 10 young female radicals lighting up their "torches of freedom". The American public was outraged and delighted, and independent-minded young women everywhere lit up their cigarettes to express their emancipation.

In other cases, Bernays created out of whole cloth an association between a product and a set of attributes that the product was in fact sorely lacking. On one occasion, his product was none other than President Calvin Coolidge, who we've heard express such gleeful enthusiasm for the practice of advertising. Coolidge was what we might today describe as somewhat challenged in the "cool" department. The terms *charismatic, warm* and *dynamic* were just not heard in the same sentence as the president's name. More likely were words like *austere, reticent,* and *solemn* if not outright *dour.* Alice Roosevelt Longworth suggested that Coolidge was "weaned on a pickle." His gregariousness was in such short supply, that the author Dorothy Parker is reported to have said upon hearing of his death, "How can they tell?"

To counteract these impressions, Bernays was charged with the task of demonstrating Coolidge's warmer and cuddlier side. Not to worry. Bernays decided that stage celebrities best symbolized the qualities of "warmth, extroversion and Bohemian camaraderie"—qualities he hoped to bathe Coolidge's image in. All he had to do was to somehow link these people with Coolidge. An invitation to breakfast at the White House was summarily issued to, among others, jazz great Al Jolson, The Dolly Sisters dancing duo, and vaudeville star Charlotte Greenwood, famous for her long legs and high kicks. The celebrities were easily lured—who could turn down a breakfast invitation with the U.S. President, no matter how dull his company? The press swooped in, and the American public was treated to headlines such as "Actors Eat Cakes with the Coolidges" and "President Nearly Laughs." No wonder Coolidge thought so highly of advertising men.

While Bernays was busy finding ways to associate products with resonant emotional content, cold hard evidence was mounting in the new field of experimental psychology to support his approach. The new research showed that arbitrary links between unrelated concepts or events could in fact be made and remembered over a long period of time. You didn't even have to be as smart as a human to do it. At the turn of the century, the Russian scientist Ivan Pavlov was conducting his famous classical conditioning experiments with man's best friend. The experiments went like this: Pavlov noticed that dogs (like humans) have a tendency to salivate before certain kinds of food actually arrive in their mouths. He wanted to see whether he could trigger this response with some stimulus completely unrelated to food. For a period of time, he would sound a bell at each meal before putting the food in front of the dog. Dog smells food, dog salivates. So far so good. After this went on for some time, Pavlov would sound the bell, without actually delivering a meal to the dog. The dog would salivate anyway, having associated the sound of the bell with lunch so strongly that the sound of it actually triggered an instinctive physical response. It turns out this worked just as well with a metronome, or whistle, or tuning fork or just about any arbitrary event, visual or auditory you can think of—you can replicate this experiment using the family mutt and your favorite ringtone. These experiments spawned an army of psychologists who got very busy performing similar conditioning experiments with even dumber animals—pigeons, rats, and fish—as well as smarter animals such as monkeys and university undergraduates.

As advertising incorporated the new ideas from psychology, its practices shifted, and advertisers stopped telling customers so much about the product, and scrambled instead to link their products to abstract ideas such as power, love, purity, and patriotism. Links like these had of course been made before in the selling of products—but now they became much more dominant, reflecting the new psychological discoveries.

Coke Tastes Better ... by That Name

Layering these kinds of associations onto your product not only helps to sell it, but actually seems to add perceived value to it—you can get away with charging more in exchange for the symbolism you've created. The value is not just (or even mainly) in the product itself, but in what the product's brand name represents.

Think of it this way. If you look in the section of the newspaper that lists stocks and bonds and other financial information, there's usually a section down in one corner listing the prices of commodities. For instance, you can find out how much wheat is going for per bushel, how much tin is per pound, and how much anthracite coal is per ton, or pork bellies per hundred pounds. Of course, these prices are for serious bulk goods—you don't run out and buy a bag of wheat or one pound of beef at these prices. You need to purchase a *lot* of it to make any kind of deal—we're talking about herds of cattle, trainloads of coal, barges full of corn, or many train tanker cars of peanut butter. Now, imagine you're a buyer for some company that uses these goods, such as a food processing plant that makes corn syrup, among other things. Your task is to purchase enough trainloads of corn to keep the syrup-making plants running at full tilt. Now, imagine further that in this position you are visited by two salesmen. One is selling "Genuine Iowa™ corn", and another is selling "Authentic Illinois™ corn". It turns out that the Iowa™ corn is priced at $4.38/bushel (provided, of course, you buy at least 100 000 bushels), and the Authentic Illinois™ corn is $5.45 per bushel (same quantity purchase required). So, the natural question you might ask, then, is "What is the difference between them? What do I get for my company's extra $107 000 per 100 000 bushels?"

Suppose, though, the answer is that, in fact, there is no difference between them—load up two trucks, one with Authentic Illinois™ corn, the other with Genuine Iowa™ corn, park them side by side in the middle of Kansas, and no amount of inspection by corn experts (of which, we imagine, you are one) could tell them apart. Same number of kernels per pound, same sucrose concentrations, same moisture contents, etc. The only difference is the name. In other words, if you choose the more expensive Illinois corn and the bigwigs at the Home Office get wind of it, you're pronto applying for unemployment. No amount of "But, sirs and madams, we are getting *Genuine Illinois*™ corn for this extra money you could otherwise be using to fatten your own Christmas bonuses" would get you out of this one. You're history with that company, and for good reason.

But, as we all know, what we call something often does matter—and at times a lot, in fact, so much we're willing to pay more for it. Now suppose the corn-syrup-making people could get the Illinois™ corn at, say, $4.33/bushel, *provided* that they agreed to call it Iowa™ corn. Obviously, they'd think this was a sweet deal—they've just saved five cents a bushel. But, would you be happy if you could get a Rolex watch for, say, $75.00 (wait . . . there's more . . .) *provided* that you had to remove the name *Rolex* from it and substitute the name *Timex*? And, also agreed to always call it a *Timex*? Even assuming you'd get a better-quality watch (though—would you really?), you might still be pretty unhappy with the deal. I know I would—the only reason I'd buy a Rolex is to flash it around so everyone would know I own a Rolex. If all I'm going to do is use it to tell me the time—I can just use my cell phone.

While few of us ever purchase 200 000 tons of iron ore, there are quite a few products we buy where we do tend to focus on the inherent functional features of the product itself—things like rakes, washing machines, calculators, diapers, and dish soap. Such products are normally advertised and sold with an emphasis on their inherent features. If you look at ads for these kinds of products, they tend to be feature-oriented, and stick pretty close to describing the actual products. You're probably not that invested in whether your washing machine has its name brand prominently featured—you just want it to wash your clothes well, use as little energy as possible, and be mechanically reliable (though you might feel differently about kitchen appliances, which are in full view of guests).

Now compare the advertising of, say, washing machines, with how perfume is advertised. Notice that perfume ads practically never include claims like "Now, with 33% less alcohol!", or "The nifty little bottle fits right into your purse!" In fact, claims that focus on the primary attribute of perfume—the fragrance—are also absent: things like "Smells great!" or "Now, new cloth-penetrating odor formula—he can smell you right through your coat!" are few and far between, to say the least. In fact, perfume ads typically include *very* little language at all (as do most high-fashion ads), and never, ever mention price—unless, of course, they're knockoffs. Why the big difference between advertising perfume and sacks of quick-setting concrete (for just $11.95) at Home Depot? Basically, it's because in purchasing the rake or the washing machine or the bag of cement, we are more like the bulk goods buyer, primarily interested in the inherent, functional properties of the goods. We're not very inclined to spend extra money just to get something that "sounds" or "feels" better if it fulfills all the functional properties just the same. I, for one, am not going to pay $6.00 more for any rake because it has the lauded *Tru-Value*™ name plastered on it somewhere. (At least, I don't *think* I would.) But give me Chanel No. 5 and not "Sears Best" perfume any day, even if I think they smell equally good.

Different types of products lend themselves to different marketing strategies. You might also notice that if you compare two products with the same function, but in very different price ranges (Rolex and Timex watches, for example, or Cadillacs and Fords), you'll tend to find that the more expensive the product is, the more likely it is to be sold in a way that emphasizes how it makes you feel—a product of associated symbolism, rather than its inherent function and properties. There is a huge economic advantage to creating this feel-good associated value, which is a product of advertising and often, advertising alone. The economic advantage is simple to state: people will pay more for this extra kick.

This might seem like trickery—the consumer is fooled by the advertiser into believing that the product is more than it is, and is induced to pay more for it as a result. But the advertisers may well argue that these added associations create not just apparent—but real—added value for the product, that they change the consumer's experience of the product into something more. Renzo Rosso, founder of the Diesel clothing company is very up front about it: "We don't sell products, we sell the emotions our products generate." And he may well be right.

In 2004, Samuel McClure and a group of colleagues at Baylor Medical School peered into people's brains while they took the Pepsi challenge. But they added a twist. They wanted to know what their brains were doing when they drank Coke or Pepsi in a blind taste test, when the subjects didn't know which was which. They then compared the brain results of the blind test to the brain's activity when their subjects were told which brand of drink they were sipping through a plastic straw in the brain scanner.

First off, they found that many people expressed clear preferences in the blind condition—however, these didn't necessarily line up with what they said they normally liked to drink best, or what they said they preferred when they knew what they were drinking. Someone might say they generally liked Coke better than Pepsi despite obviously preferring Pepsi in the blind taste test. The researchers then looked at which parts of the brain were most active by measuring blood flow in the various regions of the brain. In the blind taste test, brain activity lined up with the results of the taste test. That is, the drink that people said they preferred in the blind taste test incited more activity in the region of their brain that normally lights up when something feels good—what neuroscientists informally refer to as the "reward center". So in the blind taste test, there was a straightforward relationship between activity in the brain's reward center, and the drink that each person liked best.

Now, when people were told which drinks they were tasting, something different happened. When Coke was identified by brand, people tended to prefer this drink to a second, unidentified drink which may have been either Coke or Pepsi. And their brains responded differently as well. The scientists saw a much more complex pattern of activity for the identified Coke drink than for the mystery drink. This time, blood went rushing to the parts of the brain that scientists think are involved in developing emotional biases and memories. They even found more activity in the *visual* part of the brain. Remember, all of this activity was triggered by *tasting* the Coke.

What's interesting is that cluing people in to the Coke brand didn't seem to increase the activity in the reward center of the brain—that is, the part of the brain that lit up for the preferred drink in the blind test did not light up *more* when people knew they were drinking Coke. This suggests that identifying the Coke didn't actually make the drink taste better, from a purely perceptual point. But people's *interpretation* of what tasted best seemed to be driven by the more complex activity throughout the brain than by the reward center alone. All the extra emotionally laden information and memories associated with Coke had insinuated themselves into the very neural structure of people's brains, were triggered by tasting Coke, and affected people's overall subjective experience of the drink. Coke did deliver that extra kick. What's more, in a result that would make the marketers of Coke pump their fists in the air in triumph: letting people know that they were drinking Pepsi did *not* change people's brain activity, nor did it change their drink preferences. The Pepsi brand apparently didn't add anything more to the soda-drinking experience than the taste of the drink itself (at least for this group of drinkers).

Findings like these seem to vindicate branding guru Kevin Roberts, CEO Worldwide of the famous ad agency Saatchi & Saatchi. Roberts claims that effective branding hinges on inspiring love in hearts of the consumer, and stoking a loyalty that "goes beyond all reason." According to Roberts, it's not the economy, stupid, it's the Attraction Economy: functional advertising is dead and the best brands are "Lovemarks"—brands that move people to buy not because of the inherent nature of the product, but because of the irrational devotion they inspire. Among these, Roberts points to brands such as Coca-Cola, Apple computers, Ben & Jerry's ice cream, Kodak, and Cheerios. Anyone who's ever had the courage or stupidity to try to convince a loyal Mac computer user of the virtues of the PC has a good sense of what Roberts is talking about.

If you compare older ads to more current ones, the shift away from selling through facts to selling through associated experience becomes very clear. Here's a 1940 ad for Tide laundry detergent, singing the praises of the product: "World's cleanest wash! Actually brightens clothes! World's whitest wash!"

Reprinted by permission of Procter & Gamble Co.

And here's the Lovemark approach:

Reprinted by permission of Procter & Gamble Co.

All this is well and good. And sure, if the brand-building that's done by companies means we get greater enjoyment out of our Cokes, Starbucks lattes and iPods, what could possibly be the harm in that? And yet, at some level, we'd like to think of ourselves as consumers who make *choices*—that is, choices where we hold on to some of the control for those decisions, not just reflexive reactions to sets of pleasant associations. This seems even more important when we move from the realm of sodas and electronic gadgets to decisions about more consequential products such as homes, life insurance, or presidents. It does seem worth asking, then, to what extent we can exercise control over the effects of branding associations.

Of Two Minds

It's not hard to find examples from psychological research that show our conscious and unconscious selves galloping off in different directions, sometimes with results that may horrify us. Think you're an enlightened individual who has managed to escape being imprinted by social stereotypes of race and gender? You might want to go online and take the Implicit Associations Test (IAT) developed by social psychologist Anthony Greenwald and colleagues. The test is intended to reveal the extent to which you've absorbed common associations with various social groups, and it works like this: in a computer-based test, you're asked to categorize faces by group (let's say race, in which you distinguish between African American faces and white European American faces). You would see a face come up on the computer screen, and you might press a button with your right finger to categorize it as African American, and a button on your left for European American faces. Interleaved with this category sorting is a separate category-sorting task where you're asked to classify words such as *war, beauty, love, ugly* as positive or negative, again either using your right or left finger for each category. If you're like most of the people who have taken the IAT (yes, even the enlightened ones), you'll find that you're faster to classify the faces when the *same finger* is used to sort African Americans and negative words like *war*, than when the same finger is used to classify African Americans and positive words like *beauty*.

The researchers take this asymmetry to reveal an unconscious emotional bias in favor of whites over African Americans. The idea is that if you're faster to respond when the same finger is used for negative words and African Americans, it's because these concepts are more closely linked in your mind than *positive* words and African Americans. (Using the same technique, scientists at Harvard have developed tests to probe for associations related to gender, body weight, age, weapons, presidential candidates, and the United States versus Canada or the United Kingdom. Marketers have also picked up the ball to probe for unconscious brand preferences using the IAT.) These biases tend to show up on the IAT even for many people who claim to have no negative associations with a particular group. Now, it's hard to know whether people might simply be trying to hide their known prejudices when they report their attitudes, or whether they are revealing the attitudes they honestly think they have. Some measure of self-deception seems a likely possibility, given what I've heard from people who have shared their own experiences with the IAT. Malcolm Gladwell, author of *Blink*, reports the sense of unease he felt as a black man upon discovering, to his surprise, that his IAT results showed negative associations with African Americans time and time again.

When conscious and subconscious attitudes seem to be at odds, the million dollar question is: What best determines how people actually *behave*—the implicit biases ferreted out by the IAT, or consciously held (and openly acknowledged) attitudes? Both can be good predictors of behavior, but with some interesting differences. Some biases are more socially unacceptable than others. For example, admitting to negative attitudes about African Americans is generally frowned upon more than admitting to negative attitudes about some brand of toothpaste. The more socially unacceptable it is to admit to a particular bias, the more the implicit tests have an edge over the explicit self-reports in actually predicting behavior. Also, the explicit self-reports do best in predicting behaviors that are easily under people's conscious control—things such as brand choices and voting behavior. They don't do well at all in predicting more involuntary but socially very relevant kinds of behavior such as your body language in interacting with a black or white person, or whether you laugh at the jokes of a black or white person. What about the implicit associations that show up on the IAT? They turn out to be pretty good predictors of *both* involuntary behaviors *and* conscious ones like brand choice and voting.

So, it seems that deliberate actions can in fact be infiltrated by unconscious biases, a finding that would come as no surprise to Freud and his enterprising nephew Edward Bernays. But the extent to which unconscious biases affect deliberate decisions can vary from one situation to another. One German study led by Arnd Florack at the University of Münster focused on judgments about the guilt of a Turkish immigrant defendant. Now, legal systems are typically predicated on the assumption that such hugely consequential judgments are made on the basis of a dispassionate, unbiased sifting through of evidence, and one would hope that this kind of decision is about as dispassionate and rational as it gets. What the researchers found was that people who had a strong negative IAT bias against Turkish immigrants (compared to native Germans) *were* more likely to deliver a guilty verdict, but only when threatening aspects of the defendant were highlighted. This suggests that creating an emotionally charged situation can tilt a decision towards unconscious biases. It also suggests a clear strategy if you happen to be a prosecutor with a weak case and social biases lined up against the defendant— stimulate the jury's fears and anxieties a little. By extension, a branding strategy that is focused on selling a product based on a network of created associations rather than on the great features of its product should probably run an emotionally laden campaign that downplays the role of thoughtful evaluation. Try checking out the ad campaigns of some of the most successful "Lovemark" brands.

Everything You Need to Know You Learned *Before* Kindergarten

Freud remarked that "the mind is like an iceberg, it floats with one-seventh of its bulk above water." But about a hundred years after Freud and Pavlov first published their ideas, scientists who currently study the mind are struck by just how rarely our conscious selves seem to sit in the driver's seat of our own cognitive processes. The disconnect goes far beyond Freud's original focus on hidden drives and motivations. It runs through just about all aspects of how humans perceive and think. Most of the information we take in from the outside world gets cranked through our minds using finely-honed patterns of thought that lie beneath our awareness.

To take a simple example, look at the two horizontal lines below, and tell me which looks longer:

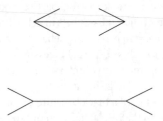

Now, whip out your ruler, and measure both lines. In fact, they're exactly the same length. Now that you've measured them, and have clear and hopefully convincing evidence of their relative lengths, look at these lines again. Do they look equal to you now? Well, no. Unfortunately, the rational part of your mind that knows that measuring lines is pretty good proof of their length can't seem to convince the other part of your mind—the part of your mind that takes in raw sensory input and spits out an interpretation. Vision scientists think that this illusion demonstrates more than the perversity of your visual machinery in the face of reason. Rather, your visual system may be responding to having learned some very robust relationships between apparent length and distance in three-dimensional space. It "knows" that when people or objects recede into the distance, they *appear* to be shorter, but don't actually shrink as they move away from you. So the visual system is smart enough to know that judgments of size and length have to be relative to depth, and not absolute. To see this, look at the drawing below which depicts a table in the foreground of a square room.

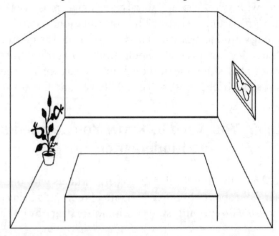

If you get out your trusty ruler one more time, you'll find that the line corresponding to the front of the table measures the same length on your ruler as the line corresponding to where the floor meets the back wall (both lines are marked in bold). Yet, when you encounter scenes like this in real life, you're apt to judge that the front of the table, which is closer, is *not* the same length as the back wall, which is farther—and if you do think they're the same length, you'll find Moving Day to be a bewildering experience. In the illusion involving the arrows, it may be that the inward and outward facing arrows serve as an unconsciously received cue about depth, so that your visual system interprets the line with inward facing arrows as being closer than the line with outward facing arrows, and adjusts estimates of their length accordingly. This may be something that you have actually had to learn as a result of lots of experience with lines in three dimensions, including walls, floors, rugs, tables, and so on. The illusion turns out to be less powerful for people whose daily surroundings don't involve angular walls, such as rural Zulu people who live in circular huts.

So, how come whatever your visual system has implicitly learned about how lines work in three dimensions seems to trump your conscious awareness of the fact that this picture is *actually* a two-dimensional drawing, and that neither of these lines is closer than the other? Well, it's probably because seeing in three dimensions is so much more common and useful to you—your brain has developed some extremely efficient and automatic routines to very quickly interpret the visual input in your surroundings. This probably confers some clear advantages from an evolutionary standpoint. For example, without such automatic responses to cues, you might not be able to duck quickly enough to avoid a crowbar swung in your direction, resulting in your expulsion from the gene pool. Your conscious knowledge may well be more brittle—more recently learned, and much less reinforced in your mind. When the two conflict, as in this particular situation, the more automatic, almost instinctive processes dominate. That's not to say that conscious and "higher-level" knowledge can never affect the more automatic kinds of processes, just that in this case, the automatic ones seem to be much more robust.

This example illustrates an interesting paradox about the mind. We're used to thinking of "learning" as something that takes some effort, and comes about through a conscious attempt to change our patterns of thinking. This sort of learning, we think, begins roughly around kindergarten, once counting and the alphabet song are foisted on us by teachers or eager parents. Before that, we get to enjoy a sort of extended vacation where we basically fool around all day with mud or finger paints, put lots of stuff in our mouths and hang out with other kids on vacation. The depressing (or inspiring) truth is that the knowledge you've acquired in the god-knows-how-many hours you've now spent in school is puny in comparison to what you've learned in the years *before* kindergarten. No question: the knowledge served up by civilization and passed on through rigorous education methods *is* impressive. But evolution has given you an extraordinarily powerful learning machine for a brain, and learning incredibly complex patterns and relationships and mental procedures seems as natural and effortless as eating and walking. After decades of study, science is still struggling just to *describe* all that you've learned in those pre-kindergarten years, let alone explain how you accomplished the feat.

Linguists in Diapers

Persuasion leans pretty heavily on language, and just like the visual system, much of the information that we suck out of language is processed in those subconscious information-processing factories. When you study language closely, it becomes really clear just how much of what you've learned is implicit and unconscious rather than *explicitly* taught and consciously learned. It turns out that your knowledge of language runs much, much deeper than what you may be taught in a foreign language class about vocabulary meanings, verb conjugations and how to form the subjunctive or the pluperfect. Every time you speak, you access a body of linguistic knowledge that is more structured and more complex than you might ever realize, using a set of procedures that your mind has optimized for efficiency, but of which you're unaware. The same goes for understanding language. Just as your visual system does its thing without any supervision from your rational self, using language "just happens." This might seem not quite right, because there are aspects of language that we do use very deliberately (for example, writing a book, alas, doesn't "just happen"). Nevertheless, the vast majority of your knowledge of language lies, like the proverbial iceberg, below the surface.

To give you a more concrete feel, here's just one example of some of the submerged linguistic knowledge lurking in your mind: Is the first sound in the word *pit* identical to the second sound in the word *spit*? If you said yes, you'd be wrong. The "p" sound in *pit* is slightly aspirated—in technical terms, there's a longer lag between the time that your lips part to release the "p" sound, and the time when your vocal folds begin to vibrate as you slide into the subsequent vowel sound. Aspirated sounds release an extra puff of air once the consonant is pronounced. You can see this for yourself with the following trick: put a lit match about three or four inches from your face and say the word *spit*. If the match is at the right distance, there won't be enough air released in your utterance of the word to put the match out. Now, say the word *pit* at the same volume, and watch the match get puffed out (you may have to experiment a bit with distance to be able to see the contrast).

But all this sounds like splitting hairs; sure, they may be slightly different variants, but they're still the same sound, right? After all, we use the same letter to mark them in writing. And substituting one for the other would make no real difference. Saying *pit* without that extra puff of air doesn't change the fact that you're saying the word *pit*. Well, not quite so to a speaker of Thai. In the Thai language, the difference between aspirated and unaspirated sounds is just as important as the difference between "p" and "b" in English (notice the difference between "*John likes to pet his cat*" and "*John likes to bet his cat*".) In Thai, whether you produce a regular or an aspirated "puffy" consonant can make the difference between admonishing Johnny not to interrupt his father, or not to bite him. And just as you might find it hard to "hear" the difference between aspirated and unaspirated sounds, Thai speakers find the difference so obvious, they might be amazed that *you* can't hear it. But if you have a new baby, she might be able to tell the difference between the two, even if no Thai word has ever passed anyone's lips in her presence. New infants in an English-speaking household can clearly hear the difference between aspirated and unaspirated sounds—but by the end of their first year, they've lost the ability to distinguish them, and treat them as if they were hearing two instances of the same sound, just like English-speaking adults do. Paradoxically, this is a form of learning. What the kids have learned is that aspirated and unaspirated sounds basically act like the same sound in English, and that they aren't used to distinguish different words (unlike the sound contrasts between *pat* and *bat*). At which point, their conscious mind learns to ignore it.

But the unconscious mind is still keeping track. This example shows something much more interesting than the simple fact that some languages treat some highly similar but slightly different sounds as the "same" sound, and other languages treat them as "different" sounds. Careful study by linguists shows that in fact, at some level, you *do* know that aspirated and unaspirated sounds are different, even if they "sound" the same to you. It turns out that you never produce aspirated sounds in the same linguistic contexts as unaspirated sounds. You pronounce aspirated sounds at the beginning of syllables that are stressed, or accented (this includes single syllable words)—for example, in words like **pit**, **pa**blum, **cas**tle, ba**tta**lion, com**pa**ssion (where the accented syllable is in bold font). You produce unaspirated sounds when they follow another consonant in the same syllable—in words like **spit**, **stairs**, **scream** and **schtick** or when they're at the beginning of an unaccented syllable—in words like po**li**tical, po**llu**tion—and in the word po**ta**to, only the first "t" sound is aspirated. And if a brand new word were to be coined in the English language—let's say, Coke, or Motorola, or Spam, or Pimbles, you would know precisely whether to pronounce it with aspirated or unaspirated sounds, just like all other speakers of English. In other words, aspirated and unaspirated sounds aren't sprinkled throughout your language randomly; they follow a systematic pattern that you must have somehow unconsciously noticed and reproduced even though you *think* you can't hear the difference between them.

Any professor of an introductory linguistics class will tell you that this is really quite an astounding feat when you consider how hard it is for bright and alert *university* students to consciously discover and describe these patterns based on a language sample. First, they have to be trained to "hear" the differences between the sounds. Then they have to apply tools of linguistic analysis to figure out the different contexts in which each type of sound occurs—first having figured out the precise definition of "syllable", and having likely entertained and thrown out many other possible hypotheses about how these sounds pattern. In decades of teaching, not once have I encountered a student who spontaneously observed "Hey, I just noticed that you can only produce aspirated sounds at the beginnings of accented syllables! How about that!" Students have to be painstakingly guided in order to consciously make these observations. And yet there's evidence that by their first birthday, infants are beginning to sort out these patterns—and without the benefit of matchstick demonstrations or explanations about what a syllable is. This points to one of the most puzzling and bizarre aspects of the human mind: that learning to be *aware* of what you unconsciously know may depend on a lot of focused effort and specialized knowledge and even some measure of aptitude, but actually *learning* it may be effortless, automatic, and require very little of what we normally think of as intelligence.

Incidentally, English speakers' understanding of aspirated consonants exactly parallels Japanese speakers' understanding of the sounds "r" and "l". If you've ever talked to a Japanese person just learning English, you'll realize what a dastardly pair of sounds this is, as it seems very hard to get them right. It turns out that Japanese speakers have as much trouble "hearing" the difference between "r" and "l" as untrained English speakers have "hearing" the difference between aspirated and unaspirated sounds—so word pairs like *arrive/alive*, *more/mole* and *rake/lake* sound like variants on the same word. But it's a mistake to think that Japanese people can't pronounce "r" or "l"—each of these shows up throughout the Japanese language (though the Japanese "r" is somewhat different from the English "r"). The reality is that just like aspirated and unaspirated sounds in English, Japanese "l" and "r" occur in completely nonoverlapping linguistic contexts. The "r" sound occurs only after certain vowels, like the vowels in *beer* and *fair*, and "l" occurs everywhere else. So, at an unconscious level, Japanese speakers know the difference between the two sounds, and have at some point in their tender infancy sorted them as to where they should occur.[1] But at a conscious level, they sound like the same sound. To extend the parallel, if you were to learn Thai, you might encounter bemused native Thai speakers, who would conclude that you can't pronounce aspirated or unaspirated sounds, or that you switch between the two in seemingly random fashion. Foreign accents generally point to evidence of the learned sound patterns of the native language colliding with the sound patterns of the new language. Therefore, pronunciation "mistakes" can provide some nifty insights about intricate patterns hidden in the mind of the speaker.

---

[1] And yes, just like the English tots do with aspirated consonants, Japanese babies start out by being able to clearly tell the difference between "r" and "l", but lose the ability to make this distinction by their first birthday.

Name-Calling

With so much cognitive action going on beneath the conscious stratum, it's no surprise that advertisers make some effort to engage consumers at this level rather than staying topside amidst all the rational deliberation. And nowhere is this seen more clearly than with the creation of a brand, beginning with choosing the brand name. Choosing a brand name used to be a pretty simple affair. It was usually picked by the upper management of a company based on some simple naming conventions. The company was often named after the founder and typically described the goods or services the company offered—for example, the *Ford Motor Company, Corning Glass Works, General Electric, General Motors, International Business Machines*, and so on. It was assumed that brand equity was built over time as the company established a reputation for itself. In some cases, this naming practice flew in the face of strong negative connotations of the name itself, as when the Czech car manufacturing company *Skoda Auto* was so-named for its founder despite the fact that the expression *skoda* in Czech translates into *"What a shame!"*

Nowadays, these practices seem incredibly naive. Who in their right mind would start a new software company called *Kowalski Computer Programming*? It's understood that the value of a brand is not just in the reputation and associations it accrues over time, but also in the associations that resonate with its name even before the first product rolls out of its factories. Branding experts now pin some of the blame for the spectacular failure of the Edsel automobile on its ugly name, and attribute the success of the BlackBerry device in part to its snappy moniker. Logitech saw a dramatic rise in sales after rechristening its bland *Scanner 2000* as *ScanMan*, and sales for Toro's *Snow Master* were much more forceful than its predecessor, the emasculated *Snow Pup*. As a result, brand naming nowadays is less often left to the linguistic ineptitude of the company's CEO, being outsourced instead to pricey branding agencies who themselves try to lure clients from their competitors with names such as *Catchword, A Hundred Monkeys, Nametag*, and *Brandshake* (though *The Naming Company* seems to buck the naming trend with a more minimalist approach). Modern approaches to branding have evolved largely as a result of the savvy intuitions and observations of marketing experts. But scientists have looked under our hoods to provide some insights as to why a BlackBerry by any other name might just not sound as fresh.

Words have something in common with lobbyists: the influence they wield often depends on the quality of their connections. Scientists sometimes talk about words being stored in a *mental lexicon*, as if our knowledge of words were some sort of dictionary. This creates the false impression that words are kept in compartmentalized bins, much as dictionary entries might be, with each entry containing information about how a word sounds, what it means, and how it combines with other words (for example, if you know a word is a transitive verb, like *kick*, you know it can precede a unit like *Billy*). If your mental lexicon worked like this, you might imagine that as you read or heard words, you would "look up" the entries that matched up to the letters or sounds of the word in order to access all of its information.

But in fact, word recognition by humans really doesn't work like this at all. It's a much more chaotic procedure than looking up words in a dictionary. Our mental representation of words seems to be less like an orderly list of separate dictionary entries and more like an interconnected mess of electric lightbulbs wired to each other. Think of your attention as a kind of electrical current running through this mess of connections. The greatest amount of electrical current flows to the words that most closely match the sounds or letters you're processing, so that this word lights up the most—but some current leaks to words that share some of the sounds (or letters), so that they too light up partially.

This means that when a word is "recognized" in your mind, it also partly activates words that overlap in sound shape with the word you're hearing or reading—a fact that companies do well to keep in mind when naming their products.

To uncover how this process works, language scientist Michael Tanenhaus and his colleagues studied people's eye movements as they listened to speech. Their study volunteers sat at a table with various objects strewn about, and heard simple spoken instructions such as "*Pick up the candle.*" While hearing and responding to the instructions, the volunteers wore an eye camera attached to a headband so that their eye movements were tracked moment by moment and preserved for posterity. The researchers discovered that people began to look at the candle well before they heard the entire word *candle*—in fact, they started shifting their attention (and their eyeballs) to it after hearing only the first two sounds of the word or so. This seems amazingly efficient but actually, people were jumping the gun a bit. Often, their eyes also flickered over to a candy on the table, presumably because *candle* and *candy* start with the same sounds. As people heard more of the word over time and the candle proved a better sound match for the word than the candy, people's eyes settled on the candle. Objects corresponding to rhyming words also drew people's attention (for example, people looked at a handle when what they heard was "*candle*"), though a bit less strongly than words that began with the same sounds. The study volunteers themselves were blissfully unaware that their attention had been momentarily lured by phonetic decoys, and were surprised when they later saw videotapes of their eye movements.

Researchers now agree that word recognition, like branding, is a cut-throat competitive process, with multiple words becoming subconsciously activated all at once and clamoring for attention until a winner is tagged as the intended word. So, hearing the word *candle* can trigger the (unconscious) activation of the words *candy, can, canteloupe, cantankerous, Canada, cancel, Cancun, candelabra, cancer, Cantonese, cannibal, canvas, candidate, cannonball, canopy, Candice*, to name just a few. A word that shares its beginning (or end) with many other words will have more competitors drawing current away from it—these words take longer to recognize and are more prone to mistakes or misremembering. And even connections to words with more oblique sound relationships than this can matter. Word scientists often measure the intensity of lexical competition for a specific word by determining its "neighborhood density". One way of doing this is to list any words that differ from the target word by one sound anywhere in the word. So, a word like *can* would count among its competing neighbors *cap*, *kin*, and *man*, among many others. Words that live in dense neighborhoods with many neighbors are harder to recognize than words that enjoy the mental equivalent of suburban sprawl.

When companies talk about creating a "distinctive" brand name, what they partly mean is a name that doesn't live in a dense lexical neighborhood. This makes sense. If your brand name sounds like many others, when consumers hear it, the names of your competitors will also light up to some extent in their minds. And when consumers try to pull your brand out of memory, the competitors will also vie for attention. Of course, you'll want to pay special attention to the words that most closely resemble your brand name, as these will light up brightest of all. All of which suggests that when naming a brand, you want to have a good look around the neighborhood before moving in—and that your own real estate value can be dragged down by an eyesore next door, or boosted by a spiffy house across the street.

Lexical Linkages

It turns out that hearing a word doesn't just light up other words that *sound* like the word you're hearing—words that are related in meaning are also partly activated. This shows up in the fleeting eye movements people make—when they hear the word *lock*, for example, they're more likely to look at a key than at some unrelated object like a shoe. Even more dramatically, people will look at the key when it's meaningfully related to a sound *competitor* of the uttered word—for example, if they hear *log*, this draws looks to *key*, presumably by way of having activated *lock*. Connections among words related in meaning are easily seen using another clever experimental technique called semantic priming. In a typical priming study, you would sit at a computer, watching strings of letters—some of them real words like *donkey* and *marvel*, and others nonwords like *sniggle* or *laste*. You'd have to make a decision, as quickly as possible, about whether you are seeing a real word or a nonword by pressing different keys for Yes or No. You can get the feel for this task by tapping your response as quickly as you can to the following words—use your right finger for Yes, It's a Word, and your left for No, You Can't Fool Me. Ready?

WORM
FRAMBLE
NISTOOD
LAYERS

BUNION
SINTENT
TROMBONE
BLODS
CRACKLING
MENDLE
FLUNK

Warmed up? OK, now do the same with this list:

STRONDER
TISTY
DOCTOR
NURSE
CAMLETE
OPIDE
FRUGAL
PRAND
SWEATER
SHIRT
GLIND

The second list contains two pairs of related adjacent words: DOCTOR–NURSE and SWEATER–SHIRT. You may or may not have noticed that you were able to respond quite quickly to the second word in each pair—in controlled experiments, your reaction time for NURSE, for example, would be measured in milliseconds by a computer, and compared to the reaction time of other subjects who saw a word like CHAIR precede NURSE instead of DOCTOR. Priming studies reliably show that it's easier to recognize a word when it comes on the heels of a related one, suggesting that NURSE was already partly lit up when you read DOCTOR, making it easier to recognize as a real word. These priming effects aren't dependent on your noticing the relationships among the words. In a version of the experiment known as *masked priming*, the first word in the pair is flashed subliminally, for such a short period of time that it's impossible to identify—subjects usually don't even realize a word has been flashed, and often experience it as a flicker on the screen. Generally, presenting the word for 50–60 milliseconds or so (and sometimes much less than that) will do the trick. Even when DOCTOR is flashed subliminally, it still speeds up the recognition of NURSE, pointing to unconscious, very rapid currents of activation surging throughout your mental word storehouse.

Priming studies—like the eye-tracking work in which people look at a key when they hear *log*, by way of activating *lock*—also show the activation of words related to sound *neighbors* of the uttered word. This effect is especially strong for neighbors sharing the same beginning sounds. So, not only does *candle* activate *candy*, *canteloupe, Canada*, and so on *ad nauseum*, it also momentarily activates *lollipop, watermelon*, and *hockey*, etc. With such noisy brains, it becomes astonishing that we actually manage to understand each other's words at all—and indeed, language disorders such as aphasia may reflect something gone terribly wrong with the delicate balance of activation of words and their competitors.

Aside from their promiscuous links to other like-sounding or like-meaning words, there's another way in which your mental lexicon is very different from dictionary entries. Suppose I ask you to "Hand me an apple." Here's how Merriam-Webster defines *apple*: "The fleshy, usually rounded red, yellow, or green edible pome fruit of a usually cultivated tree (genus *Malus*) of the rose family." You don't need any more than this to figure out what it is I want you to hand over. (In fact, you don't even need all of the information in this entry. I didn't know until just now, looking up the word *apple*, that the apple tree was related to the rose, but I don't seem to have run into any serious misunderstanding concerning apples before.) Now, given that the brain space of your average nongenius human is somewhat limited, it might make sense to conserve mental power by activating only the essential information you need to understand words as they're spoken. For example, you have all kinds of knowledge and memories related to apples. But how much of this stuff do you actually need to access in order to understand the sentence *Hand me an apple*? Just the essentials would do—you merely have to identify which nearby thing is the apple. Never mind that apples are usually juicy, crisp to the bite, nice in apple pie, make good presents for teachers, that you had one in your backyard as a child, that your ex-boyfriend loathed them, that one supposedly fell on Sir Isaac Newton's head, and so on. Ignoring all this information—which is irrelevant to the task at hand—would probably leave more room for remembering where your keys are, and what day your job interview was supposed to be.

But some studies seem to show the opposite—that you activate not just the bare meanings of words, but a variety of perceptual memories that go with them. For example, both priming and eye-movement studies show that a word like *piano* activates the word *typewriter*. The relationship between these two words is pretty tenuous. The main thing they have in common is the fact that in using each of them, you pound some keys with your fingers. In the studies in question, volunteers were simply asked to identify words and nonwords, or pick the right picture to go with a spoken word—tasks that don't really seem to require you to bring to mind a rich, detailed scenario in which you'd have to think about how you physically interact with these objects. And yet, this kind of information seems to be automatically and unconsciously activated, whether you need it or not.

To top it off, pulling words out of mental storage probably also drags along memories of how the word's been used. Nowadays, no one likes to use the word *Negro* to refer to African Americans. It's irrevocably connected to charged memories of racial prejudice and hatred. As attitudes evolved, we needed a "clean" word, unsullied by its dubious connections. The same goes for words like *imbecile*, or *spastic*, which used to commonly be used as clinical terms in the past, but became tainted by less-than-enlightened attitudes towards the disabled. And various political commentators have noted no one wants to admit to being a liberal anymore—the term *progressive* sounds much less pejorative. Linguist Geoff Nunberg quotes writer Timothy Noah as stating, in 1986: "Given the aversion this word inspires in Democratic candidates, future civilizations sifting through the rubble may well conclude that *liberal* was a euphemism for *pederast* or *serial killer*." But it wasn't always so. As Nunberg notes, there was a time when it was the word *conservative* that had odious connotations, as revealed in this 1949 *Wall Street Journal* editorial:

> *[I]f a man is described as a 'conservative' in politics . . . he is likely to be suspected of wanting to cheat widows and orphans and generally to be a bad fellow who associates with other bad fellows. Consequently very few people will admit they are conservatives and if they are accused they will go to great lengths to prove otherwise.*

So, words are deeply entangled in complex networks of memories and associations. When you use one, you can't detach it from its connections to other words of similar sound or meaning, or from the memories you've internalized from the times that word has been used in the past. The upshot of this is that getting the right word matters. A lot. All of this is good news for professional brand namers. It bolsters their sales pitch that getting the brand name right is a tricky and important business best left to the experts.

Of course, cozying up to English words with desirable connections has long been part of the branding process. Marketers hope that consumers will activate these associations for free every time your brand is mentioned—and there is every reason to believe that they do. The most obvious way to create an association parasite is to use a brand name that exactly corresponds to an actual word, a strategy that's given us strong brands like *Tide*, *Ivory*, *Mustang*, *Target*, *Sprite*, *Oracle*, *Apple* and *BlackBerry*, to name just a few. (Notice that "good" brand names are not interchangeable—naming a soap *Oracle* seems weird, and so does *Ivory* for a company that makes computers. Because of this, people are surprisingly good at guessing what kind of product is sold under a brand name they have never heard before.)

But if you pay close attention to word science, you may find other less obvious benefits to appropriating a nice English word for your brand name. By doing so, you're essentially making an English word ambiguous—suddenly the word *apple* can refer either to a fruit or a computer, just like the word *bug* can refer to either an insect or a spying device (or, more abstractly, a glitch in a computer program). Priming studies show that *both* meanings of an ambiguous word get activated even when the context makes the intended meaning perfectly clear. The word *bug* speeds up responses to *spy* even when you're hearing about fumigators and cockroaches.[2]

This raises the possibility that a casual conversation about ocean tides might serve as a kind of free product placement for the laundry detergent Tide. Indeed, in one study, scientists Richard Nesbitt and Timothy Wilson had their subjects memorize pairs of words, including the word pair *ocean–moon*. They were later asked to name a laundry detergent brand. Only 10% of those who hadn't seen *ocean–moon* named Tide, but it leaped into the minds of 20% of those who had. But those who'd been primed to think of Tide had no insight into why this had come to mind. When asked why they'd named Tide, they came up with explanations like "My mother uses Tide" or "I like the Tide box."

The Meanings in Noises

There's another byproduct of the connections in the mental lexicon that brand namers have caught on to—the potential for feedback loops between certain sound patterns and specific meanings. Here's what I mean: let's suppose that you're looking for a word in your mental lexicon that means something like "to force air through the nose with a harsh sound." As you narrow in on the word *snort*, words related in sound or in meaning become activated—and words related in *both* sound and meaning hum loudest of all in your mind. Your search is likely to send a burst of activation to nose-related words like *sniff, sniffle, snuffle, snore, sneeze, snuff, snot, snicker,* and *snout,* all of which share a striking resemblance to each other, and therefore activate each other as well, just as they have been activated by *snort.* Like geographic neighborhoods, lexical neighborhoods that are densely populated by highly similar inhabitants tend to serve as a magnet for newcomers that fit into the mold. So, suppose you now wanted to coin a word for the sudden and sharp bumping of one's nose. Well, you can actually find a word for this concept in Merriam-Webster's open dictionary, an online publication devoted to collecting instances of new words in usage. Apparently, this nose-bumping concept has been sucked into the highly resonating *snort* neighborhood—it turns out that one would use the word *snork.* This new neighbor makes the sound locale even more of a ghetto for particular meanings. To wit, the open dictionary has several other nosey newcomers in the *sn-* neighborhood:

---

[2] Things are slightly more complicated than that—whether or not people activate the unintended meaning of an ambiguous word actually depends on some subtle interplay between the context and how common each meaning of the ambiguous word is. So, the linguistic product-placement strategy likely works best if your brand is leeching off a word that is not *so* frequent in common usage that it would swamp the brand meaning of the word.

snarf (verb): to laugh so hard that you eject food or drink through your nose
snargle (noun): a rough, phlegmy catch in the back of the throat
snorphy (adjective): when you feel very sick, or have a stuffy nose
snurfle (verb): to burrow or bury your nose into something
snoz (noun): a more interesting way to say "nose"

A company interested in naming a new cigarette brand *Snock* might do well to consider relocating to a less nasal neighborhood.

It's possible to identify other examples of neighborhoods packed with words of similar meanings, leading to what looks like *sound symbolism*—that is, the association of certain sounds with a specific meaning across many words in the language. For example, a gaggle of words beginning with *gl-* have some meaning related to light: *glisten, glitter, glaze, glass, glow, glimmer, gleam, glint*; *cl-* words are often sharply auditory: *clap, clang, clink, clip, clatter, clank, clop*; many *sl-* words evoke a certain unpleasant tactile quality: *slime, sludge, slippery, slop, slip, slide, slither, slick, slobber, slug, slurp, slush*. Words beginning with *br-* are rarely timid or subservient: *brave, brassy, brash, brazen, bright, bravado, brawl, brat, brawny, bristle, brandish*. And words ending in *–ump* seem to suggest, slow, heavy, roundish, and inert kinds of objects—*lump, stump, bump, clump, hump, slump, rump, dump, plump*. So, it's probably not so good to be called a chump, or a frump, or a grump then. (How many product names can you think of that end in *–ump*?)

These word gangs are likely formed over long periods of time as a result of the resonating patterns of activation in the mental lexicon as we match up words and their meanings in regular conversation, and as we try to coin new words. Every time a new word is coined, it's somewhat more likely to be similar in sound to an existing word of similar meaning, and much more so if there's a dense sound neighborhood associated with a particular meaning. As you might imagine, many of these sound-meaning patterns are probably also highly language-specific. Words beginning with *sn-* don't, for example, elicit nasal thoughts in Spanish. This reflects the fact that, for the most part, the link between the sounds of words and their meanings is pretty arbitrary—there is nothing especially doggy about the sounds *d-o-g*, and *chien* and *pes* are probably equally effective at evoking furry, barking four-legged creatures for speakers of French and Czech. This poses a particular challenge for marketing a brand name to speakers of different languages—a very different set of sound neighbors may be evoked by the same brand name, and a brand name that is carefully crafted to exploit sound symbolism in one language may have disastrous associations in another.

However, some linguists take the sound symbolism idea further, and claim that there are some universal relationships between specific sounds and meanings that hold across all (or at least most) languages. The idea of language-universal sound symbolism has captivated thinkers as early as Plato, who explored the idea that the sound "r" universally evokes motion (presumably, the ancients had their own version of the word *vrrroom*). It can be hard—especially for monolinguals—to get an intuitive feel for what kinds of sound associations might be specific to our language, and which might be more universal. To us, *dog* may just *sound* more doggy than *pes*, since the English word automatically fires up the concept and the Czech word doesn't (unless you happen to speak Czech). But suppose we were to find certain sounds linked with the same notions across many languages? For example, which of the shapes below is the *bouba*, and which is the *kiki*?

Almost all English speakers choose the figure on the left as the *kiki* and the figure on the right as the *bouba*. If this only happened in English, we might speculate that this was caused by activation of the meanings of "sharp" neighbors like *kick*, *spiky*, or *crinkle*, and "round" neighbors like *blob*, *amoeba*, and *gloop*. But then we'd be faced with the chicken-or-egg question: Do "sharp" words in English sound like *kiki* because there is something inherently "sharp" about the their sounds, or does *kiki* sound sharp to English speakers because it coincidentally activates similar-sounding words that have "sharp" meanings? It would be worth asking speakers of languages that are very different from English. As it turns out, the same *bouba/kiki* effect works with Tamil speakers, and with tribes in the Canary Islands. Now, it's *possible* that these other languages also coincidentally just happen to have a bunch of sound words that live near *kiki* in the mental lexicon—but the argument for some inherent *kiki*-ness in the sound of the word becomes harder to dismiss. Moreover, the effect shows up in English-speaking toddlers as young as two and a half years of age, well before the kids have acquired a voluminous vocabulary or linked letters with sounds (notice that the *letters* "k" and "b" are themselves sharp and round respectively).

Where could such universal relationships between sound and meaning possibly come from? Some linguists speculate they come from either the acoustic properties of sounds, or the actual motions we use to make these sounds. For example, linguist John Ohala looked at words related to size in many languages. He was struck by the fact that words communicating smallness tend to have vowels and consonants that occur at higher acoustic frequencies than words communicating robust size. "Small" sounds include the "ee" or "i" vowels in *teeny, itty, bit, petit* (French), *mikros* (Greek), and *shiisai* (Japanese), as well as sibilant sounds like *s, sh,* and *ch.* "Large" sounds include vowels like "o" and "a" as in *large, broad, gordo* (Spanish), *grand* (French), *makros* (Greek), and *ookii* (Japanese). Ohala suggested that throughout nature, higher acoustic frequencies of sound are associated with small size, while lower frequencies are associated with larger size, and that this relationship finds its way into language. (The correlation plays out in music as well—if you were to musically impersonate an elephant and a mouse, which would be the tuba and which would be the piccolo? Russian composer Sergei Prokofiev's musical interpretation of *Peter and the Wolf* nicely illustrates the relationship between higher pitch and small size.) Of course, there are exceptions to this generalization—ironically, the English word *small* has a "large" vowel and the word *big* has a "small" vowel! This shows that arbitrariness in language *is* a real force—otherwise we might all speak the same language. But despite these counter-examples, English speakers tend to think of a *gil* as something that would be smaller than a *gol*.

It's No Accident Mice "Squeak" But Cows "Moo"

Ohala focused on intrinsic relationships between the acoustics of a sound and its meaning—in other words, properties of sounds that we *hear*. Other researchers suggest that the physical sensations we experience in *producing* a sound can have an impact on the meanings we most naturally link it to. It's no accident that your doctor asks you to produce the large sound "aaahhh" when she wants a clear view down your throat—notice how open your mouth is, and how large your oral cavity is in producing this big sound. Now say "eek!" In making the "small" vowel, your mouth is constricted into a tiny space, and the air flows through quite a narrow channel in your mouth. According to this line of thinking, the wide open space of your mouth when you say "ah" brings to mind larger spaces, and *booba* refers to the round blobby thing rather than the sharp spiky thing because when you say it, your mouth is rounded as you make the sounds.

Linguistic observations like these are driving a growing industry of marketing research aimed at wringing as many useful associations as possible from a brand name. The research suggests that this is no mere gimmick on the part of the naming experts, but a real part of the consumer's psyche. Richard Klink, of the Sellinger School of Business and Management in Maryland, subjected the idea of sound symbolism to some meticulous scrutiny. He looked at several classes of sounds that could be grouped according to acoustic frequency: (a) vowels pronounced with the tongue at the front of the mouth (e.g., *ee, i, e*) have a higher frequency than vowels made by pulling the tongue to the back of the mouth (e.g., *o, oo, ah*); (b) fricative consonants (e.g., *f, v, s, z, sh*) have a higher frequency than plosive consonants (e.g., *p, t, g, b*); (c) sounds made by vibrating the vocal folds (e.g., *b, v, g, z*) are lower in acoustic frequency than sounds made without vocal fold vibration (e.g., *p, f, k, s*). He made up pairs of nonexisting (and unlikely!) brand names that were identical except for swapping out high-frequency and low-frequency sounds—for example, contrasts like *wickle – wuckle*; *volud – golud*; *nidax – nodax.* Klink set out to check what "meanings" people associated with high-frequency and low-frequency sounds, and tested the sounds on the dimensions of size, darkness, weight, speed, friendliness, strength, prettiness, softness, sharpness, mildness, thickness, coldness, and bitterness. He recruited hundreds of people to test 124 word-pairs, asking questions such as: "*Which brand of ketchup seems thicker? Nidax or Nodax? Which brand of toilet paper seems softer? Fonib or Zonib?*" Apparently not completely benumbed by the whole experience, subjects didn't just randomly answer the questions. It seems that front vowels like *ee* sound prettier, thinner, softer, faster, weaker, more bitter, and more feminine than back vowels like *o*. Fricatives like *s* are smaller, faster, lighter, sharper, and more feminine than plosives like *t*. Plosives pronounced without vibrating your vocal folds (e.g., *t*) are smaller, faster, lighter, sharper, and more feminine than their vibrating counterparts (e.g., *d*). And nonvibrating fricatives (e.g., *s*) are faster, softer, and more feminine than vibrating ones (e.g., *z*).

It turns out that a good fit between the evoked attributes and the product is important too—just as *Oracle* might not provide exactly the right associations for laundry soap. Speed and light weight might be attractive qualities for a convertible sports car, but you might want your SUV to sound heavier and more substantial. Indeed, people seem to prefer their sports cars and knife sets with front vowel brand names, and their SUVs and hammers with back vowels. Which is the best name for a beer? *Becks, Coors,* or *Corona*? It depends on whether your ads praise it as cool, clean, and crisp-tasting, in which case go for the front vowel; or as smooth, mellow, and rich-tasting, which goes down best with a back vowel. But in any case, try to avoid the vowel *yoo* as in *puke* and *uh* as in *yuck* and *pus,* as these are the "disgust" vowels.

Poetry and advertising don't always see eye to eye, but when it comes to sound symbolism, their goals are basically the same. Both aim to layer emotions and impressions on top of the meanings of words by deliberately choosing words for their sounds as well as their meanings. Contemporary poet Christian Bök pushes this notion to its limits in his book *Eunoia* (the shortest English word to contain all five vowel letters—it means "beautiful thinking"). Each of the five sections of the book is devoted to a single vowel letter, containing poems limited entirely to the use of that vowel letter.[3] This selection from "Chapter I" nicely conveys small mental spaces:

---

[3] Notice that a single vowel letter can be pronounced with two or more different *sounds,* as is the case in the excerpted poems.

Writing is inhibiting. Sighing, I sit, scribbling in ink this pidgin script. I sing with nihilistic witticism, disciplining signs with trifling gimmick—impish hijinks which highlight stick sigils. Isn't it glib? Isn't it chic? I fit childish insights within rigid limits, writing schtick which might instill priggish mis-givings in critics blind with hindsight. I dismiss nit-picking criticism which flirts with philistinism. I bitch; I kibbitz—griping whilst criticizing dimwits, sniping whilst indicting nitwits, dismissing simplistic thinking, in which philippic wit is still illicit.

And the following selection from "Chapter U" gives a good indication of why some vowels are a brand namer's enemy:

Duluth dump trucks lurch, pull U-turns. Such trucks dump much undug turf: clunk, clunk—thud. Scum plus crud plugs up ducts; thus Ubu must flush such sulcus ruts. Sump pumps pump: chuff, chuff. Such pumps suck up mush plus muck—dung lumps (plus clumps), turd hunks (plus chunks); grugru grubs plus fungus slugs mulch up humus pulp. Ubu unplugs flux. Ubu scrubs up curbs; thus Ubu must brush up sulfur dust plus lugnut rust: scuff, scuff. Ubu burns unburnt mundungus. Ubu lugs stuff; Ubu tugs stuff. Ubu puts up fulcrums. Ubu puts up mud huts, but mugwumps shun such glum suburb slums: tut, tut.

(Reprinted by permission of the author and Coach House Books.)

Who would You Vote for?

In case you don't think of names like Reagan, Clinton, and Obama as brands, you should consider the possibility that sound symbolism may govern the selection of presidents just as it shapes your beer preference. Would you rather vote for Janice Hart, or Aurelia Pucinski? Who sounds more trustworthy—Mark Fairchild or George Sangmeister? In 1986, Illinois voters in the Democratic primaries shocked the political world by choosing the mellifluously named neophytes Hart and Fairchild over their far more experienced opponents.

English professor Grant Smith has developed a phonetic "comfort score" to capture sound patterns in surnames that he believes are associated with the traits of stability and predictability. Based on his scoring system, Clinton is graced with one of the best names in U.S. election history, while Bush is saddled with a stinker, as were the unfortunate Hughes and Dukakis. Smith's comfort scores turned out to do a pretty good job of predicting the outcome of 34 Senate and 44 House elections in 1996. Obviously, no one is suggesting that voters fall under the spell of a pretty name and abandon their political convictions. But suppose you're taking your civic duty to vote seriously enough to show up at the polling station, but haven't really had the time to follow the campaign in all that much detail. Or the candidates just don't strike you as that different from each other. Or you haven't gotten a clear sense from either candidate just what their policies actually amount to. You may be making a choice based largely on your gut impression—and that impression may well be affected, unknown to you, by patterns of electrical current set off by the candidates' names.

Words in the head are sticky and social creatures—when you finally pull one out, you're liable to get lots of bits of meanings that have rubbed onto them as a result of their palling around with other words. But the game of actually *predicting* what a brand new name will mean in the minds of consumers is much more complicated than simply sitting down with a dictionary and figuring out what words it shares beginnings with. And it's also going to be a lot more complicated than just figuring out which "meanings" are tagged onto which specific sounds. For example, any linguist will tell you that a *g* sound at the beginning of a word can be a completely different creature from a *g* sound at the end of a word in the human mind. (Ever wonder, for example, why many Russian or Israeli foreigners say *back* instead of *bag*, but have no trouble saying *gum*?) Naming agencies often use large focus groups to test associations that have been jostled loose up to conscious awareness. And more and more, they are using sophisticated software to find more elusive patterns.

Professor Smith painstakingly developed his "comfort score" for political names through trial and error, raw intuition, and by relying on observations made by other scholars about sound-meaning links. A group of word scientists led by Kimberly Cassidy at the University of Pennsylvania instead decided to see if neural network computing could do a lot of the work for them in figuring out which names sound more masculine or feminine.

Neural networks are computer models that are designed to capture the associative patterns in the human brain. Virtual neurons correspond to bits of information—for example, one "neuron" might represent a *p* sound, another might represent the first consonant of a word, and so on. The artificial neurons are linked together just like neurons in our brains connect up to other neurons. (We don't really know if our *actual* neurons really correspond to these kinds of information units, but the metaphor has been useful as a way of modeling patterns that match up well with human knowledge.) A neural network starts off like a blank slate (mostly). It has a bunch of interconnected neurons, but no information about which neurons are mostly tightly linked with each other. So, it starts off assuming a neutral state in which all associations are equal. It learns the strength of these connections during a "training" phase.

During their training phase, the Penn researchers fed their network a bunch of English names: *Eileen, Robert, Miranda, George, Ray, Franklin,* and so on. The network had to guess whether each name was male or female—and then the correct answer about the name's gender was fed into it. At first, the network's guesses were random, showing no specific link between sounds and the concept of gender. But the idea behind a neural network is that its guesses will over time become less random if there are actually patterns to be discovered—so, if boy names really do differ from girl names in sound alone, the network should discover this. Over time, the network should begin to link male gender with certain sounds, and female gender with other sounds. In fact, this is exactly what happened. Eventually, the network's guesses became less haphazard, until it could offer some reasonable predictions about the gender of a name, even for names it had never "heard" before. And it was able to come up with a "male" score and a "female" score based on its learned connection strengths, reflecting how closely a name fit with its phonetic gender stereotype.

When the researchers looked at the generalizations the network was making, they found that it had learned several patterns that various linguists had already proposed or studied: Male names tend to have stress on the first syllable (e.g. *Franklin, Connor, Chester*) and female names tend to have stress on the second syllable (e.g. *Eileen, Bernice, Colette*). Male names are more likely to have a single syllable (*Drew, Brad, George*) and female names are more likely to have three (e.g., *Barbara, Alicia, Brittany*). And everyone knows that English names ending in -a are almost always female names, so if you're named Ira, you probably have to demonstrate your masculinity in other ways. But the network also learned some patterns that hadn't been noticed before, some of them quite subtle. For example, names beginning with consonant clusters scored as more male, as did names that ended in plosive consonants (*Brad, Dick, Greg*), but only for one-syllable names—and one-syllable names ending in a vowel were scored as more female. Names with *er* in the first syllable scored as more male, and so did names beginning with *w*.

Obviously, marketers care more about what human brains do than what machines do. Do these computer-generated scores tell us anything about whether people think pink or blue thoughts when they hear a new brand name? Quite a lot, apparently. The scientists made up names like *Quop, Ponveen, Stoka*—first names that I guarantee have not yet appeared on any child's birth certificate. They ran these through their neural network to get a gender score, and then had people judge whether these were male or female characters. People tended to agree with the computer, categorizing them similarly.

Then the scientists had one group of people sort products as either masculine or feminine while a second group was asked to pick the best fake name for each product. The name was either gender matched or mismatched based on the computer scores. People liked the names to match the product types—male-scored names for power tools, female-scored names for cosmetics. Brand namers obviously think alike too. *Sports Illustrated* carries more ads for male-scoring names than does *Glamour* magazine. The folks who make their living creating names are catching on to these new computing techniques. Many namers now use hefty word databases and savvy programmers to test for the right blend of associations for a brand name. And language scientists are being snapped up by some naming firms. But the naming of a brand is still some mixture of brain science, computer programming, and black art—after all, no matter how manly it sounds, *Quop* is still a weird name for a table saw.

An Edsel by Any Other Name

The lavishly-hyped Edsel is often referred to as the Titanic of automotive history—it sank to its death almost immediately after its spectacular and expensive launch on "E-Day" on September 4, 1957. Since then, lakes of ink have been spilled to explain why this reasonably made car came to bear its reputation as the Great American Marketing Failure. Its release coincided with an unfortunate recession. Many people thought it was butt-ugly. Literally. Its oval front grille was compared to a toilet seat or a cow that had just given birth. It sure didn't get any help from its name, though. After springing for expensive name consultants, and seeking inspiration from poet Marianne Moore (whose suggestions of names like *Utopian Turtletop* were politely declined), Ford's executives grumbled about all the offerings of the word gurus. Eventually, they decided to ignore the experts and name the car in honor of Edsel Ford, son of founder Henry Ford. Not surprisingly, *Edsel* was not among the naming consultants' top 10. C. Gayle Warnock, public relations director for the Edsel wrote a memo proclaiming "We have just lost 200 000 sales" when he heard about the naming decision.

Even at the time, it was an unpopular boy's name. According to government statistics collected by *babynameshub.com*, popularity for the name peaked in 1927 when an underwhelming 220 or so babies were named Edsel *in the entire U.S.* Records list a grand total of 2399 American males as *ever* having been awarded the name, and not one since 1952. In contrast there are more than 600 000 Henrys, almost a million Jasons and over 4 million Michaels. Now, *Jason* makes a pretty crummy name for a car too, but maybe parents were on to something in giving the name *Edsel* a wide berth. When marketing polls asked consumers to free-associate with the name *Edsel*, they came up with things like *pretzel, hard sell*, and *dead cell*. The word simply does not reside in a classy lexical neighborhood. It doesn't sparkle with imagery or sensuality. Running it through a neural network model would likely pump out a fairly effeminate score. When sales tanked, it was a name easy to ridicule. In fact, the *Edsel* name is now so entwined with failure that the Webster dictionary lists the following secondary definition for the word: "a product, project, etc. that fails to gain public acceptance despite high expectations, costly promotional efforts, etc." No wonder that, amidst the schoolgrounds full of Michaels, Jasons, and (more recently) Liams, you're unlikely to have ever met an Edsel in kindergarten.

A happier story is attached to the name of *Apple*. Named through the sheer intuition of the company's founder Steve Jobs, it would make any name expert grin. It rubs shoulders with some auspicious words—*applaud, application, appeal, ripple.* It seems to snap and crackle with a fresh, fast sound symbolism. The phonetic and semantic distance between the *Apple* name and the names of its marketplace competitors (IBM, Atari, and now Dell) means it's less likely to have to compete in the lexical marketplace as well. *Apple* evokes a sensory experience of crispness and solidity. It's woven into myths of knowledge and innovation. The apple turns up in Western depictions of the Garden of Eden as the seductive fruit of the Tree of Knowledge. It inspired Sir Isaac Newton's scientific insights (the original company logo actually depicted the apple falling on Sir Isaac's head). And it was the fruit sown by that most American of entrepreneurs, Johnny Appleseed. Apple computers would just not seem the same if Steve Jobs had been a lover of plums. Think about it: the plum appears in no great legends, its name is round, heavy, and soft, has the dreaded "disgust vowel", lives next door to *plump, plumber,* and *lump,* and brings to mind squishiness and pruniness rather than a crisp, juicy byte. Names do matter.

Apple was recently joined in the fruity electronics neighborhood by the wireless hand-held device BlackBerry. The BlackBerry was named by Lexicon Branding, a naming firm that relies especially heavily on the expertise of linguists like former Stanford professor Will Leben. The makers of the device were aiming for a highly distinctive name that would set it apart from its more descriptive competitors such as Palm Pilot or Handspring. They wanted consumers to think that the technology was accessible and easy to use, so they avoided techy names like *ProMail* or *TechWizard.* Having rejected the name *Strawberry* as too slow-sounding, Lexicon seized on *BlackBerry* as the perfect alternative. Blackberries are cute, small, and not at all intimidating, just like your BlackBerry ought to be. Linguistic research had found the "b" sound to be especially relaxing, while the two vowels—especially the "e"—were deemed to be quick and light. *Berry* sounds friendly and informal, like the nicknames *Betty* and *Buddy.* The whole name has a playful quality and is certainly unexpected in the context of electronic technology.

BlackBerry doesn't mind being in the same exclusive neighborhood as super-hip Apple. But the distinctiveness of both names goes out the window if entire developments of electronics products with similar names spring up around them. That's why the makers of BlackBerry filed a lawsuit in 2007 against LG Electronics claiming the company infringed the BlackBerry trademark by selling mobile phones under the name *Strawberry* and *Black Cherry.* Now, companies can use the muscle of trademark law to keep away any copycats whose names are close enough to be likely to be confused with the original trademark. But they have no control over names that are dissimilar enough to be easily understood by consumers to be referring to different products, but that still share many of the same associations. What about another multi-media phone named *Banana*? Or an MP3 player named *Tangerine*? If products like these were to crowd the shelves of stores, the names *Apple* and *BlackBerry* would surely lose their freshness and boldness, and merely become part of one big electronic fruit salad.

In fact, just as new nose-related words are likely to begin with *sn,* new brand names do end up being attracted to successful existing brand names, whether by deliberate strategy or something more implicit in the minds of the namers. When Lucent Technologies was first named, it was hailed as a standout name. But Agilent Technologies followed soon after, as did tech companies like Avilant, Naviant, Telegent, Consilient, and Covisint. "Who could blame customers and consumers for being confusant?" wrote Rachel Konrad of CNET News about the naming glut. Pharmaceutical names fizz with fricative sounds like *s*, *v*, *f*, *z*, and *x*: Prozac, Paxil, Zoloft, Nexium, Viagra, Zyrtex, Valium, Celebrex, Dexedrine—to the point where these sounds are about to develop their own sound symbolism, if they haven't already. Trademark laws may keep your competitors from squatting on your property—but they can't prevent the entire re-zoning of lexical neighborhoods.

When is a Brand Name Not a Brand Name?

All companies want their brands to own prime real estate in your mental lexicon. But the reality is that because of the constant dynamic activity going on inside, the mental landscape is continuously shifting over time. The whole naming enterprise ends up a bit like trying to own a waterfront lot at the edge of a mudslide area, or near an active volcano. It can be hard to tell, based on existing connections, what those connections will look like in the future. Paradoxically, a spectacular naming success can actually end up back-firing over time; your brand name can become so well known, and so beyond the reach of its competitors, that it becomes a common generic word for a particular product, rather than your own proprietary brand. When people think of a type of product, that brand name will be so much more active than all others that they'll begin to use the brand name to refer to the whole category of products. When new competitors enter the market, your brand name gets applied to them too in people's everyday language use. When this happens, companies can even be in danger of losing their legal rights to the brand name. The dreaded process of losing the brand identity of a name is known as "genericide."

When your doctor tells you to take two aspirin, is he counseling you to buy the Bayer's product, or will any two tablets of acetylsalicylic acid do? If you travel to the southern United States and order a coke, the waitress might ask you indulgently, "What kind, honey? We've got Pepsi, Coca-Cola, Sprite, and Orange." If you stroll across your *linoleum* floor over to your *formica* countertop, check on the stew in the *crock-pot*, pick up the spilled *kitty litter* in the corner with a *kleenex*, pour a bowl of *granola*, and open your freezer to take out a *popsicle* before proposing a game of after-dinner *ping pong*, you are contributing to the genericide of these brand names. Even *heroin* used to be a brand name—though unlike aspirin, Bayer was probably glad to lose the rights to this one.

McDonald's has built brand identity by creating a branding McLanguage: the company has decorated a whole slew of product names with the prefix *Mc-*. You can get the special McDeal on the McNuggets or the Chicken McGrill, order a McSalad, and consider having a McFlurry for dessert. In its branding zeal, McDonald's inadvertently sent the following linguistic cues to consumers: by using *Mc-* just as if it were a prefix that could be attached to regular words, it encouraged people to decompose *McSalad* and *McNuggets* in their minds as being made up of two meaningful units. Linguists call these units *morphemes*, and it's well known that we can combine lots of them in a single word, like in the complex word *undesirables*, which has no fewer than four separate morphemes (*un-desire-able-s*). Now, once you think of *McSalad* as being formed by *two* bits of meaning, it's natural to want to mix and match and start creatively combining *Mc-* with other words too. This tendency to recombine elements in new ways lies at the very heart of your linguistic urges—your brain basically views language as a giant box of Lego blocks (i.e., linguistic units) that you can take apart and put back together in an infinite number of fascinating structures. A good thing too. Being programmed to play with your language is responsible for the fact that you can understand (and produce) new sentences that you have never heard before, a very handy trick indeed. And before you know it, along with the official line of McProducts, we have McJobs, and McMansions. In 1995, Benjamin Barber worried about the side effects of globalization in his book *Jihad vs. McWorld*. In 1998, George Ritter wrote about McUniversities—the trend towards shallow, cost-effective, convenient, and consumer-oriented practices in higher education. The *Mc-* prefix is now so promiscuous that you can think up almost any noun, run it through a search engine with *Mc-* attached and get numerous hits. I've found: McSchool, McCulture, McParents, McChurch, McThought, McJesus, and even McSex. Unfortunately for McDonald's the prefix is rarely complimentary.

Companies fight hard against this loss of control over their branded language. In 2003, McDonald's objected (unsuccessfully) to Merriam-Webster's definition of *McJob* as "a low-paying job that requires little skill and provides little opportunity for advancement." Not to be defeated, in 2006, the company launched a campaign to shift the public meaning of *McJobs* by reporting the results of a commissioned study in which 90% of McDonald's employees agreed that they were given valuable training, and 82% of workers would recommend that company to their friends as a place to work. In an attempt to re-brand the McLanguage, the new slogan was: "McProspects—over half of our executive team started in our restaurants. Not bad for a McJob."

Google is worried that the verb *to google* is being used as a general term for running a word or phrase through an Internet search engine, and in 2003, the company bullied the lexicography site *Word Spy* into acknowledging the trademark status of the word in its online lexicon. But by the time a word reaches a lexicographer's attention, the word is already being used freely on the street. Trying to control dictionary entries is more of a legal strategy than a psychological one, because dictionary entries are often considered by courts as a concrete piece of evidence documenting the common use of a word. Eliminating the offending definition is a way of getting rid of the *evidence* of generic use of the brand name, but not the problem of its actual use. You can't legislate or control the mental representation of words. That Google was fighting a losing battle became clear in 2010 when the American Dialect Society crowned the verb *google* as the "word of the decade," and filed it with the following definition: "A generic form of 'Google', meaning 'to search the Internet.'"

Ultimately, what drives patterns of language use and change, including genericide, is the set of underlying templates for linguistic knowledge that each of us has learned since well before kindergarten. Genericide is simply one price that commerce has to pay for its intrusion into the mental lexicon—the lexicon giveth, and the lexicon taketh away. And if you invent a distinctive product name like *BlackBerry*, there's not much you can do if equally inventive consumers comment on its addictive properties by referring to it as the *CrackBerry*.

Less Talk is ... Less Action?

Steven Pinker begins his book *The Language Instinct* with a reflection on the miraculous ability that human beings have to "shape events in each other's brains with exquisite precision." Pretty powerful stuff, this language. Yet, we often minimize the role of language. "Mere pretty words" are discounted as "just talk", the antithesis of "action." When I recently googled the phrase "less talk more action", I got over 65 000 hits—about 40 times more than the converse of the phrase. Surely, for marketers to be so preoccupied with the minutiae of words, they must have some reason to believe that talk and action are at least occasional bedmates, and that there is some payoff to the resonance that words set off in our minds. Indeed, some recent clever studies suggest that the associations that are triggered by words can affect our behavior in surprising ways, even when we're not aware of their impact on our actions.

Had a fight with your spouse today? Feeling sluggish and unmotivated? Trouble locating your car keys? Maybe you should think about what you were reading over your morning coffee. John Bargh and his colleagues at New York University have found that the words people are exposed to can shape their behavior in unexpected ways. In one study, they recruited students for two "language tests". In the first test, the students had to create sentences out of scrambled lists of words. (For example: *they, her, bother, see, usually.*) Some of the students had to unscramble sets of word lists in which half of the lists had a word related to the trait of rudeness: *aggressively, bold, bother, disturb, brazen, obnoxious,* and so on. Some others got lists that contained "polite" words: *respect, honor, sensitively, graciously,* etc. The rest of the students had "neutral" lists with words that were not related to politeness or rudeness. Once they were done unscrambling these lists, the students were told that they should go and find the experimenter in a different room down the hall in order to get the second test.

The researchers didn't care at all about the results of the second test, or the first one for that matter. What they were really interested in seeing was how the students would behave when they went to let the experimenter know they were ready for the second test. The experiment was set up so that invariably, the students found the experimenter involved in a conversation with someone else—in fact, unknown to them, a second experimenter in cahoots with the first. The familiar experimenter would see, but not acknowledge the student, and touch his pant leg as a secret signal to his partner, at which time the partner would start a stopwatch. The two would yak until the study subject got impatient and finally interrupted the conversation— at this point the partner would stop the watch. Just to make sure they weren't torturing the students unduly, the experimenters always called it quits after 10 minutes if they hadn't been interrupted by then. Did the students who unscrambled "polite" words languish longer in the hallway? Were the "rude" word unscramblers more assertive? You bet. All but 16% of the students primed with polite words stood meekly in the hallway *for the full 10 minutes* until the experimenter finally took notice of them. The students with the rude word list interrupted most of the time (67%), while the students with the neutral list interrupted 38% of the time. Perhaps the airlines should hand out free crossword puzzles laced with words of patience and serenity when the check-in lines get out of hand.

Other behaviors can be primed too. When undergraduate students unscramble lists with words associated with the elderly, they temporarily undergo a massive acceleration of the aging process: they walk more slowly down the hall, and do worse on a memory test. People become more belligerent when they've seen words or images that are associated with hostility—even when they are presented subliminally. They do better on trivia quizzes when they've been primed to think about college professors, and worse when they've been primed with soccer hooligans. So, words (and images) seem to prime more than just their associated words—they also prime their associated actions and cognitive processes.

A decade ago, results like these struck many scientists as novel and surprising. Nowadays, evidence of unconsciously primed behavior is turning up in journal articles faster than graduating seniors at a keg party. This research has created a resurgence of interest in the various ways in which behavior can be shaped by information that slips beneath people's level of awareness. And along with that interest is a new look at the potential of subliminal advertising. Back in 1957, the idea of subliminal advertising created a media frenzy when a market researcher named James Vicary claimed to have driven movie audiences from their seats to the snack bar to buy popcorn and Coke by flashing subliminal messages at 1/300th of a second throughout the movie. The idea of this kind of mind control created public outrage, and advertisers everywhere vehemently denied using any such techniques. (At the same time, consumers spent millions of dollars on subliminal self-help tapes that promised to teach you French or enhance your self-confidence while you sleep.)

It turned out that Vicary's results were an outright fabrication—he likely never even ran the study. In the ensuing years, psychologists for the most part pooh-poohed the possibility of the kind of behavior manipulation that Vicary described, and subliminal self-help tapes have been found to be worthless from a scientific standpoint.

And yet, there's that ever-increasing mound of newer evidence showing the effects of unconsciously processed information on behavior. All of this work seems to suggest that subliminal advertising *should* work, at least under some circumstances. This has prompted a new breed of respectable university-based researchers to take another look.

The most direct replication of Vicary's original (and bogus) study has come from a group of Dutch psychologists led by Johan Karremans. These scientists led their study subjects to believe that they would be participating in two unrelated experiments (in fact, it's pretty common for subjects doing psychology experiments to be scheduled for several unrelated studies at one sitting). The first study was described as a visual detection experiment. The subjects' mission, they were told, was to detect small changes in a string of letters on a screen: they would see a string of upper-case *B*s (BBBBBBBBB), and on occasion, one of the *B*s would be replaced by a lower-case *b* ((BBBBBBbBB). If they detected this, they were to report the change. What the subjects didn't know, of course, was that prior to each string of Bs, the computer would subliminally flash either the words *Lipton Ice*, or, as a control comparison, the same letters scrambled into *Npeic Tol*. After performing this rather arduous visual detection task, subjects were told they would now be participating in a study on consumer behavior. They were asked which of two brand names they would prefer if they were offered a drink right then, and were given the choice of Lipton Ice tea and Spa Rood, a Dutch brand of mineral water. They were also asked to report how thirsty they were.

The scientists found that the subjects who reported not being very thirsty were not subliminally swayed to prefer Lipton Ice over Spa Rood—that is, seeing *Lipton Ice* did not make them choose this product more often than those who saw *Npeic Tol*. But among those who indicated that they were thirsty, the subjects who were primed with the product name *did* choose Lipton Ice more often. In a second version of the study, Karremans and his colleagues wanted to see if the same thing would happen if they *made* their subjects feel thirsty. This time, half of the subjects first took part in what was billed as a "tongue detection" task—they were given a type of salty licorice candy and asked to detect what letter was stamped on one side of the candy (yes, this candy not only exists in the Netherlands, but is allegedly fairly popular). The other half were deprived of this "treat" and skipped this part of the study. Both groups then went on to do the same "visual detection" and "consumer behavior" tests of the previous study.

Mirroring the results of the first study, the subjects who'd been given the salty candy chose Lipton Ice more often when they were primed with the product name—but those who hadn't ingested the salt showed no preference, despite having been subliminally primed with the same words. So, subliminal priming *did* seem to tilt people in the direction of the primed product—but only if they were in a state where they might be receptive to the relevant type of product. Perhaps if

Vicary had been more diligent and actually conducted his famous fraudulent study, handing out free salted popcorn and priming the audience with subliminal messages for Coke, he might have made the same media splash, minus the subsequent disgrace. Of course, it's unlikely he would have increased sales to the extent he claimed (up to a 57% increase in sales). Subliminal priming effects of any kind in the lab tend to be quite subtle. But for many companies, even subtle nudges towards their product can translate into significant profits.

More recently than Vicary's sham study, you might remember the controversy that flared over the famous *RATS* ad placed by the Republican Party in the 2000 U.S. presidential election campaign. (And if you're too young to remember, you may still be able to YouTube it.) The ad attacked the Democratic opponent's proposed health care policies arguing that under Al Gore's plan, bureaucrats rather than individual patients and their doctors would have control over prescriptions. As the voice-over uttered the damning words "*The Gore Prescription Plan: Bureaucrats Decide*," the word *RATS* was very briefly superimposed on the screen in large letters just before being replaced by the text *Bureaucrats Decide*. Bush claimed that this was an accidental result, and brushed aside accusations of subliminal advertising as "weird and bizarre" conspiracy theories. When pressed, Alex Castellanos, the ad's creator, said he flashed part of the word *bureaucrats* as a "visual drumbeat" to create visual interest, and insisted it was coincidental that the particular letters that happened to appear spelled "*rats.*" Many people shrugged it off, stating that subliminal advertising had never been found to work anyway.

Whether or not the subliminal message was intentional, as a language scientist, I remember that I couldn't help but wonder. It seemed as if the ad *should* work. First of all, the word *RATS* flashed for two video frames—66 milliseconds—in other words, right at the upper range of your typical masked priming study, where subliminal words are activated, but not generally consciously detected unless you know what you're looking for. And I couldn't help but be impressed with the potential of the ad to subliminally reinforce lexical associations. The ad played off already-shared sound associations among *rats, bureaucrats,* and *Democrats* (though one might argue that the Dems had even bigger problems to start with by sharing beginnings with choice words such as *demolition, demonstration, demagogue*).

It turns out I wasn't the only curious scientist. Psychologists Joel Weinberger and Drew Westen actually put the matter to scientific test. They recruited study volunteers to take a test over the Internet, and showed them a photograph of an unknown person, who was presented as a potential political candidate. After looking at the photo, the volunteers had to mark how much they agreed or disagreed with statements like "*There is something fishy about this candidate*," "*There is something about this candidate that makes me feel that I can trust him*," "*I would vote for this candidate*." What the volunteers didn't know was that *before* the photo came up, a word or set of symbols flashed on the screen for one video frame.

Some people saw *RATS,* while others saw *STAR* or *ARAB* or *XXXX* (this study was run before 9/11, when attitudes about Arabs were assumed to be pretty neutral). Those who saw *RATS* flashed before the image of the candidate ended up feeling more negative about him than any of the groups who saw the other words or symbols.[4]

In this study, the "candidate" was a fictional character, and not anyone people knew when they took part in the study. Can subliminal priming affect people's feelings about a candidate they *do* know, someone they might already have strong opinions about? In a follow-up study, Weinberger and Westen found that yes, it can. This time around, instead of a word like *RATS,* people were subliminally exposed to an image of former president Bill Clinton. They then saw a photo of the then-California governor Gray Davis, and had to answer questions about their attitudes towards him. At the time, Davis (who was a Democrat) was a controversial figure. He'd taken a good deal of heat over a widespread energy crisis and the state of the economy after the popping of the dot.com bubble. The study actually took place during the week of a referendum to recall him as governor. So, people were very likely to see him in the news, and to have formed some opinions about him.

Not surprisingly, the subliminal association with Bill Clinton had different effects on Democrats and Republicans. Republicans who "saw" the brief image of Clinton rated Gray somewhat more negatively than those who weren't exposed to the image; Clinton's image caused Democrats to rate Gray somewhat less negatively. But the biggest effects were on the "swing" voters, people who hadn't registered as either Democrats or Republicans. For these people (who were inclined to view Gray negatively), the image of Clinton softened their attitudes fairly dramatically. After seeing their results, Weinberger and Westen suggested that perhaps Al Gore shouldn't have been so eager to distance himself from fellow Democrat Clinton during the Bush/Gore 2000 election.

Whether this kind of subtle subliminal association is actually more or less effective than the overt associations hammered home by your garden-variety mudslinging ad is a matter of debate, of course. What we don't know, among other things, is how long-lasting the effects of such subliminal words and images might be. Do they fade very quickly, or do they subtly change impressions until the viewer gets to the voting booth? Or do they create a bias that might color the way new information is interpreted? Until science gets to answering these questions (and no doubt it soon will), we can't tell whether the *RATS* ad might have had any impact on Bush's campaign. But the ad generated a great deal of brouhaha at the time for

---

[4] One interesting finding was that while seeing *RATS* made people agree with the negative statements more strongly, it actually didn't make them agree with the *positive* ones any less, suggesting that positive and negative feelings are somewhat independent of each other, and the negative emotions are easier to manipulate through subliminal priming. This may be related to the fact that in many cases, people tune in more strongly to negative information than positive information.

its alleged use of techniques that so obviously flew below the voters' radar. And rightly so. The word RATS *was* a visual drumbeat—one that may well have beat a certain impression into viewers' minds.

The End of Choice?

Studies like these get nice, well-behaved academics embroiled in fierce existential debates about whether there is such a thing as free will. In a recent paper, researchers Ap Dijksterhuis, John Bargh, and Joost Miedema put the question somewhat bluntly when they asked whether we think more like men and women— shaping our own destinies, and creating our own identities—or like mackerels, responding automatically like schooling fish to the cues emitted by our environment and our fellow mackerels. To what extent *can* we channel our own minds, and harness them to fulfill our conscious goals?

Sigmund Freud, for all his emphasis on the power of the unconscious, strongly believed that through conscious insight, people could eventually tame their wild hidden selves, and he was as busy showing patients how to rule their unconscious drives as his nephew Edward Bernays was marketing to them. Beliefs similar to Freud's are the foundation of many religions and educational systems—and to some extent, this book. Certainly, there's plenty of evidence in the scientific literature that shows that in many situations, we can direct and change the nature of our cognitive processes through very conscious goals. For example, memory studies dating back to the 1980s have shown that people can deliberately choose to process verbal material in such a way as to remember it better. If they read it with the specific intent of evaluating the content rather than simply memorizing it, they organize it in a way that helps them remember it. Studies of electrical activity in the brain underscore the reality of the different mental processes: when people read for understanding and evaluation, there's a good bit more activity on the right side of their brain. Anyone who's ever tried to cut corners by cramming for an exam with the goal of simply regurgitating the material for tomorrow's final is probably painfully aware of how quickly that knowledge fades. All of this shows that we're not entirely at the mercy of our own internal memory systems, with no ability to influence them—when we decide to invest the mental resources to really understand and organize content, we can process the information differently, and reap the cognitive benefits.

True enough, but the new unconsciousness research also hints that the deliberate and the unconscious may be more intertwined than we thought. Goals and intentions, which to some extent conduct the noisy symphonies within our minds, can *themselves* be activated by information that is not consciously processed. Here's an example of how this might work: John Bargh and his colleagues have found that by subliminally priming subjects with words suggesting either memorization or understanding (e.g., *retain, hold,* versus *judge, evaluate*), they were able to induce exactly the same effects on a memory task as instructing subjects to read either for rote memory or for understanding. What's more, when the scientists measured electrical activity in the brain, they found that simply exposing people to the "evaluation" words caused greater activity on the right side of the brain, just as if they were consciously trying to process more deeply for understanding. This happened even though the subjects did not know they were evaluating, and did not intend to evaluate, believing they were simply listening to a word list! All those schoolteachers who lectured Johnny on applying himself should instead have been piping in soft words like *strive, succeed, excel, mastery, brilliant...*

If brands can orient people to make certain choices, can they also activate particular goals that trigger a style of thinking, as John Bargh did with word priming? A strong enough brand may well be able to accomplish this. Apple's marketing of their Macintosh computers has focused on emphasizing the claim that its computer interface is especially well suited for creative tasks such as working with images, videos, and so on. Everything about the company's brand identity—from its "Think Different" slogan to its commercials to its product design—revolves around creating a brand that is perceived as nonconformist, innovative, and creative. You may have seen at least some of the amusing "Mac versus PC" commercials, in which a hip human personification of a Mac computer stands in stark contrast to his stodgy "PC" rival.

In one of these ads, the young, casually-dressed "Mac" has joined the middle-aged, suit-donning, hair-thinning "PC" at a counseling session to improve their relationship. In contrast to Mac's relaxed, receptive body language, PC's gestures are tense and hostile—we immediately know who the problem is in *this* relationship. PC begins the session by saying "I feel inadequate. PCs get viruses, we can't do much out of the box ..." A concerned, sympathetic Mac interrupts: "See, I don't know why you're so hard on yourself, I don't get it." The therapist cheerfully suggests, "Mac, why don't you say something positive about PC." "OK! Easy," responds Mac. "PC, you are a wizard with numbers, and you dress like a gentleman." "PC?" prompts the therapist. "Well, Mac, I guess you are a little better at creative stuff," concedes PC, but he can't resist adding "Even though it's completely juvenile and a waste of time." "Maybe you should come in twice a week," suggests the counselor.

If Apple works so hard at getting you to *think* that using a Mac computer will help you be more creative, can the mere unconscious thought of the brand actually *make* you more creative? To find out, social psychologist Gráinne Fitzsimons and her colleagues exposed students to subliminal flashes of the logos for either IBM or Apple. The subliminal logos appeared for an ephemeral 13 milliseconds, embedded in what the students thought was a simple arithmetic task; they were told that their job was to keep a running sum of numbers that appeared on a screen, and they were not aware of seeing anything else on the screen. Next, the students had to complete a test that's considered to be a standard measure of creativity. In this particular test, people are asked to come up with as many unusual uses as they can for common, everyday objects. For example, a paperclip might be creatively used as an earring, or to hang ornaments on a Christmas tree, or (unfolded) as a measuring tool. To score the test, the researchers looked for the number of uses people could think of, how different these uses were from each other, how unique each response was compared with the responses of other people, and how detailed the descriptions of the uses were. All of this added up to a composite "think different" score. They then looked to see whether students who were primed with the Apple logo scored higher on the test than those who were primed with IBM. They did.

Most people bristle at the idea of subliminal advertising. Even considering that there might be upsides to the practice—such as evoking more creative behavior—the whole thing seems pretty deceptive and unfair. To many, it's just a step away (if that) from selling beef by pumping consumers full of beef-craving chemicals, or piping trust-inducing hormones into a car dealership.

But the view from current science suggests that our minds have actually evolved in such a way that we *routinely* process information, make decisions, and take actions in ways that are outside of our conscious control and awareness. This isn't just about advertisers and consumers. It's about the way we interact with our world. It's about knowledge we've sucked into ourselves without even knowing we have it. Much of the time, it allows us to function with impressive efficiency. It probably allows us to get through the grocery store without blowing a mental gasket. But it also means that we don't always know ourselves very well, or *fully* make choices even when we think we do.

Among academics, the free will debate is likely to rage for some time. Over the past few decades, scientific study of the human mind has burst open a detailed view of the richness of the unconscious, revealing roomfuls of cognitive machinery that crank away at implicitly learned and implicitly perceived information. Scientists have been surprised and intrigued by the sheer amount of activity that goes on beneath the threshold of our consciousness and how deeply it can impact our behavior. At the same time, psychologists are also becoming aware of the fact that humans have an especially hefty part of their brains devoted to *executive control*—that is, the part of the mind that makes decisions, sifts through alternatives and competing information, and regulates impulses. In reality, we are part man (in the ideal, rational sense) and part mackerel. We judge and evaluate, and we also act reflexively. Our brains are built to do both. Science still hasn't worked out many aspects of the relationship between these two sides of ourselves—but in all likelihood, it will be complex, and the answers will be about *when* and *under what conditions* we act like men, and when and why we swim along in whatever direction our unconscious minds point us.

In the meantime, we can count on advertisers to make their pitches to our mackerel minds at least as often as to the deliberate judges within. And as the sheer volume of advertising continues to balloon on a daily basis, creating an unmanageable information glut, it seems likely that more and more of our interactions with persuasive messages will be delegated to our fast, streamlined, automatic, unconscious minds.

3

The Attentional Arms Race

Sam Aikens rolls out of bed about 6:30 every morning. He's an early riser and he has a morning routine: get up, do some exercises, shower, dress, eat breakfast, log onto his web accounts, breeze through the morning newspaper, and leave for work promptly at 8:35 AM so as to arrive at his desk at 9:00 exactly. Of course, while he's doing all these things he's also doing something else. While he exercises he has on a television morning talk show; while shaving and showering he tunes into a music radio station ("Soft rock sounds of the 1980s and 1990s"), and while preparing and eating breakfast he continues to watch the morning television show, which he puts back on after checking his email for the morning and going to several of his favorite websites. As he looks through the morning newspaper, the television remains on, and is clicked off just before he crawls into his car. In his car, he typically turns on a talk news station for the drive in. He arrives at his desk, fresh and ready for another day.

But before he arrives at his desk, he has already taken in a huge amount of information from his morning experiences. He's heard the local weather—in fact six times, and read it twice. He knows the headlines, about the dollar's continuing plunge against the euro, the warehouse fire on the East Side, the diplomatic overtures being undertaken in the Middle East, and something about some celebrity or other maybe being pregnant, or maybe not. He's heard a review of the latest action film, read about some famous author coming to town, that the city council has floated the idea of raising taxes 5.2%, and has enjoyed his favorite comic strips in the funnies section. There is something about attempts to control drugs in professional wrestling, that his town's high school basketball team won again, and a brief report about global warming and melting glaciers in Greenland.

This is only a small portion of the information he's encountered and paid at least some attention to in the first two and a half hours of the day. He has done other things that require taking in information as well: He opened an envelope from the electric company to find he had neglected to pay his bill last month. He checked the calendar to see if he had any appointments late in the day. He looked at the thermometer (38 degrees Fahrenheit, not too bad for this climate), scribbled "AA batteries" on a grocery list, and wondered if this is the day he'd return that book to

Sold on Language: How Advertisers Talk to You and What This Says About You. By Julie Sedivy and Greg Carlson
© 2011 John Wiley & Sons Ltd.

the library, deciding against it as he noticed it wasn't due for another 10 days. He received a phone call from his mother on the West Coast (a daily event for him), and placed a phone call to make a routine dental appointment. His email contained three messages he chose to read, two he decided to read later, and six he decided to ignore for as long as possible. He logged onto US Airways to see about flights to the West Coast (after his mother's call), and checked out car rental rates at Hertz. The radio had an editorial on confirmation hearings in the senate that he disagreed with, and an interview with an ex-baseball player that he found kind of boring. He learned that Ozzy Osbourne never played guitar for the Byrds, correcting a misimpression he had somehow gotten from somewhere, and that the German electorate was in a restive mood (according to one analyst, at any rate).

This, and lots more, hardly exhausts the information Sam has taken in over the course of his morning routine, though. Among all this information, there is another sort interwoven. Basically, he's been exhorted to do many many things, for a wide variety of reasons. What sorts of things has he been told to do? Well, by the time he has arrived at the office he has been told to buy a Buick from Farnsworth, to chew Dentyne Ice gum, to take out a home equity loan, to see *Vengeance at All Costs*, to shop at Ralph's supermarkets, to enjoy the friendly atmosphere at Wal-Mart, to test-drive a Dodge pick-up truck, to buy Quaker Oatmeal—good for the heart. He's been told to drink milk, not to smoke, to make his children happy by taking them to Wally's Sea World, and to give generously to the United Way; to tune into the 11:00 "Eyewitness" News ("with Ginny and Dan"), and to purchase health insurance from Blue Cross/Blue Shield. He's supposed to use Listerine, and to "Power-bank" at Lincoln Trust, eat plenty of pork, wear Hanes underwear, and on five occasions to ask his doctor about this drug (which cures bursitis) or that (the one that relieves migraines). If he's injured, he's supposed to see ("Compassionate") Sammy Betlam for legal representation, if his furnace is out to call Cole's for prompt service, and if he's feeling tuckered to drink some Gatorade.

From the newspaper he learns that Brennan's is having a half-off sale "on selected items," there's a preseason sale on John Deere lawn equipment, he's supposed to bank at Merchant's National, and to borrow for a car from First Federal. There's beautiful paint colors at Sherwin's he's supposed to buy, there's nutritious foods at Cali's Mediterranean Restaurant, and Hallmark Cards help you remember, be remembered.

His Internet site urges him to check out EverythingFurniture.com, Drugs at 70% off, Free Credit Reports (which don't quite turn out to be free), deals on plasma televisions, inkjet cartridges, and Master's Degrees. Something about a local taxi and escort service.

His email headers promise great deals on home loans, great deals on the latest drugs, and great deals on an exciting new sex life. The calendar he checks advertises the joys of his local newspaper (he got it for free).

Once he's in his car, the radio urges him to shop at Dodel's Toyota and Subaru, to "get on down" to Mr. Seconds, to play the Illinois Lottery, to think highly of the County Sheriff's crime-fighting efforts, to "buy big" at Big Roger's used trucks and vans, to click on Travelocity.com before tomorrow night for Getaway Specials, to get a cellular phone from Nokia, Internet service from Blue Tie, your cleaning supplies from Mason's, and your catered food for weddings and other events, from Leon's Catering. You should call Dave's Plumbing, and Franklin Electric, and of course don't smoke, it's bad for you. Report all crime via the TipLine (644-TIPS).

The billboards Sam looks at tell him to buy Black Velvet, to join in the fight against Child Abuse, to worship at Rev. Fox's Church of Love, to wear cotton clothing, to sail Carnival Lines to Bermuda, buy your fireworks here, buy gasoline at rock-bottom prices just ahead, and to stay at the New! Holiday Inn Express, next right. The car in front of him has a "Mary Kay Cosmetics" bumper sticker, another has two stickers both about someone's kids being an honors student at Roosevelt High, and the bus in front of him has a big grimy sign on the back—he has to stare at it for nearly five minutes locked in traffic—which (irritatingly) says "Made you Look! Transit Advertising WORKS. Anderson Outdoor Advertising 934-0098." When he passes the bus he sees on the side another exhortation to see that lawyer, and to purchase auto insurance from Geico. He passes three more busses on his way in, and numerous shops with large signs advertising everything from Grandma's Pies to Gucci purses to Goodyear snow tires. The truck next to him advertises on its side Stan's Muffler Shop, or Green Giant frozen vegetables, Merry Maids cleaning service, Swan's Ice Cream . . .

Even Sam's keys are on a keyring that tells him his "Best Bet" is Bett's Mazda. When Sam called for a dental appointment he was on hold for a time being advised by a recorded message that this dentist offers specials on teeth whitening for a sparkling smile. Sam did stop at an ATM this morning, where he was advised on the screen of low mortgage rates from his friendly "personal touch" bank.

And he walks into his office, where a full day's work awaits.

Mental Spotlights

Why doesn't Sam's head explode? Why doesn't he arrive at work exhausted, disoriented, and confused? He has gulped down an ocean of information in the past two and a half hours, he's already been exposed to several hundred commercial messages alone, yet Sam has the feeling of just beginning his day. How does he do it?

The answer is one that junior high teachers have known all along: that people ignore most of the information that surrounds them. Or rather, they shunt most of it off to the periphery of their attention, allowing only a small, select portion of it a full audience with the attentive part of their minds. Selective hearing and seeing is not just a fact about adolescent contrariness; it's a systematic human trait. It allows us to function in the Age of Over-Information, when by some estimates we're exposed to around 4 000 commercial messages daily. And the upshot of it is that there are dramatic differences in the quality and depth of information-processing that happen at the edges of our attention as opposed to its center stage.

Mental attention and vision work in ways that are very similar to each other. When you look at a scene in front of you, your feeling is that you just take it in, aware of most of whatever happens to be in your field of vision, maybe dropping off at the far edges of your peripheral vision. But in fact, you have detailed vision for only a tiny spatial area—about the size of your thumbnail held at arm's length in front of you. You don't so much "see" the scene in front of you as *interpret* it by having your eyes jump around from one spot to another every fraction of a second to take visual snapshots of these tiny regions. Your mind smoothly assembles these snapshots into a coherent scene by means of a perceptual miracle. At any given moment, you're virtually blind to most of the scene outside of this tiny area—and in the instants where you're shifting your eyes from one location to another, you *are* blind; if the head of the person you were looking at suddenly became a chicken head just as you were shifting your eyes away from it, you would miss it.

Vision and reading expert Keith Rayner can show you a compelling demonstration of the extent of your blindness to much of what's in front of you. Here is what happens in one of his perceptual span experiments: You sit at a computer screen wearing an eyetracker, and read some text on the screen. The eyetracker interacts with the software that presents the text on the screen, and sends a signal about the exact location where you are pointing your eyes. The computer is programmed to respond to this signal by replacing all of the letters outside of a small window surrounding this location with random junk. So, let's say you are reading the line below, and are focusing on the letter "t" in *analysts*:

Analysts argue that the economic outlook is quite bleak.

What would actually show up on the screen is something like this:

Ghjlysts argue that thd wooxbfsa vptulmi re cwjas ybuzl.

And as your eye lands on "u" in *argue*, the screen would show this:

Ghalkech argue that the econbfsa vptulmi re cwjas ybuzl.

As you move your eyes, this window of readable text moves as well. Now, to someone standing behind you, the text on the screen looks like utter garbage because the moving window of sensible text doesn't match up with his eye movements. But to *you* the text looks perfectly normal. You have no idea that anything unusual is happening outside of your perceptual span.

How small is this perceptual span? Keith Rayner reports that if you're an English reader, it's roughly three characters to the left and about 15 to the right of where your eyes are focused, as shown in the example here. Because you move your eyes left to right, your attention is aimed rightward—for Hebrew readers, who scan text right to left, the perceptual span is greater on the left than on the right. And the window in which you can actually *identify* the letters is even smaller, limited to a couple of characters to either side of where your gaze is pointed. You can try a version of this by holding a newspaper at arm's length, and focusing your vision very tightly on a particular character in one of the headlines. You'll find it hard to identify the words right next to where you're looking, and absolutely impossible to read any part of a headline of an adjacent article. You might be able to tell it's a headline, but there's no way you can read it.

Mental attention works a lot like this, sampling from small targeted areas to put a big picture together. There are tightly focused areas of attention, just like spotlights that can jump around at various places in the environment. People don't register awareness of much that falls outside of these spotlights. Scientists call this lack of awareness outside the spotlight "inattentional blindness."

The normally dry, technical scientific literature includes several hilarious demonstrations of inattentional blindness. In one of them, psychologists Daniel Simons and Christopher Chabris had Harvard students watch a video of two "teams" passing basketballs—there were players with white shirts and players with black shirts intermingled in a circle. The students were told to keep a mental count of the number of times a member of the white team passed the ball to another white member. To do this, they'd have to actively ignore the passes that were being made among the black-shirted members at the same time. At the end of the video, they had to give their count, and then were asked whether they had noticed anything unusual in the video. More than half of them said, "Nooo. *Should* I have?" What they failed to notice, being so engrossed in their task, was that at some point in the middle of the basketball frenzy, a person in a black gorilla suit walked from one end of the screen right into the thicket of players, stopped for a moment to face the camera, thumped his chest, and then casually ambled off to the other end of the screen. Some subjects had to see the video again before they'd actually believe the experimenter that the gorilla was there. And when subjects had to count both passes *and* throws among members of the team, they were even less likely to notice the gorilla, showing that the more effort it takes to do something, the blinder you are to the rest of your environment.

Pointing your eyeballs at something is no guarantee that you'll actually pay attention to it either. In another study, Daniel Simons and Daniel Levin had a student experimenter approach subjects on the Cornell University campus to ask for directions to a certain building. While the subject was in the midst of giving directions, two people carrying a door rudely walked right between the experimenter and the subject. What happened next was this: unbeknownst to the subject, the experimenter swapped places with one of the people behind the door. The "replacement" (who was wearing different-colored clothing) then stepped out and took his place, resuming the interaction as if nothing had happened. About *half* of all of the subjects failed to notice the switcheroo, and blithely continued giving directions, even making eye contact with the new incarnation of the experimenter just as they had with the previous one. But the researchers noted an interesting thing: almost all of the subjects who were themselves students *noticed* the switch, while most of the older subjects—presumably professors or staff—didn't. You might be tempted to suspect Cornell professors of senility, but the researchers tested a different hypothesis. They speculated that the students, being of the same social group as the experimenter, were more motivated to pay close attention to the person they were talking to. So they re-did the same study, this time using the same experimenters as before, but now dressed as construction workers instead of students, and found that student subjects noticed the switch only 35% of the time.

These studies reveal two things (other than the fact that professors really are oblivious to their students): First, that we dole out our attention in an uneven way, generous in paying close attention to some aspects of our environment, and stingy with others. And second, that we have a lot of control—though not necessarily conscious—over how we divide our attentional resources, paying more attention to things that demand more effort, or that seem more relevant to us.

This is grim news for advertisers. It means that consumers are quite good at ignoring things that don't strike them as worthy of attention. Sam Aikens can move throughout his day without imploding because he can take control over his attentional spotlight, leaving most of the unwanted advertising clutter in the dark recesses of his mind. This leaves advertisers with two main strategies they can use: They can go to extraordinary measures to get you to aim your attentional spotlight at their ads. Or they can craft messages that will manage to persuade on the attentional sidelines.

Survival Instincts and Pop-Up Ads

Of course, your chances of survival would be in jeopardy if information outside your attentional spotlight *never* had a chance to break through into your conscious awareness. Driving would be an even more lethal experience than it is if you couldn't react to a car unexpectedly barreling through an intersection while you were engrossed in navigating. Fortunately, along with your ability to focus your attention very narrowly, you're also equipped with an instinctive orienting response to sudden movements, unexpected events, and loud noises. Your instinctive mind can step in to yank control of your attention from your conscious mind for your own protection. This kind of orienting response can be cleverly exploited as a way to forcibly attract your attention. If the gorilla in the basketball videos had been wearing a cap that flashed pink and green neon lights and played "Happy Birthday," chances are, *everyone* would have noticed it. The TV advertising version of this is to make sure the first seconds of commercials are extra loud, extra flashy and with lots of extra movement compared to the TV program they're nested in, or novel and unexpected enough in some way that nabs your attention.

Pop-up Internet ads are especially aggressive in their attempts to hijack people's orienting response. And with good reason. The interactive nature of the Internet makes it a much less passive experience than watching TV or even browsing the newspaper. Though there's plenty of aimless surfing too, people mostly go on the Internet with some specific purpose in mind—to find the best deal on digital cameras, to inadvisably post their weekend photos on Facebook, to research the plot of "Wuthering Heights" for that paper due tomorrow, or to beat their high score in Tetris online. So, they tend to be pretty focused on *doing* something, not just receiving information—just like the subjects in the Harvard gorilla study. Their attentional spotlight is likely to be narrowly aimed. In fact, when researchers slap an eyetracking device on people who are browsing or searching the Internet, they find that regular, static banner ads are almost always ignored. Advertisers resort to fancy animation techniques in order to trigger those instinctive, survival-based orienting responses. Pop-up ads create an abrupt, unexpected event, often with dancing blondes, fireworks or flashing, flying, spinning, rotating, zooming text.

We often experience these ads as annoying precisely because we have to wrestle with them to regain control over our attentional resources—more attention to the perceptual alarms that are being set off by these unwanted ads means less attention for whatever mental tasks we're trying to accomplish. They act as dead weights on our cognitive processes, slowing down Internet searches and making us feel as if we're expending more mental effort, which we are. Imagine being a subject in the gorilla study, counting passes among team members while trying to ignore a flashing, bleeping gorilla on the screen. Your performance would plummet. In fact, just about every move that Internet ads make to attract attention reduces the speed or accuracy of the main task a consumer is trying to accomplish. It's a zero-sum game.

The Harvard researchers found that when people were tracking passes among members of the *black* team, rather than the white team, they were more likely to notice the guy in the black gorilla suit. Because the gorilla was perceptually similar to the players that subjects were actively tracking, it became more "visible." A study of pop-up ads by Ping Zhang at Syracuse University found a similar relationship. This time, subjects took a hit in performance when pop-up animations were similar to the items they were told to search for on the web page, presumably because they pulled away attention from the main task. And, just like in the gorilla study, where making the main task harder made it less likely that subjects would notice the gorilla, Zhang found that there was less interference from pop-up animations when the task was harder. So, the more focused people are in their interactions with the content of a website, the more extreme advertisers need to be to attract their attention.

By setting up such an adversarial relationship with consumers over control of their attention, pop-up ads have come to rival telemarketers for Most Hated Advertising status. Their tactics also put them on a collision course with the websites that host them, by making it harder and more frustrating for consumers to extract the information they need. This makes animated Internet ads very different from most other kinds of traditional ads—TV or radio ads don't compete for your attention *while* you're viewing or listening to a program. And print ads, while obviously using lots of attention-getting devices, don't normally interfere with your ability to read an article. In fact, a study by Bunnyfoot Universality, a company that does behavioral usability research, reported that pop-up ads frustrated Internet users so much that the negative vibes spread to the websites that hosted them. Users were hyper-vigilant about avoiding the ads, often managing to close them down before they were fully loaded. They remembered the content of the ads less than 2% of the time. Researchers at Bunnyfoot concluded that using pop-up ads amounted to "commercial suicide"—not just for the brands doing the advertising, but for the hosts as well.

Internet ads that rely on brute force to bust into the attentional spotlight appear to be losing the arms race. Responding to consumer demand, software developers have created web browsers that block many unwanted ads. But even when the ads do load up, our minds just may be flexible and powerful enough to learn to banish them to dark spaces and to suppress even that instinctive orienting response. Several studies have shown that over time, people can learn to tune out animated ads. Like the villagers in the story of the boy who raised the wolf alarm too often, our minds have learned to ignore these sudden movements in our peripheral vision.

Surprise Me

Let's suppose you walk into the lobby of your bank. There happens to be a lion sitting in the corner. Given that you move your eyes roughly three times a second and that your vision for any area other than your thumbnail at arm's length is dismal, how long will it take before your eyes finally land on the lion and you scream or run away?

Not as long as you might think based on what I just told you. Although you can't *see* very well in your peripheral vision, your brain can process enough of the fuzzy images to catch whether something seems wrong or out of place. You know what banks and the things inside them are supposed to look like, and that large blobby shape over there doesn't quite fit . . . better check it out. So, like flashing lights and sudden movements, unexpected or incongruent images can trigger an orienting response even before you are aware of what they are.

This was first discovered by vision researchers Geoffrey Loftus and Norman Mackworth. They showed their subjects line drawings of a familiar scene. For example, the drawing might illustrate a farm scene showing a farmhouse, barn, silo, farm equipment, and so on. Chances are, though, you've never seen an octopus in a barnyard. Loftus and Mackworth created just such images. By tracking their subjects' eyes, they found that people's eyes zoomed faster toward the bizarre object than they did towards a highly predictable object in the same location, such as a tractor. People also looked at the weird object more often, and for longer periods of time. Incongruity was a magnet for attention.

Loftus and Mackworth suggested that unexpected things attract attention because there is more information to be gained by looking at them. If you can rely on your memory to tell you that tractors are commonly found on farms and what they look like, you won't learn a whole lot by closely inspecting the tractor. But anything that doesn't fit with what you already know about farms will probably show you something you didn't already know. So your attention is efficiently guided by your acquired expertise about the world around you.

Consumers can turn this expertise to their advantage. They've adapted to their message-saturated environment by using their expectations about what ads look like and where they are placed in order to tune them out. Advertisers need to tune them back in by doing the unexpected. In one ingenious ad campaign, Folgers Coffee turned manhole covers in New York City into giant, mugs of hot coffee— images of the dark liquid in a round cup were fitted over the covers, complete with well-placed holes to let the steam out. When pedestrians walked by in the morning, this created the illusion of enormous coffee mugs embedded below street level. New York City is prime real estate for such ingenious street ads. Here's another one, from an ad campaign by FedEx Kinko's, which placed oversized highlighters and bottles of correction fluid throughout New York:

Reprinted by permission of FedEx Kinko's.

Of course, this type of gimmick is all part of the arms race between consumer and advertiser. If city streets became cluttered with giant images and sculptures of products, these would hardly draw a glance. Remember how novel (and maybe outrageous) it once felt to see ads in movie theaters or in bathroom stalls? And how short-lived that sense of novelty was? As the unexpected becomes ordinary, the spotlight shifts once again to land where your brain thinks it will get more informational bang for the attentional buck. And advertisers try even harder to sneak ads into unexpected places. Advertising has now graced airplane tray tables, drinking straws, beach sand, and eggshells. And a company that calls itself Pole Positioning will put your company's logo on the poles used as a prop by dancing strippers, promising that your ad will be at the center of attention.

More traditional ads too, use visual incongruity as a way to pull in your attention before you flip past to something else. In one such ad for Back to Nature bars, the heads of a soccer mom and her child have magically morphed into deer heads, in a perfect example of the kind of image that you feel compelled to check out, just like the octopus in the barnyard of the Loftus and Mackworth study.

But advertisers would do well to remember just how narrow the beam of attention can be. For example, it *seems* commonsensical to place an ad in a magazine or television program that attracts a lot of interest and that consumers are passionate about. Airing a commercial during a high-stakes hockey game in which viewers are aroused to heights of spectator passion would seem a great move for a company—if they could afford the TV spot. Surely, this is a better strategy than embedding it in a yawner of a TV show. Well, maybe not. True, a riveting program or magazine article means that more people will be exposed to the ads. But a number of studies show that people actually pay less attention to ads, and remember them less well when they appear in absorbing programs or articles. Remember that zero-sum game the pop-up ads were playing? And the gorilla study that showed the more attention people devoted to watching the basketball players, the less they noticed the gorilla? Same principle here. The moral of the story is that attention gets divided up very unevenly. Sometimes, the more attention viewers pay to the game itself, the more they suppress attention to anything else. And to extend this logic, I seriously doubt that ads on strip club poles actually *will* be in the center of attention of the spellbound clients, even if the star attractions are physically entwined around them.

In fact, the attention beam is so narrow that an ad that captures attention with a visually arresting image runs the risk of bleeding attention away from its actual brand. Having consumers notice the ad and even like it doesn't count for much if they don't know what it's advertising. For example, lots of studies by advertising researchers show that sexy images in ads certainly do attract attention. But while consumers remember the juicy babes or hunks in the ads, they're not that likely to remember what the ad was for.

Attention magnets in ads work best if the image that trips the orienting response is tightly linked to whatever is being advertised or to the main message the ad is trying to convey. This is the trick used by this Dodge ad:

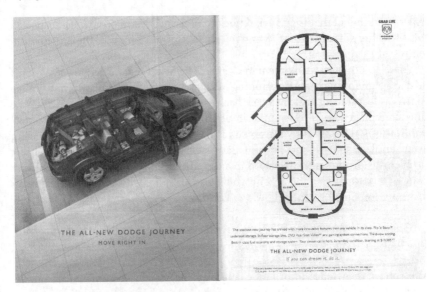

Reprinted by permission of Chrysler Group LLC.

By now, most people have a pretty clear set of expectations about what your typical car ad looks like. It rarely includes floor plans. But in this ad, the incongruity of having an architectural floor plan juxtaposed with the ubiquitous image of the car in a car ad is more than just a cheap trick to catch your attention. It's also a way to focus attention on the product itself, and to reinforce the main message of the car's roomy interior.

Brain Candy

Ads like the ones for Dodge co-opt attention in a way that feels quite different from the guerilla tactics of the wildly animated pop-up ads. They don't just use unexpected images as a cheap way to yank on our attention without offering any payoff in return. They also invite us to solve a mental puzzle. Why in blue blazes is the car sectioned off into a dining room and a living room? To solve the puzzle, the viewer has to delve deeper into the ad. The payoff is the satisfaction of having come up with some meaningful way to interpret the baffling image.

Many humor scientists (and no, that's not an oxymoron) believe that incongruity and being able to resolve that incongruity are essential ingredients in the riddles and jokes that make us giggle. For example:

Doctor: *Your husband must have absolute rest. Here's a sleeping tablet.*
Woman: *When do I give it to him?*
Doctor: *You don't. You take it yourself*

The *Aha!* moment that triggers the chuckle comes in encountering the unexpected twist that the pill is for the wife, and in solving the puzzle of why the *husband* will get rest if *she* ingests it.

There's a similar *Aha!* moment in a series of print ads that ran as part of Toyota's ad campaign for the Matrix beginning in 2008. In one of these ads, a shiny orange Matrix is featured against the black background. The eye is quickly drawn to the only copy in the ad, also featured in bright orange. It reads: **cardio-health.net/ palpitations**. The instant your eye lands on this text, your brain begins to chug away until, a split-second later, it dawns on you why a website about heart problems is prominently displayed in a car ad. And if this arouses your curiosity enough to actually visit the website, you'll find an animated diagram of the human heart accompanied by the following definition:

> *Palpitations: An abnormal awareness of the beating of the heart, whether too slow, too fast, irregular, or at its normal frequency.*

The screen then fades into a labeled X-ray diagram of a human foot on the accelerator pedal, as this text appears slowly on the screen, line by line:

Known causes:

Overexcitement
Adrenaline
Hyperthyroidism
Mitral stenosis
The all-new 2009 Matrix

The website delivers a humorous buzz in part from the twist of having this list build from the pretty ordinary term *overexcitement* up to increasingly medical and obscure language, and then abruptly shifting gears into car ad-speak (*The all-new 2009 Matrix*). The incongruous contrast creates a jolt. Notice that the list would feel less funny if it appeared in this order: *Mitral stenosis, Hyperthyroidism, Adrenaline, Overexcitement, The all-new 2009 Matrix.*[1]

There's plenty of research to suggest that people experience pleasure both in encountering the unexpected and in solving puzzles. Incongruity warms up the same part of the brain that responds to the kinds of things people are often in hot pursuit of: food, sex, money, drugs, and beauty. And some scientists think that

---

[1] When problems surfaced in 2010 with the Matrix's accelerator pedal, causing it to stick and suddenly accelerate out of the driver's control, this gave the "Palpitations" campaign a whole new meaning.

humor, which depends on incongruity, has evolved as a special kind of reward for heavy cognitive lifting.

In fact, the sheer sense of fun that humans are wired to experience from solving puzzles is probably a big reason for their domination of the planet. Far from shirking intellectual activity, people pay very good money for it. In 2007, the U.S. computer and video game industry alone took in $9.5 billion. Don't be fooled into thinking that these games are passive entertainment. They are *work*, and involve actual learning. Yes, even those first-person shooter games end up super-charging the visual attention systems of people who play them: after even modest amounts of time at the console, players develop better peripheral vision, can visually track more objects at the same time and are better and faster at sucking information out of a visual scene. Even their brains change as a result. And if shooter games aren't your thing, chances are that there is *some* kind of game or puzzle that gets your mind salivating: the *New York Times* crossword puzzle, poker, the Rubik's Cube, Dungeons and Dragons, sudoku, WarCraft, bridge, Carcassonne, the possibilities are almost endless. No other species flees from boredom with as much urgency as we do. We are far more eager to do brain work than we are to do physical labor.

So, advertisers know they can attract consumers by giving them the opportunity to exercise their mental muscles, even if the ad isn't one we think of as outright funny. In one Land Rover ad, we see an image of the vehicle in a wilderness setting in the midst of a blizzard. The caption underneath reads:

L ke y ur b ain, the n w L nd Rov r autom tic lly adj sts to anyth ng.

You're invited to feel firsthand just how smart your brain is—and by extension, the Land Rover.

These kinds of ads not only draw our attention, they persuade us to spend a fair amount of cognitive currency puzzling them out. As a result, we process them more deeply, and are much more likely to remember them. This is no small accomplishment for an ad in today's Over-Information Age. So ads can find a way past our attentional barricades by striking a bargain: they provide us with a little zap of delight or sense of smug satisfaction at our own smarts, and in return, we shine our mental spotlights on them.

The Lowest Form of Humor

Puns may be considered to be the lowest form of humor, but they're all over the place in advertising like a fierce case of the measles. One series of TV ads by the telecommunications company Comcast was built entirely around goofy wordplay. In one of the ads, a hunky young lifeguard spots something on the beach, and rushes over. A large deer with a full set of antlers is lying on the beach, apparently unconscious. The lifeguard swiftly administers mouth-to-mouth, and pounds the deer's chest. A stream of water gushes out of its mouth and its eyelids flutter. As onlookers on the beach applaud, the screen reads: "Save big bucks. Get Comcast Digital Voice and save $197 a year over AT&T."

In another, an amused bus passenger observes an altercation between the driver and a businessman boarding the bus. The businessman is trying to insert a coin into the driver's nose. "This is not where you pay," says the bus driver. "This is where I pay," insists the man. "This is not where you pay," counters the bus driver, and so on. This absurd exchange goes on for 25 seconds, until a voice-over tells you: "Don't pay through the nose. Comcast Triple Play. It's Comcastic."

In 2006, CBS hatched a strategy to squeeze its way past consumers' attentional chicken wire: it etched ads on eggs sold in supermarkets, figuring that it's hard to crack an egg without *looking* at it. Hoping to get a chuckle or at least a cluck out of consumers, the "egg-vertising" campaign produced a carton-load of puns to advertise CBS's programs. Was the campaign innovative and clever, or did CBS lay an egg? You be the judge:

CSI: Crack the Case on CBS.
The Amazing Race: Scramble to Win on CBS.
Shark: Hard-Boiled Drama

And for its Monday night comedy lineup:

Shelling out Laughs
Funny Side Up
Leave the Yolks to Us

Other (*ahem*) gems from ad campaigns include:

Make smoking history – Massachusetts Department of Public Health
Leader's Digest – The Economist, newsmagazine
Something for you and your cat to chew on – Friskies cat food
Usually, ironing leaves me flat – Moulinex irons
Hit the bar for lunch – Balance snack bars
Where's the beef? – Wendy's hamburgers
Are you up in the air about your future? – U.S. Air Force
So much about a family is revealed by its faces – Timex watches
Take your mother-in-law out and shoot her – Wix Pix disposable camera
Lashes that go to great lengths – Clarins mascara

Whether you love puns or pretend to hate them, this kind of wordplay is a nifty little brain-game. Here's a bit of a tour of what's going on inside your head when you run into a double meaning, much of the whole process lying iceberg-like below your conscious awareness:

When you meet a word or a phrase that has multiple possible meanings, you tend to activate them all, even when just one was clearly intended. You're not necessarily aware of this, and scientists only know this as a result of clever lab experiments. In fact, remember that eyetracking studies show that you even briefly "consider" all the possible meanings of a *syllable*, such as the many possible words containing *can*. With multiple meanings floating around, you recruit extra brainpower to winnow them down. You spend more time reading ambiguous words or phrases than unambiguous ones. Blood rushes to the decision-making parts of your brain. Once you've accumulated enough information to have a pretty good guess of the correct meaning, you abandon the others. Though you may not always be aware of the extra work you're doing with ambiguous language, scientists can measure it by tracking people's eyes as they read, or by measuring where the blood is flowing in the brain.

The playful double meanings in some of the examples you've just seen come from words that are ambiguous (*scramble, shoot* or *bar*, for example). Others hinge on a word or phrase that can either be used literally or as part of an idiomatic expression (*up in the air, something to chew on, hard-boiled*). But language can also be ambiguous by virtue of how the words are put together. Consider the following brain-teaser question from the game *MindTrap*:

> **Question:** *In Okmulgee, Oklahoma, you cannot take a picture of a man with a wooden leg. Why?*
>
> **Answer:** *You cannot take a picture of a man with a wooden leg anywhere – you need a camera. (Groan)*

Or here's a real-life example of dinner dialogue with my smart-ass son:

> **Me:** *Son, don't eat your meat like a dog.*
> **Ben:** *How do you eat a dog?*

My son's snappy reply reveals the ambiguity that lies in the unspoken parts of the sentence that are left implicit: *Don't eat your meat like a dog [eats meat]* versus *Don't eat your meat like [you eat] a dog*. Notice how the interpretation shifts for the parallel sentence *Don't eat your meat like a popsicle*.

The *MindTrap* example plays with the fact that the phrase *take a picture of a man with a wooden leg* can either be "chunked" like this:

> *Take a picture [of a man with a wooden leg]*
> (This means the wooden leg is attached to the man)

Or like this:

> *Take a picture [of a man] [with a wooden leg]*
> (This means the wooden leg is used to photograph the man)

You'll find exactly the same type of ambiguity cropping up in this famous joke attributed to Groucho Marx:

One morning I shot an elephant in my pajamas. What he was doing in my pajamas, I'll never know.

Ambiguity of various glorious kinds can be found in this list of allegedly real newspaper headlines taken from the website *fun-with-words.com*:

PROSTITUTES APPEAL TO POPE
GRANDMOTHER OF EIGHT MAKES HOLE IN ONE
MINERS REFUSE TO WORK AFTER DEATH
SAFETY EXPERTS SAY SCHOOL BUS PASSENGERS SHOULD BE BELTED
JUVENILE COURT TO TRY SHOOTING DEFENDANT
KILLER SENTENCED TO DIE FOR SECOND TIME IN 10 YEARS
TWO SISTERS REUNITED AFTER 18 YEARS IN CHECKOUT COUNTER

And my own personal, recently-spotted favorite:

SMOKING MORE DANGEROUS FOR WOMEN THAN MEN

which seems to suggest that if you're going to have one nasty habit, it ought to be men rather than smoking.

Let Me Take You Down the Garden Path

In order to qualify as funny, *both* meanings of the ambiguous language need to be consciously accessible, and not just setting off sparks in the subconscious. *Awareness* of the double meaning is key. But your mind works pretty hard to quickly separate one best meaning from the other possibilities, and most of the time you're never aware of the other possible meanings. So, what are the conditions under which both meanings will be hanging around in your consciousness ready to amuse you? Sometimes, both are very strongly activated so that one can't easily be rejected in favor of the other by the part of your brain that tries to resolve the ambiguity. In many of the advertising examples, something has been done to heighten one or both of the meanings in order to create just such a situation. For example, the choice of the *medium* for the CBS ads brings the eggy meanings of *scramble* and *crack* into the foreground of your attention.

But often, humor happens because you've pretty much settled on a perfectly good interpretation so that you're only aware of one of the possible meanings, and then suddenly you are made to do a linguistic U-turn and reconsider things. Your original interpretation was so strong that it stays active in your conscious mind, along with the new interpretation you've been steered into. This is ambiguity with a jolt, and is exactly what happens in the Groucho Marx joke. Language scientists call such ambiguous sentences in which you take a semantic detour "garden path" sentences. Your mind is leading you down the garden path—misleading you towards an interpretation that turns out to be the wrong one. Here are some other examples of "garden path" jokes:

Time flies like an arrow. Fruit flies like a banana.
What has four wheels and flies? A garbage truck.

Garden path sentences don't just happen in jokes—they're found in real life surprisingly often, simply because of the fact that language is often ambiguous, and we're in such a hurry to interpret it that we often take the wrong turn. In many real-life examples, people find themselves happily interpreting a string of words one way until they hit up *smack*! against a dead end that forces them to reinterpret. The following is a dramatization of an extreme garden path sentence—by far the most famous garden path sentence in cognitive science history:

The horse raced past the barn fell.

This is not word mush. There is a perfectly good, grammatical interpretation of this sentence. Don't see it? Try interpreting it so that it ends up meaning this:

The horse that was raced by its rider past the barn fell.

Still don't get it? Try to notice that the first sentence should be interpreted *exactly* like this one:

The horse driven past the barn fell.

If you had to re-read all these sentences several times through before getting it, rest assured that you're not unusually obtuse. When I show this example to students, there's usually a period of several minutes throughout which I hear "Aaah!" breaking out at various intervals as it finally dawns on people how to get that elusive grammatical interpretation.

What makes the first version of this sentence so incomprehensible? The fact that you've been cruising along through the sentence and putting the words together into a structure that was perfectly reasonable for a while, until you ran aground when you hit the word *fell*. *The horse raced past the barn* makes a lot of sense if you're reading the words to mean that it's the horse that's doing the racing (rather than being raced). The problem is, when you get to *fell*, there's no way you can attach this word to the sentence without violating all kinds of rules of grammar.

If you were wearing an eyetracker while reading the sentence, you would have read smoothly through until you got to that blasted last word. You'd gape at this word for a while before darting your eyes back to re-read the sentence several times, your eyes skipping back and forth over the sentence like fleas on amphetamines. People often end up doing funky things in their minds to try to salvage the first interpretation they've constructed. For example, you might have inserted an inaudible *and* to try to get this meaning: *The horse raced past the barn and fell.*

This particular garden path sentence is famous because it's so dramatically difficult to get to the intended meaning once you've gone after the wrong one. Language scientists have studied it to try to figure out why one of its meanings gets so deeply submerged. But garden path sentences turn out to be pretty common in real life—and often, they are so effortless to resolve that you're not really aware of any difficulty. At other times, you just experience the sentence as confusing or awkward in some way without knowing why. All of the sentences below contain a garden path that momentarily lures people to the wrong interpretation:

The psychologist told the woman that he was having trouble with to see her doctor.
The President accepted the report from the Secretary of State was accurate.
What did John read the article to find out about?

Were you aware of taking a semantic detour? Maybe not. But if your eyes were being tracked, signs of trouble in these sentences would show up at the following places: *to see, was accurate,* and *the article.* These are the spots where your favorite interpretation of the previous string of words turn out to be impossible to continue. The sentences would give you no trouble if they instead took a direction that was consistent with your (not necessarily conscious) first attempt at interpreting the ambiguity:

The psychologist told the woman that he was having trouble with her husband.
The President accepted the report from the Secretary of State before filing it.
What did John read in the newspaper?

Now, garden path sentences like the ones I've shown you here don't feel funny. They just feel annoying to read. But if both meanings are consciously noticed, and one of the interpretations is absurd or off-kilter in some way, the magic ingredients for humor are there.

What might trick your mind into heading down the garden path in pursuit of the less sensible meaning? Language scientists have identified a slew of factors. For example, some kinds of structure might be more commonly found in language than others, leading to a bias in your expectations. There may be tendencies for specific individual words to be "chunked" with other specific words. For instance, look again at the garden path sentence: *The President accepted the report from the*

Secretary of State was accurate. The verb *accept* likes to have a direct object. This is important, because the ambiguity hinges on whether you interpret *the report from the Secretary of State* as a direct object or as the subject of a second clause that's embedded within the first. But the verb *think* prefers not to have a direct object, and likes to lead into an embedded clause instead. Notice the distinct lack of a garden path effect if you substitute *thought* for *accepted* in the example you just saw: *The President thought the report from the Secretary of State was accurate.*

There may also be pressures on your short-term memory system that lead you to pursue one interpretation over another. Consider the headline TWO SISTERS REUNITED AFTER 18 YEARS IN CHECKOUT COUNTER. In the "sensible" interpretation, it's the reunion that happens in the checkout counter. This means that you have to relate the phrase *in checkout counter* to the much earlier word *reunited.* But by the time you get to the checkout counter bit, *reunited* will already have decayed in your memory somewhat. So instead you stick *in checkout counter* together with the much fresher phrase *after 18 years.* Then you notice how bizarre this is, and cast about for another way to interpret the sentence. It's funny only if *all* of this has happened. But notice how much harder it is to get the sensible reading in this version: TWO SISTERS REUNITED IN SEATTLE AS A RESULT OF FACE-BOOK SEARCH BY MOTHER AFTER 18 YEARS IN CHECKOUT COUNTER. Here, by the time you get to *in checkout counter,* the word *reunited* has not only decayed in memory, it's fully rotted and is attracting flies.

So, in order to work, ads that use wordplay have a tricky balancing act so that neither meaning becomes lost to the audience. Sometimes the visual context gives a needed boost, as in the ad for British Airways on the following page.

Without the graphic, you likely would only be *consciously* aware of the kind of showers that everyone normally associates with London, even if the other meaning were activated unconsciously. The picture in the ad nudges the second weaker meaning across the consciousness threshold, you become aware of the semantic tension, and then, maybe the pleasure of the pun motivates you enough to spend some time reading about all the creature comforts—such as hot showers—that await you at Heathrow Airport.

Once an ad has pumped up two meanings in your mind, it can do some neat things with them. The least interesting strategy is just to use the ambiguity as an attention-getting device, like the CBS "egg-vertising" campaign. The goal there was to make the ads fun enough that you'll actually make a point of reading your eggs (and therefore the ads) before making an omelet. But the pun doesn't do anything else to enhance or strengthen the message. Ads rarely use such shamelessly gratuitous punning—they normally put the double meanings to work in some more useful way.

One common strategy is to use the pun as a way to draw attention to a company's slogan or main message. This is what Comcast did with its "Save big bucks" and "Don't pay through the nose" ads. It put its take-home message dead center on the wordplay stage, right where you're beaming your attentional

Reprinted by permission of British Airways.

spotlight. Think how much less effective the ads would be if the elaborate pun revolved around something less central or irrelevant to its persuasive message. Still funny, and you'd remember the pun—but maybe not the sales pitch. This would be the equivalent of wrapping nude girls around the ads on strip poles.

Ads can use ambiguity in even more sophisticated ways. Often, punning is a way of getting the consumer to roll together both meanings of the ambiguity. A clever example is the "Make smoking history" public health campaign in which the viewer is invited to help bring about a historical moment by making smoking a thing of the past. In the early 1990s, Volvo put out a controversial print ad that asked the reader: "Is something inside you telling you to buy a Volvo?" This text appeared next to a sonogram image of a fetus. The reader was obviously intended to take the "something inside" to refer both to her parental instincts and to her unborn child, who, if he could talk, would surely beg her to keep him safe on the highway by driving a Volvo. The Friskies ad (*"something for you and your cat to chew on"*) brings to mind food for thought for you and food in the bowl for your cat, implying great taste and good nutrition in one pun. The U.S. Air Force ad (*"Are you up in the air about your future?"*) cleverly uses an ambiguous question to identify a problem: your aimlessness about your future; and a solution: joining the Air Force.

Other times, ads create a garden path effect to startle or shock you into wondering: Did they just *say* what I thought they said?? Examples include the "Take your mother-in-law out and shoot her" disposable camera ad, and the "Hit the bar for lunch" ad for Balance snack bars. You're obviously meant to throw away one of the two meanings in the end, but the ad draws you in by first shocking you, and then creating the experience of a jolting semantic U-turn. This is a souped-up version of Groucho Marx's joke.

A *really* skilled pun can even get you to think of two meanings, and use the contrast between them as a way to position a product by highlighting a key difference between the advertised product and its competitors. Think of the impressive work done by the two-word wordplay in *The Economist* ad: "Leader's Digest." It brings to mind the mass-marketed *Reader's Digest,* a magazine that has long been a staple of medical waiting rooms and the bathrooms of your average American home. It also brings to mind the short, simple articles and abridged literature you find in *Reader's Digest.* The word "leader" encourages the audience to imagine what society's elite would subscribe to—surely not simple, light low-brow articles, but in-depth, trenchant analyses and reports, like those found in *The Economist.* Finally, the reader is flattered into imagining herself among this elite group, and feeling smugly superior to the *Reader's-Digest*-flipping masses. *Reader's Digest,* now defunct, was probably never a direct competitor for *The Economist,* but subscribers to the latter magazine may be eager to put some extra psychological distance between themselves and those who read lower-end magazines—including perhaps *Time* or *Newsweek.* All of this information is spring-loaded into a bit of compact wordplay; punning at this level is hardly a primitive form of anything.

Marketing researchers sometimes caution that using puns or puzzles can be risky, because they rely on the consumer deciding to spend enough precious mental resources to actually solve the puzzle and get to the message. If the consumer doesn't commit these resources, she'll never get the ad's message. This might seem especially worrisome in today's marketing environment, where zillions of ads compete for a smaller and smaller share of consumers' brain space.

But interestingly, over the past few decades, ads have come to rely *more* on puzzle-solving, and have offered *less* in the way of verbal explanation of the puzzle. And studies show that consumers like ads best when they present a brain-teaser, and they don't want the ad to do the work of figuring it out for them. It's a testament to human curiosity that even in this age of too-much-information, advertising built around puzzles runs a greater risk of boring consumers than of mentally overtaxing them. At least for now, providing some brain candy still goes a long way in getting past the consumer's attentional barrier.

Linguistic Spotlights

Next time you find yourself in a grocery store or a bookstore, try doing a bit of people-watching. How often do customers stoop to look at the products on the bottom shelf or crane their necks to see what's on the top shelf? The products on the shelves at eye level have an extraordinary advantage, especially when people aren't armed with a list of specific items and just happen to be browsing. Retailers are well aware of this fact, and treat the prime shelf space as the housing market might treat waterfront property: scarce, and expensive. It's no wonder that shelving decisions aren't made willy-nilly by the stock-boys. The shelving plan in a retail outlet is the result of a complex set of decisions and negotiations. Retailers reserve the choice spots for items that have the greatest profit margin or products that have garnered a special fee from suppliers who pay for the privilege. (If you see someone who habitually scans the very bottom shelf, ask them if they've read this book.)

It seems pretty intuitive that stores would have "hot spots" that capture more attention from the strolling customer. What may be less apparent to you is that, just like supermarket displays, *sentences* have attentional hot spots as well. Attention to sentences is in some ways a lot like attention to a visual scene—it focuses more tightly on some information rather than being evenly spread out. Speakers and writers can use all sorts of subtle linguistic cues to make important information pop out from the linguistic background. Though you likely don't realize it, when you speak, you probably make use of a varied menu of sentence arrangements that help your hearer focus his attention on whatever it is that is at the center of yours.

In an English sentence, the equivalent to shelf space at eye level is linguistic content that's displayed at the beginning of a sentence. To illustrate, here's a snippet of a conversation I overheard by a group of young women checking out the sights at a downtown café on a warm summer day:

> **First woman:** *Kali, I think that guy two tables down is trying to get your attention. He's kinda cute, don't you think?*
> **Kali:** *Nah. Not my type. But the guy standing at the bar I wouldn't kick out of bed.*

All eyes swiveled over to appreciate the young man at the bar.

Notice how Kali's chosen syntax played a role in beaming a bright spotlight onto the fellow. Her remark would have sounded a bit less compelling had she used the more common way of styling a sentence, as in: "But I wouldn't kick the guy standing at the bar out of bed."

These kinds of cues, where parts of a sentence are shuffled around for effect, are just part of our vast, implicit knowledge about language structure. Most people use them, at least some of the time, but would be at a loss to articulate *how* they use them. Even linguists who have intimate knowledge of them generally use them without thinking about it. For instance, linguist Gregory Ward, who has written extensively about these kinds of structures with co-author Betty Birner, once told an anecdote in which Dr. Birner remarked, "You know Gregory. These unusual sentence structures, I don't think I use."

In the hands of highly skilled writers or public speakers, linguistic techniques for focusing attention can be elevated to practically an art form, and are sometimes used deliberately as a result of specific training in copywriting or rhetorical technique. They can even be used to create certain visual effects.

For example, try to come up with a picture in your mind for each of these sentences:

> *Bees swarmed in the garden.*
> *The garden swarmed with bees.*

You might conjure up slightly different images. In the first, the focus is on the bees, and you might imagine a cluster of bees flying in a garden, and follow their trajectory in your mind. In the second, maybe you see the garden in more detail, and have the impression that every nook and cranny of the garden has bees in it, possibly evenly distributed throughout. The only difference between these sentences is which word takes center stage and sits at the beginning of the sentence in the *subject* position. (You probably learned in school that the subject is what the sentence is "about"—hence the name *subject*).

While I'm on the topic, let me leap at the opportunity to discredit a flawed piece of advice many people get at some point in their writing lives. Has an English teacher or writing instructor ever told you to use active sentences and avoid sentences in the passive voice? For example, rather than writing "*The deer was killed by the hunter,*" you should write: "*The hunter killed the deer.*" The two sentences mean the same thing. But active sentences are usually described as stronger and punchier—and therefore better. This common piece of writing advice is perfectly sound much of the time. But language evolved passive sentences for a reason. When languages offer a menu of options to say the same thing, the various choices usually are there to allow for different bits of information to be swapped around to positions in the sentence where the spotlight shines brightest. Slavishly avoiding passives would deprive you of the opportunity to play around with subtle, but effective ways to shift attention.

In figuring out whether to use an active or passive sentence, what it comes down to is a decision about which part of the sentence should be under the spotlight. This obviously depends on the content. Imagine you're a newspaper headline writer. Should you write *"Poachers kill last remaining snow leopard"* or *"Last remaining snow leopard killed by poachers"?* Ignore your English teacher: now would be a good time to break the ban on passive sentences. This lets you highlight the most important information on center stage. And here, the "passive" aspect of passive sentences works for you: the sentence downplays the action itself, and plays up the *outcome* of the action—the irrevocable, irreversible death, not the specific action of killing—just what you want in this case. On the other hand, if the person doing the killing is more newsworthy than whatever is being killed, the active version of the sentence is the better choice. For example: *"Toddler kills deer on hunting trip with dad"* is better than *"Deer killed by toddler on hunting trip with dad,"* where the precocious hunter is buried in the middle of the sentence where a reader might barely notice it.

These might seem like high-level decisions that take thoughtfulness and more than an ounce of linguistic sophistication. But it turns out that choices like this are made on-the-fly by regular people uttering ordinary sentences, in situations where they couldn't give a hoot about literary merit. Linguist Russell Tomlin dreamed up an ingenious experiment to test how attention affects speakers' choices to use active or passive sentences to describe an event. He created animated video clips in which two fish of different colors swam toward each other. As they approached, one of the fish opened its mouth and swallowed the other. Study volunteers watching these clips had to describe the event quickly, before the next fish-eating scenario came up on the screen, so they didn't have time to mull over their choice of phrasing. In order to orient their attention to one of the fish, Tomlin had an arrow flash briefly above it as it swam towards the other. The flashing arrow made it more likely that people would mention this fish first, and it affected the type of sentence they used. So, if the black fish was the predator, and was marked with the arrow, people would say "The black fish ate the red fish." But when the arrow flashed over the victim in the same event, people were more likely to use the passive sentence "The red fish was eaten by the black fish."

This works even when people's attention is captured in extremely subtle ways. In a variant of the Tomlin experiments, language scientists at the University of Pennsylvania oriented attention by subliminally flashing a square over one of the characters in a scene for about 6/100ths of a second, and found the same effect. People were more likely to mention this character first, despite the fact that they weren't aware of anything flashing on the screen at all, or that the experimenters were manipulating their attention in any way.

Most copywriters very deliberately tailor their writing to take advantage of attentional hotspots, even if they aren't aware of the language science behind them. In ad language, a fair amount of care is devoted to the optimal use of a sentence's shelf space. For example, if you take a close look at ad copy, you'll find plenty of examples of passive sentences where the product name is strutting in the center of the stage:

> *This exclusive ACTIVE NATURALS® oatmeal formula, with scents of lavender, chamomile and ylang-ylang, has been shown to calm and relax (Aveeno Stress Relief Body Wash)*

Here, the product has been promoted to the coveted subject slot, and whoever it is that has shown the calming effects of the body wash is nowhere to be found in the sentence. This structure is similar to the famous Ronald Reagan remark *"Mistakes were made"* which de-emphasizes the actor in the sentence to the point of omission. Other examples:

> *These innovative kitchen mats are scientifically engineered to absorb shock and reduce pain-causing pressure. (GelPro chef's mats)*
>
> *Extra Sweet Watermelon lasts longer and is preferred over Trident® Watermelon Twist®. (Extra Fruit Sensations chewing gum)*

Another device commonly found in advertising copy is the technique of loading up the important features of a product at the beginning of the sentence. For example:

> *With a stunning large display and up to 8 GB external memory, simplicity has never been so productive. (LG Decoy phone)*
>
> *With available XM Navtraffic®, the future of the crossover knows the future of your commute. (Nissan Murano)*
>
> *Now with Lotus Milk and Jasmine, our revolutionary formula is enriched with moisturizer complex. (Veet hair remover)*

The well-heeled copywriter knows not only how to get the right information *into* the spotlight, but also how to keep the wrong information *out* of the spotlight. Sometimes ad writers just have to include certain words they'd rather not—the words make their claims weaker, but without them, the ad would run the risk of being flagrantly deceptive. For example, qualifiers like *may help, up to, virtually* and so on (often called "weasel words") are often relegated to the wings of the stage. If they're buried somewhere in the middle of the sentence, it's probably because they've been sent there, like the awkward relatives at a wedding.

In one ad I saw for a breakfast cereal, a clever graphical device was used to accentuate some parts of a sentence more vividly than others. The second half of the sentence appeared in high-contrasting white against a black background, popping out visually, while the first half was in red, creating a slightly more subdued visual contrast against the black. Reproducing the text in grayscale, the general effect was something like this:

A Bowl
of Cereal May
Help Reduce
The Risk of
Osteoporosis

It was the boldest part of the claim "reduce the risk of osteoporosis" that stood out visually while the namby-pamby words "may help" kind of blended into the background.

TV and radio ads can use intonation to create the right spotlights and shadows. You can bet that you'd never hear a commercial with the following intonation:

> Now our revolutionary SOON-to-be-patented formula MAY actually HELP reduce the APPEARANCE of unsightly wrinkles.

Instead, you'd get:

> Now, our REVOLUTIONARY soon-to-be PATENTED FORMULA may ACTU-ALLY help REDUCE the appearance of UNSIGHTLY WRINKLES.

And in print, a weak qualifier can be surrounded by stronger words in more privileged positions of syntax, like in this ad for an automobile anti-theft device: "In all probability, you or one of your family members may have your car stolen this month." With its clever syntactic structure and specific phrases like "you or one of your family members" and "this month," you have the impression of almost certain impending disaster, rather than merely the possibility of a theft. The wimpy word "may" is stuck in the attentional sinkhole right in the middle of the sentence. Like the gorilla studies of visual attention, you're so busy paying attention to everything else in the sentence that this word escapes notice.

Henry James and the Art of Copywriting

You may also have noticed that your average print ad doesn't exactly read like a Henry James novel. If you haven't read any Henry James lately, here's what it sounds like:

> He had none the less to confess to his friend that evening that he knew almost nothing about her, and it was a deficiency that Waymarsh, even with his memory refreshed by contact, by her own prompt and lucid allusions and enquiries, by their publicly partaken of dinner in her company, and by another stroll, to which she was not a stranger, out into the town to look at the cathedral by moonlight – it was

a blank that the resident of Milrose, though admitting acquaintance with the Munsters, professed himself unable to fulfill.

Henry James, *The Ambassadors*

In the hands of a zealous copy editor, this passage might read:

A mystery woman. Two friends—Waymarsh and Strether. They all share dinner together, a moonlit walk. She has a history with Waymarsh. His friend is eager to know more. Why can't Waymarsh remember anything about her? Their evening together triggers no memories. But she seems to know him well.

Every copywriting manual will tell you to use simple words and short sentences, trimming away any verbiage that doesn't absolutely have to be there. Copywriting guru Robert W. Bly suggests that ad copy should aim for sentences that are on average 6–16 words long. The Henry James passage is a single 92-word sentence. It takes a serious mental toll on the reader, and is certainly not something you could read casually over breakfast before you've had your first dose of caffeine. No ad can afford to make a reader work that hard—without at least offering up some fun brain candy in return. Bly tells aspiring copywriters that crisp, simple sentences are easier to understand and add rhythm and drama to the writing. In *Guerilla Advertising*, Jay Conrad Levinson advises: "Don't worry about sentence fragments. Sometimes they make for copy that is readable. And clear. And even motivating."

Clipped sentences and fragments also accomplish something else. Since attention is spread out unevenly over a sentence, this means that in a longer sentence, much of the material will be languishing in the shadows. The longer the sentence, the less material can be under the spotlight. Even within a simple sentence, some positions of focus are more "visible" than others. When extra phrases and clauses are tacked on, the contrast between the focused and blurrier parts of the sentence increases. In sentences with more than one clause, only one of them is called the *main* clause. This is because only one clause conveys the central idea. Other clauses dangling off the sides are called *subordinate* clauses and they play a supporting role to the starring main clause. Notice the contrast between these two sentences, which express exactly the same information. (The main clause in both of these sentences is the first one.)

The new Achieva has several design flaws, even though it won the award for Best Mid-Priced Sedan.
The new Achieva has won the award for Best Mid-Priced Sedan, even though it has several design flaws.

In the first sentence, the focus is on the design flaws rather than the award, and it feels as if the flaws might be more significant than those mentioned in the second sentence.

In an ad that extols the virtues of a product, the copywriter would like the reader to treat *all* of the virtues as important. To do this, the writer can give each idea its own sentence. This means that rather than having just one hog most of the attention, each idea gets its moment in the spotlight, as in this bit of ad copy from a L'Oréal ad for mascara:

> New Le Grand Curl.™
> Lift and Curl Mascara
> It's enough to curl your lashes.
> Really.
> All by itself.
> Even without an eyelash curler.
> For the Flirtatious eye.
> Instantly.
> L'Oréal Paris
> Because I'm worth it.™

All of the techniques so far in this chapter—from pop-up ads, to puzzles and incongruity, to subtle linguistic phrasing—provide ways for advertisers to eke out the most from consumers' stingy attention. They're all ways to deal with the very finely-tuned human attention system in which some information is invited into the inner chambers of the mind, while other information has to hang around at the gates. And the crowd of advertising that clamors at the gates keeps getting bigger and bigger.

It says something about our adaptability that we're able to function in an environment that's overrun with information—the narrow beam of our attention has a great deal to do with this. But it's worth pausing for a moment to think about what happens with the information that's pushed to the periphery, the information that doesn't command our full, undivided attention. Because as it turns out, some part of our mind continues to process that information. It still has the potential to impact our choices and actions. It's just that we're a lot less aware of how it does so.

Persuaded by Truthiness

Remember Calvin Coolidge's 1928 speech to admen, in which he bubbled with confidence that "more and more, advertising seeks to tell the truth?" Coolidge argued that consumers would be best persuaded by truthful appeals to reason. Almost a century later though, advertisers seem to rely more on "truthiness" than on truth to sell their wares.

The word "truthiness" burst into the popular lexicon in 2005 after comedian Stephen Colbert used it to describe the sense of certainty that comes from feeling rather than thinking. Aiming his wit at then-reigning President Bush, he riffed:

Face it, folks; we are a divided nation. Not between Democrats and Republicans, or conservatives and liberals, or tops and bottoms. No, we are divided between those who think with their head, and those who know with their heart. Consider Harriet Miers. If you 'think' about it, of course her nomination's absurd. But the president didn't say he 'thought' about his selection. Notice how he said nothing about her brain? He didn't have to. He said this: 'I know her heart.' And what about Iraq? If you think about it, maybe there are a few missing pieces to the rationale for war. But doesn't taking Saddam out feel like the right thing? Right here in the gut? Because that's where the truth comes from, ladies and gentlemen, from the gut. Do you know you have more nerve endings in your stomach than in your head? Look it up. Now somebody is gonna say—'I did look it up and it's wrong.' Well, mister, that's because you looked it up in a book. Next time, try looking it up in your gut.

Here are some examples of how truthiness works in advertising:

You are at your local grocery store scanning the mind-numbing array of choices of breakfast cereals on the shelves. You see a box of granola in green and brown colors, with photographs of various grains and nuts. The words "nature" and "fiber" appear in large print. Next to this, you see a box in eye-bruising pinks and purples with a leering cartoon character. You want to choose something healthy, so you go for the box of granola.

A commercial for cough medicine features an actor who plays a respected doctor in a daytime soap. The ad has a different feel than if they'd hired the actor who plays the violent drug dealer.

An ad lists 22 reasons to buy a stereo. You don't have time to read all the copy, but you feel impressed by the body of evidence the company can marshal for its product.

You buy a L'Oréal hair coloring product "because you're worth it." And because it sounds French.

You need a life insurance policy. You buy one from MetLife, because this is the company you've heard about the most, and you feel they must be reliable.

All of these advertising strategies work on consumers' knowing in their gut, rather than thinking with their head.

Maybe Coolidge was naive about the rationality of his fellow consumers. But in all fairness, consumers weren't blasted with the same volume of information as they are now. This ends up mattering in some very profound ways. The sheer *amount* of information people are exposed to may actually change the *way* in which they think about most of it.

Thinking deeply about something is expensive for the brain. We do it with zest and superb concentration when there's likely to be a big payoff, but we're incredibly selective about how we spend our cognitive energies—just as our decisions about where to aim our eyeballs are driven by the brain's best guess about what information will provide the greatest reward or best odds for survival. When you think with your head and fire up your brain's impressive horsepower to ponder, analyze, and evaluate, your quality of thought is a lot like the quality of vision you get in that small area directly in your line of sight. It's detailed, sharp, and crunches through loads of information. Peripheral vision isn't just less good than your central vision. It's qualitatively different. It responds to different cues, and is lousy at detecting color and shape, but pretty good at detecting motion and at recognizing very familiar objects. Peripheral vision doesn't do a whole lot of higher-level analysis. It handles low-level cues, and depends on lots of accumulated knowledge about what things look like in order to send signals to your brain to look directly at anything that's worth further investigation.

It's the same with peripheral thinking. It's not just less thinking. It's a kind of thinking that doesn't really do any serious analysis at all. It's more about instinctively reacting to low-level cues and knowledge that comes from repetitive experience. And because deep thinking costs a lot more brainpower than peripheral thinking, the more information we have coming at us, the more we fall back on peripheral thinking. This is where truthiness comes in.

The upside of advertising clutter (for advertisers) is that when people push ad messages into the realm of peripheral thinking, they can be swayed by incredibly superficial "reasons." Ellen Langer and her colleagues suggested that people flip into auto-pilot mode when something triggers a well-known social routine or "script" as they called it. For example, we all have a script for how requests get made and granted: whoever is making the request is usually expected to come up with some reason or justification for imposing on the requestee (assuming it's really a request, and not a disguised command) who then either grants it or nixes the favor. Typically, the better the justification, the better the odds that the request will be granted. But when the requestee is thinking peripherally, what counts as justification is pretty minimal, and almost any reason decorated by the word "because" will do.

In Langer's study, an experimenter interrupted students who were just about to photocopy some papers at the library of the City University of New York, and asked to use the copier ahead of the student. Sometimes, the experimenter gave no reason for the interruption at all, simply saying, "Excuse me, I have five pages. May I use the xerox machine?" New Yorkers have a wholly undeserved reputation for being unhelpful to strangers, so let the record show that 60% of the students agreed to the request even when the experimenter made no attempt to explain why he thought he should butt in front of the student. Let the record also show that 94% of the students agreed to the request when the experimenter provided a reasonable justification, ("May I use the xerox machine because I'm in a rush?"). What really interested the authors of the study, though, is what happened when the experimenter gave the flimsiest nonreason dressed up as a justification: "May I use the xerox machine because I need to make copies?" The students granted the request *just as often* as when they were given a real reason. As long as it *sounded* like a justification, they didn't seem to evaluate it at all—provided the experimenter had fewer copies to make than the students themselves.

This picture changed quite a bit depending on how many copies the student and experimenter each needed to make. Sometimes the experimenter asked to make 20 copies instead of just five. When the students had fewer copies to make themselves than the experimenter, they were much more likely to actually pay closer attention to the justification. Now, when the experimenter explained he was in a rush, only 42% of the students agreed to the request. And when the experimenter provided the lousy reason (which the authors called "placebic information" because it was devoid of active ingredients) he got only 24%— which was exactly the same as when he gave no reason at all. So, when the personal consequence of the request was higher for the students, they were more likely to actually notice whether the justification was reasonable.

Thought Prevention

According to Richard Petty and John Cacioppo, who have been main characters in the research on persuasion for decades, peripheral thinking is a useful survival mechanism, just like peripheral vision. It's there for those times when you can't afford the mental resources to carefully deliberate over a decision—given how expensive these mental processes are, you'd run the risk of constant decision paralysis. Peripheral thinking gives you a cheap, quick-and-dirty way of making a snap decision that has a reasonable shot at being OK. For example, chances are that if someone has used the linguistic trimmings that go along with justifying a request, there's likely to be an actual justification in there somewhere. Similarly, if someone can come up with 20 reasons why you should do something, maybe you should consider doing it. If a product is named *filorazine*, chances are, it's been approved by the FDA. And a politician who looks confident and sounds intelligent is more likely to have solid arguments to make than someone who is hesitant and garbles his speech.

Peripheral thinking taps into these kinds of "chances are" cues, and chances are, it'll be right much of the time because these cues reflect something about actual patterns in the real world. That's why it "feels" right. But in any specific instance, it can fail spectacularly. All the more so if these cues are being deliberately manipulated for persuasive intent, in which case, the cues can be completely disconnected from the patterns they normally link to in the actual world. For instance, a politician can be carefully coached for a debate to sound confident and smooth while spouting nonsense. And the name for a diet supplement put out by a shady company might be deliberately chosen because it sounds like it belongs in the trusted medicine name neighborhood. Though it's better than nothing, relying on truthiness puts you on much shakier ground than thinking with the head and evaluating truth.

After collecting a whopping body of data, Petty and Cacioppo can tell you when you're most likely to be thinking with the head. First of all, you need to feel that the message is worth spending big brainpower on. You'd probably think more deeply about which mortgage to bind yourself to than which breakfast cereal to buy. And some people seem to be inherently more driven to think deeply than others—the scientists called this trait a "need for cognition." Second, you've got to have enough free brainpower to spend. If you're racing to finish up grocery shopping in time to get Billy to the doctor to extract that pebble that's lodged in his nostril while little Sally is screeching and wriggling out of the grocery cart, you won't have many neurons to spare. You'll be a packaging designer's dream customer.

Today, the thick information soup we swim around in almost guarantees that we'll do proportionally more peripheral thinking that people did in Coolidge's era. And this matters enormously, because our thinking style in turn shapes the information that's aimed at us. Peripheral thinking rewards persuasive messages that use superficial cues, many of which we're not even conscious aware of. Messages that focus on building a decent argument and presenting solid evidence are at a competitive disadvantage in this environment.

A typical study from the Petty and Cacioppo lab illustrates this point. The scientists wanted to see how a peripheral thinking cue—using a famous person to endorse a product—would stack up against using strong arguments for the product. They made up ads for the fictitious Edge razor, and listed either five strong arguments ("*Special chemically formulated coating eliminates nicks and cuts and prevents rusting*") or five crummy ones ("*Designed with the bathroom in mind*"). Each ad also showed an endorsement—either by two famous athletes, or by a bunch of unfamiliar average joes and jills. Lured into the lab with the promise of a free gift, subjects were either told up front that after the study, they could choose a brand of razor or a brand of toothpaste (it apparently doesn't take much to get undergraduates into a lab). The scientists reasoned that they could nudge the subjects who'd be choosing a razor (called the "high involvement" group) to pay more attention to the ad. In fact, the "high involvement" subjects were also told that the new Edge razor would soon be launched in their area, while the "low involvement" toothpaste-choosing subjects were told that the Edge wouldn't be sold in their area. All this made the personal relevance of the ad very different for the two groups. After the subjects looked at the ads, they were probed for their attitudes towards the Edge razor.

The "high involvement" subjects were thinking with the head. They couldn't care less whether the endorsers were famous or not, but their attitudes showed they were really paying attention to the strength of the arguments, and they thought very little of the Edge after seeing the weaker ad. The "low involvement" subjects did exactly the opposite—they were less swayed than the other group by the quality of the arguments, and more dazzled by the famous endorsers.

For advertisers, the moral of the story is this: if you're saddled with creating a campaign for a mediocre product, and can't make a strong case for it, get the consumer to think peripherally. The easiest way to do this is by distracting them.

The persuasion research shows that distractions disrupt thinking with the head. This means that if a message has strong arguments, distracting people will water down their positive opinions about it. But if the arguments are lousy, distraction will make it more convincing. You can do this by peppering an ad with anything that pulls attention away from the actual claims—a little game within the ad, humor, flashy pictures, music, unusual camera angles and edits. In fact, most of the things that create fun in an ad and that actually draw our attention to it in the first place also keep us from thinking too deeply about it. (You might keep this in mind next time you see a lecture served up with plenty of jokes and jaw-dropping PowerPoint animations.)

You've probably noticed that as a TV or radio program yields to a commercial, the speech rate often revs up. The reason for this can be purely practical, to squeeze in as much information as possible into a pricey 30-second commercial slot. Sometimes, when the taped commercial runs slightly over the allotted time, it's compressed to fit in, so it runs faster than actual life. Researchers began to notice that time-compressed commercials could actually be more effective than the same commercial run at normal speed. When they took a closer look they found that surprisingly, people use less brainpower, not more, in listening to time-compressed ads. Since thinking takes more time than reacting, it may be that people just gave up on it when the speech ran faster than cognition. In that case, we'd expect to see signs that people were thinking peripherally when they heard time-compressed ads. Sure enough, ads that sounded like they were on amphetamines led to people relying less on the strength of its arguments, and more on a general impression of how credible the announcer seemed.

Over the last decades, the average commercial time slot has moved away from a standard 60-second slot to the more typical 30-second and 15-second slots. And if you think that's alarming, you should consider the recent trend towards one-second "blink ads," like the one Miller aired for its High Life beer during the 2009 Superbowl.

Incidentally, social stereotypes are a prime example of peripheral thinking—categories based on repetitive experience (even if most of these experiences come from TV) that lead to snap, not-at-all-thoughtful "friend or foe" decisions. Given the extreme time pressures on an ad to capture attention and convey information, heavy stereotyping is inevitable. If a character is supposed to be gay in a commercial, the ad has about two seconds to convey this to the viewer. Piling on every possible stereotypical trait allows the viewer to quickly sort characters into their categories so the commercial can move through its plot without wasting any time on establishing who the characters are. Of course, the rampant use of social stereotypes just feeds right back into the repetitive experiences that help shape the categories in the first place, branding them all the more deeply in viewers' minds.

There are probably many tools for shifting people into peripheral thinking that remain unknown. But so far, scientists have uncovered some downright bizarre ways to manipulate how much thinking you do about a message. For example, putting people in a good mood is a great way to persuade them—especially if you have weak arguments. For some reason, when people are in a happy mood, they tend to rely more on peripheral thinking. Some scientists think that an upbeat mood serves as a signal to the brain that everything is copacetic, that there's no immediate threat on the horizon, so go ahead and let your guard down. A feeling of unease, on the other hand, might signal that some vigilant information-processing is warranted. This extra processing translates into the capacity to sort out good versus bad arguments, among other things.

And who knew that your physical posture could cause you to lean towards truthiness over truth? Apparently, subjects who listened to a message over head-phones while reclining paid more attention to the quality of arguments than those who were forced to stand. And getting subjects to either shake or nod their head while listening to a message mattered as well. Head nodding made a strong argument more persuasive and a weak one less persuasive. The idea seems to be that nodding reinforces whatever internal monologue is going on—whether it's "That's the lamest argument I've ever heard" or "Hmm ... that's pretty convincing." Head shaking had exactly the opposite effect, making a strong argument less persuasive and a weak one more effective, perhaps by throwing people into a state of self-doubt about their own thoughts. The subjects, by the way, were clueless about the real point of the experiment, having been tricked into believing that the study was funded by a headphone company looking to test the effects of various bodily positions and movements on headphone comfort and performance. Which goes to show that mental processes can be pushed around in ways you'd never dream of.

The Escalating Arms Race

Calvin Coolidge argued that the demands of discerning, thoughtful consumers would induce advertisers to present truthful, cogent arguments for the products they sold, which of course is more pleasant for the advertisers than resorting to sleazier techniques. Perhaps what he had in mind was the kind of advertising that shows up in a classic 1959 ad for Rolls Royce.

The whole ad describes in amazingly attentive language 13 details that make the Rolls a superbly crafted vehicle. Here are some of them:

Detail#2: *Every Rolls Royce engine is run for seven hours at full throttle before installation, and each car is test-driven for hundreds of miles over varying road surfaces.*

Detail#5: *The finished car spends a week in the final test shop, being fine-tuned. Here, it is subjected to 98 separate ordeals. For example, the engineers use a* <u>stethoscope</u> *to listen for axle-whine.*

The Rolls-Royce Silver Cloud—$13,995

"At 60 miles an hour the loudest noise in this new Rolls-Royce comes from the electric clock"

What makes Rolls-Royce the best car in the world? "There is really no magic about it— it is merely patient attention to detail," says an eminent Rolls-Royce engineer.

1. "At 60 miles an hour the loudest noise comes from the electric clock," reports the Technical Editor of THE MOTOR. Three mufflers tune out sound frequencies—acoustically.

2. Every Rolls-Royce engine is run for seven hours at full throttle before installation, and each car is test-driven for hundreds of miles over varying road surfaces.

3. The Rolls-Royce is designed as an owner-driven car. It is eighteen inches shorter than the largest domestic cars.

4. The car has power steering, power brakes and automatic gear-shift. It is very easy to drive and to park. No chauffeur required.

5. The finished car spends a week in the final test-shop, being fine-tuned. Here it is subjected to 98 separate ordeals. For example, the engineers use a stethoscope to listen for axle-whine.

6. The Rolls-Royce is guaranteed for three years. With a new network of dealers and parts-depots from Coast to Coast, service is no problem.

7. The Rolls-Royce radiator has never changed, except that when Sir Henry Royce died in 1933 the monogram RR was changed from red to black.

8. The coachwork is given five coats of primer paint, and hand rubbed between each coat, before nine coats of finishing paint go on.

9. By moving a switch on the steering column, you can adjust the shock-absorbers to suit road conditions.

10. A picnic table, veneered in French walnut, slides out from under the dash. Two more swing out behind the front seats.

11. You can get such optional extras as an Espresso coffee-making machine, a dictating machine, a bed, hot and cold water for washing, an electric razor or a telephone.

12. There are three separate systems of power brakes, two hydraulic and one mechanical. Damage to one system will not affect the others. The Rolls-Royce is a very safe car—and also a very lively car. It cruises serenely at eighty-five. Top speed is in excess of 100 m.p.h.

13. The Bentley is made by Rolls-Royce. Except for the radiators, they are identical motor cars, manufactured by the same engineers in the same works. People who feel diffident about driving a Rolls-Royce can buy a Bentley.

PRICE. The Rolls-Royce illustrated in this advertisement—f.o.b. principal ports of entry—costs $13,995.

If you would like the rewarding experience of driving a Rolls-Royce or Bentley, write or telephone to one of the dealers listed on the opposite page.

Rolls-Royce Inc., 10 Rockefeller Plaza, New York 20, N. Y., CIrcle 5-1144.

March 1959

Detail#7: The Rolls Royce radiator has never changed, except that when Sir Henry Royce died in 1933 the monogram RR was changed from red to black.
Detail#8: The coachwork is given five coats of primer paint, and hand-rubbed between each coat before <u>nine</u> coats of finishing paint go on.

Detail#10: *A picnic table, veneered in French walnut, slides out from under the dash. Two more swing out behind the front seats.*

There's no rugged landscape, no celebrity spokesperson, no beautiful people living a beautiful life, and no sexy name hand-crafted by pricy name consultants. Looking at this ad, you can almost believe Coolidge's "advertising-as-education" schtick. The copywriter probably *did* go to the company to ask, "What good things can I say about this car?" With a list like this one, the ad probably wrote itself.

But Silent Cal's everyone-wins scenario hasn't exactly panned out.

It's not that advertisers have a special gene for sneakiness. It's that Coolidge forgot that consumers don't keep the porch light on and the door open to advertising. It's human nature of a highly adaptive sort to resist messages that are intended to persuade. The will to filter out persuasive messages combines with a superbly selective attentional system. This is put to good use in an age where everyone suffers from a bad overload of information and too many choices.

In his 1983 book, the late great adman David Ogilvy (who happened to be the creator of the Rolls Royce ad you just saw) bemoaned the fact that most ad campaigns of his time provided far too little information to the consumer. He also detested the amount of advertising clutter in the American media. When pressed to make predictions about the future of advertising, he went out on a limb and foresaw that clutter would come under control, and that advertising styles would become more factual. He was dead wrong on both counts.

Robbed of a rapt audience, advertisers know that influencing how you spend what's in your wallet depends a lot on having some control over how you spend the resources in your head. And thus begins the battle for control over your attention.

In *Under the Radar: Talking to Today's Cynical Consumer*, authors Jonathan Bond and Richard Kirshenbaum wallow in the language of warfare as they write:

> *[P]ersuasive marketing should be invisible, with the consumer feeling the benefit rather than having to uncomfortably digest its overt message . . . The real threat [to the advertiser] is the consumers' mental machine guns, their very own personal defense departments that can shoot down messages at any given point. And there are only a handful of techniques today that are sophisticated enough to act as stealth bombers, dropping new messages behind the wall—escaping detection by consumers' ever present radar!*

This sentiment might not line up with how Coolidge and Ogilvy would have liked to see things go. But it's right up the alley of Freud's nephew Edward Bernays, who was captivated by his uncle's writings about the less rational side of the human mind. Believing that people are seldom persuaded by arguments and reason—even when they think they are—Bernays enthusiastically pioneered ways of enhancing the "feeling of knowing." Flying under the radar was his specialty. Not one to sit in his office creating crisp, informative copy, Bernays targeted the peripheral mind instead, luring stylish debutantes into being spokeswomen for cigarettes, and packaging the dour President Coolidge as a fun guy who consorted with Broadway stars.

As in any arms race, both sides quickly evolve in response to the other's advantage. Consumers become even more selective, and advertisers adapt with newer attention-getting techniques. When consumers aggressively divide their attention, it becomes all the more motivating for advertisers to understand where these divisions lie and how to best use them. And advertisers are honing some of their best weapons; they're finding ways of making their messages work in the shadows of the periphery. As the attentional arms race escalates, this is more and more becoming the meeting ground for consumer and advertiser.

4

We Know What You're Thinking

Why Squier wasn't Fired

Dick Morris, who managed Bill Clinton's 1996 re-election campaign, relates the following anecdote in his book, *Behind the Oval Office*:

> *[Clinton's] achievements were a problem. In strategy meetings, he often complained that he had created seven million jobs and cut the deficit but nobody seemed to notice. In speeches, he referred to the achievements awkwardly. Our polls showed audiences either already knew about them or didn't believe they were true.*
>
> *At one strategy session, Bob Squier suggested a better way to draw attention to what he had done. The key, Squier explained, was to cite the achievement while talking about something he was going to do. For example ...*

... Now let's interrupt Morris here for a moment. Squier seemed to be suggesting that if you focus the audience's attention on something else, this would (by some miracle) draw attention to some "oh, by the way" remark you make along the way. But this is pretty strange. If focusing people's attention on the achievements won't get them to understand, then how on earth is diverting attention going to be any *more* effective? Now, as you already suspect, Clinton didn't choose Squier to be his media strategist for testing high on the dopiness scale. And, you may also suspect, it's the *way* you present the information that makes for all the difference. Let's return to the Morris quote and let him finish. He continues:

> *For example: 'The hundred thousand extra police we put on the street can't solve the crime problem by themselves; we need to keep anti-drug funding for schools in the budget and stop Republicans from cutting it.' Or: 'The seven million jobs we've created won't be much use if we can't find educated people to fill them. That's why*

Sold on Language: How Advertisers Talk to You and What This Says About You.   By Julie Sedivy and Greg Carlson
© 2011 John Wiley & Sons Ltd.

I want a tax deduction for college tuition to help kids go on to college to take those jobs.'

These changes may have been superficial. But in Bill Clinton's case, they made a real difference.

Superficial, schmuperficial. I beg to differ. Linguists recognize that these examples are loaded with language that's used to signal information that is *presupposed.*

Presuppositions have a distinctly "backgrounded" nature. The references in the campaign ads to a hundred thousand extra police, or the seven million new jobs have something of this character—they serve as the backdrop for what feels like the main point of the statement. In everyday life, we rely on a vast number of backgrounded, taken-for-granted assumptions. To take a perfectly mundane example:

Each morning I go out to the mailbox to get the local newspaper (OK, I confess, I still like to read actual paper newspapers). It's usually folded up so it would fit the mailbox. As I walk back to the house, I unfold it to look at the headlines. My attention is focused on finding out the news—what's going on in the world? I'm not wasting any of my precious attention on whether I can unfold the newspaper, though—why on earth would I ever do that? I simply assume I can do it, and it does not arise as even a glimmer of a question in my mind whether I can. None of us have time to think about stuff like that and if we did, we'd quickly go bats. There are zillions of little assumptions like this that allow us to operate on some sort of automatic pilot while focusing our attention on the things at hand that require it.

These "zillions of little assumptions" are the reasons we learn to expect things to happen normally without focusing our attention on those expectations, or even being aware we have such expectations. It's why Whoopee! Cushions work: it's that we expect, way down inside and without thinking about it, that sitting on the couch will *not* create a rude noise. And when this humdrum expectation proves embarrassingly false, everyone else gets a really good laugh out of it. Lots of humdrum expectations of this sort are squarely behind the "home team" advantage in sports. If you're at home in a familiar environment, you can just go on blithely assuming all kinds of things without any "Whoopee-cushion" effects. But if you're the "away" team, you do need to divert some of your precious attention to where the bathroom is, how to operate the hotel snooze alarm and the shower adjustment, that the elevator button marked "M1" is where the hotel restaurant is located, etc. Even the bed doesn't quite "work" like it's supposed to. Each item on its own (with the possible exception of figuring out how to set the alarm on the hotel clock radio) is a perfectly trivial little task not requiring many resources at all—but pile them up, big and little, hundreds and hundreds of them, and presto! Home team advantage. It becomes just that much harder to focus on the main purpose of your visit—winning the game. (Naturally, the cheering of the crowds and maybe some friendly refereeing don't hurt, either.) We're all happier when things work as they should without our having to pay them much attention. Listening to language is like this too; we tend to focus on the point and not worry about the things we already know.

Let's get back to Squier's brainstorm. Note the way the information about extra police and job creation is phrased in the examples: even though it's not taken to be the main point of the sentence, it does an impressive amount of persuasive work. That's because the way the sentences are crafted *presuppose* the creation of jobs and putting extra police on the streets. This presupposed information has something of this taken-for-granted background flavor. However, there's more to the story of presuppositions than that. Presuppositions also signal *shared* information. In fact, they're backgrounded precisely because it's presumed that the information is already known not just to the speaker, but also to the hearer, or "people" more generally. This fact gives presupposition a curious property of undeniability.

To get a sense of the presupposition dynamic, let's look at a couple of scenarios. Suppose you're visiting relatives and somehow the topic of conversation wanders into your hosts' furnishings, bought from an upscale store called Stickley's. There comes a point in the conversation when your nosey brother-in-law, who you've never liked much anyway, says:

The quality of Stickley's furniture is legendary. You can afford it.

There are two obvious points where you have the opportunity to openly agree or disagree. So, for instance, after the first sentence you might respond "I didn't know that," "Oh", "Stickleys!? That's dime-store stuff." Or whatever. Similarly for the presumptuous claim about what you can or cannot afford—"No, it's way out of my price range," "Yes, with my recent promotion, you're right!" and so on.

Of course in conversation it's probably more normal to not openly respond to claims being made—the key point here is when you have the *opportunity* to deny or confirm openly. We often choose to forgo these opportunities in order to be polite, or to get on with the conversation, in which case we may keep to ourselves that fact that we've accepted or rejected certain statements in our own minds. But these opportunities exist anyway. They're structured by the ways *assertions* are typically presented in conversation. Assertions are what we are given the opportunity to openly agree or disagree with in conversation.

Now, let's change the scenario just a bit. Instead of this information being delivered to you by your presumptuous relative, you see an announcer in a TV commercial telling you the exact same thing. Of course, what with the announcer being on TV and all, you cannot meaningfully respond to her as you might have been able to respond to your relative since, obviously, the announcer can't hear you. And this is where the notion of having an *opportunity* to respond plays a role. You can still evaluate and, if you wish, mentally agree or disagree with the two assertions made about quality and affordability, on TV as in real life.

Stickley, an actual upscale furniture store, did run a series of ads in the local media, both on television and in print. But the ads read somewhat differently from "The quality of Stickley's furniture is legendary. You can afford it." Instead, the attractive announcer came on TV and presented the information in a slightly different way, assuring us that:

Yes, you can afford the legendary quality of Stickley.

There is now only one assertion not two, but the same two bits of information remain presented. At the end of the sentence you have the opportunity to agree, or disagree, but only with a part of the information presented—the asserted part. You can easily locate the asserted part of an utterance by simply asking yourself the following: if you (mentally or verbally) respond to this assertion by saying "No," or "I do not agree," or "that's not true," which part are you disputing? In this case, the answer is clear that you're only disputing the affordability of the furniture, and not whether Stickley furniture quality is legendary. This is because the bit about legendariness is *presupposed* content, and not a part of the asserted content.

The point is not that it's impossible to wonder if Stickley quality is in fact legendary. It's that the structure of the utterance presents the asserted part as what you have the opportunity to respond to, and we're most keen to attend to information that is presented that way.[1] There's a simple reason for why we think the asserted contents should be what we're keen to attend to, and the presupposed contents should be backgrounded in our attentional space. It's because in normal real life, the things that are presented as presupposed are, 99 times out of 100, humdrum familiar information that is already considered entirely uncontroversial, the same way nobody needs to tell you that you can unfold a newspaper. And if there's anything that's new or controversial, it's signaled by being asserted. Consider an everyday situation where, say, you pass two coworkers standing by the water cooler, and you hear Bill saying to coworker Alex,

The problem with my car turned out to be the battery.

There are several bits of information in this utterance: (a) that Bill has a car, (b) that the car has a battery, (c) that the car had a problem, and (d) that the battery was the source of the problem. But Bill did not say to Alex: "I have a car. It has a battery. The car had a problem. The problem turned out to be the battery." This is

[1] If you've been especially alert, you may have noticed that information that's presupposed can still appear in parts of the sentence that normally *do* receive a lot of attention. For instance, the Clinton ads place the information about new jobs in the subject of the sentence. Presupposition, at least in English, tends to be marked by very specific bits of language, not general position in the sentence, so that information can still have this backgrounded feel regardless of where in the sentence it appears. More on this later.

what happens when all information is presented assertively—it gets real boring, real fast, because you already know or can easily assume most of it, and instead you're being treated as something of a dolt. Rather, people normally take what's already known and mark it linguistically as presupposed, in order to focus on what is taken to be the new bit that demands the most attention. So the language of presupposition allows the speaker to partition a sentence into what's taken to be already known, and what's not.

Every native speaker of English has an intuitive, implicit sense of how this kind of partitioning works. Of course, just because information is coded in presuppositional language doesn't automatically mean that it's already known by everyone, or even by the person who's being addressed. But it can actually turn out to provide a lot of information about what the speaker *thinks* the hearer knows (or ought to know). For example, in passing the water cooler you might have known Bill well enough to know he had a car, and that his car had a battery (duh), but you may not have known that his car had a problem. This, to you, was new information. But because Bill was talking to Alex, and not you, you surmise that the reason Bill presented the information this way is because he had reason to think Alex already knew about it. And you can also figure out that the reason he put the actual source of the problem as the asserted part is that he thought Alex didn't already know about his battery trouble.

In short, to understand the structure of the presupposed/asserted contents, you need to construct a scenario in which it makes sense for the speaker (or writer) to have presented it that way in the first place. So, while the fact that the car had a problem turned out to be new information to *you*, you understood that had you been in Alex's place, Bill would have expected you to have already known this. Linguists use the term *accommodation* to refer to this process of updating information that is unknown by the hearer but presupposed by the speaker—the hearer enters it into memory with a tag that says "shared information."

Presuppositions are, 99 times out of 100, things that are already known or taken as boringly obvious to the people conversing. So we tend to accommodate them quite readily, not bothering to examine very closely whether the information conveyed in them is accurate or not. That accuracy is presented as having already been established between people, in contrast to the assertion, whose accuracy remains up for grabs. In the end, evaluating presupposed information is a tiresome and unrewarding exercise—it's like looking under every cushion you ever sit on to see if there just might be a Whoopee! Cushion there. You can live that way if you like, but for most of us it's a tedious way to do things.[2]

---

[2] Obviously, there are limits to accommodation. If a speaker refers to "the girl who lives next door to me," the hearer is likely to accommodate this without batting an eye. Things would be a bit different if someone referred to "the dragon that lives next door to me."

And since we are so very used to not paying much attention to the contents of presuppositions, taking them instead as already established facts that we can rely on as "known," we can see why Squier suggested wording Clinton's accomplishments in the form of a presupposition. In saying "The seven million new jobs we've created . . .", those seven million new jobs were presented as if they were an established fact that, oh by the way, if you follow politics at all you'd clearly be aware of. So once you heard and understood it and it's gone by without too much thought, it becomes one of the "background" facts that we take to be true, but aren't inclined to think about very much or even to wonder *why* we think it's so. And Squier kept his job long enough to help usher Clinton to electoral victory.

Presupposition Smorgasbord

We've seen that savvy political operatives and the whiz kids at Stickley furniture seemed to have caught on about presuppositions. But have advertisers as a whole clued in? Well, as they say in Minnesota, "You betcha."

Presuppositions in ads are abundantly abundant. Language offers an appealing sampling of options when it comes to packaging information up as presupposed. In English, much of the time, presuppositions are signaled by specific words or phrases. They can also be triggered by certain types of grammatical structures. Below is a partial menu.

Definite descriptions are phrases like *the suitcase in the trunk; the legendary quality of Stickley; the battery; the person who got the lowest mark on the dentistry exam*, and so on. They consist of the English definite article *the*, followed by some descriptive material, and the effect is to assume the existence of something fitting that description. For example, notice the difference between these two minimally different sentences:

> *Jonas searched, without success, for an honest politician,*
> *Jonas searched, without success, for the honest politician.*

The first sentence makes perfect sense even when the entire universe is devoid of any honest politicians whatsoever. But in order for the second sentence to be sensible, there's one who's gone missing, and moreover, a specific one that is mutually known to the hearer and speaker. An example of very small words making a big difference.

The ad on the next page for Altoids mints packs a great deal of persuasive power into this compact little word. Without it, if the product had been pitched simply as "curiously strong mints," the ad would have merely told you something about the taste of the mints. Add the *the*, and all of a sudden, the ad creates the impression of buzz—you have the sense that everyone's been talking about those mysterious, curiously strong mints, and now the ad tells you what they are.

Reprinted by permission of Wm. Wrigley Jr. Co.

Definite descriptions can also begin with other types of words, particularly possessives such as *Joe's, his, mine, their,* and so on, so that if someone refers to "Larry's older sister" the presupposition would be that Larry has an older sister.

Once you start looking in ads, you trip over definite descriptions all over the place. Here are some snippets of ad copy that use them—it's worth pausing to recognize what's being presupposed:

The solid choice.
Ad for Toyota Corolla (presupposes there's a single, specific solid choice)

With our strong capital base, global reach, and extensive expertise we can offer the stability and security you are looking for.
Ad for Credit Suisse (presupposes that the bank *has* a strong capital base, global reach, extensive expertise)

Fauxbesity: the half-hearted claims other fast food chains make about helping kids eat better.
Ad for the Subway sandwich chain (presupposes that other chains make half-hearted health claims)

Finally, a low fat cereal that meets your high expectations.
Ad for Quaker cereal (presupposes that you have high expectations, demonstrating flattery as a common use for presupposition).

Another way of coding presupposition is through a class of verbs (linguists call them *factives*) that express someone's mental state towards a presupposed fact. Among these are verbs or phrases like *regret, realize, is aware, was proud, think it strange, it's your fault that . . .* and so on. These expressions presuppose that the fact is already known to be true. For example, if you came back from vacation in a remote location, and the front-page headline of your local paper read: "*PRESIDENT REGRETS SELLING TEXAS TO SAUDI ARABIA,*" you'd feel you'd missed some pretty significant news while away—presumably, everyone else already knew about the actual *sale* of Texas, if not about the President's misgivings after the fact, and you might ask the cab driver for an update. And when Apple put out an ad in which a polished young woman said, "I used to think it was my fault that Windows didn't work properly," the company was cleverly signaling that the shortcomings of the Windows operating system were presupposed, common knowledge.

There is also a collection of verbs that communicate a change of state or a continuation of a state—in both cases, some existing state is considered to be part of the background knowledge. Hence the absurdity of an organization dedicated to "stopping illegal immigration from Mars," or my doctor advising me to "keep running five miles every day."

In ads, we have:

Start treating the appearance of wrinkles, age spots, and discoloration in your sleep.
Ad for Olay night cream (presupposes you haven't been treating these signs of aging in your sleep, perhaps even if you've been using other creams)

No wonder Dove's the one that dermatologists recommend most to keep your skin looking healthy and feeling soft.
Ad for Dove soap (presupposes—flattery will get you everywhere—that your skin looks healthy and feels soft. Notice there's a second presupposition, coded by a definite description. Catch it? It's the presupposition that there's one particular soap that dermatologists recommend).

Then there are iterative expressions, like *again, return, anymore, another.* Suppose you've promised your wife that you will only have one drink at the office party due to various embarrassing occurrences in the past. Your friend slips you a glass of whisky in private, having been sworn to secrecy. You know your friend has blabbed when later, your wife observes you sipping a glass of wine, and remarks "I see you're having another drink."
These bits of language are often found in ads that promise the recovery of a lost youth:

Bring back vibrancy.
Ad for Estée Lauder cosmetics (presupposes you were once vibrant)

Feel young again.
Ad for GENF20 diet supplement (presupposes—somewhat trivially—that you once felt young).

When a clause is introduced by temporal expressions like *before, after, during,* or *when,* the events it describes are usually presupposed. This can lead to a statement feeling less controversial than if it were asserted. Imagine a political analyst responding to a question about his opinion of the Bush Presidency by saying: "While President Bush was preventing further terrorist attacks, he let the economy slide." It feels as if there is widespread agreement that Bush prevented attacks. But suppose the analyst had responded by saying, "He prevented further terrorist attacks, but let the economy slide." Now, the actual prevention of attacks feels a bit more like just once person's opinion. It's open for denial.
And when an ad for Westin hotels informs you: "Earn unlimited free weekend nights when you stay at Westin," it expresses a confidence that you are in fact a current or future customer. This has more swagger than saying, "Earn unlimited free weekend nights *if* you stay at Westin."
Sometimes it's a certain grammatical structure rather than a word or phrase that triggers the presupposition. These syntactic structures often serve to put special focus on certain parts of the sentence, with the result being that the remaining material is treated as background information. "*It was Suzanna who ran off with your husband*" can only be said to someone who already knows she's in marital trouble, and not out-of-the-blue to break the bad news that all is not well on the domestic scene. Likewise with "*That's how your car ended up on fire,*" or "*What the*

builder did to cause your roof to cave in was use improperly poured concrete." The person who uttered these sentences is assuming that you already know that your car was on fire, or that your roof caved in.

Advertising language is positively laced with these types of structures. Often, glowing things about the advertised good are said in the form of a presupposition (the presupposition-triggering structures are underlined):

> *Elbow grease is overrated. That's why Brawny is soft, with the classic strength you* *expect.*
> Ad for Brawny paper towels

> *The energy from algae might someday produce biofuels that are compatible with* *those made from conventional crude oil. That's why ExxonMobil is committed to a* *major long-term research and development program aimed at developing algae as* *a viable fuel source.*
> Ad for ExxonMobil

> *Visit myslimquick.com to see how SLIMQUICK^{TM} appetite control works in 6 ways* *to help women fight temptation.*
> Ad for Slimquick weight loss supplements

> *Our trained experts will show you how the superior comfort and unsurpassed* *support provided by our proprietary Tempur® pressure-relieving material will help* *you fall asleep faster and wake more refreshed.*
> Ad for Tempur-Pedic beds (notice also the two definite descriptions for extra presuppositional *oomph*).

There are a good many more ways to signal presupposition, but this gives an idea of the range of possibilities—a pretty wide range, it turns out. Of just the examples provided by Dick Morris, Clinton's campaign recruited the use of definite descriptions ("the hundred thousand additional police we put on the street"), iterative verbs ("keep funding for schools in the budget"), and syntactic constructions ("That is why I want a tax deduction for . . ."). Here are the things you (and the world at large) are presumed to know about Bill Clinton: That he put a hundred thousand new police officers on the streets; that his budget includes anti-drug funding for schools and that Republicans will cut the funding unless some action is taken; that he's created seven million jobs; and that he supports a tax deduction for college tuition. When you think about it, a pretty powerful package to have people listening to and treating as if these were established fact. And there's a fair bit of experimental evidence to point to presupposition's special blend—its backgrounding effects and the signaling of communal information—as an especially potent mix for the human mind.

Leading Questions

Let's say you happen to have the misfortune of standing trial for murder, and are being cross-examined by the prosecution. The judge is already exasperated by the evasive verbosity of several witnesses, and has instructed you to keep your answers to a simple "yes" or "no." Seizing the opportunity, the prosecuting attorney fires these questions at you:

> —*Was it with this letter opener that you stabbed the victim? (May I remind you, a simple "yes" or "no," please.)*
> —*When the mailman came to the door, did you stop stabbing the victim?*
> —*Do you regret murdering this innocent girl?*

Basically, you're screwed. The astute prosecutor is well aware that, whether you answer "yes" or "no," you're accepting the highly incriminating presuppositions in these questions. You can't reject them simply by answering "no."

Just like statements that contain presuppositions, questions don't give you the opportunity to reject their presuppositions either. In the same way that statements are partitioned into the asserted bits and the presupposed information, questions are too, and the *question* part only applies to the nonpresupposed portion. The presupposed part is, of course, already presumed to be true. Again, while of course it's generally *possible* to deny the presupposed material in a question (unless you've been limited to a "yes" or "no" answer), it has the feel of objecting to the premise of the question, not actually answering the question.

Of course, any defense lawyer would do just that, wearing out his shoes jumping up to raise objections to these questions, and no judge with a pulse would allow a prosecutor this kind of linguistic latitude. In a courtroom, the wording of questions *is* carefully scrutinized. But outside of the courtroom— when statements are first taken from witnesses or suspects, sometimes during a long and grueling interrogation—the rules of the game are much less clearly set out. This has some scientists worried. They worry because in remembering an event, people can be quite vulnerable to outside influence and will often accept information that is presented to them in a suggestive way as if it were part of their original memory. Presuppositional language is often part and parcel of this suggestive packaging.

Think of how you go about sneaking into a building or room that you have no business being in. The *last* thing you do is make a show of presenting your fake ID, and you neither lock eyes with the person in charge nor conspicuously avoid eye contact. You simply saunter in with utmost confidence, looking intent on some specific goal, as if having to prove your right to be there was the furthest thing from your mind. You act like you assume everyone already knows who you are and what you're doing there (which, naturally, is what everyone who is actually *supposed* to be there is doing).

What you're doing, of course, is using body language to signal the presupposition that you belong in that room—just as certain words or sentence structures signal the presupposition that a specific bit of information belongs in your storehouse of knowledge or memory. Unlike assertions, they don't bother displaying their ID cards.

The metaphor of memory as a storehouse is fairly accurate. Many people think of memories as photographs or video recordings of events that they've experienced, which, other than becoming somewhat faded with time, preserve a record of the original event. We often talk about "replaying" events in our minds like movies. But lots of scientific study since the 1970s shows that this intuitive sense of memory is deeply wrong. Like the contents of a somewhat chaotic storehouse, only some of the details of the actual event make it in; sometimes things get in that weren't part of the event at all, and the entire contents of the room are subject to endless revisitings and shufflings about, with things getting lost or new things brought in from outside. The memory movies we experience aren't recordings of the events—they're more like shows recreated with the contents of the storehouse as props.

Elizabeth Loftus is one of the world's busiest memory researchers, and her long career has been devoted to showing just how changeable memory is. Early on in her research, she became very interested in how leading questions used presuppositions to shape memory. Can presuppositions slip material into your mental storehouse even when it's at odds with what really happened out in the world? To find out, Loftus and her colleagues simulated an accident eyewitness scenario for their study volunteers: people saw a one-minute film of a five-car pileup, and filled out a questionnaire afterwards to test their memory for the event. The scientists were most interested to see whether people's responses would vary for questions such as "Did you see a stop sign?" versus "Did you see the stop sign?" In the second version, of course, the presence of a stop sign is presupposed. What happens when there was in fact no stop sign? Can a small word like *the* influence people's responses? Apparently, it can. When people heard the more neutral question "Did you see a stop sign?"—when there was no such thing in the film— they answered "yes" about 6% of the time. This number more than doubled when the question used the definite article *the*.

But showing that people say "yes" to the question doesn't necessarily show that their memories were altered. An alternative explanation might go like this: maybe the people who answered "yes" were somewhat unsure about whether there was a stop sign. But because the question containing the presupposition made it clear that the *questioner* took its presence for granted, they may have thought, "Well, I didn't see a stop sign, but because there obviously was one, I'll go along and say I saw it." These people may have been eager to please, or willing to change their responses in order to look smarter—both dangerous qualities in an eyewitness, to be sure—but their actual (somewhat fuzzy) memories may have been the same after hearing the leading question as before.

But Loftus then launched a full-throttle investigation into memory, and showed that false information that was slipped in via presupposition could in fact change how people remembered an event. Here's a particularly convincing demonstration.

Subjects watched a traffic accident unfold over a series of video slides, and then filled in a questionnaire supposedly testing their memory for what they had seen. This questionnaire was actually just a decoy—its real purpose was to smuggle in some presuppositions. Loftus wanted to see whether these would actually change what people remembered, as measured by a later memory test. On the decoy memory questionnaire, subjects answered questions such as "Did another car pass the red Datsun while it was stopped at the stop sign?" Half of the time, the presupposed information was misleading—the traffic sign had been a yield sign, not a stop sign. The other half of the time, the question referred to the correct sign. The subjects then spent 20 minutes being distracted from their eyewitness role, reading an unrelated story and answering some questions about it before taking the real memory test. In this actual memory test, they were shown pairs of slides that were identical except for one critical detail. For example, instead of the original yield sign, one of the slides showed a stop sign in the same place. They then had to say which of the slides was the one they had actually seen as part of the accident sequence. So the test in this case was whether a *previous* leading question in the decoy test would taint how their memories matched up to true or false photos of the event.

Their responses would make a traffic court judge throw his hands up in the air: misleading presuppositions caused correct responses to plummet from 70% to 43%. That is, people were actually "recognizing" the wrong sign 54% of the time when they'd read a misleading presupposition much earlier. At the end of the study, the experimenter admitted to the subjects that the point of the research was to look at the effects of misleading questions, and asked the subjects whether they remembered how the earlier question had been worded. Most people couldn't. And whether they did or didn't recall the leading question had no impact on the memory test, so it seems unlikely that they were responding the way they did just to placate the experimenter or to look good.

It seems that the best explanation for what the subjects did in their minds is that they treated the "taken for granted" presupposition as taken for granted—they "accommodated" it. To do this, they altered their own memories.

Remember Those Crimes You Committed?

Still. Getting people to misremember yield signs as stop signs is hardly in the same league as implanting memories of murder. Presuppositional language doesn't mesmerize people into accommodating just anything into their memories. Being greeted with a cheery "I'm so glad you've stopped selling crack to school kids!" would likely bring the conversation to a grinding halt rather than induce you to believe you had a past as a drug dealer. When memories are truly clear and strong, or when the presupposition is outright preposterous we do tend to challenge it. All true, but it may surprise you just how shape-shifting human memory can be. One of the most extreme cases is the story of Paul Ingram, who in 1988 pleaded guilty to sexually abusing his two daughters. Though originally denying his daughters' allegations, Ingram eventually came to admit to not only abusing his children, but also to holding satanic cult rituals with other police officers and members of the community. According to his confessions, he and his fellow satanists engaged in horrific acts such as killing small animals and babies, and burying them on his property.

None of these confessions lined up with a shred of hard evidence from the extensive criminal investigation. What's more, shortly before his guilty plea, a psychologist named Richard Ofshe visited Ingram, and, suspecting his confessions to be false memories, decided to see if he could implant one that *was* clearly false. He told Ingram that his family accused him of forcing his children to have sex with each other—family members in fact agreed that this had never happened. Ingram came forth with a written confession of the event, complete with many details that he claimed were as vivid as any other memory. Ultimately, Ingram was convicted on the basis of his guilty plea. Some time later, he recanted, saying that he had been deluded into "remembering" these events. However, constrained by Washington State law, an appeals board refused to overturn his guilty plea, and he was jailed until he completed his prison sentence in 2003.

Was Ingram simply crazy (assuming he was in fact innocent)? Elizabeth Loftus would say no, that this bizarre case is in line with how we might expect normal people to respond under extreme pressure. In a line of studies that had some eerie similarities to the Ingram case, Loftus recruited family members of study volunteers to help implant false memories about childhood events. Relatives provided three true stories, and then helped construct a fourth that never actually happened, but that *could* have happened. Since it's generally considered unethical scientific practice to try to convince your study volunteers that they committed heinous crimes, the false memories revolved around events that were much more benign, such as getting lost in a shopping mall. About a quarter of the subjects could be led to "remember" the event, even garnishing it with details of their own. When told at the end of the study that one of the childhood stories had been cooked up, a number of the subjects guessed that one of the *real* events was the false memory.

Using this technique, researchers have been able to implant false memories not only of very common events like getting lost, but more unusual ones as well. People have been hoodwinked into remembering spilling a bowl of punch on the bride's parents at a wedding, taking a nonexistent ride in a hot air balloon, having to evacuate a grocery store when its sprinkler system accidentally went off, and being attacked by a vicious animal. False memories can even convince people that they like asparagus.

In these studies, subjects found it hard to resist their family's claims that certain events had occurred. In *trying* to remember them, they likely spent some time imagining what might have happened, until their minds misinterpreted the experience of imagining as the experience of the actual event. In the same way, Paul Ingram apparently could not reconcile his own initial belief in his innocence with the belief that his daughters would not lie (even though one of them had made false accusations of sexual abuse on two earlier occasions). Moreover, police interrogators, and the community at large behaved in a way that presupposed his guilt.

False confessions aside, can more mundane persuasive messages such as advertising cause people to imagine memories into being? Sit back in your chair, relax, read the copy for this Disney ad, and let the memories flow:

It's time to remember the magic

Take a look back into your childhood . . . Try to recall the first time you visited a Disney theme park . . . Bring that image to mind . . . See Cinderella's castle glisten in the bright sunlight . . . feel the breeze that cooled off the sweat you worked up as you ran from ride to ride to fit the most excitement into your day. Recall the pride you felt as you cleared the height requirement indicated by the character's wooden hand . . . that allowed you to go on the really cool rides like Space Mountain.

You were in your element—festival food, scary rides, and exciting shows. With the song 'It's a Small World After All' in your mind, you ventured back to your hotel to rest up for another day. Just then, you spotted one of the characters, looks like Bugs Bunny! He waved you over. Adrenaline rushed through you and you somehow managed to move your feet in his direction. He shook your hand. The perfect end to a perfect day.

There. Floating in nostalgic reverie yet? Were you one of those lucky kids who got to go to Disneyland or Disneyworld for spring break? And were you lucky enough to shake hands with Bugs? If so, you have fallen prey to a false memory. Bugs Bunny is a Warner Brothers character, not a Disney creation, and if he were spotted strolling through Disneyworld trying to shake hands with children, he'd more than likely be removed by security guards.

The text you just read comes from a fake ad concocted by Loftus and her colleagues. The people who read it believed they were taking part in a study to test the effectiveness of various marketing techniques. And sure enough, when asked about their own childhood memories of visiting a Disney park, about a fifth of them reported that they had met Bugs Bunny.

In this phony ad, the false information about your childhood memories isn't coming from any credible person who would actually have been there with you. And yet, the ad, by triggering the *imagining* of a memory, is able to create a false sense of familiarity to a number of readers. Notice too that the ad is loaded with presuppositional language—the text is acting as if your memories were truly real. This likely lowers your guard in the act of "remembering" your Disney park visit.

Language that is more tentative about the content of your memories seems to have much less power in immersing you in a constructed reality. Try this instead:

Do you remember feeling some magic?

Take a look back into your childhood ... Can you remember visiting a Disney theme park for the first time? If you did, bring that image to mind ... Was Cinderella's castle there? If you ran from ride to ride to fit the most excitement into your day, you might have felt a breeze that cooled off the sweat you worked up. There would have been a height requirement indicated by the character's wooden hand that allowed you to go on some really cool rides like Space Mountain—were you able to clear it? Bugs Bunny is a Disney character—did you spot him? And if you did, did he shake your hand in a perfect end to a perfect day?

This contrasts with the fake ad created by the Loftus team—the copy used in the study assumes you visited a Disney park, and has many more presuppositions sprinkled throughout: *the first time you visited a Disney theme park; the breeze that cooled off the sweat you worked up; the pride you felt as you cleared the height requirement; back to your hotel,* and so on.

In fact, there's an uncanny resemblance between the language in the fake Disney ad and the following chunk of real ad copy for the Porsche 911:

The first time you experience a Porsche 911, you notice a degree of purpose to the car you may not have anticipated. Every component, every technical advancement is there to advance one cause: the drive. You notice the key is on the left; it was put there originally so a racer could start with one hand, shift with the other and hit the track faster. You, car and road bond like brothers. You suddenly remember driving can be a thrill. Is a thrill. You feel alive every time you get behind the wheel. You note, amazed, that a 385-horsepower car returns 27 miles per gallon. You appreciate its founding belief of getting more for less. You strain to think of something else that has stayed this true to its ideals for 46 years. And you come to the realization that, in the age of the superfluous and the superficial, the unrooted and the unserious, the 911 is necessary. Very necessary.

If you've never been to a Disney park, or you've never driven a Porsche 911, the ads are unlikely to make you think you have. But if you have done either, the copy may add some convincing (and sexy) flesh to your skeletal memories.

The Emperor's Clothes Effect

Presupposition is powerful in part because it communicates that certain information is presumed to be shared and generally agreed upon. What Bob Squier was communicating, in his crafting of the Clinton ads, was that *people know* that Clinton created seven million jobs, put a hundred thousand police officers on the street and so on. Sticking this *people know* tag on an idea makes it very hard for someone to reject it. Conformity is a dirty word in many Western cultures, and we would really love to see ourselves as independent thinkers who are not swayed by the opinions and beliefs of others. But this self-image is hard to maintain in the cold, hard light of scientific evidence. Human beings, even those living in extremely individualistic cultures, seem to be wired for a great deal of social conformity. This was apparent in the way that Paul Ingram and Loftus' subjects tried to align their own memories with those of the people around them.

Research in the late 1940s and 1950s spawned much of the work on the science of conformity that is still being done today. At that time, still deeply affected by the fallout of World War II, some psychologists were disturbed by how easily entire populations of educated people in Western democracies gave themselves over to oppressive fascist regimes. It seemed urgent to understand when and why people would subordinate their own thoughts and actions to those around them. Many of their early experimental results were startling—all the more so because they involved undergraduates at elite American institutions, students who had presumably been taught to cherish freedom of thought and should have been among those most capable of practicing it.

Solomon Asch demonstrated that under social pressure, Swarthmore college students could be swayed to proclaim that the sky was green—or close enough. The students thought they were participating in a vision experiment testing their ability to discriminate lengths of lines. They sat in a room with a number of other subjects who were secretly colluding with the experimenter. The experimenter showed the group pairs of cards with one line on the left, and a series of three lines on the right, like this:

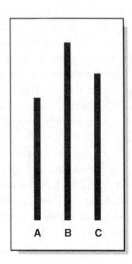

A   B   C

The students were asked to say out loud which of the lines on the right was the same length as the line on the left. As you might imagine, this is pretty easy ("C")—when tested alone, subjects were about 99% correct. But in the social version of the study, the experiment was rigged so that the real subject always responded last, and after a couple of trials in which the conspirators gave the right answers, they suddenly and unanimously began to give wrong ones. About a quarter of the real subjects resisted the urge to agree with the crowd. But most of them buckled under the pressure and began offering up the same wrong answer as their peers on a good portion of the test items, yielding an average error rate of 37%. When questioned afterwards, many of them admitted that they knew the others were wrong, but decided to go along with their responses anyway. A small number of the subjects said they began to question their own perception. Later research showed that if the task is harder, and people show more uncertainty in their answers even when questioned alone, conformity rates are even higher, and the responses of others change not just their responses, but their perceptions.

Asch found that it only took about three others acting as a unified group to induce conformity in subjects, and, like the fairy tale in which one little boy breaks through a crowd's willingness to pretend the naked emperor is splendidly dressed, one dissenting member in even a large group was enough to break the spell.

Similarly, there's often a barrier against challenging a presupposition. When you do so, you are backing away from the agreed-upon starting assumptions of the conversation. Because of its cues about the general acceptance of these assumptions, questioning the content of a presupposition amounts to declaring the emperor has no clothes even though you may you have the impression that others are silent on this point.

Since Asch's classic experiments, social psychologists have piled up evidence of conformity in a wide variety of situations. Ralph Waldo Emerson, patron saint of American-style individualism, penned the free thinker's manifesto *Self-Reliance* in which he declared that "imitation is suicide"—but it turns out that often suicide is imitation. It's now well known that suicide rates leap up after prominent media reports of a suicide, especially if they cast a romantic light on the victim. Between 1984 and 1987, subway suicides in the city of Vienna spiraled upwards, and then dropped abruptly after the Austrian Association for Suicide Prevention managed to get the media to agree to accept voluntary restrictions in reporting them. Mental health agencies now routinely publish media guidelines intended to minimize copycat suicides.

More recently, researchers James Fowler and Nicholas Christaker studied social networks in detail and found that obesity and happiness spread within networks. If your friend's friend (whom you've never met) becomes overweight, you are more likely to gain weight, even if your *friend's* weight stays the same (the scientists suggest this may be because her attitudes about heavy people have changed as a result and subtly get communicated to you). Having a happy friend within a mile of you can apparently increase your likelihood of happiness by 25%, a far greater impact on your well-being than getting a hefty pay raise. And depression can spread too, showing that misery loves company so much it tends to create it.

There are countless ways in which persuaders can exploit social contagion and the tendency to conform. Collection plates in churches are sometimes spiked with large bills to give the impression that others are donating generously. Laugh tracks *do* make sitcoms feel funnier, though we may think we're far too sophisticated to be affected by them. When you go shopping on Amazon, the page you browse helpfully tells you what *other* products have been purchased by people just like you.

And master persuaders like Edward Bernays understand the phenomenon of social influence inside out. On one occasion while working for Lucky Strikes cigarettes, Bernays produced a report revealing that women often rejected Lucky Strikes because the green-and-red packaging clashed with their clothing, neutral tones being the fashion of the day. When his suggestion to change the packaging was greeted by howls of protest from the company, Bernays calmly suggested a different tack: he would change the fashion to favor green, a feat he handily accomplished on a budget of ten thousand 1934 dollars, without ever taking out a single ad for Lucky Strikes—and without anyone realizing he was working for the cigarette company. The key to his success was throwing one strategic, high-profile New York charity ball for a hospital, with green as its theme color. This well-publicized event triggered an imitative spread of fashion that was so complete that *competitor* cigarette companies, in an attempt to ride the fashion wave, ran ads featuring models dressed in green with red accessories—the colors of Lucky Strike cigarettes.

Defining Normal

If a high-school teacher hands out a form for an upcoming class trip saying "Be sure to give this form to your parents," she can be forgiven for having made an understandable error if one of her students turns out to be an orphan—though her remark may have served to remind him of this stark difference between himself and his classmates. But imagine sitting in the classroom and having your teacher say, "Be sure to give this form to your parole officer." You might look around at the other kids in the class and start calculating your chances of making it through to the end of the day un-assaulted.

As in this scenario, presuppositions in advertising language often do more than just signal that certain beliefs are generally shared. In many cases, they also communicate subtle information about social norms that are so common as to fail to raise an eyebrow. It doesn't make sense to refer to a parole officer using presuppositional language (*your parole officer*) unless you can assume that the people in your audience have one. In the same way, an ad for K-Y LiquiBeads assures you that "the days of worrying about dryness are officially over," letting you know that even if *you* haven't been worried about this problem, lots of other people are (and maybe you should too). So presuppositions can communicate something about social norms, and examples abound where advertising uses this to its advantage.

A browse through magazine ads reveals that it's normal to have high-end gadgets and be technologically savvy:

> *Download to your iPhone or iTouch now!*
> Ad for People *iPhone* app

> *Personalize your home page. Stay connected to TIME's influential bloggers.*
> Ad for Time.com BlackBerry app

To be internationally connected:

> *Sound like a million bucks when you talk business with Brussels.*
> Ad for Blue microphones

> *Before you travel the globe, for business or pleasure, switch to Verizon Wireless, America's Largest Wireless Network.*
> Ad for Verizon Wireless

To have accumulated a nontrivial amount of wealth:

> *It's important to keep your investments secure.*
> Ad for TD Waterhouse

> *When it comes to your home, auto and business, you know you need insurance protection.*
> Ad for Chartered Insurance Professional

To have questionable dietary habits:

> *This year, start getting five servings of vegetables every day.*
> Ad for V8 vegetable juice

To take time off work:

> *Vicks NyQuil provides multi-symptom cold and flu relief. That way you can enjoy a good night's sleep, and wake up tomorrow for your vacation, staycation, or whatever the day brings.*
> Ad for Vicks NyQuil

And to be a regular user of the advertised products:

Have you had your can a week?
Ad for Blue Diamond almonds

Now get it from your Mary Kay Independent Beauty Consultant.
Ad for Mary Kay cosmetics.

What people *think* others are doing—whether or not they ever see them doing it—shapes their behavior. Teachers who try to get their students to behave by sternly telling them "The behavior in this school is appalling, and I expect that to change," are basically saying that it's normal to misbehave. And like kids, when adults are told that others are misbehaving, it can be an invitation to do so themselves. Persuasion expert Robert Cialdini reports his experiences in working with Arizona's Petrified Forest National Park which was slowly being denuded of its main attraction—petrified wood—due to thieving visitors eager for souvenirs. In an attempt to staunch the flow of stolen wood out of the park, signs were posted with the impassioned plea: "Your heritage is being vandalized every day by theft losses of petrified wood of 14 tons a year, mostly a small piece at a time." Cialdini conducted a little experiment: with the Park's blessing, he and his colleagues placed secretly marked pieces of petrified wood along the pathways, and then measured how much of the wood was stolen depending on the type of message posted on signs at the entrance to the pathway. When the signs drew attention to people's bad behavior by saying "Many past visitors have removed petrified wood from the Park, changing the natural state of the petrified forest," about 8% of the marked pieces of wood were stolen over the five-week period—a rate which would require a name change for the park in the not-too-distant future. But when the signs simply requested "Please don't remove the petrified wood from the Park, in order to preserve the natural state of the petrified forest," less than 2% of the wood disappeared.

On the flip side, emphasizing people's good behavior can nudge people in the desired direction. Taking its cues from the social psychologists, the state of Minnesota ran its own experiment in an attempt to get more people to properly pay their taxes, trying out various techniques such as telling them the good things their tax dollars were providing, threatening punishment for noncompliance, and directing them to helpful resources in preparing their taxes. But the most effective strategy turned out to be simply informing them that 90% of people in Minnesota were law-abiding citizens who paid their taxes in full.

"Everyone's Doing It"

Social norms can drive behavior when they're communicated indirectly or even inadvertently. In the 1980s and early 1990s, Nancy Reagan consulted with psychologists to create the "*Just Say No*" anti-drug education campaign which emphasized teaching kids how to resist peer pressure and avoid illegal drugs. But as research on social norms evolved, scientists became aware that these programs sometimes inadvertently create the impression for kids that offers of drugs are around every corner, and that "everyone is doing it." For some kids, these perceptions can actually increase the likelihood that they will use drugs. Good intentions, road to hell.

Another such sobering tale for prospective do-gooders comes from psychologists Anne Stuart and Hart Blanton at the University of Albany. They cooked up the following public service announcement, which looks more like a sincere effort to encourage safe sex than an evil plot to spread STDs throughout the population:

> I want people to think of me as a success. It's for that reason that I use condoms each and every time I have sex. Bottom line, using a condom when you have sex is smart. People who use condoms have thought about the responsibility of being sexually active. They think with their brains instead of their genitals. People who use condoms are usually those individuals who are goal oriented, conscientious, responsible, and careful. I think people give their partners more respect when they use condoms. Using condoms means that you've taken the time to think about AIDS, about pregnancy, about venereal diseases and all that, and that you're going to be one of those people who keeps your life on track. I'm clean now and have always used good judgment. I plan to stay clean and so I use condoms whenever I have sex. This isn't just the right decision, it's the smart choice.

But Stuart and Blanton cautioned that an educational strategy linking good behavior (e.g., using condoms) with a positive trait (being smart) can backfire because it gives the impression that using condoms is not a usual, normal behavior. Their logic went like this: normally, we assume that behavior reveals something about a person's character only when it's out-of-the-ordinary in some way. Stuart and Blanton pointed out that it would be bizarre to describe someone as "self-conscious" because they chose to wear clothes to work—that's just the norm, we *expect* everyone to wear clothes, even on Casual Fridays, so inferring much about their character based on this behavior is weird. (Try it: describe a co-worker this way, and prepare for the intrigued questions about your company's liberal dress code.) On the other hand, describing a person as outrageous for *not* wearing clothes is perfectly natural. By the same token, describing someone as smart for using condoms signals that condom use is not a normal, expected behavior—and we've just seen what can happen when people become aware that other people are behaving badly or stupidly. In the public service ad, the effect of social norm perception could well water down or even override the positive associations linked with the desired behavior. For maximal persuasiveness, the researchers suggested making statements about the negative traits that are revealed by *bad* behavior—this conveys that the good behavior is the more expected norm.

Stuart and Blanton tested this hypothesis by comparing the above passage to the one below:

> *I don't want people to think of me as an irresponsible individual. It's for that reason that I never once have had sex without a condom. Bottom line, not using a condom when you have sex is stupid. People who don't use condoms haven't even thought about the responsibility of being sexually active. They think with their genitals instead of their brains. People who don't use condoms are usually people who just don't have any goals, are thoughtless about their person, are irresponsible, and are careless. I think people give their partners less respect if they have sex with them without a condom. Not using condoms means you haven't even thought about AIDS, about pregnancy, about venereal diseases or any of that, and that you're not even going to keep your life on track. I've never screwed up with this stuff or used bad judgment. I don't plan to get a disease and I will never have unprotected sex. Having unprotected sex isn't just the wrong decision, it's stupid.*

Indeed, people who read the first passage, which commented on how smart it is to use condoms, estimated that fewer students on campus used condoms during sex than those who read the second passage.

In these examples, the audience gleans information about social norms by speculating (probably unconsciously) as to why the speaker or author is communicating this information. Kids infer that their teachers are providing them with skills to refuse drugs because they'll have plenty of opportunities to use these skills. People hearing the condom-use ads infer that when someone comments on the intelligence of condom use, it is noteworthy, not to be taken for granted—otherwise, it wouldn't make sense to draw attention to it. In these particular cases, information about social norms ends up being conveyed even though it's not intended, and even though it appears to be entirely absent from the message itself. People are reading between the lines—a practice I'll talk about more in the next chapter.

If even such subtle ways of communicating social norms can have an impact, it seems likely that social norms would pack a really powerful punch when presented in the form of a presupposition—as they are in the advertising examples I've pulled from magazines. Not only is the information about social norms explicitly there in the language, rather than simply being read between the lines, but it's coded as something that is common knowledge. Not only does everyone do it, but everyone *knows* that everyone does it. An anti-drug campaign built around messages like: "Stay away from your drug dealer" and "Never do cocaine again" is unlikely to be a success. And if you ever see an anti-smoking ad telling you that "quitting smoking is smart," check to see if it's being run by a tobacco company.

Mindless Agreement and Unconscious Individualism

Presupposition is a way of dressing information up as uncontroversial background stuff that is assumed to be already known by the hearer or readily accepted by the world at large. The studies of false memory show that presuppositions are especially effective at slipping past memory's doorman to become entrenched as inaccurate recollections of a scene or event. Presumably, *accurate* presuppositions are also less likely to be stopped at the door by a suspicious, hyper-vigilant doorman—this resistance is exactly what Bob Squier was hoping to get past in crafting Clinton's campaign messages. To push the analogy a bit further, this is likely because the doorman doesn't scrutinize presuppositions as carefully as assertions, which don't stride in with the same casual confidence and look of belonging. He may never directly point his eyeballs at presuppositions for very long, lulled by superficial cues into believing there's no reason to examine them very closely.

In psychological terms: if presuppositions are thought about *peripherally* rather than centrally, they engage our gut feelings of truthiness, dampening more thoughtful, critical means of evaluating their message. When we read a sentence like "That's why ExxonMobil is committed to a major long-term research and development program aimed at developing algae as a viable fuel source," are we less likely to ask detailed questions about the presupposed information than if the same information were asserted outright? Are we less likely to be skeptical about it, and ask what a "commitment" means, how viable a fuel source this would be anyway, and by the way, is this a sensible way to spend money, or just a nifty way to buff up the company's public image by linking it with a (literally) green energy source? When Clinton offhandedly refers to "the hundred thousand police officers I've put on the street," by way of background knowledge that he assumes we're all familiar with, do we just take it for granted that this was a good thing to do? If he informed us directly: "I've put a hundred thousand police officers on the street," would we be more likely to wonder where all these police officers are, what all that cost us as taxpayers, and whether that's going to really reduce crime?

No one has specifically looked to see whether presuppositions escape critical thought more readily than assertions. The differences are more likely to be subtle than stark. But some suggestive data out there lend plausibility to the idea by showing that people think less deeply about information that they think most people agree with. This is very interesting, because one of the important functions of presupposition is to suggest there is some consensus about its truth.

Persuasion researchers use a gold standard to determine whether people are thinking centrally or peripherally: they look at the extent to which their attitudes are sensitive to the difference between a strong argument and a weak one. If people are as convinced by a flimsy argument as they are by a solid one, they must be thinking pretty shallowly—and sure enough, they are least discriminating of good and bad arguments under conditions that discourage deep thought (for example, if they're distracted by another task they're doing at the same time, or if the issue is one that's largely irrelevant to them personally).

Some scientists have used this technique to look at how deeply people evaluate opinions they believe to be accepted by the majority. Robin Martin and Miles Hewstone had volunteers read a passage summarizing various arguments in favor of animal research, and told half of them that the passage reflected the views of 82% of survey respondents, and the other half that it expressed the views of 18% of survey respondents. Within each of these groups, half of the volunteers got a bunch of compelling arguments in the passage they read, while the other half read weak ones. All of the volunteers then reported how they felt about animal testing after reading the passage. People were more convinced by the strong arguments than by the weak ones only if they thought the arguments reflected a minority view—when the same arguments were thought to be held by the majority, people just glossed over them, showing no distinction between good and bad arguments. This pattern showed up whether or not the volunteers themselves were for or against animal research at the outset.

The tendency to take mental shortcuts in evaluating majority views seems to interact with a number of factors. When the issue is one where people have something concrete and personal at stake, when it's likely to affect them directly, they do think deeply about the content of the majority opinion as well. And at times, the effect can even be reversed, so that people are *more* sensitive to the quality of an argument when the opinion is held by the majority. This tends to happen when there is some reason to be quite surprised that the majority would take that position—for example, if most people seem to be arguing for a position that goes against their self-interest, or if the majority opinion is startlingly out of line with the opinions of the subjects. In these cases, subjects are fairly motivated to find out *why* so many people unexpectedly hold this view. (And the minority view is glossed over under the same conditions—presumably because the minority position is so obviously at the fringes that it's hardly worth figuring out why some people hold this strange view.)

The connection to linguistic presupposition is indirect. But it's an intriguing one, given that presupposition serves as a signal that certain information is already part of the common ground. It suggests that packaging a statement in presuppositional language may have multiple advantages: people will accept it more readily, entering it into their memory as something that is already known, and they may spend less time putting it under the microscope. Bob Squier should have asked for a raise.

This tendency for people to become absorbed into the Common Mind may seem troubling. To the red-blooded individualists out there, the fervent Emersonians: it may comfort you to know that herd-following instincts aren't fully hardwired—culture and context matter as well. In 1996, researchers Rod Bond and Peter Smith sifted through 133 studies in which people were subjected to the same kinds of "perceptual" tests under peer pressure as in the original Soloman Asch studies. They found a steady rise in independent-minded behavior since the 1950s, with people conforming less and less over time—this would reassure Solomon Asch, who was rattled by his own findings. It also mattered *where* the studies were conducted. Conformity levels were higher in countries that tend to emphasize the importance of groups and communities, and lower in countries like the United States which put great value on individual choice and achievements. Score one for Emerson.

But maybe even these moments of individualistic triumph are really just knee-jerk, possibly even subconscious responses to the social norms that happen to pervade our culture, the subtle and often superficial cues that tell us to be like just everyone else in bucking the trend and thinking for ourselves. Ask U.K. researchers Louise Pendry and Rachael Carrick: they showed their subjects a photograph of either a punk rocker or an accountant—pretending that these were materials that were being prepared for a different and unrelated study that was to be run later in the lab—and then inflicted an Asch-type task on them. Astoundingly, this seemingly irrelevant trivial cue had the power to tilt independence of thought. People who'd briefly stared at a punk rocker were less swayed by the responses of their peers than those who'd seen the accountant. So much for looking to your higher principles and ideals for guidance in the face of peer pressure—the mackerel mind strikes again.

5

Why Ads Don't Say What They Mean (Or Mean What They Say)

Dear Mr. Language Person:
I am curious about the expression, 'Part of this complete breakfast.' The way it comes up is, my five-year-old will be watching TV cartoon shows in the morning, and they'll show a commercial for a children's compressed breakfast compound such as 'Froot Loops' or 'Lucky Charms,' and they always show it sitting on a table next to some actual food such as eggs, and the announcer says: 'Part of this complete breakfast.' Doesn't that really mean 'Adjacent to this complete breakfast' or 'On the same table as this complete breakfast.' And couldn't they make essentially the same claim if, instead of Froot Loops, they put a can of shaving cream there, or a dead bat?
Answer: Yes

Dave Barry, Tips for Writer's

Words Don't Mean Things—People Mean Things

If you're a typical speaker of English with native-like proficiency, congratulations: you probably know somewhere in the range of 50 000 and 100 000 English words. Even at that, your brain is not crammed so full of words that you *couldn't* learn more—most people max out at that point because they're simply not *meeting* new words anymore. A look at the website "Word Spy," dedicated to documenting new coinages of words and phrases, shows how

Sold on Language: How Advertisers Talk to You and What This Says About You. By Julie Sedivy and Greg Carlson
© 2011 John Wiley & Sons Ltd.

eager people are to add even more words to their stash. Of course, you're not content to just have all those words lie there to be pulled out one at a time when you need them. Like all humans with reasonably intact cognitive capabilities, you're constantly combining them in new and unusual ways, allowing you to implant new and unusual ideas in other people's minds. Fifty thousand words give you a *lot* of expressive potential. The periodic table has (at best) only 118 elements, but like words, they combine with each other in a mindblowingly large number of ways—currently, databases contain trillions of known molecules. Just think what you can do with 50 000 units.

With all these linguistic parts at our disposal, you'd think we'd easily build sentences to precisely express any thought that could possibly cross our minds. And yet, language sometimes seems maddeningly imprecise, embroiling people in heated and even expensive debates about the meanings of words.

Remember the famous impeachment trial of former U.S. President Clinton, in which taxpayers were treated to discussions about the meaning of the word "is"? Clinton was accused of lying about his sexual relationship with White House intern Monica Lewinsky. At one point in his testimony before the Grand Jury, he was pressed about the truth of a statement his attorney had made at a deposition asserting that there was no sex of any variety between him and Lewinsky. Clinton claimed that, according to his recollection, the question had been put in the present tense, and had this to say about the statement:

> *It depends on what the meaning of the word 'is' is. If the—if he—if 'is' means is and never has been, that is not—that is one thing. If it means there is none, that was a completely true statement . . . Now, if someone had asked me on that day, are you having any kind of sexual relations with Ms. Lewinsky, that is, asked me a question in the present tense, I would have said no. And it would have been completely true.*

How is it even possible to have this kind of discussion? Surely, with all those words, we ought to be able to simply say exactly what we mean, and mean exactly what we say.

The truth is, we almost always mean quite a bit *more* than we actually say. Take the perfectly ordinary sentence *"Simon is a very nice man."* From the mouth of a prospective mother-in-law, this might be a ringing endorsement of Simon's suitability for marriage into the family; when spoken wistfully by his girlfriend, it might be the prelude for a break-up; in the boardroom at a hiring meeting, these words might signal the kiss of death for Simon's hopes for an executive position.

On the whole, even though this mismatch between what we say and what we mean is a less precise way of going about things, it actually enhances—not hinders—communication. It's true that every now and then, it really *is* crucial to spell everything out carefully in the language you use—you probably want to avoid any wiggle room for interpretation in a legal contract, or in technical instructions for the use of an atomic device, or in the assembly manual for a backyard barbecue unit. But in most situations, making sure that the language you use expresses the intended meaning, the whole meaning, and nothing but the meaning would end up sounding stilted, pompous, or downright absurd. Not to mention, it could take a long time.

Imagine asking someone out on a date by saying:

> *I hereby request your attendance at a film or other comparable activity in a public social setting, as arranged by mutual agreement. Should the request be granted, I will accept financial liability for the evening's activities to the amount of a reasonable sum that would normally be incurred during such activities. The purpose of the proposed social activity is to ascertain mutual compatibility for further social interactions and possible sexual activity, as mutually agreed upon by both parties. If the request is granted, neither party is under any obligation to engage in further social interactions, nor to engage in sexual activity at the conclusion of the proposed social activity.*

I doubt that "Dating for Dummies" would advise you to use this kind of language, and an invitation like this would fall flat with any but the most unusual of invitees. But probably *all* of this information is in fact both intended and understood by the much more casual and indirect "Hi. I was thinking of going to a movie or something on Friday. Do you have any plans that night?" That's a pretty big gap between what the words mean, and what is being communicated.

In his self-help book *Take Control of Your Life*, Myron Downing has this to say about the gap between what words mean and how we understand them:

> *If you and I met in a social setting and sometime during the first few minutes I said to you 'You need a good counselor,' what would you hear me saying? That something is wrong with you and that you have some kind of a problem or need help? Look up these words in the dictionary: 'you' 'need' 'a' 'good' 'counselor'. Did you see anything there about you having a problem or needing some kind of help? So, where did you get that idea? Those meanings are not in the dictionary, and I didn't say anything about you having a problem or needing help. 'You need a good counselor,' was all I said. If I didn't say you needed help and it is not in the dictionary, where did those thoughts or ideas come from? It must have come from your thoughts, the meanings that you put on those words.*

Downing goes on to suggest that we can become happier people by *choosing* the way in which we frame messages—by taking responsibility for the parts of any meaning that aren't there in the words themselves, we can ultimately choose to perceive messages in a positive rather than negative way, and control how these messages affect us. In other words, Downing puts the "extra" aspects of meaning squarely into the hands of the hearer rather than the speaker, stating that "the message is in what the listener hears, and not what the speaker says."

After all, as he points out, there are many times when our own beliefs or attitudes may garble a perfectly innocent message into a hurtful one. Through an insecure person's filter, a well-meant compliment such as "You look really nice today" might be transformed into a veiled insult (leading her to wonder, "Why, what was wrong with the way I looked yesterday? Do I normally look like a slob?") or a suspicious accusation of flirting with the boss. By putting a positive spin on what people say, and taking charge of what we understand them to mean, we can immerse ourselves into a kinder, gentler social environment more conducive to our well-being.

If you were to take Downing's advice literally, though, you may well end up a happier person—but likely a seriously deluded one. If you ask someone on a date, only to be met with the remark "I'd rather have a root canal," trust me on this one, choosing to take this remark as an enthusiastic recommendation of the surgical prowess of your crush's dentist would entail some significant peeling from reality on your part.

Advertisers, like dating partners, often count on the fact that people *will* read between the lines to get exactly the meaning that was intended (in fact, this is often what makes ads enjoyable). This allows them to use startlingly sparse language. The meanings don't have to be spelled out, and are elaborated in the consumer's fertile imagination. In fact, ads can provide some of the best examples of communication where the meaning in the addressee's head has travelled a large distance from the meanings of the words. For example: one ad shows a photograph of a lion-trainer gingerly inserting his head between the jaws of a powerful lion. The caption reads:

Trust.
(One word rarely seen in the same sentence with "car dealer".)

A logo for Mercedes-Benz appears in the lower right corner.

In another ad, we see a spoon and an emptied container for Häagen-Dazs ice cream lying on its side on top of rumpled satin sheets. The caption smirks "Who needs mistletoe." The consumer is certainly filling in a lot of blanks in these examples. And in some ads, language is barely used, if at all, as in this ad for Tide laundry detergent:

Reprinted by permission of Procter & Gamble Co.

But if these meanings were left entirely to the consumer's *choices*, advertisers would lose control over the messages in these ads. Imagine a world in which ads had to use words to fully spell out their meanings. The advertising copy we read would be a lot more boring and would deflate the humor right out of the ads: "Tide will get your clothes clean even if you spill ketchup on them." "You can't trust other car dealers, but you can trust Mercedes." (As for the Häagen-Dazs ad, the message spelled out in words would be ... oh, never mind).

Obviously, the "extra" meaning layered on top of the words is not really left to the whims of the consumer. This is true just about any time people say less than they mean, a situation that routinely turns up in advertising and normal conversation alike. When language is used in real life, hearers do read between the lines—but in most cases, they read exactly what the speaker intended them to read. Usually, you can tell with stunning accuracy when you've been complimented or insulted, and when you have been handed a veiled threat dressed in pretty words, and you know when someone has been damned with faint praise. How are these telepathic feats achieved, if the meanings are not packed into the words?

Language Contracts and the Clintonian "Is"

In the 1970s, philosopher Paul Grice developed some ideas that caused language researchers to begin to pay very close attention to the dividing line between what is said and what is meant. He proposed that we rely on two separate, but individually very powerful systems for interpreting meaning. The first is knowledge of language itself—all that stuff you learned before kindergarten about how the sounds in your language pattern, which words can join up with which others in a sentence, what the words mean individually (and which words they're associated with) and what they mean when they're joined up together in a sentence.

The second is a body of knowledge you have about rational, sentient beings and how they go about achieving certain goals. The second system really isn't about language at all. It's all about interpreting the purpose of people's actions in context, a skill our hyper-social species has perfected. It allows you to know what your girlfriend means when she dangles a piece of lacy underwear in front of you, without saying a word (as they say, brevity is the soul of lingerie). In the right context, you read this as an invitation, or a reminder of a pleasant evening. Now, the meaning of this action could be completely different if it's your wife dangling the underwear, and it isn't hers. If a sales associate in a fancy lingerie store does the same thing, she's suggesting an item you might want to consider buying. And if it's your boss—well that's probably sexual harassment.

The same kind of reasoning about what the communicator must have *intended* to mean comes into play for ads that conserve words to the point of silence, much like the Tide ad you saw earlier.

Thinking like this is easily mastered even by those few people who have no language—for example, deaf children in isolated communities who don't use any signed or spoken languages at all. They can still point, gesture, and use eye gaze and actions to convey many things. And decoding intentions is what allows people who don't speak a word of the same language to be able to communicate with each other at least to some extent. But it's more than just a way to compensate when people can't use language to communicate with each other. Even when they wallow in the full mastery of 50 000+ glorious words, this kind of reasoning still plays a central role. In a sense, the words are just a starting point, a clue to what was *really* meant.

Although reasoning about people's goals and intentions is separate from language, when it does meet language, it can become so intertwined with it that it's often hard to tell which part of the meaning of a sentence is the linguistic meaning, and which part comes from reasoning about goals and intentions.

The last time I walked into a classroom of 100 students and truthfully announced "Well, some of you passed the midterm exam!" my words were met with a stony, apprehensive silence. The tension in the room cranked up a few notches. The pre-med students began to sweat visibly. Apparently, the students were under the impression that I had just told them that a number of them had *not* passed the exam, probably quite a large number of them. They were relieved, but not amused when I later informed them that not one student had failed the exam, and that in fact, the entire class as a whole had done very well. They also didn't buy my argument that their initial spasm of pessimism and anxiety at my announcement of the exam results was entirely due to their reading between the lines of my perfectly innocent statement "Some of you passed the midterm exam." Had I *said* "Not all of you passed the midterm exam?" No. The students weren't impressed. "*Some* can't mean *all,*" they countered. "*Some* means *only a small number.*"

But does it? Paul Grice's insight about meaning was to show the difference between what *words* mean, and what *we* mean to convey by using them. Words do have inherent meaning, and this aspect of meaning isn't negotiable—in fact, you might think of it as the part of meaning that's contractually binding. If we try to use language in violation of this contractual type of meaning, the end result is utter nonsense. This type of meaning is coded right there in the language. But the meaning that we add on through inferences about what the speaker must have meant by using the words that he did is not like a contract—it's more like a set of presumptions—and these can be removed without making the language completely senseless. So does the word *some* mean "only a small number," or were the students presuming that I meant "only a small number" by using the word *some?*

My students legitimately felt misled by being told that some of them had passed, without any further qualification. But the point is that you *can* qualify *some* to include *all.* If I'd strolled into the class and said cheerily, "Well, some of you passed the exam—in fact you all did splendidly," I likely would not have been charged with misuse of the word *some.* It's the fact that I just left the word *hanging* there, inviting a presumption that I meant "only a small number" without doing anything to dispel this very reasonable belief, which led to the students' grievance that they'd been misled.

If you stretch your imagination hard enough, you can also come up with examples of unusual contexts in which the statement, even without qualifications, wouldn't have been met with the same dread, or the same feeling that *some* means *only a small number.* Imagine this scenario:

The public at large believes that universities are churning out illiterate and ignorant graduates while squandering tax dollars. As a result, the government has decided to make all students take a government-designed exam. It has also announced that instructors will be fired on the spot if none of their students pass the exam. But as long as at least some of their students pass, the instructor's job is safe. Now, it turns out that the exam is laughably easy. Nevertheless, the day after the exam, a student asks me whether I'll get to keep my job, and I snidely say, "Well, some of you have indeed passed the exam" and get on with the business of teaching. I haven't used the word *some* to mean *not all*. I've used it to mean "more than none," and while I'm at it, to make a sideways comment about the low standard of achievement set by the government.

The moral of the story is that if the meaning can shift depending on the context, then it's not part of the meaning that's written into the contract—in other words, it's not part of the meaning of the word. Rather, the speaker has used the word to communicate that particular meaning.

You can see this more clearly by comparing the *not all* meaning of *some* with an aspect of the word *some* that truly is written into the contract. No matter what the context, you can't eliminate the *more than none* meaning that's built right into the word. For example, you can say "some of my best friends are Republicans—in fact, *all* of them are" without being outright self-contradictory.[1] Your second statement is taken as a refinement or clarification of the first. But try saying "Some of my best friends are Republicans—in fact, *none* of them are." Your listener will just stare at you, trying to figure out if she's misheard or if you actually know English. If you're not convinced yet, try to come up with some unusual context where a person might use the word *some* in a way that's consistent with *none*. You can't, because it's part of the contractually understood meaning of *some* that's shared among all speakers of English. It *has* to mean *at least some* all the time, across all contexts. On the other hand, *some* merely implies *not all*—another way of saying this is that most of the time, the speaker uses the word *some* to mean *not all*.

So how does the hearer figure out what the *speaker* means? According to Grice, by working off of a set of expectations that can be summed up as: *WWRSD? What Would the Rational Speaker Do?*

In the first classroom scenario, the students expected that if *all* of them had passed, I would have explicitly said so—in that particular context, it would certainly have been relevant. Saying that *some* had passed if I knew they *all* had would be uncooperative, and I would be deliberately withholding relevant information. And because we can normally count on speakers to be cooperative, and give us all the relevant information we need or expect (unless they're specifically trying to deceive us), the fact that I didn't say *all* the students had passed, or *most* of the students had passed must mean they didn't.

---

[1] The expression "in fact" is very commonly a signal that an implication is being withdrawn or rectified.

The trickiness in separating the meanings of words from the meanings of speakers shows just how little room there can sometimes be for personal taste or choice when it comes to reading between the lines. Most of the time, given the right context, just about everyone will read *some* to mean *not all*. This happens so automatically, that we have the illusion it's part of the word itself. My students had trouble excising this part of their own interpretation from their understanding of what the word *some* means.

They were in some elite company, actually. Grice, who after all was a philosopher by trade, applied surgical linguistic techniques for separating what words mean from what speakers mean, thereby solving some really thorny problems in the philosophy of language. For example, logicians since Aristotle have been using the tools of logic to talk about the meaning of language. But like my students, they'd often ignored the difference between what *words* mean and what *people* mean by using certain words. Subtle point, but in doing so, they'd painted themselves into the following logical corner:

Suppose you accept as true the premise that *It's certain that the Yankees will win the World Series*. If you accept this premise as true, you must also accept as true the statement *It's possible that the Yankees will win the World Series*. This seems reasonable. To say that it's certain that the Yankees will win but it's *not* possible that they'll win seems a logical contradiction. Now, suppose you also accept that *It's possible the Yankees will win* means *It's possible that the Yankees will win, and it's possible that the Yankees won't win*. This also seems reasonable, capturing the intuitions we have about the meaning of the word *possible*. Well, if that's what *possible* means, then you put the two steps together to get the following nonsensical conclusion: If it's true that *It's certain that the Yankees will win* then it must also be true that *It's possible that the Yankees will win, and it's possible that the Yankees won't win*. Huh?

Long after Aristotle's time, logicians were still scratching their heads over this one until Grice pointed out that the second step in this reasoning process was wrong. *It's possible that the Yankees will win* actually *doesn't* mean *It's possible that the Yankees will win and it's possible that they won't win*. When speakers say this, they're just using the word *possible* to *imply* that the Yankees might not win. They do this for the same reasons that speakers use *some* to mean *not all*: they assume that the hearer can figure out that the speaker doesn't think that a Yankee victory is a dead certainty or even highly probable. If he did think that, he would have used *those* words instead. Because he hasn't, he must not believe them to be true.

Splitting apart the meanings of words from what people mean to imply causes the logical conundrum to simply evaporate. If we remove the implied sense of the word *possible* from the actual meaning of the word, there's no quandary, and the logic works out just like it's supposed to. The philosophers can all go home knowing that the logical universe hasn't in fact imploded on itself.

This kind of semantic surgery might strike you as academic hair-splitting—handy for wriggling out of logical mousetraps, but pretty far removed from any meaningful daily concerns. On the contrary, questions of just this sort are fundamental to our understanding of truth and falsity and the ethics and legality of deception.

I've been talking about the meanings that are packed into words and sentences as contractual—this seems to suggest that when it comes to being accountable for your language, you should be held to what you say, rather than what you might mean by implying. But, looking back at my students, it's not clear that people really think about truth in this way. An ad for orange juice points out: "Other brands of orange juice give you some of the Vitamin C your body needs." You're obviously meant to work out that they don't give you all the Vitamin C you need. Let's suppose this *isn't* the case, and *all* the OJ brands on the market actually meet your daily Vitamin C requirement. Has the ad lied? After all, the word *some* just means *more than none*, right?

In fact, most people seem to judge truth and falsity in a way that includes the implied meaning. If you ask people whether it's true or false that "some elephants have trunks," most of them will say it's false—and would presumably react in the same nonliteral way to the orange juice ad.

Getting back to Clinton's exegesis on the word *is*, one might try to make the following argument: the word *is* in the present tense, just means *right now*. Now, most of the time, people use the word in a broader sense—they use it to refer to some relevant time span *overlapping* with the present. But this isn't, strictly speaking, what the word means. Going by the contractual meaning of *is*, the statement made in the deposition was perfectly truthful.

Now, if your wife finally finds your credit card bill, and confronts you about the affair you've been having for two years by asking "Are you cheating on me?" and you say "No—absolutely not!" because, well, you're not cheating on her *right then*, even though you did meet your lover yesterday—you won't exactly get points for honesty. *Technically*, you've been truthful as far as the meaning of the words goes, but you've violated every expectation about how a cooperative speaker should behave. Any rational communicator has got to know that, without extra qualifications, his wife will interpret his reply as meaning "No cheating has happened in a time frame relevant to this conversation." You might not have outright lied, but you sure haven't been honest.

When Clinton defended his reply to the questioning, he was trying to move the interpretation of his answer closer to the strictly linguistic interpretation of the words. However, even he had to admit that it would be absurd to go entirely by the meaning of the words. When the prosecutor asked whether he was actually claiming that he'd been truthful in his statement simply "because you were not engaging in sexual activity with Ms. Lewinsky during the deposition"

Clinton had to acknowledge that this would be an unreasonable way to interpret the question:

> No sir. *Anyone generally speaking in the present tense saying that was not an improper relationship would be telling the truth if that person said there was not, in the present tense—the present tense encompassing many months. That's what I meant by that—not that I was—I wasn't trying to give you a cute answer to that.*

The point Clinton was trying to make was that there was some debate as to exactly how the word might be used by a rational speaker.

What Would the Rational Speaker Do?

When people open their mouths to talk, as listeners we apparently hold them to a pretty high set of standards. According to Grice, we behave as though we expected the speaker to follow a set of Four Commandments of Conversation (Grice actually called them "conversational maxims"):

1. Be truthful (don't say what you believe is false or for which you have no evidence).
2. Be relevant.
3. Make your contribution as informative as required but no more.
4. Be clear (avoid obscurity or ambiguity, be brief, be orderly).

This isn't supposed to be an English teacher's wish list—it's supposed to be a set of *assumptions* about what ordinary-educated-or-not-people *actually do* on a regular basis. Now, we all know that there are people who wield language far more effectively than others, and that they are the ones who are the most virtuous in following these Four Commandments. We admire these linguistic Olympians, and would love to have their expressive skills. But the point is that actually, the average person follows these conversational expectations to a surprising degree, and has—you guessed it— pretty much learned to do this before kindergarten (or very soon after).

You might doubt that we really are so trusting as to assume people are being truthful. But how would you react if I told you that actually, none of what you've read so far in this book is true? I just made it all up for the fun of it, and have absolutely no reason to believe any of it. If you'd suspected this from the outset, chances are you wouldn't have bought this book or any nonfiction book for that matter. In terms of sheer plot and entertainment, I can't really compete with the latest Dan Brown novel. More likely, you probably assumed that the entire contents of the book so far were based on my telling the truth as far as I know it, in accordance with Grice's First Commandment.

Next time you have dinner with someone, pay close attention to what they're saying. How much of what they say do you normally assume is true? If you were to transcribe the entire conversation, and assign every single sentence a True or False, depending on whether you think the person is lying, chances are, the Trues would vastly outnumber the Falses. And even when someone you know has lied once, it's simply not the case that you simply stop trusting anything that comes out of their mouth, even if the lie is a big bad one. Think of a really horrible important lie someone might make to your face—like lying about an affair. Imagine having dinner with this liar. How many Falses would you tally up against their Trues? You'd probably still give this deceitful SOB the benefit of the doubt on most of the things he says. You'd suspend belief about things related to infidelity, or maybe even general moral behavior. But you probably wouldn't assume he was lying about things like what bus he took to work, what he had for lunch, whether the Joneses in fact had put an offer on a new house down the street, and so on. Your suspicion would be pretty narrowly targeted. In fact, if you truly did meet someone who didn't tell the truth most of the time, you'd take that to be more a sign of mental illness than of garden-variety deceitfulness.

It's pretty striking that assuming truthfulness is the *default* setting—though perhaps language would have had limited evolutionary benefit otherwise ("Look out! There's a saber-toothed tiger behind you!"). We generally go around believing that the whole point of language is to approximate reality, and we suspend this assumption pretty much only when we think of some other good, purposeful reason why the speaker might have said what he did—like being entertaining, getting us to fork over money, enjoying humiliating us through trickery, or preventing us from ending a relationship. And when we know for a fact that the speaker said something that's obviously false, rather than assume he's lying, we often assume that the real point was to broadcast some entirely different meaning from what the words mean. Try this:

Slick guy on the make: "*Do you come here often?*"
Attractive blonde: "*No, I just beamed down from Pluto.*"

The blonde is being frosty, not a liar. The whole fine art of sarcasm is based on the fact that you can say something blatantly untrue and be deemed witty rather than dishonest. Such is the faith of the hearer in your essential truthfulness.

All of this is really terrific news if you're an advertiser. It means that, unless consumers are hyper-aware of the reasons you might have for lying, they'll likely take your truthfulness as a starting point. Claim your car gets 50 miles to the gallon? That a bowl of your low-fat ice cream has less fat than a side salad? Consumers will generally believe that you have good reason to be making these claims. Sure, people's enthusiasm for taking something to be truthful gets dampened when it's obvious that there's a collision of interests between them and whoever has made the claim—and even more so if they believe that there's no penalty for lying. Certainly, there are plenty of studies showing that we're most persuaded by people who seem to be acting outside—or better yet—*against* their own self-interest. But in the great scheme of human communication, lying is anomalous and is treated as the exception by the hearer, not as the rule. Advertisers can exploit this default assumption, especially if they dial down any cues that make their persuasive intent apparent.

The Search for Relevance

Imagine getting a letter like this from your *adult* son:

I am writing on paper. The pen I am using is from a factory called 'Perry & Co.' This factory is in England. I assume this. Behind the name Perry & Co. the city of London is inscribed; but not the city. The city of London is in England. I know this from my schooldays. Then, I always liked geography. My last teacher in that subject was Professor August A. He was a man with black eyes. There are also blue and gray eyes and other sorts, too. I have heard it said that snakes have green eyes. All people have eyes. There are some too who are blind. These blind people are led about by a boy. It must be very terrible not to be able to see. There are people who can't see, and in addition, can't hear. I know some who hear too much. One can hear too much . . .

This actual letter from a schizophrenic man sounds more like really terrible performance art than a letter. It doesn't seem to do any of the things we normally expect a letter to do: let Mom know how you've been since you last wrote or talked to each other, give highlights of recent happenings in your life, ask how she is, talk about people you both know, and so on. It strings together thoughts in the order in which they popped into the writer's mind, completely missing the purpose of the communication. It goes without saying that having a conversation with someone like this would be utterly exhausting—you'd probably end up tuning most of it out, since there'd be no *point* to it.

The point is, we expect communication to *have* a point. The reason it's exhausting to listen to someone who can't stay focused on a communicative goal is that we're wired to wrack our brains trying to figure out what they meant based on why they've said what they've said. When someone says something apparently irrelevant, we don't usually just dismiss it as a total non sequitur. Imagine two guys talking together at the office Christmas party after they've had a few. One says loudly to the other: "Did you *check out* the boss' wife? Man, what would *you* give for five minutes with her in a dark room?" The other guy says, very intently, "These crackers are really really good." If the first guy isn't too drunk, he'll understand that what his buddy really means is: "Shut up before you make an even bigger ass of yourself, and possibly lose your job, because, don't look now, but the boss is standing right behind you."

Or, suppose you get a brief letter of recommendation for a prospective employee who's applied for a position in upper management in your company. The letter consists entirely of the following glowing words: "Stan wears the most superbly original ties I've ever seen, and is a brilliant master at cooking mushroom risotto." It's obvious that what this seemingly irrelevant information is supposed to mean is "Don't touch this guy with a twenty foot pole—he's completely incompetent."

Advertisers are virtuosos at meaning a great deal by saying very little. This elegant economy of words would be completely lost on the consumer without the constant engagement of WWRSD reasoning. Think about what the Mercedes-Benz ad with the lion was able to communicate with a grand total of 11 words and an eye-catching image: "You can't trust *other* car dealers—doing so would be as foolish as inserting your head between the teeth of a lion. On the other hand, we're different, and you can certainly trust us."

Now, think about all the knowledge you have to activate to get the message. First of all, you have to understand the purpose of ads. They normally try to get you to buy their stuff instead of the other guys' stuff. So, they're likely to try to get you to think good things about themselves, and bad things about the other guys. Whatever message they're trying to get across is likely to put them in a better light than the other guys. Second, you have to understand that when people comment that two things are rarely seen in the same sentence, this isn't literally true. After all, there are lots of sentences like "You just can't trust car dealers." The ad is really using a cute way of saying that car dealers aren't normally trustworthy. Third, you have to notice the Mercedes-Benz logo, know that it's a company that makes cars, and that this is an ad aimed at getting you to buy *these* cars, and not some other cars. Fourth, you have to put the first two things together, and infer that even though other car dealers aren't trustworthy, this one is. Finally, you have to get that when ads have a picture, they're related in some way to the text and the overall purpose of the ad to get you to buy their stuff, so it dawns on you that this image is supposed to be a metaphorical representation for what will happen if you go to the other car dealerships instead.

This is *quite* a nifty feat of verbal reasoning. The advertisers obviously assume you're pretty smart if you can work all this out—and chances are you can, though the meaning would probably elude the schizophrenic author of the letter you just read. (Actually, it's possible that this ad might be attributing just a bit too much reasoning power to the consumer. Sure, the average consumer could work this message out, but it takes a fair bit of brain juice, so can they be counted on do it every time? Maybe they're tired or bored, and don't fully engage with the ad, and then what they're left with is an association between Mercedes-Benz and the experience of sticking your head in a lion's mouth.)

Of course, the flip side of WWRSD reasoning is that the advertiser has to be able to accurately predict what the output of your WWRSD computing would be. This means that just as you have to have a good theory about what's in the head of the person who designed the ad, the advertiser has to have a good theory about what's in yours in order to be confident that you'll get the intended meaning. The whole ad could be pretty puzzling to someone who didn't know what kind of company Mercedes-Benz was. Or about the stereotypes of sleazy car salesmen.

When an ad gets it just right, playing to a highly specialized body of knowledge can create a sense of intimacy between the advertiser and the consumer. One ad that appeared in *Urban Climber* magazine shows images of a climber on a steep rock wall, with the following text:

> *5.11*
> *+5.10* ®
> —————
> *5.9*

Unless you're a rock climber, this ad seems to involve some seriously fuzzy math. But show the ad to any climber, and he'll get its meaning right away: "Oh, the ad says that if you wear (brand) 5.10 climbing shoes, a really hard climb with a grading of 5.11 will seem like an easy climb with a grading of 5.9." Obviously, this message depends on the familiarity of climbers with the brand name (5.10), and the North American system for grading the difficulty of climbs, where many fairly casual climbers can achieve a climb that is graded at 5.9, but a 5.11 takes some real skill and training. It actually works to the ad's advantage that the message is incomprehensible to nonclimbers—it emphasizes the specialness of the climbing community and the shared knowledge between the advertiser and the climber-consumer. It creates an emotional bond between the company and the climber-consumer.

The search for relevance often depends quite a bit on culturally specific knowledge. I remember being perplexed several years ago, when I read a letter of recommendation for a female applicant from Taiwan to our PhD program. After saying reasonably good things about the academic abilities of the applicant, the letter finished by stating "Ms. X dresses impeccably and has a very pleasing personal appearance." Now, from a North American academic, this would be code for "She's easy on the eyes, but not the sharpest tool in the shed." Our culture (at least in *my* academic field—and at least officially) doesn't consider appearance to be a relevant asset of PhD students, so mentioning it at all sends a strong negative message. Letter writers, reluctant to say bad things directly about the students they've mentored, rely on an intricate system of inferred meanings. But when I checked with an Asian colleague, she assured me that this was by no means a slight on the applicant: it would be considered a genuine plus to have a good-looking student, and it would be OK to say so. Huh.

My culture-centricity bit again when a teaching assistant showed me a Japanese commercial that had me completely flummoxed. In the TV ad (which aired at a time when the video game company SEGA was being trounced by Playstation), a Japanese executive of the SEGA video game company is seen wandering through the streets and encountering jeering kids who hurl insults at him and shout that they all use Playstation, not lousy SEGA. He looks distressed and humiliated. The kids pelt him with rotten fruit and vegetables. The last shot is of his wife crying out as he stumbles through the door and collapses, a truly pathetic sight. Then, the company logo fills the screen: SEGA

This ad violated everything that I expected the rational advertiser to do. My Japanese assistant swore that the ad was perfectly sensible—it played off the natural sympathy that typical Japanese viewers would feel for the underdog, and induce them to buy SEGA products. When we showed the commercial to my American individualistic, winning-is-everything students, they had "I don't get it" expressions plastered all over their faces. The explanation offered by the teaching assistant appeared to have no effect on this. I don't think they believed her.

The New Ford is 700% Quieter

A couple of decades ago, Ford put out an ad that stated, incredibly: "The new Ford is 700% quieter." That sounds like a pretty impressive claim. But 700% quieter than *what*? Applying WWRSD reasoning, we can come up with some relevant claims for an ad to want to make: Quieter than the previous model. Perhaps quieter than the competitors. When ads make claims, the companies are supposed to be able to provide at least some basis for them. The Federal Trade Commission, the U.S. body that oversees deceptive advertising, got a bit curious about how Ford might support such an extraordinary claim. At the hearing, it came out that what Ford *actually* meant was that the new Ford was 700% quieter on the inside than on the outside.

Like focusing on the purely literal meaning of the word *is*, this comes across as a sleazy way to be communicating. But it's pretty interesting that of all the possible ways of interpreting the language in the claim, only a couple come to most people's minds. Many other logical possibilities never seem to pop up: "The new Ford is 700% quieter than flying in a Concorde." "The new Ford is 700% quieter than a jackhammer." "The new Ford is 700% quieter when the engine is turned off than when it's running." For fun, you *can* imagine bizarre contexts where these might actually be the first meanings that come to mind. But these would be strange claims for an ad to make. Your mind passes by all the weird but logical possibilities and eagerly leaps at those that would be most likely to be reasons to persuade someone to buy a Ford. And you assume that this is what the ad must mean.

The Ford example is a famous one, and is included in many a Consumer's Guide to Avoiding Being Tricked by Advertising manual. But this kind of mental filling-in-the-blanks happens all the time with advertising. Many claims turn out to be exceptionally weak once you distil their literal meaning from their implied meaning. Claims that rely on the consumer inferring reasonable meanings come in all varieties and flavors. Here are some of my favorite kinds.

Comparison is in the mind of the beholder

Decades after the famous Ford case, claims that rely on the consumer to come up with the relevant comparison are as ubiquitous in ads as mushrooms after rain. A recent ad for Estée Lauder SuperTan Spray reads: "Faster. Darker. Without the sun. And now—easier." *What* is faster than *what*? And is the *what* that is faster (and easier) than the *what* the same *what* that is darker than *what*? These fill-in-the-blanks comparisons crop up in many places, but seem to be especially prevalent in ads for beauty products—a flip through *Glamour* magazine will likely yield lots of examples.

Another kind of build-it-yourself comparison is when ads tell you that a product is *like* something else—you normally assume that the comparison is along some particular *relevant* dimension. If an ad tells you that drinking a brand of orange juice is like taking a multivitamin, you assume they're talking about nutrition, not taste, even though the latter would be perfectly consistent with the language used. Taken at a literal level, these kinds of comparatives tell you about as much as the Ford ad—they're completely open-ended. Like the off-color joke that asks what all men have in common with a linoleum floor, you can come up with *some* way to draw a comparison between even the most far-fetched examples. (An ad for Nicky Clarke shampoo played with the riddle-like possibilities of comparisons by pointing out: "*Hair should be like men: Gorgeous, rich and full of life.*") But when an ad seems earnest, you don't treat the comparison as a riddle, and rule out many logically possible—and likely amusing—ways to compare the two things. You focus on the ones that you assume would make you want to buy the product.

The gap between the implied comparison and the "actual" comparison that the company is able to defend can veer into the absurd—the Ford example is by no means an isolated example. You'll often find packaging for food or shampoo, or laundry detergent prominently displaying words such as "30% more!" "Now with an extra 8 oz!" Ever thought about exactly what these claims are supposed to mean? It's worth taking a closer look at some of these packages, with a magnifying glass if necessary. The April 1998 issue of Consumer Reports sneered at a "purr-fectly ridiculous" claim on a 16 lb bag of *9 Lives* cat food announcing **"2 LBS MORE"**—and then in *much* smaller print: "than other 14 lb bags."

Reasons to buy

If an ad goes to the trouble of mentioning something about a product, it must be one that would make the product more appealing to the consumer, right? And likely, one that competing products probably don't have, right? Again, that's your WWRSD reasoner talking. You assume rational communicative choices and create a back story in your mind to justify the feature's mention. An ad in the late 1800s for Marseilles soap told housewives "It will not shrink your flannels." If housewives hadn't been anxious about soap ruining their clothing up to then, the ad gave them food for thought. The same ad also boasted: "Marseilles soap is made solid. It will not float." Funny thing is, around the same time, Ivory soap was advertising itself as "the soap that floats." Casting about for why it would be a *good* thing for soap to either float or not, the attentive housewife likely seized on the fact that these claims about floating appeared next to other claims that seemed relevant: "Marseilles soap is made solid." "Ivory soap is 99 $^{44}/_{100}$% pure." Why is solid (or pure) soap better? From there she probably leaped to other, *really* relevant inferences. Maybe solid soap lasts longer. Maybe pure soap is gentler on the skin. Floating (or not) must be a diagnostic for these desirable qualities. The soap wars are a great example of how some pretty trivial feature of a product can be used as the focus for differentiating a product from others—and along the way, inviting consumers to imagine all kinds of other (more important) differences. (While we're at it, 99 $^{44}/_{100}$% pure *what*? And what's the other $^{56}/_{100}$%? Is that the air that's whipped into the soap to make it float?)

One classroom assignment I gave was for students to create their own print ads for a fictional product that would clean up smelly household spills and messes. One of the students cleverly produced an ad that included the line, "Now, with Blue Crystals!" There was absolutely no mention of what the blue crystals were supposed to *do*. Nearly everyone in the class agreed that this innovation sure sounded good, though, and that they'd fully expect the crystals to enhance the product's effectiveness if it were a real commercial for a real product. Such is the power of relevance.

All of this is related to why "*part of this complete breakfast*" is not taken to mean "*on the same table as this complete breakfast*." Your mind generously elevates the claim to something that would amount to a persuasive reason to buy the advertised breakfast compound.

Don't try this demonstration at home

Like a good illusion, an ad can focus you so intently on what you assume to be the whole point of a demonstration that you forget to wonder whether the elaborate demonstration has any point at all. In 1970, the Federal Trade Commission put Colgate-Palmolive on the hot seat for the following TV commercial for Baggies plastic sandwich bags: The ad showed two women wrapping sandwiches in plastic bags, dunking them into aquariums filled with water, and then pulling out the bags to inspect the sandwiches. The sandwich from the Baggies bag came out dry—the one out of the competitor's bag came out sodden.

Now most of us, unless tormented by a bully who makes a habit of tossing our bag lunch in the toilet, don't have great concerns about submerging our lunch underwater. Obviously, the point of the demonstration is to use this as a way to draw our attention to something we do care about—for example, whether air enters the bag and makes the sandwich stale. Well, Baggies were really good at keeping out water. But it turns out that air enters a sandwich bag through the pores in the plastic, and not just through the seal, and Baggies plastic was just as porous as everyone else's. But since testing a sandwich bag for its impenetrability to *water* is pretty irrelevant, you readily assume the demonstration is providing information about something you would care about.

Connect the dots

You generally take it for granted that people's statements are linked together in some coherent way, that they're not just lists of sentences in random order. So, when Ivory puts its claim about floating right next to its claim about purity, it can expect its readers to infer a relationship between them—a causal relationship is a handy candidate.

Here's some text taken from an ad for Tropicana orange juice. The ad pictures a heavily pregnant but clearly athletic woman in workout clothes tossing back a tall glass of O.J. Give the text a quick read through:

> *Craving more Calcium and Vitamin C? Tropicana Pure Premium with Calcium has a calcium your body absorbs better than other common sources of calcium. Just one glass has as much calcium as milk, plus an entire day's worth of Vitamin C. And with the great taste you expect from Tropicana Pure Premium, it's easy to give your body what it expects when you're expecting.*

Without looking back at the text—did the ad claim that the calcium in the orange juice is more readily absorbed than the calcium found in milk? If you answered yes, go back and look carefully. If you happened to mentally fill this bit in, you'd be in some spiffy company in drawing this inference—more than half of a group of students at an elite Ivy League college drew the same conclusion, even *after* studying language and advertising for nearly a semester.

The ad seems to be communicating to the consumer that drinking this brand of orange juice is healthier than drinking milk. Is this an intentional claim the company is making? Is it a true claim? Should the company be held responsible for it? Given that this ad is targeted at pregnant women, with the bones of our future citizens at stake, these kinds of questions are far from mere academic hair-splitting.

There's a distinct possibility

You may have witnessed the following kind of interaction between a child and parent: The child asks, "Mom, can I sleep over at Jesse's tonight? Can I? Can I please?" Mom answers "Maybe" and the kid gleefully shouts "Yes!" Mothers everywhere know to be sparing with this little word, since kids generally take it to mean a real possibility, a *likelihood* even. It's almost as good as a Yes. But of course, the meaning of the word *maybe* is merely to rule out an absolute impossibility. The stronger meaning is creatively added by the child.

Kids aren't the only ones who strengthen statements of possibility—trial lawyers know that they've scored big if they can get a witness to acknowledge that yes, it *was* possible that the sudden death on the operating table of a generally healthy patient who came in for routine minor surgery was really caused by a fluke undiagnosed blood disorder rather than surgical incompetence. Unless the witness qualifies her answer by saying "It's possible, but extremely unlikely," the jury is likely to conclude that it's a *significant* possibility (and is often tempted to do so even with a qualification).

This courtroom strategy is illustrated in this amusing story involving an unusually persistent attorney:

Lawyer: Doctor, before you performed the autopsy, did you check for a pulse?
Witness: No.
Lawyer: Did you check for blood pressure?
Witness: No.
Lawyer: Did you check for breathing?
Witness: No.
Lawyer: So, then, is it possible that the patient was alive when you began the autopsy?
Witness: No.
Lawyer: How can you be so sure, doctor?
Witness: Because his brain was sitting on my desk in a jar.
Lawyer: But could the patient have been alive nevertheless?
Witness: Yes, it is possible that he could have been alive and practicing law somewhere.

And of course, advertisers are well aware of how consumers strengthen claims in their minds. I heard a radio ad for insurance that warned "In all probability, you or one of your family members may be the victim of a house burglary this month." The literal meaning is ridiculously weak: it's *probable* that it's *possible* you'll have your house broken into? This is even weaker than saying that there's a possibility of a burglary—there's only the *probability* of a possibility. But what sticks in the consumer's head is much more frightening—helped, of course, by the fact that the little Possibility Word *may* is buried right in the middle of the sentence, with the spotlight-grabbing beginning and end positions reserved for the more forceful and specific *in all probability* and *this month*.

When Eli Lilly Pharmaceutical tells us that Prozac can help alleviate depression, we're inclined to take a decidedly optimistic view of this claim: that it probably *will* help, and moreover that it will help more than marginally—and that just taking Prozac on its own will do this. Presumably, if you have to take Prozac along with some other medicine, and while on a special diet in order for its chemistry to kick in, you would have been told.

I have to nominate a certain Paramol ad for the dubious Paul Grice prize for the sheer number of claims made through implication. I don't think there's a single substantive claim in the ad that *doesn't* require the consumer to read between the lines to get a meaning that's quite a bit stronger than what is actually said. Here's the ad copy:

The power to hit pain. Precisely.

There's now a pain reliever that contains dihydrocodeine, a highly effective ingredient that has never before been available without a prescription. PARAMOL tablets bring you a different way to fight pain. They contain dihydrocodeine with paracetamol to create a powerfully effective combination that targets your pain. Precisely. Sometimes your pain needs a tough answer. So when you need powerful relief from headache, migraine, period pains, backache, toothache and other aches and pains, you'll find there's no stronger pain relief your pharmacist can offer you. The power of dihydrocodeine now without a prescription.

And here's a line-by-line dissection:

Said: The power to hit pain. Precisely.
*Meant: This medication **will** hit your pain precisely (whatever this means).*

Said: There's now a pain reliever that contains dihydrocodeine, a highly effective ingredient that has never before been available without a prescription.
Meant: PARAMOL contains dihydrocodeine. And it has enough of the drug to actually be effective.

Said: PARAMOL tablets bring you a different way to fight pain.
Meant: PARAMOL tablets fight pain more effectively than other pain relievers.

Said: They contain dihydrocodeine with paracetamol to create a powerfully effective combination that targets your pain. Precisely.
Meant: This combination of drugs doesn't just target the pain—it gets rid of it. And it doesn't do other things you don't want a drug to do—like upset your stomach?

Said: Sometimes your pain needs a tough answer. So when you need powerful relief from headache, migraine, period pains, backache, toothache and other aches and pains, you'll find there's no stronger pain relief your pharmacist can offer you.
Meant: PARAMOL is not only as strong, but stronger than other drugs you can get from your pharmacist.

Said: The power of dihydrocodeine now without a prescription.
Meant: *PARAMOL has dihydrocodeine, not just its "power." PARAMOL has enough of this drug to have required a prescription before now.*

You have to really train yourself to get good at noticing which claims are implied rather than stated outright. Even then, the exercise of separating out the two kinds of meaning takes a lot of focus and effort. A slew of experiments run since the 1970s tells us that it usually takes a bit more mental computation to grasp implied meanings than when the same meaning is laid out in the open. But once those meanings are built, they stick. If people are asked afterwards to remember what was said, they'll roll in the implied meanings too, and claim to remember that they were actually part of the original wording. Their memory has obscured how they arrived at the meaning—whether it was built into the language, or whether they reasoned it out. These implied meanings can be so sticky that even overt disclaimers that later contradict the implied meanings can have surprisingly little effect (maybe that extra computation actually makes them even stickier).

We behave this way not because we're lazy, careless consumers, but simply because we're built that way.

Wired for Mindreading

In his book *The Language Instinct,* Steven Pinker makes the point that humans are so innately hardwired for language that they can no more suppress their ability to learn and use language than they can suppress the instinct to pull a hand back from a hot surface. But as Grice pointed out, knowing the nuts and bolts of language is just one half of what's involved in communicating—the other half involves decoding the beliefs and intentions of others, often working with extraordinarily subtle cues. This ability often seems just a shade away from sheer telepathy—scientists have even taken to calling it "mindreading." Study of this everyday variety of mindreading is now one of the hottest areas of cognitive psychology. And the bulk of this work seems to be showing that, like language itself, this ability is instinctive—and specifically human. Even young babies are driven to read minds, and as a species, we are far more sophisticated at this than our closest primate relatives.

Mindreading is involved in understanding even the most basic forms of nonverbal communication. Take pointing. In terms of the pure physical mechanics of the action, pointing is almost identical to, say, moving a hand towards an object so that it brushes against it. But think of how differently we interpret the two actions. Pointing is obviously purposeful, never accidental. More than that, its intent is to draw another person's attention to something for the purpose of communicating—it could be a request, or a remark on something interesting going on, or an answer to a question. To get all this, you have to first be able to know the difference between intentional and accidental action, you have to figure out from the general direction of the point exactly what it is you're supposed to be paying attention to (more likely to a three-legged dog than its two-legged owner, or to a coffee cup on a counter than the *handle* on the coffee cup), and *then* you have to guess why the pointer is directing your attention to that thing. None of this happens when you notice someone's hand brushing up against an object—you just don't get inside the other person's head in the same way.

It seems inconceivable that we might not be able to "get" pointing—most of us have mastered the art as toddlers. It's a supremely compelling gesture. Pointing was the subject of one episode of "Just for Laughs Gags," a Canadian comedy show in which unsuspecting people on the street are filmed by video cameras as they respond to actors who behave in socially bizarre ways. In this particular episode, the victims would come across a man standing on a busy sidewalk, emphatically pointing at something in the distance. They would stop in their tracks and turn to stare in the direction of the point, trying to figure out what they were supposed to be looking at. While they were staring, the man would swivel around about a hundred and twenty degrees, and suddenly point in that direction. Sure enough, the hapless observers would also swivel around and stare in this new direction—until the man pivoted again, and so on. This would typically continue for quite some time, with the victims persisting for a hilarious length of time, absolutely certain that there was something really interesting and important to look at.

Understanding pointing is a capacity not shared by our chimpanzee cousins though. If you put food into one of two opaque containers, letting the chimp choose only one, the ape will be oblivious to the fact that you're pointing *right at* the container with the food in it, and will choose randomly between them. Chimps (and other primates) also ignore helpful cues like someone gazing at the right container, tapping it, or deliberately placing a wooden block on it. Despite being highly intelligent, highly social animals, they seem not to have evolved some basic abilities to decode communicative intentions.

What's fascinating is that dogs *do* get pointing, and treat it as a blatant hint in these food-finding experiments. Since chimps are usually smarter than dogs, what gives dogs a leg up when it comes to understanding intentions? You might think that it's the canine pack structure that makes them so sensitive to communicative cues. But actually, *wolves* don't do any better than chimps—it's domesticated dogs, bred to be man's best friend, who show the ability to read these human cues. And this trait appears to be bred in, and not just learned as a result of being around humans. New puppies do as well as adult dogs, and puppies raised by other dogs do just as well as puppies raised by humans, all of which makes it seem that such mindreading abilities can be written into the DNA. As a result of interacting with people, over time, dogs have mutated to become more *like* people.

Like language, mindreading is beginning to look like an essential ingredient in passing knowledge down from one generation to the next. The human combination of *both* abilities gives us an incredible edge over our fellow species. Everyone knows that young children are great mimics, but they don't just imitate all actions indiscriminately. They pay special attention to actions that are clearly intended. We know this from ingenious experiments such as the one designed by Malinda Carpenter and her colleagues: the scientists had an adult play with various interesting toys in front of babies who were between 14 and 18 months of age—for example, a box that had a flip top to lift and a ring to pull on. The adult would both flip the top and pull the ring, but after one action, she would say "Whoops!" and after the other, she'd say "There!" with satisfaction. Then she'd hand the toy to the baby to play with. The babies were far more likely to imitate actions that were followed by "There!" than the "accidental" actions. Even kids this tiny can clue in to the difference between purposeful actions and random or unintended actions, and put special weight on the intended ones. (If you're a parent reading this, you may well recall your toddler's fascination with expressions such as "Uh oh!") It's easy to see how other primates who lack this ability hit up against some pretty rigid limitations in terms of building up a cultural body of knowledge that extends across generations. Teaching by example becomes a lot harder if the pupil can't separate purposeful actions from random, incidental ones. Imagine watching someone in order to learn how to create a baked Alaskan Flambé if you had no way of understanding that the stirring and pouring and flaming actions were somehow more crucial to the finished product than any variety of nose-blowing, head-scratching, and foot-shuffling that might go on during the whole thing.

We remain exquisitely attuned to evidence of intentional and unintentional actions throughout our lives, of course, and the difference between them can have enormous consequences, legal and otherwise. I'm reminded of a story related by a friend while in medical school: as part of being litigation-proofed, the med students were trained that, when performing a procedure, one was to never, ever, *ever* utter "Oops." One should always instead emit a soothing "There."[2]

Kids also perform a mental check on the communicative goals of adults before linking new meanings with new words. In talking about how children learn new words, Yale psychologist Paul Bloom likes to compare two theories about word learning, one by the seventeenth century philosopher John Locke, and the other by the fifth century philosopher and theologian Saint Augustine. Locke wrote: "To make children understand what the names of simple ideas or substances stand for, people ordinarily show them the thing whereof they would have them have the idea and then repeat to them the name that stands for it." The idea is that the adult makes sure that the child is paying attention to whatever is about to be named—when little Lily hears "teddy bear" uttered at the same time she's looking at it, her brain's powerful associative machinery will link the two in memory. This is a very reasonable theory, one that, as Bloom points out, was pretty much taken for

---

[2] Needless to say, I now become unreasonably alarmed whenever a medical practitioner concludes a procedure by saying "There."

granted as a theory of word learning until very recently. It makes sense, given the rich associations we can store for any word. And it also seems to make sense that adults, in an effort to instruct their children, would try to make sure to talk about things that the child is paying attention to, to make sure they form the right links.

Saint Augustine, writing about a thousand years earlier, had a somewhat different view. Relying either on keen insight or extraordinary memory, he introspected about how he likely learned the meanings of words and suggested that it was the *child* who figured out what the *adult* was paying attention to, rather than the other way around: "When [my elders] named any thing . . . I saw and remembered that they called what they would point out by the name they uttered. And that they meant this thing and no other was plain to me from their body . . . indicating the affections of the mind, as it pursues, possesses, rejects and shuns."

About fifteen hundred years after Augustine's writings, modern psychology has indeed shown us that, rather than passively trusting their elders to supply just the right words at the right times, even babies take responsibility for checking to see what the adult is intending to talk about. Dare Baldwin, who pioneered some of the most influential studies of young children's understanding of intentions, made the following observations: if you hold a bucket with a hidden object in your lap, wait until an 18-month-old child is looking at another object on a table in front of her, and then say "It's a modi!" the child won't simply assume you're talking about the thing that's front and center in her own attentional space. She'll look up at you, and if she sees your eyes pointed into the bucket in front of you, she'll peer into it too. Later, if you show her both objects, and ask her "show me the modi," she'll pick the object that was in the bucket, even though she was actually looking at the other object at the moment you said "modi."

Kids also tend to assume that when they hear a new word, the speaker must be referring to something whose name the child doesn't already know. If you put a familiar object in front of a child (say, a ball), along with an unfamiliar one (say, a belay device, which is a specialized piece of climbing equipment), and ask "Show me the blicket," the child will almost certainly pick the climbing gizmo. Many researchers suggest that this is an example of kids making inferences about new meanings of words based on their expectations about how a reasonable speaker would behave. The idea is that the following thoughts whir inside the kid's head (presumably not fully consciously): "Hmm, if that nice lady had meant to be talking about the ball, she would have said *ball*—since she didn't, she must mean that other thingy." You can probably test a version of this with the nearest adult too—wave in the general direction of a common, familiar object that has a well-known ordinary name to it next to another more unusual object, and say "Can you hand me the thingamajig?"

In fact, thinking along these lines probably led to an important misconception for many consumers when a product named Excedrin Migraine hit the shelves, right next to Excedrin in the drugstores. You might easily be excused for being one of the confused. Like the shrewd tot with the ball and the climbing gizmo, you might have thought to yourself that any product with a slightly different name than Excedrin was in fact a different product. Why else would it have a different name?

But Excedrin Migraine was in fact the same product as Excedrin. It was so-named only because the makers of Excedrin had gone through a series of controlled clinical trials to specifically test its effectiveness against migraine pain. It was found to work better than a placebo, and this gave the company the right to advertise the fact. But it was *exactly* the same formula as the original Excedrin. The new name was just a way to market it to migraine sufferers.

The confusion from thinking that two bottles of pills with different names don't contain the same pills could have some real consequences for consumers. What if someone took a dose of Excedrin for a backache, and then a dose of Excedrin Migraine for a migraine, thinking they were a different medication that acted on different bodily systems? They would have ended up taking double the recommended dose. This possibility may have raised some concerns, because some time after the product was released, a new set of ads came out, presumably to prevent the faulty inference. The new ad showed a picture of Excedrin and Excedrin Migraine side by side, and the text clarified:

> *An announcement to physicians and migraine sufferers: Clinical research has just proven that the formula in Excedrin actually relieves migraine headache pain. And because of the distinct nature of migraines, the FDA worked with Excedrin to develop a different package with specific information for migraine sufferers. So now next to Excedrin, there's a new package—same medicine—called Excedrin Migraine.*

Explicit as this disclaimer seems, an informal survey of my students revealed it had shockingly little effect. I compared this new ad to an older ad for Excedrin Migraine. The older ad had none of these disclaimers and clarifying information. It simply showed a box of Excedrin Migraine with the caption: "Excedrin Migraine. The only nonprescription medicine approved for the relief of migraine medicine pain."

I showed some students the older ad and some the newer one, asking the same question to both groups: "Does this ad claim that the medicine in Excedrin Migraine is different from regular Excedrin?" As many students answered "yes" to the newer ad with all the disclaimers as the older one without the clarification—about *80% in both cases*. The bias to take different words to mean different things can be so strong, that on a casual read, it may override even the explicit statement that the two products are identical.

When you consider that mindreading is likely sandblasted into our DNA, it becomes less surprising that it's woven into just about every communicative act we're involved in, and that it leads us to read between the lines of what is said at every turn—often without being at all aware where the language ends and our own mindreading thoughts begin. Contrary to Mr. Downing's views that reading between the lines is a matter of personal choice (maybe tainted by personal neurosis), we seem to efficiently run a set of programs that allow us to get inside each other's heads and pretty accurately decode intended meanings that aren't part of the actual language. Sure, we may misinterpret some of the time, especially when interacting with someone outside of our culture, but there are systematic patterns to our "between-the-lines" inferences. And reading these meanings is possibly as automatic, as unconscious, and as reflexive as decoding the actual language itself.

You Can't Tell the Truth Deceptively

If what you do for a living is create policy to define and constrain deceptive advertising, all of this discussion about what is said versus what is meant puts you in a bit of a quandary. On the one hand, there seems to be a clear separation in the quality of the meaning that's built directly into the language as opposed to the stuff that's read in between the lines. You just can't overturn or withdraw meanings that are directly stated; they're part of the language itself, just like the explicit wording in a legal contract. If you claim outright that your car is 700% quieter than last year's model, you have exactly zero wiggle room to later turn around and say that what you really meant to do was draw a comparison between the inside and the outside of the car, and not between this year's model and last year's version. If you do that, you're flat out contradicting yourself.

Implications seem softer. They can be retracted, and though the speaker's intent and the hearer's interpretation line up most of the time, there *can* be some question as to whether the inference made by the hearer is actually a fair representation of what the speaker meant to imply. So it would seem reasonable to hold advertisers more accountable for directly stated claims than for implied claims.

On the other hand, this move leaves the field uncomfortably open to sneaky and misleading advertising practices. Recent science makes it pretty clear that a whopping amount of communication between humans happens through a form of highly sophisticated mindreading. Meanings that come about this way aren't "chosen" by the hearer. They're rational re-constructions of what the speaker likely meant based on a set of shared assumptions about how rational speakers behave. Once they're constructed, these meanings often can't be distinguished in the hearer's own mind from meanings that are contractually built into what the speaker has actually said. Given that implied meanings are a predictable and systematic aspect of how communication works, giving advertisers free rein to imply anything at all would result in an utterly toothless policy when it comes to truth in advertising. There'd hardly be a point to having one.

In the United States, the law firmly declares that truth is in the mind of the beholder. Advertisers are responsible for any reasonable meaning that's likely to be inferred by consumers, even if it wasn't intended by the advertising company, as long as that meaning is relevant to the consumer's decision to buy or use the product.

For example, in 1986, Thompson Medical was ruled to have acted deceptively in its advertising for a product called Aspercreme, which you were supposed to rub on your skin to relieve arthritis pain. In a TV spot for the product, an announcer held aspirin tablets in her hand, which were replaced by a tube of Aspercreme as she delivered the following monologue:

> *When you suffer from arthritis, imagine putting the strong relief of aspirin right where you hurt. Aspercreme is an odourless rub that concentrates the relief of aspirin. When you take regular aspirin, it goes through your body like this. But, in seconds, Aspercreme starts concentrating all the temporary relief of two aspirin directly at the point of minor arthritis pain ... [Voice-over:] Aspercreme. The strong relief of aspirin right where you hurt.*

Got the impression that Aspercreme contains aspirin? And that it works even better than aspirin? That's not what we claimed, said Thompson Medical, when hauled into court by the Federal Trade Commission. And if you look closely, you'll have to admit that that's not what they *said*.

It turns out that Aspercreme doesn't contain aspirin. It does contain trolamine salicylate as its active ingredient, which is a chemical cousin of aspirin, but sadly, without its pain-relieving properties.

The court accepted the FTC's argument that by using a name that was so similar to aspirin, by using language like "the strong relief of aspirin" and by invoking repeated comparisons to aspirin in its language and its graphics, the ad invited the consumers to make inaccurate inferences. You'll notice that the language in this commercial was quite similar to the text you saw for Paramol, our unofficial recipient of the Paul Grice implication proliferation award. Applying the same legal standards would require Paramol to be able to provide evidence for every one of the implied claims in the ad that were listed earlier.

More recently, the FTC launched a complaint against R.J. Reynolds over their "No Bull. No Additives" campaign for Winston cigarettes. In a number of print ads, the tobacco company focused on what it *didn't* put into its cigarettes. For example:

> *Yours have additives. 94% tobacco 6% additives. New Winstons don't. 100% tobacco. True taste. No BULL.*
> *Winston just got naked. No additives. No BULL.*
> *Thank you for not smoking additives. No BULL. 100% tobacco. True taste.*
> *I get enough bull at work. I don't need to smoke it. WINSTON NO ADDITIVES. TRUE TASTE. No BULL*
> *Still smoking additives? Winston straight up. NO ADDITIVES. TRUE TASTE.*
> *I'm not all sugar & spice. And neither are my smokes. WINSTON NO ADDITIVES. TRUE TASTE. No BULL.*

The FTC argued that the ads could mislead consumers into thinking that Winston cigarettes were safer because they didn't contain additives. This is an interesting argument, because there's little in the actual text of these ads to lead to that implication. Unlike Aspercreme's constant references to aspirin, these ads make no explicit mention of any health-related aspects of the cigarette. If anything, they tend to focus on taste instead. But the FTC felt that because additives in food are commonly linked with health issues, there was the potential for reasonable consumers to be misled by the focus on additives in these ads. Evidently, R.J. Reynolds thought the FTC might be able to make a case—the company settled out of court, agreeing to include prominent disclaimers stating "No additives does not mean a safer cigarette."

These standards seem pretty stringent, and they are—the rule of thumb is that if roughly 20–25% of consumers can be shown to be misled by an ad, it's considered deceptive. But it's wishful thinking to believe that sneaky implications are mostly a thing of the past. By its own admission, the FTC can only pursue a small number of the complaints it gets from consumers. It tends to pick and choose, singling out the most egregious offenders, or those industries where deception is rampant, or where claims are made that are related to consumers' health. And in practice, it sucks up many more of the FTC's resources to make a solid case for deceptive implications than to nail a company for explicitly deceptive assertions. If an ad makes a direct statement that's false, all you have to do is point to the text. The meaning will be obvious to any judge who can read (or hear). But when the deception hinges on an implication, especially one that's less glaringly obvious, the courts need some convincing that the implication actually would spring into the minds of consumers. This might mean rounding up actual consumers to do surveys, or dragging in expensive expert witnesses (and experts to counter the other side's experts). What's a financially strapped federal agency to do? Making it illegal to tell the truth deceptively only has real impact if enough of the advertising industry actually obeys the law. In the end, the real constraints on deceptive advertising probably come from the consumers' own sense of outrage.

Why Not Just Say What You Mean?

Advertisers, then, can obviously count on a specialized bit of human cognitive machinery that causes unspoken meanings to settle in consumers' minds in fairly predictable ways. The question is: why do they so often choose to convey these meanings indirectly, rather than just come out and say them? Aside from the fact that it's harder to prove the deceptiveness of implied meanings than directly stated ones, using implication changes the psychological orientation of the consumer to the ad in a fairly deep way.

First of all, even if the law treats deception by implication as morally equivalent to deception by assertion, it's pretty clear that people don't. Despite the fact that most of the time, people are good at getting the "right" implied meanings, these meanings may not have the same hard contractual *feel* to them that the literal language does. The end result is that it's more believable for advertisers to claim not to have intended them—or for someone to claim not to have understood them, for that matter. When Clinton weaselled his way out of a difficult line of questioning by claiming to have interpreted the present-tense question about his relationship with Monica Lewinsky in an uncooperatively literal-ish way, he was ridiculed. But let's suppose he'd answered "no" to the question "Are you now, or have you ever been sexually involved with Ms. Lewinsky?" This would have been more than mere sneaky communication—it would have been a bald-faced lie, and would have prompted more outrage than ridicule.

It's the same with ads. When Ford finally tells us what 700% quieter *really* means, no one believes it was actually what the company intended the consumer to believe. But the company seems to have violated the public's trust to a lesser degree than if it had lied outright and said "the new Ford is 700% quieter than it used to be" when it obviously wasn't. People are willing to accept greater responsibility for their understanding of implied meanings than literal ones. This is likely because there is certainly *some* degree of subjectivity involved—it's easy enough for people to imagine that someone else, under certain circumstances, or with a different body of knowledge or cultural background, might not interpret the ad in the same way. In other words, people are somewhat inclined to believe that, as the self-help writer Myron Downing suggested, something inside *themselves* caused that interpretation. All of this allows advertisers to count on a forgiving buffer in consumers' minds when they do imply stronger claims than they would be able to state outright.

To imagine a less flagrantly deceptive scenario, let's suppose that the new Ford was actually 700% quieter than one of its competitors. By leaving the comparison implicit, there's the possibility that consumers will infer other favorable meanings from the ad, including, for example, the claim that the new Ford is 700% quieter than it used to be. In fact, this meaning may be inferred alongside the intended claim, creating an overall stronger impression of the product in which a number of plausible claims are activated together. Quite a few ads seem to have the effect of triggering a fairly diffuse set of flattering implications, all of which may serve to reinforce each other. For example, one ad, proudly advertising Toyota's hybrid car technology, features an image of a green leaf appearing over the word *Why?* The answer *Because* is accompanied by a picture of a fish obviously drawn by a child. The main point of the ad is to create the general impression that driving a Toyota is good for the environment. But contained inside this impression is any number of more specific inferences that may be activated to some degree. For example: Toyota as a company *cares* about the environment; Toyota cars generally (and not just the hybrids) are easier on the environment than their competitors; driving a Toyota is a good way to express your concern for the environment you'll leave to the next generation. And so on. This broad set of potential implications creates a halo around the product that just couldn't be achieved by directly stating any one specific claim.

There are other reasons—aside from trying to skirt charges of deception—for advertisers (or anyone for that matter) to use indirect language as a way to avoid the unpleasant consequences of stating things too directly. Most people would *rather* work out for themselves why it is that Tampax tampons allow women to bike, swim, and ride horses— getting a more direct explanation would be Too Much Information. It's perfectly clear why all those women are smiling in the Viagra ads. No need to humiliate the men with an explicit description of their shortcomings prior to medication. So to speak.

Some unmentionables are a little less obvious. Communications professor Paul Messaris argues that Americans are much less squeamish about sex (unless it's between adolescents or people of the same gender) than they are about social status. Of course ads pitch social status all the time—but they almost always do it in very subtle and indirect ways, often shunning words altogether and relying entirely on visual implications or imagery. It would be incredibly crass for an ad to come right out and say "If you wear a Rolex, people will think you're wealthy and successful." Messaris speculates that this is such a touchy subject in part because American society has bought into the belief that your social standing is the direct result of your own efforts and qualities. Commenting directly on social standing feels especially loaded and judgmental. An ad might as well call its prospective customers losers who need certain enhancements to be socially respected. Or elite snobs who want to flaunt their wealth and power.

In a way, using indirect meanings allows both parties to play an elaborate game in which either has some freedom to pretend that the intended meaning was not intended at all, while at the same time relying on the meaning actually being understood. This goes far beyond avoiding social taboos. Across cultures, indirectness is a tool used by social subordinates to communicate suggestions and opinions to their superiors—because subordinates are not really expected to give their opinion, both parties can pretend it never happened. If you're the boss in an office, it's perfectly socially acceptable for you to walk into an employee's office and point out "You should probably get to the meeting now—if you don't go right away, you'll be late." But if *you're* the employee, you'd be much more likely to say something circumspect to your boss, like "What time was that meeting supposed to be?" You and your boss know perfectly well that *you* don't need reminding of the meeting's time. But you both pretend you do, to hide the fact that you've just told your boss what to do, and that she's let you.

The subtle advantage of this subterfuge also explains why people ask each other out on dates in oblique ways rather than in the form of legal contracts. A rejection stings less (and is easier for the other person to deliver) if you're both allowed to pretend that one of you hasn't just put your whole ego on the line but was really just idly wondering what the other person was doing for the weekend.

This mutual game of pretend also allows advertisers to make overblown hints about what their products can do without risking embarrassment over exaggerated claims. The copy for one ad for Finesse hair conditioner reads as follows:

> <u>Monday</u>. *Condition as usual. Get soft hair. Get flat hair.*
> <u>Tuesday</u>. *Condition with Finesse. Get Softbody. Why? Two conditioners. One*
>   *penetrates for softness. One penetrates for body.*
> <u>Wednesday</u>. *Use Finesse. Get Softbody. Get unbelievable job offer.*
> <u>Thursday</u>. *Use Finesse. Get Softbody. Get unbelievable counter offer.*
> <u>Friday</u>. *Use Finesse. Win lottery. Quit job. Move to Paris.*

This example is littered with connect-the-dots inferences: You got flat hair *because* you used a competitor's product. You got an unbelievable job offer *because* you used Finesse. If the ad came out and said this, it would be hard to take it seriously. But it's more subtle, so it gets past your inner skeptic. And by the time you read about Friday, the connection between conditioning your hair and winning the lottery is so absurd, that you take the implied claims to be playful, not in earnest. But of course, the ad would be completely pointless if you took the claims to be *only* a joke. At some level, you *are* expected to believe that using the conditioner will improve your life. The ad has managed to plant this seed in your imagination without opening itself up to seeming ridiculous. And you, the consumer, can accept the claim at this level, without overtly admitting your gullibility over an outlandish claim.

So, indirectness provides cover for advertisers. It allows them to psychologically offload some of the responsibility for their message. They can pretend that they didn't make that strong (and untrue) claim you dreamed up. It's a lot like having someone make a slightly offensive innuendo. If you understood it, well, it's partly because of how *your* mind works. Ever laugh at a subtle off-color remark, only to be told by the speaker (with phony innocence) to get your mind out of the gutter? At some level, you *do* have to accept that you're just as capable of smutty thoughts as the guy who made the remark. And advertisers can pretend that they didn't just tell you what to do, or what to think—*you* arrived at that conclusion yourself.

Do-It-Yourself Meanings

One of the most famous ads of all time is Apple's 1984 commercial, aired only once during the Superbowl. Even if you weren't alive in 1984, there's a good chance you've seen it—at the time of writing this, YouTube registered the ad as having over two and a half million hits. This was almost twice as many as the number of hits for Barack Obama's historic presidential acceptance speech.

The ad is a one-minute piece of dystopian sci-fi cinema, created by *Blade Runner* director Ridley Scott. It opens with a line of shaved, pallid men (people?) in drab uniforms, marching in perfect conformity down a bleak tunnel and into a room with a giant screen, where more people in uniform are seated. The screen is filled with a joyless face intoning a steady stream of propaganda, with references to the workers living in a "perfect garden of ideology", etc. As the catatonic crowd sits, bathed in a bluish haze, it is told "We are one people, with one will, one resolve, one cause." Intercut with this drab scene are brief images of a young, athletic woman racing straight towards the camera. Her skin is a vibrant pink, and she is wearing a tight white t-shirt and red shorts. Troopers in uniforms and masks are in pursuit. The woman charges into the room, and with a primitive cry, swings a long hammer straight at the face on the screen, shattering it. A voice-over makes the first mention of the product: "*On January 24th, Apple Computer will introduce Macintosh. And you'll see why 1984 won't be like '1984'.*"

Like an art film, this ad has many layers, and the viewer has to work to get at the underlying message. The references to George Orwell's novel *1984* evokes a rich set of connections to a soul-eating totalitarian society. Clearly the woman is supposed to symbolize Macintosh, as the sexy, brimming-with-life liberator who saves everyone from this grim fate. What are people supposed to be liberated from? Perhaps the computer technology of the time, which turned people into lifeless drones? Some viewers saw the blue color of the uniformed workers and the face on the screen as a subtle reference to IBM, known as "Big Blue" in the business world.

Even with the North American tolerance for direct comparisons in advertising, the implied messages in this ad would have been too aggressive for the company to get away with, had it come out and stated them more directly. But more than that, a direct statement of the ad's meaning would have undercut its impact. It captivated audiences precisely because of its mystery. It got media commentators to talk about its interpretation long after its one-time airing. People were *engaged*. To a large extent, the persuasive power of the ad came from the fact that it got people to persuade themselves.

This kind of advertising is a bit like coming across a guy on a sidewalk pointing at something. You can't help but want to figure out what he's trying to tell you. It captures your attention in a way that makes it impossible for you to keep walking by. One of the lessons from Saint Augustine and from Dare Baldwin's word-learning babies is that we're wired to actively participate in reconstructing meaning. We run through guesses as to what's in the head of the speaker—we don't just sit back as passive receptacles and wait to be told. This makes us co-agents of our own persuasion.

And without this trait, we couldn't understand pointing, or sarcasm, or why *some* often means *not all*, or the symbolism in a Truffaut film. We'd probably date a lot less too.

6

Acting Out

News Item: "Present Participle Banned in Brazil Federal District"

In October of 2007, the use of the present participle form of the verb was banned in the Brazilian Federal District (a district akin to Washington, DC) by Governor Jose Roberto Arruda, to increase governmental efficiency. Turns out—surprise!—that Brazilian civil servants and politicians were using the form to weasel out of committing to anything clear and definite. So, instead of saying something concrete like "We will increase access to medical care," they'd say something slipperier, like "We'll be taking steps to increase access to health care," (though since Brazilians speak their own brand of Portuguese, they of course would say it in Brazilian Portuguese and not in English). Apparently this kind of phrasing, made possible by the Portuguese present participle (which corresponds to the –ing form of the verb in English), had become so commonly used that poor Governor Arruda got really, *really* sick of hearing it, in fact so sick of it that he "fired" it from all government branches in the 2000 + square miles of the Brazilian Federal District. Including telephone operators.[1]

Naturally, Arruda got an earful for this attempt to legislate language, however good his intentions, but the idea of banning certain language forms was hardly his brilliant new idea. After all, societies have been doing much the same thing since who knows when, though through more informal means with social sanctions rather than governmental pronouncements backed by legal consequences. Don't know what I mean? Try this: next time you interview for a job, use "ain't" whenever possible, sprinkle in phrases like "shit-kickin' good,"

---

[1] A similar example turned up in 2008, when local councils in Britain banned their staff from using Latin words and phrases, on grounds that they are elitist and discriminatory. Among the objectionable examples: *bona fide, ad nauseum, vice versa, etc.*, and *status quo*. This prompted one Latin scholar to denounce the move as "linguistic ethnic cleansing."

Sold on Language: How Advertisers Talk to You and What This Says About You. By Julie Sedivy and Greg Carlson
© 2011 John Wiley & Sons Ltd.

add a hearty "f**kin' A!" for good measure, and you'll get the picture real fast. It's bad behavior in the situation, not all that different from farting or hacking up a big loogie and spitting on the floor during your interview for that brokerage VP position you've always coveted.

Speech, the use of language, is a form of social behavior. And what we do with it can turn out to be wise, kind, foolish, or even, as we've just seen, illegal. Never mind Arruda's ban on the present participle—there are plenty of ways to break the law simply by uttering words. There is just no other way to perjure yourself in court, thereby committing a crime, than to say something in testimony that you know to be false. Add to that many other juicy language crimes such as conspiracy, racketeering, libel, slander, forgery, aiding and abetting, price-fixing, insubordination, sedition . . . you get the picture. In all of these cases, how you use language is considered to be an action for which you can be fined or jailed. Nor is legal responsibility for language limited to the criminal domain. If you can figure out a way to get married—or unmarried—without saying or writing certain things, you'd do what no one else has done. There is no way to enter into contracts, take on a mortgage, create a will, dissolve a company, adopt a child, give someone power of attorney, than by using language—by saying or writing the right things under the right circumstances at the right times.

In fact, once you start thinking about all the things you can do with words, whether or not they're entangled with legalities, language *actions* number in the thousands. You apply to college, christen a ship, organize a banquet and many, many other things that can bring you glory or disgrace. Without language? Impossible.

This idea of language as constituting action can be a bit remote from the way we often think about it. If you ask the average person what language is (and somehow get past the weirdness of asking the question in the first place), they might tell you something like, it's a means of communication, and if pressed on what "communication" is, they might offer that communication is the exchange of information. Wikipedia seems to agree. The first line of the Wikipedia entry for "Language" is:

A language is a system of symbols for encoding and decoding information.

This is all pretty much common sense. If someone tells you it's raining outside, then what's been communicated? The answer seems to be simple: what's communicated is that it's raining outside, something you didn't know before but know now as the result of being told so.

This commonsense line of reasoning seems to lead to the conclusion that what's communicated is identical to what a sentence means. Obviously, this isn't the whole story. As you've seen in Chapter 5, hearers understand that speakers often mean a lot more than they actually say with words, that they communicate much more than the meaning of the sentence itself. This comes in part from understanding that to speak is to act. You can't really understand what someone is communicating unless you have a pretty clear idea of the action they're trying to accomplish by using language in the way they did.

So what *is* being communicated when someone says "It is raining outside"? That depends. Think about how odd this would seem if you were, say, shopping in a store at a mall and a random person came up to you and said this. Yes, you understand what's being said, you may even take the person as saying something that's true, so you have gained the information that it is, in fact, raining outside. But something's ... amiss. Namely, of course, *why* someone would choose you to say this to at that time. What might they be leading up to? Is this their idea of how to start a conversation? Are they flirting? Do they work at Umbrella City next door and are looking for a quick sale?? Unless you can resolve what it is they're trying to *do* with their words, the communication is far from a resounding success.

Most of the time, it's perfectly easy to figure this out, so much so that it doesn't feel you have to wonder about motives at all. Let's say you and your wife have picked a restaurant to eat at, and you're debating whether to drive or walk. Your wife says, "Oh, it's raining out." It makes perfect sense here because the reason for saying this is transparent—she's telling you why it would be best to drive and not walk. Of course, the same sentence could be put to other uses. It could be used to advise you that you can't mow the lawn this morning as planned, or that we don't need to water the garden after all today, or to answer the question "What's that funny noise from upstairs?"

When it comes to legal sanctions on language, Governor Arruda's ban on specific grammatical endings is actually a bit of an anomaly. Normally, sanctions apply to *acts* that people perform with language, and not to the language itself (one very notable—and widespread—exception is the prohibition of words that are considered "obscene"). This means that responsibility is assigned not on the basis of the words themselves, but what people do with them. This is why, for example, charges of slander involve extensive evidence and arguments about the speaker's state of mind and intentions. It's only a crime if the words were uttered with the intent of committing a malicious, destructive act. By the same token, when advertisers are charged with deception, it's not simply because they printed or broadcasted something untrue. It's because they did so with the intent to persuade the public into buying their product.

Form Versus Function

If you scratch the surface, it's not hard to see just how tenuous the match can be between the form of your utterances and the acts you perform in uttering them. True, some types of speech acts pretty much wear their identity on their sleeves. In school, you may have learned about the functions that go along with the sentence types of declarative, interrogative, and imperative—you use them to make a statement, ask a question, and issue an order:

> Declarative: *"The Amazon River is in South America."*
> Interrogative: *"Will the Lakers win tomorrow in Philadelphia?"*
> Imperative: *"Get off the bus at the next stop."*

All human languages have sentences like these. But even these forms can't be taken at face value. The speech acts of stating, asking, and ordering can each appear in a number of different guises. For example, if you think that a statement can't be used to pose a question, you probably shouldn't work at an airline ticket counter, where you might get "disguised" questions such as these:

> *I wonder whether the flight to Detroit is on time.*
> *I would like to know if my suitcase can be carried on.*
> *My travel agent told me this flight was full.*

The appropriate responses (in case you're wondering) sound like "It arrives at 5:05," "No, you'll have to check that suitcase," or "Yes, the flight is full," and not "That's nice." People with normal social skills understand that they're expected to provide answers like this even though the question was never overtly asked. This kind of mutual understanding leads to a lot of slippage between form and function. Similar mis-matches happen with imperative and interrogative forms. "Would you care to sit down?' is really a polite way to say "sit down"—it would be unsettling if someone responded by saying "yes" and remained standing.

There *is* one sure-fire way to align language form with the speech act you're performing. You can come out and attach a tag—called a *performative* verb—that clearly identifies your speech act. When garnished this way, and spoken under the right circumstances, your sentence has the effect of accomplishing what it is you're describing. If you say "I **thank** you for your generosity" or "I **congratulate** you on your promotion to head waiter," then the speech acts of thanking and congratulating have been thereby accomplished. Note that to accomplish the speech act, you're not required to actually be sincere, or to have the types of feelings and attitudes that typically prompt the act. The new head waiter that you've just congratulated may well be someone you'd just as soon see rot in the flames of hell for all eternity, or you may even be uttering the sentence sarcastically—doesn't matter. He's been congratulated—albeit insincerely or sarcastically—even if both of you are well aware of your spiteful attitude. A congratulations has taken place by virtue of the form of the sentence.

Sentences with performative verbs used in this way are not normal declarative sentences. "Normal" declarative sentences describe certain facts. If I say "I detest cashews" or "The inauguration is next Thursday," I'm describing a dislike I have and the time of an event, but not *accomplishing* a dislike or an inauguration by virtue of having said what I did. For a good intuitive way to figure out if a verb that describes a speech act is being used performatively, try using that good old lawyerly adverb *hereby* with it. So, compare:

> *I hereby detest cashews.*
> *I hereby congratulate you on becoming head waiter.*

The first is pretty strange. In fact, most sentences with *hereby* in them are going to sound strange. They'll sound like this: "Max hereby shopped at Target last week." "M&M's hereby melt in your mouth, not in your hand." "Unemployment was hereby up .02% for the fall quarter." You'll also notice, when you start slapping this word onto sentences, that not all sentences that contain verbs like *thank* and *congratulate* use them performatively. Try:

> *Millie hereby congratulated Bill on his promotion to head waiter.*
> *I will hereby thank Frank tomorrow for the lovely fondue set he gave us for our wedding.*

That's because *hereby* is now being attached to descriptions of past and future acts of congratulations and thanks—it's not accompanying a sentence that's bringing these acts about. What the *hereby* test does is to home us in on the inventory of types of speech acts to be found out there. "I hereby pronounce you man and wife." "I hereby request your resignation." "You are hereby notified that your parking privileges have been terminated." All of them represent things that can be accomplished via the use of language, under appropriate circumstances. Some of them are very highly structured circumstances, requiring a lot of social backing, legal sanction, and just generally a lot of bureaucracy.

Consider what it takes to have someone appropriately and successfully sentence a person to five years in prison by saying "I hereby sentence you to five years in the state penitentiary." The guy that walked up to you at the mall can't say that, the prosecution lawyer can't, the judge herself can't do that unless it's done after an elaborate and highly regulated series of other events have taken place. No matter how angry the judge might be at the teller at the bank that has just refused to cash her check, she cannot sentence that person to five years in prison by saying so at that time. But put a felon in front of her after the jury has deliberated etc., etc., and the words when uttered become effective. Or consider all it takes for a minister to pronounce two people husband and wife. Even in Vegas it takes quite a bit to get that all set up right! At the other end of the scale there are all sorts of speech acts that don't require much in the way of structured context. I can convey my thanks to people all the time for things large and small, by simply saying so: "I thank you for loaning me the twenty bucks." "I thank you for holding the door for me." Or, one can assert something under just about any old circumstances: "I hereby assert that it's raining outside/that unemployment is down/that one of my cats likes bacon . . ."

An inventory of English verbs (not all languages have such an array, it turns out) that can be gainfully used with *hereby*—and are thereby designated "performatives"—includes a wide variety of actions, some requiring little background, others quite a bit: warning, advising, promising, betting, asking (but not wondering), commanding, christening/dubbing, declaring, accusing, blaming, crediting, denying, ordering, suggesting, voting, encouraging, dismissing, postponing, firing, hiring, bidding, summoning, apologizing, adjourning, ordering, selecting/choosing ... But again, while I might bequeath things to my heirs performatively ("I hereby bequeath my stamp collection to my cousin Maude ..."), which involves transfer of property and/or money, I can't *pay* for things by simply saying so (don't we all wish ...) even though that involves the transfer of property or money as well. And, of course, you can't sneeze by *saying* you sneeze, or repair the car, or walk the dog or get thirty miles to the gallon—while most things we typically want to do cannot be done performatively via language, many can.

But the vast majority of the time, even if we're performing these acts whose function *can* be marked in such an unambiguous way, we choose a much more oblique form. A person can easily congratulate someone by saying "Way to go there, kid" without resorting to the use of the verb *congratulate*. Promises can be made by saying "I promise ..." but far more often simply saying "I'll pay you back next Wednesday" (technically, a declarative sentence in the future tense) will take care of the job as easily.

Partly this is because our ability to reason about the intentions of others makes it so easy to figure out the intended speech act from the context. This allows us to avoid the clunky, more formal-sounding performative sentences. But partly, it's because there are times when we don't want to draw too much attention to the speech act itself.

Performative sentences are used not just to perform the act itself, but to underline it, often in a very solemn or ceremonial way. "I sentence you to five years in prison" almost sounds like it has the drop of the gavel built into the *language*. When the minister announces "I now pronounce you man and wife," this is the cue for applause (or whooping and hollering if that's the sort of wedding it is). And note how much more ominous it feels to get a letter from the government saying, "You are hereby notified that you owe $33 000 in back taxes," than it does to get a letter that simply states "You now owe $33 000 in back taxes." Both accomplish the same speech act, but the first has a gravity that the second lacks.

As you saw in Chapter 5, there are times when it seems more socially appropriate to structure a speech act *as if* you intended to communicate something other than what you actually are, even if this is obvious to both you and the hearer. In reminding your boss that it's time she got going to her meeting, you coat the reminder with a request-like veneer ("What time was that meeting supposed to be?") This innocent pretense lets her know that you are well aware of the corporate pecking order. But try saying this instead: "I hereby remind you that it's time to go to your meeting." Same speech act, very different effect; unless you have a very casual relationship with her, and this is said in humor, it seems badly out of place. So there are some real consequences to any decision to either make your intent glaringly obvious or understated.

For obvious reasons, here's a phrase you won't often hear at the start of a TV commercial: "Procter & Gamble will hereby attempt to persuade you to buy Tide laundry detergent." This has less to do with social niceties, and more to do with the fact that P&G would prefer the persuasive intent of the message not to be at the front and center of your attention. That has an inconvenient way of reminding you of the troublesome gap between the company's interests and your own. At times, ads have gone to extremes to mask their true intent. One woman showed me an envelope she'd received in the mail; it was bright yellow, looking just like the kind of envelope that birthday cards are tucked into, had her name and address handwritten on the front, and a real stamp affixed to it. When she opened it, there was indeed a greeting card inside. On the front was a picture of a telephone, with the words "Missing You . . ." Inside the card, she read the following "greeting":

WE MISS YOU.
Our new lower rates make it easier to stay in touch.

And below this text, there was a *handwritten* note: "Wendy, place the enclosed stickers on or near your telephone and start saving. Thanks! Linda Bell."

Many other ads can be like this, masquerading as anything *but* advertising. Sales pitches have arrived in people's mailboxes disguised as: a tax refund check (really an offer for a loan at a staggering interest rate—you send the check in to initiate the loan), a jury duty summons (really a request for donations to a political cause), and an envelope that looks like an official government document, with the words "Form M283-31: Attention State Property Owner—Urgent Financial Notification" (really a pitch for a mortgage loan). In these cases, the point might be to do more than just create a bit of psychological distance from the intended speech act—there's the real potential for actual confusion about it. One such incident was documented on the website of the National Advertising Division, a division of the Better Business Bureau:

> *The buyer was livid. He had received in his office mail a page ripped from a magazine with an article touting a book on public speaking. Ordinarily, he would have thrown the article away—but this one had one of those familiar yellow 'stickies' attached, addressed to him by name. 'Try this. It's really good!' the handwritten note said, with the signature 'J.' 'J' happened to be the first initial of his supervisor's name, so the employee promptly ordered the materials, forking out almost $300 for what he assumed to be 'obligatory' professional reading.*

These are egregious examples, and they go well beyond what most advertising does in the way of downplaying its persuasive intent. They feel sneaky and get our hackles up. But there's a cornucopia of methods that advertisers use—many of which feel perfectly acceptable to us—that make it *feel* as if their purpose was to accomplish something other than persuade. Like the pretense between the employer and her boss who was in danger of being late to her meeting, ads are good at creating small fictions for us, fictions in which we readily participate. As it turns out, we're willing to participate in quite a few fictions that are assembled by advertisers.

Action/Reaction

Many speech acts come in pairs. This is because, by definition, social behavior involves more than one person, and language, as a social medium, normally takes place in situations involving more than one person. One person acts and the other reacts. The most obvious social uses of language are when people interact in direct face-to-face conversation, still a reasonably common occurrence even in this day and age. Suppose Sal meets Hal and says Hi. Hal has been thereby *greeted*. In saying Hi back, Hal has *returned* the greeting. A greeting and its return are just one such pair of speech acts. Others nearby may hear the "Hi" and absorb the information that a greeting has taken place, but none of them except Hal has actually been greeted. None of them, therefore, feels any compulsion to greet Sal in return because there is no "return" to be had—*they* were not the ones greeted in the first place.

Now suppose Sal then says something like: "My nephew is having a birthday party at our house next Monday, and we'd like you to come." Sal's speech is, again, addressed to Hal. In this case, Hal has been *invited* somewhere, and Hal having been invited, has the obligation to *accept* or *decline* the invitation Sal has just extended. These other people nearby may also hear the invitation, but since they're not *participants* in the conversation, the invitation is not addressed to them. They have (and feel) no need to respond to Sal, even though they understand the information being conveyed perfectly well. But, Hal, being a participant, needs to respond at risk of being seen as uncooperative or a social misfit. Maybe he says, "Gee, I'll have to check my calendar and get back to you," declining to respond right away but, at the same time recognizing the need to give an answer eventually. Even then, he's still on the hook for a response, and if he eventually fails to accept or decline, he owes an apology (another type of thing one can accomplish via language), which can then be *accepted* (or declined) by Sal.

Pairs like greet/return, invite/accept (or decline), and apologize/accept (or decline) govern much of our social behavior. If you're asked a question, you should answer. If someone says good-bye in leave-taking, you return the good-bye. This is what it means to be a part of a conversation—to abide by these "rules" that govern how interactions take place. In the above scenarios, the onlookers who could hear everything plainly, were not part of the conversations, and so not only did they not respond, but, even more important, they didn't even *feel* a need to respond.

The "rules" of conversation are so deeply engrained in us that most of the time we just go with what feels right if we're a conversational participant.

It turns out there are special bits of language that go along with being a conversational participant—the ability to use first-person and second-person pronouns. All languages have these pronouns in one form or another. In English, the first-person forms *I* (*me*, *my*, *myself*, and *mine*) are a way of pointing to the person who's doing the talking; the second-person forms *you* (*your*, *yourself*, and *yours*), represent the person being addressed (these also have plural forms I'll come back to later). These two pronoun types mark the conversational participants. That's it. The other pronouns (the third person forms, *he*, *she*, *it*, *they* . . .) point to people or things that aren't conversational participants at that moment. Since very little advertising is carried on via face-to-face conversation (when's the last time you had to deal with a real door-to-door salesman?), we shouldn't expect to see these pronoun forms cropping up much in ads, right? Well, not so fast. For starters, let's look at this rather well-known example:

The use of *I* and *you* in this image doesn't feel all that strange. In fact, it feels downright natural. Advertisements are peppered with *you*'s and *I*'s and *we*'s and *your*'s—especially the *you*'s. A glance through the ads in a local glossy publication that came in yesterday's mail bears this out. I didn't have to look beyond this single magazine that was lying on my kitchen counter, nor did I have to go beyond page 19 to find the following examples:

"*Find your vehicle at John Holtz*" (who, in case you were wondering, "...
brings *you the world*")
"*Call for your tour today*" at the Highlands at Pittsford
"*To us, your kitchen is no place for cutting corners*" Charlotte appliances
[note: "Charlotte" here is pronounced "shar-LOT"]
"*So you'll experience nothing but intense performance . . .*" Dorschel Infiniti
"*You're a real eye-opener!*" (Eye Openers optical fashions)
"*You say you can't find the home theater in this Rochester living room?*" (The Stereo Shop)

Not hard to find at all. If digging up ads that used first and second person forms were a classroom assignment, it would be among the easiest of the semester (finding ads that use the word *persuade* would be the hardest).

Fine. But who's being addressed in these ads? Put another way, in seeing ads like this, do you feel more like a bystander who happened to overhear, or do you feel more like you yourself are being addressed? To make this question a bit more concrete, imagine you go to the office and find a balled-up piece of paper on the floor. You idly pick it up and see that it has a note written on it which reads, "See your supervisor immediately." You don't know who it's addressed to, but you assume it's not yourself, so you wonder who might be in trouble. Compare this with finding the same unsigned note, not in a wad on the floor, but placed neatly on your desk. Even if you pretend not to have seen the note (Note? What note? I didn't see any note), you still feel the obligation to see your supervisor in a way you simply would not had you found it crumpled on the floor, leaving you to wonder what poor sap this had been addressed to.

Now, compare this to the way you interpret the ads that urge "you" to do something, such as finding "your" vehicle at John Holtz Honda. Do you interpret this as directed at someone else, and you're a mere bystander, or do you feel like *you* are being urged to do something?

Most people, possibly after some thought, would say, yes, *in a sense* they themselves are being addressed. They're not pure onlookers.[2]

There's something odd about this. If you *are* being addressed by the ad, and words like *you* are reserved for conversational participants, this seems to bring us

---

[2] There are times when ads use the word *you*, and are nevertheless clearly pitching something that is totally irrelevant to you. It's still not quite like an onlooker situation. It might be a little bit more like a case of mistaken identity. I'm reminded of the time my teenage daughter took a call from a telemarketer, and dutifully answered several questions that were rather forcefully put to her. Finally, she managed to break the flow of the interrogation to say: "Look. I'm fifteen. I don't *buy* insurance."

to something of a nutty conclusion: that we're conversational participants with ads—we're engaged in a conversation with a poster! Obviously, that's not the case—if advertising is a conversation, it seems to be one in which *your* side is deprived of the chance to converse. When that loud and ridiculously dressed used car salesman comes on local TV and tells you he wants to see YOU at Buckin' Benny's Ford, right out on Route 31, you can't answer him and decline the invitation, or ask directions, or tell him to tone his act down about three notches. The inability to talk back would certainly seem to be one major strike against the idea that we're "participants." But this leaves us with something of a dilemma, since you interpret the YOU as, well, you, and equally importantly, you *feel* like you've been addressed.

   To use a nonlinguistic example: in the poster of Uncle Sam, are you being pointed at? Are you being looked at? The right answer seems to be something like: well, *in a sense* yes, but in another sense, no. There is, of course, no Uncle Sam. He's in the same category as the Easter Bunny and Santa Claus. In this sense, the used car guy on local TV has a serious leg up on Sam. But still, why do we *feel* like we're being looked at by this seriously nonexistent Uncle Sam creature? Paul Messaris, in his book *Visual Persuasion*, argues that the way we understand images, such as pictures, is to instinctively treat them as if they are real. He uses the Uncle Sam poster as his lead example. We know there is no real "Uncle Sam" person—looking at the poster doesn't change this belief. We know this is an image that has been dreamed up and painted (actually, it's based on the painter James Flagg himself). We're keenly aware of all this. Nevertheless, in order to interpret the picture, we take our cue from reality. Someone who's old looks pretty much like Uncle Sam does. If someone's wearing a hat, it looks something like that. If someone is (really) looking at you, then their eyes look about like Uncle Sam's eyes. And if someone is really and actually pointing at you, that's about what it looks like. And, we use these real experiences to interpret the actions in the picture.

   But, Messaris points out, this process of interpretation isn't just an idle exercise we do in our heads like a little puzzle to be solved. It engages all parts of how we interpret the situation: our *reactions* to what we encounter are the reactions we would have if the depicted scene were real. For instance, one reaction that seems to hold across cultures is the instinct to look back at someone who's looking at you (*initiating* eye contact, by the way, is oftentimes considered rude). Most people gazing at the Uncle Sam poster look first and longest at the eyes and face, but not, say, at his left shoulder, just as they would in real life. This "reaction" is not confined to overt behavior. The *emotions* triggered by pictures are also based on the emotions you would have in the real world. They are part of the "reaction," and in this case, since the image engages those emotions so effectively, it's why the poster is as famous as it is.

   Just about any art form relies heavily on these wired-in reactions. In films, high camera angles are often used to draw from us the kinds of feelings we might associate with looking down on children (look at the camera angles in ads seeking charitable donations for victims of natural disasters for instance—they make the victims seem especially vulnerable). On the other hand, lower angles that suggest a child's viewpoint may be used to elicit respect for certain characters, the people we "look up to." It's no accident that Gary Cooper in the film *High Noon* (he portrayed the good guy, that's all you need to know if you somehow missed it, and yes his hat was white) was filmed from an angle about four inches below eye level.

There's a story that in the early days of motion pictures, an onrushing train was shown on film to a theater audience in France, leading to a near-stampede out of the theater as people attempted to flee. This story turns out to be an urban legend, but it captures something of the visceral reaction that can overtake you even when you know that you're watching a flickering two-dimensional insubstantial image. And you don't have to be a movie *naïf* to experience it. I for one have seen gazillions of movies and TV shows and all that, and I'm well aware of how the images are produced, as is everyone in this day and age. I can't be fooled in that regard. But a funny thing happened when I was at a screening of an Imax 3D movie (with the huge screen and the 3D glasses). At one point in the short film, cartoon characters (*obviously* not even *remotely* real, right?) were chasing one another around, and one escaped by climbing a telephone pole. The other character then got an ax and chopped the pole down. The pole fell right at me! Of course it's a movie—it was even in a mall multiplex, for heaven's sake—but what did I do? I ducked! And what's more, as I was ducking (and self-consciously noticing I was doing so), I also noticed everyone else in the same row was doing the same thing. In other words, I did much the same thing I would have done if the pole were a real one—and so did everyone else. And this was in the late 1990s.

More recently, there were some reports of audience members sinking into bouts of depression after watching James Cameron's film *Avatar* in 3D. Seems the fictional world of Pandora was so beautiful that after experiencing it, people found it hard to tolerate living in the real one. One viewer even said, rather melodramatically:

Ever since I went to see 'Avatar' I have been depressed. Watching the wonderful world of Pandora and all the Na'vi made me want to be one of them. I can't stop thinking about all the things that happened in the film and all of the tears and shivers I got from it. I even contemplate suicide thinking that if I do it I will be rebirthed in a world similar to Pandora and that everything is the same as in Avatar.

This kind of response, though admittedly overwrought, would be impossible without the ability to experience the unreal as if it were real. You just couldn't have the same yearning for a world if your only knowledge of it came from reading lists of its features or an encyclopedia entry (try reading the 8000 + word Wikipedia entry for "Earth" for example—there's no *romance* to it).

So we have this delightful ability to experience alternative "realities" in a way that is completely unencumbered by our knowledge of the fact that these realities simply don't exist. Our feelings and our intellect can run on quite different tracks here, and the *knowing* doesn't make the *feeling* much less real at all.

Like art, advertising can leverage this wonderful human property to create the feeling of alternative realities. And this is how you come to be a conversational participant in many of these ads, how the person on the screen in front of you, with whom you have no personal interaction at all, is talking to you as well. Much of the time, we inhibit our responses to such situations by not talking back to the image. But most of us, at one time or another, have also reacted to someone on television as if they're real. Ever scream back at the politicians, crane your neck in heightened interest, or laugh out loud at a joke someone just told on TV? It's the equivalent of ducking when the 3D telephone pole comes crashing down on you.

So, that same sense in which there was an onrushing train, or there was a telephone pole about to bash in my head, is the same sense in which Uncle Sam is in fact looking at you and pointing at you, and addressing you; less compelling, but along the same lines, it's also the same sense in which Dorschel Infiniti, the Stereo Shop, the Highlands at Pittsford, and so forth, are addressing you as well. You are in a virtual conversation, and as the addressee in that virtual conversation, you are the "YOU." No matter that there's no beaming salesman at your door—you are involved in a human interaction.[3]

Exploding Roles

One very important thing that sets apart a created reality like a film or a book or an ad from actual reality: we're aware that it has been *created*—by *somebody*. And that makes all the difference in terms of how we assign responsibility for the speech acts it seems to contain.

In order to hold someone responsible for an action, whether a speech act or anything else, we need to be able to think of them as an agent—that is, as someone whose action springs from intention and free choice. Actually, an agent need not be a person. We breezily attribute agency to higher animals, to groups of people or groups of animals (we can say, for example, "*the wolf pack harassed the sheep*"), and to human organizations such as clubs, governments, corporations, and so on. Our legal system enshrines this—you can sue a company as easily as you can sue an individual.

Nonhuman animals could never have a system of law because, aside from being bereft of language, they lack brains that are programmed to think of all actions in

[3] You will no doubt have noticed, that the word *you* has appeared throughout this book many times for pretty much the same reason it appears in ads—to create a reality in which you and I (the I actually being an amalgam of Julie Sedivy and Greg Carlson) are in a conversation.

terms of agency. Which is why we understand pointing, and chimps don't. In fact, we're so hard-wired to think about the *purposes* behind actions that we tend to go overboard. We talk as if computers don't "want" to do what they're told, and just the other day I heard someone tell me that her word processing program "had it in" for her. In experimental studies, people have been shown to breathe agency into geometric *shapes* moving around a computer screen. A subject in one such experiment described the scene this way:

> *The blue dots would not let the green rectangles pass. However the green rectangles did not seem to mind and didn't try that hard. All of a sudden, red rectangles came flying in to the scene, and carried away the green rectangles. The blue dots seemed frustrated by this and still tried to get to the green rectangles. The red rectangles were very fast-moving and did not let the dots touch the green rectangles.*

Obviously, the viewer doesn't honestly believe that the shapes have minds and feelings. This is simply another way of interpreting images *as if* they obeyed the rules of reality. And in the real world, the intentions that underlie actions are every bit as important to us humans as laws of physics. They're what allow us to perceive Lady Macbeth as first consumed with ambition and then wracked with guilt, and Hamlet as driven by the desire to avenge his father. Without this understanding of agency, Shakespeare would cease to captivate. So would soap operas for that matter.

Our agency-obsessed brains allow us to do much more than simply bestow intentions upon drawings or fictional characters. Our grasp of the concept of agency is so nuanced that it also allows us to understand *layered* intentions and *embedded* agency. These layerings and embeddings can create interesting textures in fiction (and, as it happens, in ads). But you don't even need to look as far as that. They also turn up in communication that's squarely planted in the real world.

Let's take a crack at dissecting agency in speech acts: A conversation between two people is a conversation between two agents, each acting willfully and intentionally as part of the conversation. Other things involving two people might not be intentional. Suppose you're standing on a crowded bus and it lurches unexpectedly. You bump into the person next to you. That involves two people—you and the person next to you—but not two agents. If the person, offended by the jostle, then bumps you back, then an agent has suddenly entered the picture, and if you, angered by the rudeness, then bump *him* back, you now have two agents in the picture. If this continues, it could devolve into something called a "fight," which is exactly like a conversation in that two (or more) agents are involved, though the actions themselves are a bit different.

In normal face-to face conversation between two people, there are two agents, but the number of actions involved is somehow more than meets the eye. As with nonlinguistic actions, one *action* can correspond to more than one *act*. For instance: One way of voting is to flip a small lever in a voting booth (or mark an X in a box), and you've done two things by apparently doing only one: in flipping the lever (or marking the X) you were also voting. In other contexts, that same lever-pulling may not have also been a voting—if you repair voting machines, for instance. Or, you raise your hand in class, and in doing that, ask to be called on by the teacher. Other times, the same hand-raising is not a request to be recognized (maybe you're reaching for something on a high shelf), and there is only one act, and not two.

The same applies to language. In saying things, you make certain noises with your mouth, but you also convey meanings. So each agent in a conversation is actually playing a number of different *roles* and intentionally performing a number of different acts, all balled up into one. This is the insight of philosopher Erving Goffman. Goffman refers to these different capacities as *speaker roles*. He outlines three of them. The first, which he calls the *animator*, is the agent who actually makes the noises we experience as speech (or, if using a signed language, signing, or if writing, creating the written form to be read by others). But the person who creates the physical forms is also usually the one who figures out how to say what needs to be said. This agent is responsible for the choice of words, the phrasing of the sentiments and ideas, and the entire collection of linguistic details that go into shaping the message. Goffman calls this role the *author*. Then, above and beyond these, is the agent who's responsible for the fact that the speech act is taking place at all and for the *contents* of the message—not its shape. This would be the *principal*.

In normal conversation, all three roles get fused together into the same person, so it's easy to miss that they involve separate acts. But at other times, they pull apart more clearly. Some of the roles can be delegated. Take, for example, someone giving a political speech.

It's taken for granted that the speaker (let's call him Senator Foghorn) has to claim responsibility for what's being said; listeners assume he's expressing his own perspective and positions. If he says "The proposed tax on pet otters is unfair," then he's taken the public position that that tax is unfair. Sure, in his own private thoughts, he might be pulling like mad for the new tax, or maybe he doesn't care or even understand what it is. But whatever his private thoughts and feelings may be, he is now publicly committed to that position. In other words, he's clearly the *principal*. He's also the *animator*, since it's his mouth and other organs that are moving to create the noises that his audience interprets as speech sounds.

But, Foghorn is probably not the *author*. Political bigshots typically hire speechwriters to write their speeches for them. The speechwriters don't get up and give speeches themselves, so they're not the animators, and when a speech they've written is delivered, nobody comes after them when the perspectives and positions expressed turn out not to be their own, so they're not the principal either.

Whoever wrote Sen. Foghorn's famous "otter tax speech" takes no public stance at all on the otter issue as a result of Foghorn giving that speech. What speechwriters do is to find the most ringing phrases, select the most pungent and memorable arrangements of words, and generally say well what the senator would likely have said much less well if left unsupervised on his own. They are the *author* in a typical political speech. Most of the time, the audience never fully knows if a speech was written by the politician or whether it was farmed out to a speechwriter whose identity is not divulged. In fact, the public is encouraged to mentally merge the two. This illusion is easy to maintain, since we're so used to the animator, author, and principal all being one and the same. So, even if everyone knows consciously that speechwriters are likely involved, Senator Foghorn's sonorous phraseology still gives the *appearance* of an eloquent person. Foghorn is, of course, quite pleased with all that.

It's easy enough to find other cases where the roles diverge. When a messenger reads (or recites from memory) a message to some group of soldiers written by a general, it involves the messenger as the animator, but the general as both the author and principal. The soldiers are inclined to obey because they recognize that the general is the principal—none of them would probably care much what the messenger himself thinks ought to be done. Or, the animator and author might share the same body in the form of a company spokesperson; the principal, however, is the company itself. It's even possible to find situations where all three roles inhabit different people. These happen more commonly than you might think. Suppose that on the night of his "otter tax" speech, Senator Foghorn comes down with a terrible case of laryngitis. Unable to croak a word, he asks his friend Bill Gates to stand in for him. So then Bill will be delivering a speech as the animator (it's his intentional control over his own vocal apparatus that produces the noises addressed to the rapt audience) and Foghorn's speech writer is the author, as before (Gates didn't write this stuff), but it's still Foghorn's public positions that are being established and not the speechwriter's or Mr. Gates'.

A curious thing: when three different people take on each of these three roles, the only one who really needs to know the language is the author. Parrots, assuming they merely mimic human sounds, can be animators, but never authors (ever have a parrot suggest a better way to word a phrase it was taught?). And since they presumably have no concept of accomplishing things by way of language, they can't be principals. But even the principal need not know the language—the otter tax speech by Foghorn may well end up translated and published in a Mongolian volume of great political speeches. Or, it may have been originally written and delivered in Mongolian by Foghorn himself (via benefit of a phonetic transcription set before him. Last Christmas the Pope conveyed Christmas blessings to the world in 65 different languages, most of which he does not know, so this type of thing does happen). But Foghorn is still on the hook for whatever it is he pronounced in that speech that he himself did not understand. He's still the principal.

The Buck Stops Here

This profusion of speaker agents raises an interesting question: what happens when the pronoun *I* is used, if the roles are split among different people? Who gets to claim the pronoun that's reserved for the speaker participant?

Is the "speaker" the animator? It doesn't look like it. Suppose Sal gives Jane a note to read to Hal, and Jane reads the note out loud, Hal would probably be startled to find Jane waiting for him at the appointed time. And we can rule out the author—Senator Foghorn's ghostwritten speech in which he boldly proclaims "I will never yield in my eternal efforts to bring justice to all otter owners, wherever they may be!" is not even secretly committing the poor speechwriter to that position. It's Senator Foghorn himself who will be viewed as inconsistent if he turns around and votes for the Pet Otter Tax bill. And in that case, no one would consider it even the lamest of lame excuses if he explained his sudden reversal by pointing out, "Oh, I hired a new speechwriter." The speechwriter may have *written*, "I will fight any new taxes with all my life and strength," but Foghorn is the one who *asserted* it.

It's apparent that not all speaker agents are created equal. The right to use the first person pronoun *I* (and its kindred forms, *me, my, myself, mine*) is awarded to the principal. These unequal linguistic rights line up with our intuitions about responsibility. It's the principal who takes on the responsibility for what's communicated, and not the animator or author. In the political phraseology of the late 1980s, the animator and author are "Teflon" roles—nothing sticks to them.[4]

When you stop to think about it, it's pretty remarkable that as a species, we manage to keep track of such intricately structured notions of agency. You might think there'd be room for a lot of confusion when the three speaker roles are taken up by different people. But somehow, we manage to dish out the right levels of responsibility to whoever's involved, and we do this effortlessly and without thinking about it. It may have never have entered your mind before now to mull over the fact that every act of communication splinters apart into a number of different smaller acts, possibly with different agents involved. And yet you've certainly been confronted with such complex speech acts before, and intuitively knew just how to interpret them. No one ever had you fill out worksheets in school in order to teach you how to interpret the pronoun *I* in these situations. It's just one of those things you learned before kindergarten. All this from a species whose closest living genetic relative (the chimpanzee) has trouble with *pointing*.

---

[4] It turns out that for all the common talk about computers having thoughts and intentions, people actually don't like it when computer-generated voices use the pronoun "I." Even though in many ways there is the feeling of talking to a real person (more on this in Chapter 7), our knowledge that computers can't be true agents means they're not quite entitled to the pronoun. All of which adds special interest to the title "I, Robot" by sci-fi author Isaac Asimov.

When it comes to modern-day advertising, of course, we're almost always dealing with a proliferation of speaker roles. If a company like Penney's has something to sell, they go to an ad agency, where the actual ads are created. After a good deal of back-and-forth in which many of the ad agency's ideas get nixed by company officials, the agency eventually comes up with something that everyone is pretty happy with. Copywriters at the ad agency take on the role of author. The final copy gets sent to the graphics people who end up producing the ad you see. This makes the graphics people the animators. And the principal? Naturally, it's who you'd go after for any false statements in the ad. Suppose a Penney's White Sale ad in the newspaper reads in part: "40% off all towels and bedding! Wednesday and Thursday only!" You go down to your local Penney's store bright and early Thursday morning, and . . . no sale! The clerks and even the store manager tell you the sale ended Wednesday night. Going to the newspaper print shop to complain would get you no satisfaction. Nor would going to the ad agency—they'd say the clients approved it and gave them that information in the first place. The people at Penney's are left holding the bag, without anyone else to blame. Penney's is the principal, and if you filed a complaint with the Better Business Bureau or the Federal Trade Commission (FTC), that's who you'd file it against.

Naturally, along with Penney's legal responsibilities come certain linguistic privileges; Penney's and not the ad agency or the graphics people get to refer to themselves in the first person in the ad. Of course, because the principal in an ad is almost always a company rather than a single person, the plural form (*we*) of the first person pronoun gets used, almost in a formulaic way in commercial messages. When General Electric used the slogan "We bring good things to life," the *we* referred to GE, and not the iconic Madison Avenue agency BBD&O that authored it, and certainly not the various animators who transformed the phrase into something that could be seen or heard by human sensory organs. At Merrill Lynch, "*We* are" (or used to be at any rate) "bullish on America." And companies everywhere tell you "We care" or "Our stores are open 24 hours a day, for your convenience." Even when the company is referred to by an individual spokesperson or CEO speaking on its behalf, the plural form of the pronoun is always used—the instant the spokesperson shifts to using the singular form *I*, she's no longer speaking for the company, but for herself, as a private citizen. The language form provides the cue for the shift of agency. Now she is the principal of whatever speech act she's setting in motion.

Since we humans are such virtuosos of tracking agency, mostly all of this goes smoothly and we can move between roles with stunning ease. We might have the *feeling* that speaker roles merge, so that we attribute eloquence to Senator Foghorn, or a cool sense of humor to a company (when it's really the folks at the ad agency who are funny). But we usually are clear in our knowledge of who's responsible for what part of the speech act. However, when it comes to ads specifically, it's getting harder and harder to keep the principal straight, as nowadays, corporate entities can be structured in extremely complicated ways. This allows advertisers to play a little fast and loose with our beliefs about who's responsible for what's being communicated. At the time of the 2004 American elections, Miller Beer represented itself in a series of spoof ads as running for president against Budweiser (personified in some ads by a mute horse standing behind a podium to "debate" the Miller spokesman), and proclaiming itself "President of beers," an obvious allusion to Budweiser's slogan, "The king of beers."[5] Anheuser-Busch, the St. Louis-based maker of Budweiser, retaliated by pointing out that the patriotic self-presentation was disingenuous—Miller Brewing wasn't even *American* anymore, being owned by a South African company. However, the company that owned *that* company, SAB Miller, charged that Anheuser-Busch's retaliatory ad was misleading because SAB Miller is based in London, and South African-based Miller Brewing is only a subsidiary of the company. Miller has subsequently merged with Coors brewing, to become MillerCoors.

Often, we're perfectly happy with a slightly fuzzy or abstract idea of who the advertiser's *we* refers to—it's good enough to just think about the principal in terms of the company that makes and distributes a certain product. Decisions to buy or not to buy a product rarely hinge on understanding exactly how all the companies that are involved are stacked inside each other like Russian dolls. And we can file a complaint against the company with the FTC or the Better Business Bureau regardless of whether we've identified who the parent company is—this all gets sorted out by whichever body investigates the complaint.

But sometimes, it does matter. Many companies nowadays advertise less on the merits of their products, and more on the merits of the company's image. This is especially true when an ad campaign works by creating good will towards the company. This was exactly the strategy for selling the Dove brand of soaps and beauty products. In 2004, Dove launched its "Campaign for Real Beauty," featuring "Dove beauties" endowed with the proportions of normal women rather than runway models. The campaign was pitched at women who were sick of the typical beauty industry tactic of displaying out-of-this-world gorgeous women as the standards of beauty. As part of its campaign, Dove uploaded onto YouTube a 75-second commercial titled "Evolution." In this spot, a pretty but reasonably ordinary-looking model sits down in a studio and is worked over by hair and make-up experts. Once they're through with her, her photo is taken, and then electronically "tweaked"—a little neck elongation here, a little eye enlarging there—and soon the image is unrecognizable as the woman who sat down for the photo shoot. This much-transformed paragon of femininity is then placed on a billboard where it's seen by people walking around on the street. The screen fades to the caption: "No wonder our perception of beauty is distorted. Take part in the Dove Real Beauty Workshop for Girls."

---

[5] The "king of beers" is *itself* a play on the slogan "The beer of kings" of the Czech beer Budvar, which was at one time owned by a branch of the Busch family that did not immigrate to the United States.

In another Dove spot titled "True Colors," the camera shows a series of lovely young pre-pubescent girls, each of whom is shown as having a specific gripe about her looks. One hates her freckles, another wishes she were blonde, another is afraid she's fat (she's not). Accompanied by the sentimental song "I see your true colors shining through," inspiring text rolls on the screen: "Let's change their minds. We've created the Dove self-esteem fund because every girl deserves to feel good about herself and see how beautiful she really is."

The ad campaign pushed back against the unhealthy advertising practices of the beauty industry. And it worked. Dove not only won a fistful of advertising awards, it gained the loyal following of many women, eager to reward a company that spoke to them with such respect and empathy.

These same women probably loathed the "Axe effect" campaign for Axe body spray for men. The Axe campaign was hardly built around the notion of enhancing female self-esteem. In fact, the makers of the ad campaign seem not to have had any women at home to answer to; the campaign revolved around the "Axe effect" in which supermodel-like women fall under the spell of the scented body spray, lose all self-control and go to any lengths to touch or make out with the lone male in the ad, who has, of course, sprayed himself with the product in question. In one commercial, titled "Billions," hordes of beautiful, long-limbed women in bikinis run and swim through a panoramic landscape, shoving and clawing at each other to get to one man standing on a beach and spraying himself with Axe in a pose of utter ecstasy. The viewer is told: "Spray more, get more." It doesn't take much imagination to infer what "more" is supposed to mean. In another commercial, a woman, clearly entranced by the Axe product, is sitting zombie-like in front of a nude dancer at a strip club, thanking him for taking her to the club for her birthday. Evidently, a touch of Axe body spray has the power to take over the female mind. To enhance the Axe brand, the company created a downloadable program called V.I.X.E.N.S. (Very Interactive Xtremely Entertaining Naughty Supermodels)—the user could issue a set of voice commands and see the super-models do his bidding.

All the women I know detest these ads. None of this seemed to matter much to the company, seeing as Axe was marketed to young men. (Yes, women could pressure their boyfriends not to use the product, but I suspect that men inclined to like the Axe ads would continue to use them in secret as an act of defiance.) This probably left women with the option of doing a slow burn, and buying products from "good" companies like Dove, who treat women with a little more respect.

The catch is: Dove is owned by Unilever. And so is Axe. Buying Dove products benefits the same company that made the "Axe effect" ads, and vice versa. Ultimately, the same company is responsible for both ad campaigns. Some consumers have caught on to the relationship between the two. But others haven't. On the blog *G-Wave* (supposedly created by a nonprofit organization dedicated to the health and well-being of girls and women), one 14-year-old blogger commented on Dove and Axe in the same blog post. She gave Axe a "thumbs down" for "discriminating against women, saying that all women are good for is to look at." Apparently unaware that the two are owned by the same company, the blogger gave Dove a "thumbs up" for showing how "the beauty industry is harming girls today by telling them to be skinny, taller, have bigger boobs, no wrinkles, tan skin, and blonde hair." It's the case of the blurry principal.

"Hello, I'm a Mac ..."

More fun with pronouns. If the principal of an ad is the company that makes the product, and the principal is the only agent who's entitled to use the first person pronoun (always in the plural *we* form), then there's a puzzle: what's the first person *singular* form doing in the famous commercials by Apple in which a mellow hipster introduces himself by saying "I'm a Mac" while his counterpart—who is sorely lacking in coolth—chirps "And I'm a PC"?

It's doing the same thing in the Macintosh ads as the first person singular *me* is doing in *this* ad:

Reprinted by permission of Sun Products Corp.

Once again, looking at how pronouns are used in ads is a convenient jumping-off point to understanding how ads are structured as communicative acts. The Snuggle ad gives us a clue with the use of quotation marks: there's a smaller speech act embedded within the larger speech act. The company that makes Snuggle is the principal only of the larger speech act, and the word *me* refers to the principal of the embedded speech act.

Quotation marks are interesting here. Normally, quotation marks in writing are used to report verbatim utterances. If golfer Tiger Woods is reported on a given day, February 19, 2010, as having said at a press conference, "I have a lot of work to do, and I intend to dedicate myself to doing it," then the quote is accurate if he uttered *exactly* those words, and inaccurate otherwise. If he said instead, "I need to do more, and will do it in the future," then he would have been *mis*quoted, a serious journalistic error, even if the gist of the message was preserved. There are rules about quotation marks, and using them commits you to capturing someone's literal words (even if in direct translation, such as a British news article quoting what Russian Prime Minister Medvedev said to his Olympic officials).

But in the Snuggle ad, the "person" being quoted is a *teddy bear*. It would be a bit hard to argue that journalistic integrity is at stake in this use of quotation. Teddy bear's quote here has less in common with Tiger Woods, and more in common with Hamlet, who we might quote by saying "Hamlet rejected Ophelia by telling her: 'Get thee to a nunnery.'" It's a misquote to say that Hamlet told Ophelia, "Get yourself to a convent," even though it means pretty much the same thing. Except of course Hamlet never actually *said* anything, being a character in a play.

Shakespeare it's not, but what the Snuggle ad is effectively doing is creating a spare little play for our consumption, and in the framework of this little drama, we're playing along with the idea that inanimate objects can talk to us. In the context of this miniature fiction, the teddy bear *is* the animator, the author, and, of course, the principal as well. But only in the context of this pretend world.

When you pull back and evaluate the teddy bear's quoted utterance from the perspective of the real world, things are different: The animator in this ad is whatever graphics printing place produced the ad—that's who actually produced the forms we see. The author, well, that's the team back at the ad agency, the people who finalized the ad and its contents before sending it off to the print shop. And the principal? It's not the teddy bear, he doesn't exist in the real world. And, it's not the parent company Sun Products (formerly Unilever)—if it were they'd use the word *us* instead of *me*—and besides it's the cute teddy bear we're supposed to love, not the cold impersonal corporation. So who's the principal? In the real world, there is none. In the real world, *no one* is responsible for saying that you'll love the teddy bear. It's how drama and fiction and anything make-believe work. Bottom line is, you can't hold Shakespeare responsible for Hamlet's statements. He's the author, but not the principal of Hamlet's words, and if Hamlet vows to kill his uncle within earshot of witnesses, no one sends the police after the bard for uttering a death threat.

So there's a disconnect between how rules of responsibility apply to speech acts in the embedded fictional world, and how they apply to the real world. In a play, if one actor says to another, "I promise to raise your son as my own," whether or not he's made a promise depends on the frame of reference. In the play frame of reference, the character who said this is the animator, author, and the principal, all rolled into one, just like in normal conversation. It's clear that he's the principal because, within the frame of reference of the play, a promise has been made, and if he breaks his promise, he'll be responsible for the consequences. But we understand that the structure of agency is completely different in the real world frame of reference. Words have been spoken by actors (they're the animators), but they were put into their mouths by a playwright (the author). And, critically, *no promise has been made* in the real world, even if there was a promise made in the play. It's like the ads put out by the Nevada tourism industry—what happens in Vegas, stays in Vegas. Same goes for fiction.

So a speech act in a fictional world doesn't actually result in any speech act at all being made in the real world. Some *components* of the speech act are happening in the real world: there are individuals making noises to each other in the real world, saying words that have been carefully put together by someone real. But the key ingredient is missing. There's no principal, so no one is *doing* anything in the real world like making promises, threats, invitations—there are no thanks and congratulations. There are lots of other things they're not doing in the real world, of course. In the play, they might find a bag of money hidden in a wall, but in the real world an actor reaches in and grasps a bag full of worthless stage-money (the grasping is real, the getting rich is not). Or, Luke Skywalker might do in Darth Vader and save the world, but in the real world nothing was saved and nobody was done in. It's the same with the talk.

It takes an incredibly sophisticated understanding of the world to keep all this straight, and it's no surprise that children sometimes take a while to sort out the whole boundary between reality and pretense (I have an early childhood memory, for example, of watching the chariot race in the movie *Ben Hur*—a character died during the race, which prompted me to remark that they must have paid the actor a lot of money to allow himself to be killed during the filming of the movie). Adding to the challenge is the fact that there's nothing in the language to help make the distinction—exactly the same language forms are used to describe fiction as reality. There's nothing in the way *Juliet* is pronounced that shows that the name's owner is a fictional person. Or in the form of the sentence *Dirty Harry put away six bad guys in the gunfight* to clue us in to the fact that it's about a scene in a Hollywood film. We use exactly the same type of language to talk to kids about Santa Claus as we would about any other person. To peel fiction away from reality, we have to rely on our grasp of the facts of the world. That, and a profound but completely intuitive understanding of how invented worlds work—how agents in the real world can intentionally create embedded worlds in which agents reap what they sow in the fictional world, but are insulated from real world consequences. We can even understand embedded worlds within embedded worlds—as in Shakespeare's famous play-within-a-play scenarios. One more impressive feat to tack on to the human cognitive resumé—right there along with pointing, reading between the lines, deciphering veiled and indirect speech acts, and keeping track of multiple speaker agents.

All of this cognitive power keeps you from being confused when a couple of obviously human creatures casually introduce themselves as computers. You get that they're introducing fictional characters (and not themselves), and that that's why they can get away with saying they're computers without being considered crazy or outrageous liars. They're not making real-world claims. And you also understand that Mac and PC owe their existence to a real-world principal whose goal it is to persuade you to get a Mac.

The Leaky Insulation of Fiction

Fiction acts as a protective layer around an invented world that keeps certain actions from getting out into the real world. But in art and advertising both, what makes fiction *really* interesting and really *useful* are the ways in which the real and the unreal have a way of bleeding together. The wall between the two has certain leaks. And it's these leaks that give fiction a power that goes well beyond mere amusement.

The barrier separating the two, for example, applies selectively to what we *know*—we know that the events that are happening in the pretend world aren't happening in the real world. But this doesn't stop us from *feeling* as if they were real. So where fiction falls short as a way to convey information, it more than makes up for this by being just about the best way there is to simulate an experience. It's a way of making you duck at an oncoming object that is a pure figment of invention.

The feelings triggered by fictional experiences can go beyond all reason. You've experienced this if you've ever stayed up all night because you couldn't put down the detective novel you were reading, or if you groaned in frustration when your favorite TV series ended on a cliffhanger. You were gripped by the *need* to know what happens next. If you lean in close, I'll whisper what happens next: *Nothing happens. None of it's real.*

Doesn't matter. The light stays on all night. You call your friend to argue about what will be revealed in the next episode. None of this urgency is dissipated one iota simply by being reminded that, in fact: nothing does happen. Shamelessly manipulating the need to find out what happens next is how daytime soaps manage to create addicts out of viewers despite being hobbled by flimsy budgets, cheesy acting, and not-always-crisp writing.

Of course, soap operas were created specifically as a vehicle to sell . . . well, soap.[6] The narrative formula guaranteed a steady audience of rapt (mostly) female viewers to serve as advertising targets. But a few decades ago, Nestlé went even further in leveraging the power of a gripping love story to create one of the most successful ad campaigns of all time. Between 1987 and 1993, the company distilled the soap opera formula into a series of TV commercials for Gold Blend instant coffee. Over 13 compact episodes, viewers watched a slow romance smolder between a classy professional woman and the suave neighbor from whom she borrows a jar of Gold Blend instant coffee. The chemistry between actors Sharon Maugham and Anthony Head (of *Buffy the Vampire Slayer* fame) was masterfully exploited in cliffhanger episodes—you might not think that 45-second commercials could end in cliffhangers, but they did: Who was that attractive man Anthony found prowling in Sharon's apartment while she was in the bedroom getting dressed one evening? (Her *brother*, the next episode revealed.) When Sharon found a woman in *his* apartment, would she retaliate by dating a cultured Italian? (She did, but Anthony interrupted the date by showing up during dinner and forcefully dragging her away.)

The commercials became so popular that they not only held viewers' attention over *six years*, but were listed in the local TV Guide so that people could be sure not to miss one. Thirty million viewers—half of the population of the United Kingdom—watched the climactic first kiss episode. The TV spots led to a spin-off novel (*Love Over Gold*), and the series was adapted for the U.S. market under the brand name Taster's Choice, with slightly more complicated plot twists—a college-aged son and lovestruck ex-husband turned up to muddy the waters. Devoted viewers reported that the commercials restored their faith in romance— and the restored faith led to restored coffee sales. The series finally ended its run in 1998, but in 2010, Nestlé announced that it would revive the concept with a brand-new story line, featuring a younger and funkier couple in a warmed-up version of the old advertising classic.

Don't tell the viewers that *nothing happened* between Sharon and Anthony— their emotions say otherwise.

Not many commercials are quite as absorbing as the Sharon–Anthony romance. But advertisers would have little use for the device of fiction if it couldn't be counted on to trigger real emotion. Often, the advantage lies in being able to simulate an experience while taking cover under the insulating blanket of fiction. There's no doubt that Mac and PC are characters who stand in for certain products. But the unreality of PC doesn't stop the viewer from having the very real experience of thinking "loser" whenever she sees him onscreen, just as she might if she met dorky PC at an office party. Of course, Apple hopes that this very real feeling of

---

[6] Some of the longest-running serial shows in history—*Guiding Light* and *Another World*—were produced by Procter & Gamble.

contemptuous pity will be linked by association to the competitors' products (and maybe even their users).

When you look at them this way, the Macintosh ads turn out to be quite nasty little commercials. But they don't *feel* nasty, they feel clever and amusing. Imagine what would happen if Apple tried to get the same point across without the cover of fiction. Having a spokeperson for Apple come onscreen and *assert* that PC owners are losers would be a nonstarter. Not only would viewers never actually experience PC owners as losers, but they'd likely be alienated by Apple's attempt to make that claim. But by creating the fiction of a pulled-together Mac and a hapless PC, the viewer is led to feel that PC is a drip, without any such assertion ever having taken place in the real world. The advertiser wins on two counts: more emotion, less responsibility.

Try this at home: Keep a tally of the number of ads you see that introduce a world-within-the-ad and compare this to the number of ads that make do without embedded worlds. For each ad that creates a little fiction, re-write the ad copy so that it states directly whatever it is the ad is trying to achieve through fiction (as with the Mac ad above). You'll quickly see just how broad the cover of fiction is.

Even the most mundane fictional ad scenarios benefit from this protective cover. Fiction allows you to suspend disbelief; when a movie action scene shows a city bus full of passengers leaping over a 50ft gap in a bridge, you set aside your skepticism, and experience the thrill. The fact that laws of physics are violated doesn't detract from the experience for any but the annoying few. Ads that use fiction get to indulge in similar extravagant exaggerations. On a miniature scale, exactly the same suspension of disbelief happens in a commercial like this:

A bank has a TV ad expounding on the joys of online banking. The scene shows a woman at the kitchen counter on a stool with children running around and a man—presumably a husband—apparently getting some breakfast. Everyone is alert and cheerful. Even the teenager. The woman, dressed in a robe, sits serenely at a computer; every now and again she taps a key, takes a sip of coffee, taps another key, and eventually closes up the computer to say something to her children. Who listen. (Even the teenager.) The voice-over tells us that "this woman" is paying her bills online. Now: I pay bills online and I have no idea how the woman does it. I need passwords (I tend to lose or forget them); I need to type in amounts; I need to select payment options; I need to click that, yes, I agree with everything in the fine print that's on the screen that I never read but assume I am not signing away my firstborn or joining a cult; I need to deal with the fact that I've been overcharged, or that the bank's website is undergoing maintenance; I need to interrogate my spouse about why the credit card bill is so high, and scold the kids for not doing their bit to reduce our energy bill; and most of all I am never, ever, nearly that relaxed when challenged by paying bills, and I wouldn't be even if drugged.

(The commercial, as if to add insult to injury, also shows that this woman has something like $7000 left in her account, a result I'm unfamiliar with.) But this is all my problem—the fictional woman on the screen (who, by the way, is *not* paying any bills) can go ahead and dwell in a world where she can actually pay her fictional bills that way. And I get to have the vicarious experience of serenely paying bills. I sit through all this just like I would through the bus-jumping action scene, without feeling compelled to say to the person sitting next to me: "That would never happen."

Truth and The Fiction—Reality Barrier

You might think of the barrier between fiction and reality as being a bit like the blood-brain barrier, which allows only some kinds of molecules to pass from the bloodstream into the brain. Emotions can easily pass from the fictional world into the real one, so that fiction can feel as if it were real. But *beliefs* are blocked. We *know* the events have no bearing in the real world.

All this puts an interesting spin on the issue of truth in advertising. As a society, we've decided to agree that it's not all right for advertisers to be deceptive. They're responsible for the information they convey. There are even laws to punish them if they're found to be lying. But a second's thought shows that these laws apply only to beliefs, and not to emotion. A company can quickly be hauled into court for running an ad that makes you believe that something untrue is true. But when it comes to emotion, we're all libertarians. No sanctions come into play if an advertiser—or a novelist for that matter—makes you *feel* as if something untrue were true. This doesn't seem remotely controversial. Morris Zapp, a character in David Lodge's novel *Small World*, is saying something weird when he declares, "Novelists are terrible liars. They make things up. They change things round. Black becomes white, white black. They are totally unethical beings."

It's the novelist's moral prerogative to manipulate your emotions any way he can, and in the same vein, advertisers have the blessing of the law when it comes to creating an ad in which a man can attract sexy and immediately available women because he uses the right (take your pick) aftershave/razor/deodorant/toothpaste/mouthwash/hair dye/chewing gum/dandruff shampoo/body spray . . . all without saying a single word. No one, it seems, wants to legislate telling stories out of existence, or even out of TV commercials.

It would be one thing if the decision-making part of your brain treated beliefs as trusted advisors and emotions as the court jester—there to lighten the mood, but not invited to the meeting. But as it happens, emotions get at least an equal voice when it comes to making choices, all of which makes it very interesting that we're willing to apply strict rules of truthfulness to one domain while leaving the other an unregulated Wild West. Not that you'll find me advocating the legislation of fiction. I'm just saying: It's *interesting*.

But in fact, the barrier between reality and fiction turns out to be more complicated than this—not all beliefs *are* blocked. Some aspects of what we know about the fictional world and what we know about the real world pass back and forth. All of which can make the legalities of truth a delicate thing.

Even though fictional worlds are self-contained and insulated from the real world, any writer knows that you can't have just anything happen within them. There are certain rules about where fiction and reality need to line up. This applies even if you're writing a science fiction or fantasy novel in which you get to take quite a few liberties with reality—for example, you're allowed to assume that interstellar travel happens. But what you *can't* do, according to sci-fi icon Orson Scott Card, is simply wish away the lightspeed barrier, which dictates that nothing can travel faster than the speed of light. This leaves you with the following options for getting around from one star system to another:

1. You can exploit hyperspace, in which space is folded and curved—so that two points that are far apart in three dimensions can actually be close together if you manage to jump out of three-dimensional space and then back again. You might not even need a spaceship. "Portals" between points in space can do the trick neatly.
2. You can launch a ship at sublightspeed, and equip it with whatever's necessary to sustain the multiple generations of people it will take to travel from one star to another.
3. You can put your crew into suspended animation for the duration of the trip.
4. You can travel at almost the speed of light, in which case time aboard the traveling ship would be compressed relative to time outside of the ship, so that a trip might feel like three months for those onboard, even though 30 years have elapsed in the universe.

You might have a few other alternatives, but all of them have to take seriously the basic constraint on the speed of travel or the reader will toss the book aside in disgust.

The constraints differ depending on the sort of novel you're writing. If you're setting a character in late nineteenth-century London (let's say he's a contemporary of Sherlock Holmes), there's a whole pile of things that you're not allowed to have happen: your character can't take an elevator up to his office, he can't drive around in a car, and he'd better not have a PDA that he uses to check his email for the latest NFL football scores. The events in your fictional world need not be true, but they have to be believable. In order to be believable, they need to import just the right structures from reality into the fictional world. Without these structures, readers feel let down; the writer has resorted to cheap tricks. This is why writers spend a lot of their time *researching* the background for books in which—remember?—*nothing really happens.*

What's interesting is that the rules about what aspects of reality need to be imported into the fictional world depend on the reader's understanding of the writer's agenda. Is she writing a piece of historical fiction? A fantasy novel? A piece of postmodern surrealism? Different rules.

Or an advertisement? Ads too, sometimes require their fictional worlds to import pieces of reality. For example, here's one of the Mac versus PC mini-dramas:

Mac: Hello, I'm a Mac ...
PC: ... and I'm a PC, and here at PC Innovations Lab ...
Mac: Wait, wait, wait. PC Innovations Lab?
PC: Well, you know how you have your patented MagSafe cord that pops out anytime someone trips over it?
Mac: Sure, sure.
PC: Well, we're protecting PCs with this new air-cushioned enclosure.
Mac: That's bubble wrap.
PC: And you know how you have your revolutionary new battery that lasts almost an entire work day?
Mac: Mm.
PC: Well, we are offering this new extremely long cord. (Points to assistant wearing an orange construction-style extension cord looped over his shoulder.)
Mac: PC, shouldn't innovations make people's lives easier?
PC: Well that's exactly why we've developed these. (A man walks by wearing cup holders with paper coffee cups attached to his sleeves. PC lifts a cup out of its holder.) Cheers. To innovation.

Most of this ad is understood to be safely inside the fiction-reality barrier. There's no PC Innovations Lab (there is, after all, no *company* named PC). Apple's competitors are not selling long orange extension cords along with their products as a way to deliver power to the computer. They're not proposing bubble wrap to avoid damaging your PC when you trip over your cord. None of this is true. But two things do have to be true in the real world: Macs have to come with those nifty patented magnetic cords that pop out when you trip over them; and the new battery in the Mac has to be able to stay alive for close to eight hours. If not, consumers have a right to feel betrayed and lied to. Somehow, words spoken within the cocoon of fiction have crossed the fiction-reality barrier: an assertion has been made in the real world.

This means that *beliefs* are involved, not just emotions, so the truth of the claims about the Mac's power cord and battery now enter the legal realm. Apple could be made to answer for them in a court of law, even though the claims were made by fictional characters who in the same breath, also uttered a number of false claims for which Apple is *not* on the hook legally.

Psychologically, this actually makes sense. Apple of course intends consumers to interpret the claims about the cord and the battery as factual, to be able to separate them from all the fictional stuff that's meant to be felt but not believed. The ads are a masterful blend of the real—which provides you with some factual reasons for getting a Mac—and the unreal—which gets you to feel contempt towards Mac's competitors, while shielding the Apple from accusations that Apple is *telling* you to feel contemptuous.

But again: notice that there's nothing in the language to make this separation. If you listen to the ad, PC talks about the innovations in the Macintosh in exactly the same style, tone of voice, loudness, etc. that he uses to talk about the fictional PC "innovations." There are no vocal italics or quote marks to allow you to know what's real and what's not. So what's going on inside your head that allows you to separate fact from fiction? It's subtle.

One clue is that Mac has a closer counterpart in reality than PC does. The character of PC is a made-up amalgam of all the personal computers on the market that compete with Mac. PC is a somewhat abstract entity. But Mac is recognized as representing a specific line of products, so its toehold in reality is just that much stronger. As a result, statements about Mac need to have a bit more in common with the structures of reality.

Novels work in the same way. Set your story in the city called Venice, and you'll have to dig out your map, use actual street names, and get the details of the appearance and history of landmarks just right. One mistake, and someone's bound to play Gotcha! But put your story in an unnamed city that *feels* vaguely like Venice, and you have a lot more room to play around—your characters can stroll through nonexistent museums, and you have license to conjure up, say, a completely fictional war that left the city scarred many years ago. For exactly the same reason, readers demand much more hard truth in historical novels than in fantasy novels. For instance, some readers took to task the author of one popular historical novel set in Japan for fabricating the name of a sixteenth-century master artist rather than using the name of an existing artist.

In fact, creating fiction around a character that's perceived to have a real-world counterpart can get the novelist in as much trouble legally as an advertiser who inserts falsehoods between the lips of a made-up character. In the 1932 MGM film *Rasputin and the Empress*, there is a scene in which the historical character Rasputin rapes a character named Princess Natasha. Princess Natasha was transparently based on the person of Princess Irina Alexandrovna of Russia, whose husband ended up successfully suing the filmmakers for defamation of her character over this fictional scene.[7] So these leaks from fiction to the real world do come with some real-world responsibility.

---

[7] This is why every work of fiction is now preceded by words such as: "All characters appearing in this work are fictitious. Any resemblance to real persons, living or dead, is purely coincidental." However, whether this disclaimer actually has any *psychological* impact on the viewer is highly debatable.

The fact that truth has a way of adhering to people and places with real-world counterparts is reflected in the policies of the Federal Trade Commission on endorsements and testimonials. In the FTC's eyes, there's a big difference between using an actor in a commercial, as opposed to using a recognizable celebrity, or someone who's been presented as a real-world customer giving a testimonial. If a no-name actor shows up in a commercial for a certain brand of golf balls, there's no legal requirement for that actor to own any of those golf balls. It's perfectly legitimate for him to use a competitor's brand instead whenever he shows up on the golf course. No real-world claims stick to him. But if Tiger Woods stars in the ad, then he must in fact be a "bona fide" user of those golf balls. Same goes for someone who's introduced as a real-world enthusiast of that golf ball brand. This applies even if Tiger Woods or the happy customer take part in a little dramatization in the ad. In practice, of course, it can be a bit tricky to sort out if someone does have a real-world counterpart or if they're meant to be an entirely fictional character, just as it might be hard to tell in a historical novel. Ads will often blur the lines—a character might be "interviewed" as if in real life, but some ambiguity remains about whether the person is a real person or merely an actor's representation.

But there's more going on in the Mac commercial than just the fact that Mac has a real-world counterpart. Part of what's at play is the plausibility of each statement in the real world. This means you have to access a whole body of knowledge about facts in the world. You easily recognize that the new developments coming out of the "PC Innovation Lab" are just too ridiculous to be viable candidates for reality. But you can't know this unless you have some experience with computers, unless you know that a 50ft extension cord is just not practical for most uses of a laptop computer, you know what bubble wrap is and that wrapping it around a computer would impede its use. And you have to also be able to see the claims about Mac as *within* the bounds of reality: a detachable power cord is not past the reach of current technology, nor is an all-day battery. No one's claiming that Mac broke the lightspeed barrier.

Because so much knowledge is involved, it's easy to see how things could be different if, for some reason, you didn't know all these things. Suppose you saw the ad for the first time right after waking from a coma you'd been in since 1955. You missed the invention of home computers *and* bubble wrap. Suddenly, sorting out fact from fiction in the ad would be a lot harder.

This dependence on real-world knowledge can lead to some degree of ambiguity about whether a claim's been made in the real world. Sure, the ads in which a man attracts multitudes of galloping, Amazonian women by spraying himself with Axe product is *obviously* fiction. But what happens if the fiction moves a little closer to reality? Suppose a character looks straight into the camera and says earnestly, "I never used to be able to get a date before. Since I started using this body spray, I've met someone really special." Does *that* get through the fiction-reality barrier? And what if you were aware (or believed) that the cosmetics industry was reaping the benefits of new breakthroughs in pheromone research? For every case where it's easy to predict what gets through the barrier and what doesn't there's another case where it's not so clear. People might disagree on what passes between worlds. Start asking—you might be surprised at the lack of consensus. Responsibility, therefore, gets fuzzy.

Children, whose grasp of facts can be a bit shaky, are especially vulnerable to fictional claims. In a couple of cases brought before the FTC in 1991 against Teleline, Inc. and Audio Communications, Inc., children were exhorted to call a 900 number, for which they (or rather, their parents) would be charged at least $2.45, and normally more. The voice-over of one ad went like this:

> Hi, I'm Harry the Easter Bunny. I have your Easter basket. But I'm lost and need your help! Call 1-900-909-2345 and I'll give you a secret code so you can play a push-button computer game and help me find your house!

The commercial showed the (minimum) price of a call and was clearly in the format of a regular advertisement. Similar ads appeared using Santa Claus as well. It's not hard to imagine being a child again and either believing, or partially believing in the Easter Bunny. In the ad's mingling of the real and the imaginary, some kids might fall prey to the implicit threat in the ad that the Easter Bunny will not come to your house unless you call that number.

But there's one more essential ingredient to your ability to spot the real claims in the Mac commercial. You have to know who the principal of the ad is and you have to know that the whole point of this little play is to persuade you to get a Mac. Clear-eyed about these facts, you can rely on your past experience with persuasive messages—you know that ads often list the appealing features of their products, and you assume that the talk about the Mac power cord and battery falls into this category. But notice that without awareness of this persuasive intent, any belief that these statements are true goes up in smoke. Let's transport this *exact* snippet of dialogue out from a Macintosh commercial and into an actual play that you happen to see in a theater. Think of this snippet as just part of a longer plot line about the misadventures of two "computers" named Mac and PC. The number of assertions now made in the real world: zero.

Understanding the persuasive intent changes everything. In this case, it changes the porousness of the fiction-reality barrier.

Memory's Creative Destruction

It's not such a simple thing then, to sanction acts of language. Judging who's responsible for speech acts is a complicated business: Collaborating agents need to be pulled apart into those more and less culpable. And beliefs (but not feelings) about the real have to be untangled from beliefs about the unreal. The whole thing pushes our species' capacity for thinking about agency right to its limits, and sends our legal systems into vast shades-of-gray territories.

And even when we get it all sorted out just right in our minds, the frailties of human memory conspire to blend it all together again. This suggests that for all our best efforts in pinpointing responsibility for speech acts, we haven't even begun to grapple with the implications of the effects of *time* on our beliefs.

For example: When MGM was held responsible for defaming Princess Irina's good name, presumably what was legally relevant was whether viewers who saw the movie would be likely to take the rape scene as being based on a factual event. I don't know what evidence was trotted out, but I suspect that MGM would have been in the clear had they been able to produce a study like this: 100 normal people watch *Rasputin and the Empress*, and as they file out of the theater, an unbiased interviewer takes each one aside and asks about a number of events in the movie: Do you believe that Princess Natasha in the film represents Princess Irina in real life? Do you believe that Princess Irina was raped by Rasputin in real life? Suppose quite a few people answer Yes to the first question, but out of 100, only one answers Yes to the second. It would be hard to make the case that Princess Irina's reputation has been sullied (leaving aside the whole issue of why being the *victim* of a rape should sully one's reputation in the first place).

But let's leap ahead two years or fifteen. Now, let's ask those same 100 people who saw the film whether they believe Princess Irina was raped by Rasputin. Unless the movie was an incredibly memorable piece of filmmaking in which each scene left a permanent imprint on viewers' minds (it wasn't), chances are, people's memories of the actual film have since turned into the kind of sludge that has a tendency to slop over onto other sludgy memories. Especially vulnerable is the part of memory that tells us where a memory originated in the first place. This is called a failure of source memory, and it's extremely common. For example: what people think of as some of their earliest memories are often not in fact their own memories, but memories of having those events described by family members who witnessed them. But over time, you feel as if you're remembering the event rather than the *telling* of the event. You forget where the information came from. And as people age and memory deteriorates, it turns out that their memories for content are less affected than their memories for where that content came from—you know you heard that Tammy and Brett are getting married, but you can't for the life of you remember who told you.

It's not hard to imagine how Princess Irina might become defamed in people's minds *over time*. The question is whether the insulating blanket of fiction is woven tight enough to keep memories about the source securely contained within the fictional world. Some experimental work suggests that it is not.

The seeds of the problem are evident even when you probe memory almost immediately after people are exposed to fiction. Language scientists Richard Gerrig and Deborah Prentice found this by looking at the *response times*—and not just the actual answers that people gave—when they were tested on statements that were made within the fictional world. The study went like this: Subjects read a 20-page story that revolved around a series of kidnapping capers at a fictional college. Some subjects read a story in which one character made a claim that mental illness could be virally transmitted. Others read the same story, but in that particular scene, the character talked about how in the past, people *used* to mistakenly believe that mental illness could be physically contagious. And still others read a completely different story that made no mention of mental illness anywhere. After reading their assigned story, the subjects were asked a bunch of decoy questions about how well written the stories were, how well they captured the reader's attention, and so on. They then spent five minutes writing an essay on a prescribed topic. Once done, they were told they would participate in a separate study that tested their world knowledge. They were told to respond as quickly as possible by pressing one button for Yes, and another for No, in response to questions like:

> *Eating chocolate makes you gain weight.*
> *Penicillin has had bad consequences for mankind.*
> *Most forms of mental illness are contagious.*

The people who had read the false statement about mental illness being contagious in their story were slower to respond No to this last question. They didn't *believe* it was true—but they took longer to reject the statement, showing that already, their experience of the statement from the fictional world was intruding somewhat into their representations of the real world.

A more recent study adapted the stories used by Gerrig and Prentice, and looked to see whether the intrusions from fiction to reality became greater over time. They did. People were more inclined to agree with a false statement such as the one about contagious mental illness if they'd read it in their story than if they hadn't—and this effect became much greater if they were tested two weeks after reading the stories than if they were tested right afterwards.

This line of research makes it clear that we're fooling ourselves a bit to think that we can draw a sharp line in the legal and moral sand between the *feelings* that cross over from fiction to reality and *beliefs* that presumably don't. Over time, memory may well blur the distinction between the two, and the experience that you had some time ago—all the while knowing *then* that it was unreal—may gradually *become* real to you in your memory. So fiction may, in the end, be even more than just a means of simulating reality. It might actually have the potential to *construct* it in your memory. Paradoxically, it does this by corroding the barrier that separates fiction from reality, experience from belief.

Obviously, you're not ever going to "have" the memory of having lived on the alien world of Pandora in James Cameron's *Avatar*, no matter how vividly you experienced it in 3D. But as with so much when it comes to persuasion, the action is at the edges, in the subtle internal shifts that are so undramatic that they escape notice. In the end, *was* that pimple cream recommended by a real doctor—or just by someone who plays one on TV?

7

Divide and Conquer

The McDonaldization of Advertising

McDonald's has an image problem. It goes something like this: For many years now, McDonald's arches have been crawling through the landscape like armies of two-legged yellow spiders spreading a web of bland uniformity over the globe. Along with millions of faceless consumers, you are lured into McDonald's stores[1] as a result of bland carpet-bombing ad campaigns. Cheerfully bland robotic staff activate a verbal script to take your order, and automaton workers execute their series of assembly-line tasks to serve up your bland, uniform, and very fattening food. As the arches proliferate all over the world, they trample local customs and symbols, offering as replacements a tepid homogenized version of Americana.

McDonald's is the official cultural icon of uniformity. As such, it is required loathing for all those who profess to value individuality, authenticity, and diversity. More than any other company, it's the lightning rod symbol for social critics who warn about the downsides of mass production and globalization. In *The McDonaldization of Society*, George Ritzer talks about how the McDonald's business model of efficient mass production is infiltrating education, medicine, and the criminal justice system—with dire results. Political scientist Benjamin Barber uses McDonald's as a stand-in for all national-identity-ignoring, local-culture-smashing multinational corporations in his book *Jihad vs. McWorld*, and warns that such forces trigger desperate counterreactions, often based in tribal and

---

[1] I still can't bring myself to call them "restaurants," as McDonald's seems to insist I should (look under "Restaurants" in your local Yellow Pages).

Sold on Language: How Advertisers Talk to You and What This Says About You. By Julie Sedivy and Greg Carlson
© 2011 John Wiley & Sons Ltd.

fundamentalist mentalities. As if that weren't enough to establish McDonald's as Public Enemy #1, the documentary film *SuperSize Me* traces the medical history of filmmaker Morgan Spurlock as he eats three meals a day at the golden arches. After a month on this McDiet, he winds up gaining 24 pounds, suffering from heart palpitations and depression, and losing his sex drive. This bland stuff can kill your love life *and* trigger a clash of civilizations.

McDonald's gets no respect from the English language either. McPrefixes are scuttling through the linguistic landscape like all of those yellow spiders, with new McWords popping up at least as often as new McDonald's drive-thrus. They're rarely flattering to the home of the Big Mac. The words McMansion, McJob, McUniversity, McDoctor, McJustice all bring to mind low-quality mass-produced goods, and impersonal and robotic service. And in the McArts, originality has gone into hiding. Blogger Lynn Viehl pegs the following symptoms that you are writing a McNovel: your novel features Brother McVampires ("a manly, aggressive, somewhat homoerotic group of male vampires controlled by a female deity who passes off torture and mind games as wisdom and guidance"), centers around a dragon McQuest, opens with a Dark and Stormy McNight scene, and ends Happily Ever McAfter.

Everyone knows that in the McUniverse, everyone and everything is predictable, bland and indistinguishable from everyone and everything else.

Tell that to the advertising industry. In 2009, the Association of National Advertisers bestowed a Multicultural Excellence Award on the company that brought you McNuggets and Ronald McDonald. That's right. *Multicultural. Excellence.* And tell that to McDonald's. In 2004, the company's chief global officer, Larry Light, declared that mass marketing was dead, a thing of the past for the great McD. Given that McDonald's hawks its products to a select niche market limited to those individuals who consume calories, what could this possibly mean?

What it means is that McDonald's has ditched the once-revered marketing strategy of brand positioning. This is the practice in which a company decides on a coherent identity for its brand and then communicates that image consistently and repetitively. So what is replacing McDonald's old identity? Well, what do *you* want it to be?

If you're African American, *your* McDonald's website can be found at 365Black. com—so named because McDonald's believes "that African-American culture and achievement should be celebrated 365 days a year—not just during Black History Month." You can read many success stories of African Americans who made it thanks to a McDonald's scholarship program, or a stay at Ronald McDonald House, or a job at McDonald's that put them through college, or ownership of a McDonald's franchise, or an ad campaign that helped bring them to prominence as artists and musicians. You can hear R&B artists Dwele and Conya Doss croon about the new McCafé flavors. You can check out the highlights of the Essence

Music Festival, which showcases African-American musical talent, or buy tickets to the McDonald's *Inspiration Celebration Gospel Tour*. There's plenty of that lovin' community feeling to go around.

There's a separate website for McAsians (myinspirasian.com) and for McHispanics (meencanta.com). The Asian site has a cerebral bent: a graphic for its McCafé line of beverages features a coffee bean representing a brain, while a precise voice intones in the subtlest of accents "When I think of great coffee, my rational side says go for quality ingredients, while my emotional side says I'm falling in love. No matter how I think, McCafé is always on my mind." The site lists a series of college workshop events, with recruiters and admissions officers from various schools offering helpful tips and information on video clips that you can watch.

The Hispanic site is slanted to the sensual and the social—an interactive feature invites you to explore McCafé drinks with all five senses, videos feature young partiers joyously whooping it up to popular Latino songs while munching McDonald's fries, and there's a link to a Facebook application that allows you to "send" a hot McDonald's beverage to your friends. You can download "Latin Pride" graphic images to print as posters or iron-on T-shirt designs. Ethnic artists are prominently featured on all three sites.

McDonald's is also getting more personal in its choice of advertising media. At the turn of the millennium, the company was still spending the bulk of its ample advertising budget on TV spots. A mere five years later, half of its TV budget was siphoned off into media such as closed-circuit sports programming shown in Hispanic bars, custom-published magazines distributed to black barber shops, and ads on in-store video networks of sports equipment stores—each with ads custom-designed for a specific target demographic.

Tailoring itself to specific audiences is a critical aspect of McDonald's globalization strategy—or as the company likes to call it: *glocalization*. A McDonald's in Ohio is not quite the same as a McDonald's in Bavaria or Dubai or Tel Aviv. McDonald's has kosher offerings in Israel, serves up halal beef in numerous Middle Eastern countries (you can inspect the authenticity certificates online at mcdonaldsarabia.com), lamb *instead* of beef in India— along with plenty of vegetarian fare—and of course, beer in Germany, and wine in France. Mincemeat pie is on the menu in the United Kingdom and Guatemalans can indulge in a piece of tiramisù with their McCafé. In Malaysia, the menu offers the Bubur Ayam McD, described as "juicy chicken strips in mouth-watering porridge, garnished with spring onions, sliced ginger, fried shallots and diced chillies. Just like mum's cooking!" Ohio is a long way off. And it's not just the menu that's tailored to the market; McLanguage mutates as well, with Ronald McDonald becoming Donald McDonald in deference to Japanese accents, with their distinctly un-English distribution of r's and l's.

At one level, all of this customized marketing can be seen as yet another energetic attempt by McDonald's to polish a tarnished image. The company does depend on tremendous standardization of its food supply and production, and it has an undisputed history of an aggressive, imperialist policy in the fast-food industry worldwide. The fact that these aspects co-exist with the cozy, community feeling created by the company's marketing department is no paradox; the custom marketing is *necessary* so that consumers will feel the slightest personal attachment to a behemoth like McDonald's, or even just avoid picketing its stores.

At another level, though, McDonald's shift away from mass marketing is simply part of a larger marketing trend of mass customization. This trend is likely to continue and to deepen. It has its roots in several changes gathering steam over the last few decades. First, consumers have much more choice than they used to. Technological changes in production and in communications have given them more options as to what to buy, who to buy it from, and where to listen to their sales pitches. Second, techniques for predicting the behavior of consumers (and of voters, for that matter) have sharpened, with pollsters and marketing researchers devising new ways of collecting and crunching data from individuals. Third, demographic changes have made the Western World much more culturally diverse, so that companies can no longer count on the same values, the same symbols, or the same language resonating as broadly throughout the population as they once did. All of this means that persuasive messages are likely to get even more intensely personal.

Your Own Personal Advertising

Pop quiz: How many of these famous ad slogans or jingles can you link with the company that created them? And how many of them can you sing?

Think different.	*We bring good things to life.*
It's the real thing.	*Mmm Mmm Good.*
Good to the last drop.	*Look Ma, no cavities!*
Does she or doesn't she?	*Let your fingers do the walking.*
The pause that refreshes.	*You deserve a break today.*
I'm lovin' it.	*Do you eat the red ones last?*
Breakfast of champions.	*Just do it.*

Many of these are no longer alive on the air, but they linger in the minds of consumers, sometimes for decades. Most of these entered our bloodstream during the golden years of mass marketing, brought to us by the former queen of advertising, the television commercial. These slogans were broadcast during the most-watched shows on TV, and they were broadcast repeatedly. For the most part, people roughly of the same age will score about the same on this little quiz.[2]

In 1974, historian Daniel Boorstin made the observation that advertising in America had become the new folk culture. Advertising language had sucked into itself the stylistic features that are typically found in folk cultures: repetition, a plain style of language, hyperbole and "tall talk" (think Paul Bunyan), and folk music. All these features normally make folk culture highly contagious, prone to flowing easily throughout a community. But as Boorstin pointed out, the new folk culture no longer sprouts organically from the earth, or villages, or even cities. He wrote: "We are perhaps the first people in history to have a centrally organized mass-produced folk culture."

A mass-produced folk culture has a shorter shelf life than the kind that gets handed down through the generations. If you have grandchildren, ask them how many of these advertising gems they can identify, especially the older slogans. Chances are, you've probably sat them on your lap as toddlers and recited nursery rhymes such as "Hey Diddle Diddle" or "Little Baby Bunting." But you'd be an oddity if you spooled off toothpaste commercials while putting them to bed. If you don't have grandchildren (or children for that matter), any that you do have in the future may well be unable to peg a single one of the above slogans that seem so familiar to you. In a commercial environment obsessed with innovation, ads look and sound dated after they've been out for only a few years. The pressure for advertising to constantly replace and reinvent itself leads to a strangely discontinuous type of folk culture with fewer links between generations.

But the implications of advertising as the replacement folk culture are even deeper than Boorstin originally thought. It's not just that your progeny will know *different* jingles that will be the ear-worms of the next generation—they may not know *any* jingles that have spread uniformly throughout the consumer body. Advertisers will speak to them in small groups, or even one on one. The current re-shaping of advertising suggests that ad-folk culture will be fractured *vertically* by social group as well as horizontally by generation.

The pressure to provide highly specialized ad messages comes from the same source as the pressure to provide constantly changing advertising: the escalated warfare for consumers' attention in a world where ads cram every sliver of consumer brain space. As discussed in Chapter 3, cognitive self-preservation dictates that most ad messages will be ignored. Which of course leads to ever more energetic (and novel) attempts on the part of advertisers to break through the

---

[2] Answers: *Think different* – Apple; *It's the real thing* – Coca-Cola; Good to the last drop – Maxwell House coffee; *Does she or doesn't she?* – Clairol hair color; *The pause that refreshes* – Coca-Cola; *I'm lovin' it* – McDonald's; *Breakfast of champions* – Wheaties breakfast cereal (General Mills); We *bring good things to life* – General Electric; *Mmm Mmm Good* – Campbell's soup; *Look Ma, no cavities!* – Crest toothpaste; *Let your fingers do the walking* – the Yellow Pages telephone directory; *You deserve a break today* – McDonald's; *Do you eat the red ones last?* – Smarties candies by Nestlé (not marketed in the U.S.); *Just do it* – Nike.

consumers' defenses. Which of course leads consumers to ... well, you get the picture. As Canadian radio advertising celebrity Terry O'Reilly puts it, advertising is the only modern industry that is frantically creating its own worst problem, multiplying ad clutter with each attempt to break through it. One way out of the attentional standoff is to actually reduce the number of ads that will be lobbed at consumers—by targeting them with ads that they might *want* to pay attention to.

Using demographic information is a fairly crude pass at solving this problem. For example, young married women are more likely to buy diapers than 70-year-old widowers. They're also more likely to read *Family Circle* magazine than they are to read *Guns & Ammo*, hence the higher proportion of Huggies diaper ads in the former publication than the latter. But there are many products for which the connection between product type and demographic group is much less clear. What's more, ads are rarely focused on selling the product itself rather than the layered-on symbols and meanings that are linked with the brand. How can marketers choose a target audience for a product, and then design messages that will resonate with that particular audience?

In the 1970s, while Daniel Boorstin worried about the discontinuities of a mass-produced folk culture, consumer futurist Arnold Mitchell was busy analyzing an already fragmenting consumer market, and laying the groundwork for an even more fractured folk culture. Working at Stanford Research International, Mitchell developed new refinements in the practice of audience targeting. He noted that a single demographic group might contain people with widely different consumer behavior, reflecting very different psychological profiles. Mitchell understood that in an age of plenty, how people chose to spend their money was related not just to their material needs, but to their deepest values, attitudes, and aspirations. Survey tools were needed to tap into these. As a result of his research, Mitchell published *The Nine American Lifestyles* in 1983, in which he identified a set of nine "psychographic" groups, each defined by the resources they had available to them and the motives that drove them to spend. Here are some of the survey questions that Mitchell used to sort people into their psychographic groups:

I want to live every moment to its fullest.
I would rather spend a quiet evening at home than at a party.
My greatest achievements are ahead of me.
I like to think I'm a bit of a swinger.
Women should take care of their homes and leave running
    the country up to men.

Mitchell's Values, Attitudes and Lifestyles survey (VALS) provided a detailed portrait of each of his nine groups. For example, *Belongers* were described as family-oriented, conservative, "moral,"[3] patriotic, sentimental, and generally

---

[3] Mitchell's scare quotes, not mine.

contented. Mitchell noted that they were heavy users of soap operas and romance novels, tended to avoid alcoholic or caffeinated drinks, bought more freezers than dishwashers, had little interest in home computers, and, Mitchell noted, "their use of gelatin desserts is substantially above average."

Experientials were a different lot altogether. Ralph Waldo Emerson might have been one, as might Sir Edmund Hillary—can you see them bringing a Jell-o mold to a potluck party? Experientials were more likely than other groups to be self-reliant, politically liberal, to favor legal marijuana, and oppose the Vietnam War, to head out on climbing expeditions, and to study Eastern religions. They owned small foreign cars, drank a lot of wine, ate more ethnic food than the average American, and filled their garages with piles of recreational equipment.

The VALS tools are still being used in an updated form by Strategic Business Insights (a spin-off of Stanford Research International). The basic premise behind the classification—that there are stable relationships between people's goals and identities and the products they buy—applies today more than it ever has. Armed with detailed datasets, companies have become more and more sophisticated at defining their products for specific segments, and marketing to them in a way that connects more intimately with their values. As a result, advertising now does more than simply cater to audience segments; it often has the power to reinforce or even create them. Recently, friends of mine were in the market for a new car. They're thoughtful, thorough types, and did a lot of research before ever setting foot in a dealership. They had narrowed the field down to two station wagons they were interested in: a Volkswagen Passat and a Subaru. Over dinner, they reported that they'd made a list of the features they wanted in a car, and had pored over consumer reports. They were going to test-drive both cars, but their research already suggested that the Passat was the car that was providing the greater number of their desired features for the best value. Two weeks later, they pulled up in their shiny new Subaru. "What happened to the Passat?" I asked. The husband looked slightly sheepish. He admitted: "When it comes down to it, we're just not Passat people."

For the record, their garage is crammed with outdoor gear.

The Big Sort

My friends the Subaru people probably don't have a whole lot of Passat people over for drinks. In fact, chances are that when they stroll through their neighborhood on their way to the fabulous bakery on the corner, they won't see too many Passats, let alone any Cadillacs, Humvees, or Corvettes. There are no city bylaws banning these vehicles in their particular neighborhood. But Cadillac folks just aren't likely to feel at home there, no matter how much they love the sticky buns from the local bakery. They'll go and buy a nice house in the Cadillac end of town instead. Now, when they talk to a real estate agent, they're not likely to ask what cars people drive in a particular neighborhood. They'll ask all the rational questions about re-sale values, schools, recreation centers, transportation, nearby hospital facilities, parks, and so on. But when they go look at a place, it'll either resonate for them or not—and part of their vague feeling of being at home may well be affected by the cars in people's driveways.

Several researchers who study migration patterns are making the argument that just as practicalities take a back seat to identity in people's choice of cars, more and more, people are choosing where they live on the basis of whether they feel they fit in, rather than for purely practical reasons such as cost of living or proximity to a job. Not surprisingly, when place becomes linked with identity, people often choose to live among those who are similar to them, leading to the paradoxical outcome that the more freedom people exercise over where they live, the more segregated the landscape is becoming. This is true not just of visible markers such as race, ethnicity, age, and car ownership, but also—in fact, *especially*—of less visible traits like values and attitudes, levels of education, political beliefs, and even personality types. This self-sorting has a number of important consequences.

One of these is the potential for self-sorting to create economic peaks and valleys. In a series of books beginning with *The Rise of the Creative Class*, urban theorist Richard Florida explores the economic implications of these population shifts. Florida argues that as economic growth is driven more and more by the creation of new ideas and knowledge, economic potential is concentrated in those areas that manage to attract members of the so-called "Creative Class"—the educated, innovative segment of society that includes scientists, engineers, artists, architects and designers, and so on. The tendency for these folks to cluster together is leading to growing disparities in the economic health of urban areas. Some cities, like San Francisco, Toronto, Austin, and Portland (Oregon) suck in more than their share of young, educated people, and have emerged as the powerhouses of economic growth, while others—Pittsburgh, Buffalo, and Cleveland—are losing this critical segment of their population, and are staring down economic stagnation as a result. When new companies that trade in information and knowledge think about where to locate, they tend to start up in places that have a large Creative Class concentration, so as to be able to draw from a healthy pool of workers. This of course provides more opportunities for this particular group, leading to an even greater influx of Creatives. The whole sorting process snowballs.

Florida points out that this dynamic has occurred despite the fact that advances in computer technology and telecommunications should have made location less relevant in many ways. Where we might have expected technology to have made the world "flatter," spreading out the opportunities for economic strength, social and cultural forces have been pulling strongly in the other direction, causing it to become "spikier" instead—innovation has become sharply concentrated in a small number of areas, if you count things such as the number of new patents, for example, as shown in the map on the next page.

This trend seems to be linked with people sorting themselves into distinct "personality regions." We tend to accept without a second thought that specific

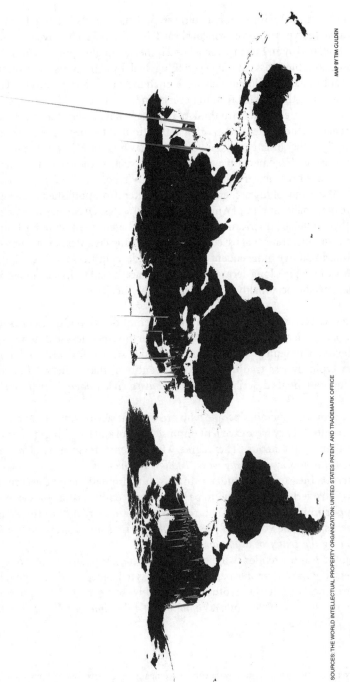

Reprinted by permission of Richard Florida and Basic Books, a member of the Perseus Book Group, New York.

traits are identified with national cultures, and these traits become fixed in our minds as stereotypes. You've probably heard the joke in which heaven is defined as being populated by an Italian lover, a French chef, an English policeman, a German mechanic, and the Swiss running everything; hell, by contrast, is what you're in if you are subjected to an English chef, a French mechanic, a Swiss lover, a German policeman, and the Italians running everything.[4]

Within countries, we tend to think of regions as having distinct "types" as well. Southerners in the United States often complain that the people in New England are as chilly as the climate and Manhattanites may find the Midwest too sedate and unadventurous. How pervasive are stereotypes such as these? And why would a single country become carved up by personality type?

In 2008, a group of researchers led by Peter J. Rentfrow published the results of a massive personality survey of Americans in all 50 states. Over a period of six years, more than 600 000 Americans filled in Internet-based questionnaires testing for stable personality traits that psychologists call The Big Five. Personality researchers have found that five independent over-arching domains seem to best capture the structure of people's long-term personalities; these broad traits subsume a variety of more specific personality traits. Here are the Big Five:

Openness captures an appreciation for art, emotion, adventure, curiosity and variety of experience. People who score high on the Openness scale tend to prefer complexity, ambiguity, and subtlety over the straightforward and obvious. They're typically less traditional and conventional than others. They feel the following statements describe them well: *I have a vivid imagination; I use difficult words.*

Conscientiousness includes people who are dutiful, self-restrained, and achievement-oriented. They have excellent impulse control and like things to be planned rather than spontaneous. They agree with statements such as: *I am always prepared; I am exacting in my work; I follow a schedule.*

Extroversion measures the tendency to seek out stimulation and the company of others. Extroverted people tend to be high-energy enthusiastic types who leap at the opportunity for action. You're probably an extrovert if the following statements describe you: *I am the life of the party; I start conversations; I don't mind being the center of attention.*

Agreeableness is the tendency to be compassionate, cooperative, and considerate of others. If you're a "people person" who tends to believe the best of people, and often reaches out to help others, you likely score high on Agreeableness statements such as: *I feel others' emotions; I take time out for others; I make people feel at ease.*

---

[4] However, a recent global sex study by the condom company Durex leaves one to doubt the aspersions that this joke casts on the lovemaking abilities of the Swiss.

Neuroticism is a measure of emotional instability and the tendency to experience negative emotions such as anger, anxiety, or depression. Neurotic people are often moody, highly reactive to stress, have trouble regulating their emotions and may find ordinary situations to be threatening or even overwhelming. They agree with statements such as: *I have frequent mood swings; I am easily disturbed; I worry about things.*

No one falls into just one "type," but most people tend to show clear differences in their scores across these traits, with one or two predominating over others. You might score highest on Openness and Extroversion, for example, be moderately Neurotic, with pretty low scores on Agreeableness and Conscientiousness. Rentfrow and colleagues wanted to know whether states, like people, would show a characteristic personality type. What they found was that these traits did indeed separate by geographic area, as you can see in the map on the next page—in fact aligning pretty well with some common stereotypes. States high on *Openness* massed mostly along the coasts, with highest concentrations along the whole of the West Coast, and in the Northeast and Mid-Atlantic states. *Conscientious* states clustered in the Southwest, the Midwest, and South Atlantic, with New Mexico, North Carolina, and Georgia taking the top three spots. States in The Great Plains, the Midwest, and the Southeast scored high on *Extroversion*. North Dakota, Minnesota, and Mississippi took top prize for *Agreeableness*, whereas *Neuroticism* was concentrated in the "stress belt" of the Northeast.

How do regions come to be stacked by personality type? Rentfrow and colleagues suggest that a number of mutually reinforcing factors spiral together to produce pockets of neurotics or epicenters of extroversion. Early on, a region may start off leaning towards a certain personality type simply because of the kind of people who first migrated there. For example, the American culture of innovation and can-do self-starter spirit may be rooted in the fact that much of the founding population was made up of individuals who had the gumption to uproot themselves from familiar surroundings and strike out to a strange and harsh environment to build a completely new life. Or, a personality imbalance might start out being shaped by the physical environment; it turns out, for instance, that people who live in areas where there is little sunlight for long periods of time are more prone to anxiety and depression.

Once a region starts tilting towards a particular trait, the imbalance continues and can easily become magnified for a number of reasons. The trait might have a genetic component, and be passed on through the generations, leading to a gene pool with a distinct flavor. It can also get transmitted socially through people's interactions with each other. Personality affects not just how people think and feel, but also what they do, and as you saw in Chapter 4, people's actions are often socially contagious. People who aren't especially agreeable might start acting like many of the agreeable people they see around them. So it won't surprise you to learn that along with differences on personality scores, Rentfrow also found

Personality

Extroverted   Agreeable

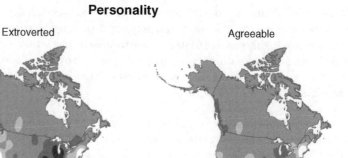

Neurotic   Conscientious

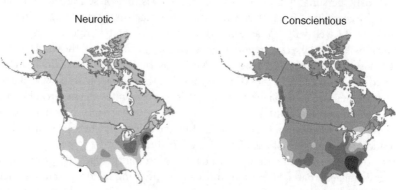

Open to Experience

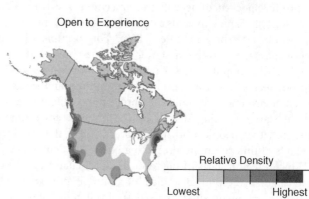

Relative Density

Lowest   Highest

Source: Jason Rentfrow and Kevin Stolarick
Maps by Paulo Raposo

Reprinted by permission of Richard Florida and Basic Books, a member of the Perseus Book Group, New York.

differences in behavior patterns across regions. For example, highly *Agreeable* regions had lower crime rates than others. People in the *Agreeable* states also lived longer, presumably because being nice to people and having strong social networks is actually terrific for your health. People in the *Extroverted* regions tended to spend a lot of time entertaining guests, hanging out in bars, and gravitated towards social occupations such as sales or nursing. Taking part in religious groups was more common in the *Conscientious* states, participating in *any* type of social activity was low in the *Neurotic* stress belt, and regions high in *Openness* had large numbers of new patents, people with liberal political views, but a low level of church attendance or social involvement in general. It was clear to the researchers that personality differences accounted for these patterns; these patterns held even after other demographic factors such as race, income, and education were pulled out of the equation.

Because personality affects behavior, and because people are exquisitely sensitive to social norms, even small differences in how personalities are distributed can end up leading to very large differences over time. Let's say a region starts out with a large number of *Open* people who appreciate art and intellectual pursuits. Going to concerts and book clubs becomes the socially expected norm. Those who, left to their own devices would really just love to watch sitcoms all evening in their pajamas, start to feel vaguely guilty about their "lazy" impulses, and join in to avoid being isolated. Eventually, a large population of people who value art and knowledge might lead to, say, establishing a university in the area, or attracting companies or industries that are looking for people high on the *Openness* scale. By providing new opportunities, these institutions draw in newcomers with precisely this personality trait. Those who just can't stomach all the artsy fartsy eggheads may throw up their hands and go elsewhere. And the artists and creatives will have plenty of opportunity to meet others just like themselves, form couples, and make babies that will likely also share their personality traits.

The exact mix of causes that exaggerate the sorting is probably quite complex and subtle, with different factors affecting different personality traits. For example, *Agreeableness* is an especially socially contagious trait, so people who move to an *Agreeable* area from elsewhere may quickly assimilate. *Openness* tends to increase as a result of education, so the presence of strong universities in the area might really boost this trait for a region—not only does the university attract *Open* people, but it shifts the existing population in the direction of this trait. Other traits, like *Extroversion*, may have a stronger genetic link, and hence, build up more slowly over time, and get more readily diluted by newcomers with a different genetic makeup.

What's certain, though, is that all of these factors work together to produce the same effect, so that an increase in any one of them has the potential to have a cascading effect on the other factors as well. So, if people continue to choose where they want to live based on a feeling of where they fit in and where they find opportunities, the sorting is likely to become sharper and sharper over time. This element of choice is probably especially important for people high in *Openness*, since it's this group of people that is most likely to uproot and move away from family and friends to seek a new life in a more stimulating environment. And it's this group of people that tends to make up Richard Florida's Creative Class. In a Creative economy, it's a recipe for even greater divisions between regions that prosper and those that flounder.[5]

The Sorting Blues (and Reds)

My Subaru friends are upstanding members of the Creative Class. They are also fervent Democrats. As it turns out, Republicans in their neighborhood are about as rare as Cadillacs. According to Peter Rentfrow, this is not mere coincidence. Personality traits can predict not only the jobs that people seek, but also their voting behavior. In fact, the personality trait of *Openness*, aside from being the strongest trait associated with the Creative Class, also turned out to be the strongest predictor of political leanings: *Open* people have tended to vote Democrat in the last three Presidential elections, with *Conscientiousness* somewhat less strongly predicting voting Republican, and *Extroversion* being mildly linked with voting Republican.

All of this worries Bill Bishop, author of the 2008 book *The Big Sort: Why the Clustering of Like-Minded America is Tearing Us Apart*. Together with statistician Robert Cushing, Bishop looked at the results of presidential elections by county between 1976 and 2004. What they found was that over time, counties have tended to settle more and more strongly into either Democrat or Republican majorities. In 1976, 38% of counties were won by a landslide with a spread of more than 20 percentage points, whereas by 2004, that number had grown to 60%. In some counties, the spread between counties has increased dramatically: In 1976, 44% of people in San Francisco voted Republican, but by 2004, only *15%* did, partly because Democrats sorted themselves in, and Republicans sorted themselves out (all while maintaining the same population count). All of this may explain why it's so hard to find people who disagree with you politically, despite the fact that, year after year, elections are nailbiters won by puny percentages of the vote.

Bishop, who lives in the Creative ghetto of Austin, Texas, describes how alienating it can to be to live in his ultra-liberal neighborhood if you happen to lean politically towards the right. On one occasion, a resident posted a remark on the neighborhood listserv; all he did was express his support of a conservative candidate for local elections to the board of a nearby community college. "Within

---

[5] For the record, the two U.S. authors of this study, Samuel Gosling and Jeff Potter work in Austin, Texas and Cambridge, Massachusetts, respectively—two creative class hotspots. Richard Florida has fled Pittsburgh, lured by the bohemian charms of Toronto.

the day," writes Bishop, "the newsgroup reacted in a way that wasn't as much ideological as biological." One member posted:

> Okay, as a member of this list, I'd really like to see this kind of political discussion disappear. . . As a resident of Travis Heights and a member of this neighborhood list, I'm not interested in having this kind of discussion here. I have to defend myself against my government pretty much daily these days, and one place I don't want to have to do that is on this list.

Another member chimed in to support the muzzling of the offending opinion:

> A-men. Stephen, you're in the minority politically on this list and in this neighborhood, and while your opinions are your own to have, this list isn't the place for them . . . This is my home, and this list an extension of that . . . I hope we can all agree to prevent it from becoming a battleground.

It's not hard to see how a reception like this would prompt Stephen to think about de-camping to more Republican pastures.

So what's wrong with people sorting themselves into like-minded communities? Doesn't this just make for stronger neighborhoods, where residents interact with each other, feel invested in the community and work towards shared goals? Possibly. But at the same time, it gouges deeper rifts *between* communities so that the next neighborhood over feels like a foreign country. This is because simply living in a community with a common set of views actually leads people to take more extreme positions on issues than they would be inclined to take on their own. Interacting with like-minded people doesn't just reinforce your point of view—it actually shifts it to a more extreme position.

The tendency for people to become polarized when they talk to people with similar views is really striking. This even happens on *juries*, where the whole point is to have jury members discussing a case together because we assume that they'll challenge and question each other, tone down the extreme views, and all around make it more likely that they'll arrive at the unbiased truth. But it doesn't always work as planned. When jury members start out with similar views, group discussion doesn't move members towards the center, but out to the edges. In one simulated jury study, jurors read descriptions of the evidence against a mock defendant, and provided their initial opinions about the guilt or innocence of the defendant. Then, they discussed the case with other jurors, and were polled again for their opinions. If the group as a whole leaned towards thinking the defendant was guilty at the outset, individual jurors felt more sure of his guilt *after* the discussion than before the discussion. And if the group was more inclined to believe in his innocence, individuals moved even further from a guilty verdict after the discussion. So two different groups that start out with somewhat different attitudes would actually pull apart from each other after talking the issue over.

What's interesting is that this shift to a more extreme viewpoint happened even for jurors who *started out* having more extreme views than the rest of the group. Rather than moving to the middle of the pack, the most extreme jurors became even more extreme in their opinions. In fact, it's those who have the most extreme views at the start that tend to shift the most towards an even more extreme view—provided the group as a whole is fairly uniform in its views.

This phenomenon has been demonstrated time and time and time again with groups of all kinds. In one early study, young French men who on the whole started out with a mildly positive view of their own president and slightly anti-American views were told to discuss their opinions. The chat led to them liking their president quite a lot more and America a great deal less. In another study, church members showed more extreme opinions on various church-related issues after they were shown what the average member thought. If they saw that most people felt the way they did, their opinions changed after seeing the poll results; again, rather than safely adopting the group average, their initial position became more firmly entrenched. It's not hard to see how viewing poll results might turn a mild preference for a political candidate into a fervent one.

Other studies have turned up the same result with opinions about racism and gender equality—so if your girlfriend objects to you going out for drinks with some of your male chauvinist friends, well, she has a point. But the issue doesn't have to be emotionally loaded to show the effects of group polarization. The effect's been found when people were asked for their opinion about what moves *someone else should make in a chess game.* And group polarization affects actions as well as opinions: intervention programs that throw young delinquents together have led to higher crime rates among members than those that treat them separately. Group polarization dynamics can turn an attractive woman into a knockout, a weak employee into dismal one, and conscientious medical efforts to save a life into heroic measures. And not surprisingly, they impact consumer behavior. The effects are most powerful in groups of people who like each other, and who have limited access to outside opinions—it's very much in the interests of marketers to create cohesive subcultures.

This group dynamic is so powerful, that it can affect even those decisions that should be the most impartial of all—rulings made by judges. Only the most naive would believe that a judge's decision could be entirely sealed off from her ideology. When the law is unambiguous, political views have very little room to play, but the law can be maddeningly unclear in many cases, and it's in these spaces that a judge's leanings can affect her interpretation of the law. As a result, appointing judges to the Supreme Court is politically charged; presidents see these appointments as opportunities to shape how the law is interpreted and, because the appointments must be approved by Congress, there is often vocal pushback when a candidate is deemed too politically extreme.

But an important study led by Cass Sunstein shows that even moderate judges can become more extreme in the company of other judges who lean in the same political direction. A Democratic judge on an appeals panel was more likely to vote like a stereotypical Democrat when the other two judges on the panel were also Democrats than when there was at least one Republican on the panel; the same was true of Republican judges.

In most situations, then, it seems that the more surrounded we are by like-minded people, the less we act like individuals and the more we act like mackerels. The real problem that Stephen from Austin had was not just that he lived in a neighborhood made up mostly of liberals—it's that he lived in a *friendly* liberal neighborhood where people talk to each other.

Zip-Code Marketing

McDonald's is right: the mass market is dead. We're a long, long way from the 1950s and 1960s when large companies advertised a relatively small number of products on *The Ed Sullivan Show* or in *Life* magazine, reaching the majority of Americans. We no longer all covet the same status symbols: I know quite a few kids who wouldn't be caught dead in Abercrombie and Fitch clothing, and wealthy adults who think big suburban houses with foyerage are tacky. Two households of similar income levels might share very little in the way of their location, style, products, and leisure activities. It's nonsensical to talk about the "average American consumer" and advertisers know it. Instead, consumer society has splintered into smaller and smaller distinct subcultures, each with its own specific tastes, attitudes, preferred media and consumption patterns.

A laundry list of factors have all contributed: An influx of immigrants with relatively high birth rates has made the population more racially and ethnically diverse over the last few decades. But most of all, the balkanization of America— and indeed, the rest of the world—comes from the proliferation of choice in our lives. Selective migration within countries has led to greater clustering. Techno-logical changes have made it easier for new companies to make goods, taking the innovation of new products out of the hands of a small number of large companies, so the sheer number of consumer goods has exploded. Consumers have learned to pick and choose from this cornucopia of products by using them to not only meet practical needs (after all, most of those brands of shampoo aren't all that different from each other), but to express their identities, making products visible markers of group membership. The advent of cable TV and the Internet have pulled mass audiences apart, so that people no longer share a common source of information. All of this has made it possible for us to cocoon within our own idiosyncratic tribes.

And technological advances have made it easier than ever for advertisers to track and store information about which tribe we belong to, and where our tribe shops, eats, gets our hair cut, drinks coffee, exercises, and vacations. Several specialized companies make it their business to collect and store data about the geographic location, income levels, and buying and reading habits of consumers. In the United States, Nielsen Claritas has identified 66 distinct consumer segments tagged with cute names like *Pools & Patios, Beltway Boomers,* and *Multi-Culti Mosaic.* This number of segments is a sharp rise from the 40 identified in the 1970s and 1980s. The largest group—*Traditional Times*—logged in at a mere 2.9% of the population in 2008. (In case you're wondering, *Traditional Times* folks are mostly white, small-town couples nearing retirement with upper-mid incomes and college educations who like to travel by RV, watch Antiques Roadshow, and read magazines such as *Country Living, Gourmet,* and *Forbes.* They are Cadillac people.)

All this data is harvested from public sources such as census data, car registries, birth and marriage records—and from data that consumers have agreed to provide on warranty cards, frequent shopper cards, and surveys. Companies like Nielsen Claritas can provide information on clusters even more precise than the level of the zip code—if advertisers need it, they can buy information tuned finely to the level of a postal ZIP +4 code (roughly 10 households), or in some cases, even down to the individual household.

These datasets can be worth their bits in gold. They take the guesswork and expensive legwork out of figuring out the answers to questions about where to locate a new store, or which households to target in a direct mailing ad blitz. And as creepy as it may seem that someone out there has a pretty good guess as to the contents of your fridge, closet, bookshelves, and medicine cabinet, there's no question that you—and society as a whole—often reap the benefits. Stores you actually want are more likely to set up shop near where you live, helping you avoid the long car schleps to your favorite stores and do your bit to save the planet. Your mailbox is more likely to contain coupons that you actually clip, and to be less cluttered. The TV programs you watch will have commercials for products that you would actually consider spending your cluster-specific income on. In the long run, all this micromarketing probably reduces the amount of advertising you're blasted with, freeing up more of your attention to think about the ones in front of you. In the best cases, it doesn't seem that dark after all.

Cluster marketing has been used in truly creative ways. Author Michael Weiss has collected a slew of intriguing case studies. In one case, the Pratt Institute, a fine arts college in Brooklyn, used clustering data to help solve its high freshman dropout rate. It turned out that culture shock, and not academic stress, was mainly responsible for the fact that 20% of students defected after their first year. The dropouts tended to come from highly privileged exurban communities with sprawling supermarkets and large homes on leafy streets (the *Second City Elites* and the *Upward Bounds*). These kids had a hard time coping with the grime and graffiti of an urban setting—not to mention the startling absence of Toyota Sequoias.

Pratt tackled the problem by focusing its recruiting efforts on clusters of students who would have less trouble adjusting to the school's setting, kids from closer-in suburban clusters and mid-scale urban clusters. They tailored their recruiting messages to each cluster. Parents in the upscale suburban clusters of *Pools & Patios* and *Winner's Circle* received soothing letters about the safety measures that the college had put in place. Parents in the midscale urban clusters (*Old Yankee Rows, Latino America*) were told about financial aid and job prospects. By shifting its recruiting efforts away from the tony exurban areas, Pratt saw its application numbers almost triple, its attrition rate plummet, and the size of its freshman class swell to double its original size. Other colleges are using cluster data not only to tailor their messages to potential recruits, but also to match up applicants with alumni recruiters to show off graduates who are cut from the same cloth, and to assign roommates in an attempt to minimize friction in close quarters.

Dastardly uses of the cluster data exist as well, of course. Companies that sell potentially harmful products like tobacco, alcohol, and unhealthy foods can and do use the data to identify market segments that are especially receptive to their products, and tailor their messages to these groups. This can deepen serious health problems in already vulnerable communities. But public health agencies fight back—also with the help of cluster datasets. In Georgia, health officials have used clustering to identify people with lifestyles that put them at risk of heart disease, and to craft their education campaigns accordingly. Members of downscale urban clusters were warned about the health hazards of cigarettes, pork, and fast food; upscale *Money & Brains* residents were admonished to cut back on their alcohol, snacks, and buttery foods at restaurants. Presumably, it's easier to get people on board with healthy habits if instead of handing them a list of 300 things that are bad for them, you focus them on a relevant few. And you can even imagine governments using cluster data to develop higher-level health policy, given that you can predict to some extent which diseases a cluster is likely to have 20 years from now.

But whether cluster marketing is used for dubious, virtuous or seemingly morally neutral goals, one thing is certain: its commercial practice as a whole can't help but contribute to the growing fragmentation of society. The more that products are pitched in ways that hinge on people's sense of their identity as members of a particular group with a specific lifestyle and attitudes, the more visible the divisions among groups will become. Remember Bill Bishop's conservative neighbor in Austin? If Stephen's neighbors can predict that his opinions will offend them just by looking at his shoes, car, and the landscaping of his yard, why would they ever bother to even talk to him?

Actually, if they did decide to start a neighborly conversation, they might quickly find that his style of speech is just one more way of signaling which tribe he belongs to. The shape of his vowels might give away his politics as much is his choice of clothing or interior decorating choices—even if all he talked about was the weather. If you listened closely, you just might find that Stephen speaks a different American tongue than many of his neighbors.

Nucular Reaction

Linguists who study dialects and language variation are fascinated by the differences among speakers of a common language, and by how these differences evolve. The language we call "English" is really an umbrella term for an assortment of dialects—some of them so distinct from each other that speakers of one English dialect may need to turn on the subtitles to understand movie dialogue spoken in another. And just like loyalties to Macintosh computers or Subaru station wagons, people can get pretty attached to their dialects as a way of telling the world who they are.

Back around 1880, Mark Twain riffed on the theme in his essay "Concerning the American language." In the essay, he offers up an anecdote in which a British train passenger compliments him on his "English," noting that most Americans don't speak English as "correctly" as Twain. Twain brushes aside the compliment, claiming that he speaks American, not English, and proceeds to list some distinguishing features:

> *I have heard English ladies say 'don't you'—making two separate and distinct words of it . . . But we always say 'dontchu.' This is much better. Your ladies say, 'Oh, it's oful nice!' Ours say, 'Oh, it's awful nice!' We say, 'Four hundred,' you say 'For'—as in the word or. Your clergymen speak of 'the Lawd,' ours of 'the Lord'; yours speak of 'the gawds of the heathen,' ours of 'the gods of the heathen.' When you are exhausted, you say you are 'knocked up.' We don't. When you say you will do a thing 'directly,' you mean 'immediately'; in the American language— generally speaking—the word signifies 'after a little.' . . . Your word 'stout' means 'fleshy'; our word 'stout' usually means 'strong.' Your words 'gentleman' and 'lady' have a very restricted meaning; with us they include the barmaid, butcher, burglar, harlot, and horse-thief. You say, 'I haven't got any stockings on,' 'I haven't got any memory,' 'I haven't got any money in my purse'; we usually say, 'I haven't any stockings on,' 'I haven't any memory!' 'I haven't any money in my purse.' You say 'out of window'; we always put in a the. If one asks 'How old is that man?' the Briton answers, 'He will be about forty'; in the American language we should say, 'He is about forty.' However, I won't tire you, sir; but if I wanted to, I could pile up differences here until I not only convinced you that English and American are separate languages, but that when I speak my native tongue in its utmost purity an Englishman can't understand me at all.*

To which the Englishman responds by saying, "I don't wish to flatter you, but it is about all I can do to understand you now."

In his essay, Twain dismantled the myth that there is one "correct" English language, and that anything that deviates from this standard is a form of language decay that had better be corrected in order to keep the language from going to hell in a handbasket. Way back in 1882, he lamented that "esthetes in many of our schools are now beginning to teach the pupils to broaden the 'a,' and to say 'don't you,' in the elegant foreign way."

More than a hundred years later, teachers and language pundits still deliver stern lectures about proper English grammar and pronunciation. Language teachers and language writers get wound up about the fact that many speakers say "she was like" when they mean "she said," and that people no longer seem to realize that to say you feel badly really means you have a poor sense of touch. But most *linguists*—the people who actually study the science of language—think of these examples more as genetic mutations than as errors and signs of ignorance.

The idea that language doesn't have *one correct form* is not the result of academics being brainwashed by a political correctness craze sweeping through the ivory tower establishment. It's the result of centuries-long fastidious observations about languages and how they split off from each other. These observations all point to the same conclusion: all languages change. Sometimes they change quickly, and sometimes they change more slowly, but over time, language is in constant flux and change, just as biological life forms of any species inevitably change over time. And just as there's good evidence that we share a common ancestor with chimpanzees, linguists believe that English, Spanish, Czech, and Hindi all descended from a common ancestor language, which they've christened Proto-Indo-European. Current English, like other languages, has all sorts of organic mutations roiling within it—some variants of English, could, over time, split off and become different enough that they would be classified as different languages, just like Spanish and Italian are different but similar languages that have split off from each other more recently than say, Spanish and Urdu.

Using the language of evolutionary biology is no cheap intellectual trick. These views of language evolution were well accepted *before* Darwin formulated his theory of biological evolution. In fact, what linguists knew about language change served as inspiration and analogy for Darwin's biological theories. All of this is why, when George W. Bush pronounces the word "nuclear" as "nucular," linguists don't see this as evidence of mental deficiency, but as a marker of his aligning himself with a dialect group where this word is undergoing a pronunciation change. In the words of linguist Steven Pinker, to describe particular dialects of English as collections of mistakes is as scientifically bizarre as saying that modern-day dolphins are not executing their swimming strokes correctly because they swim differently than their genetic ancestors.

A case in point: Mark Twain's "American language" no longer exists as he described it a little over a hundred years ago. If you're American, when's the last time you said "I haven't any money?" And the differences between Twain's version of American and his fellow passenger's English don't seem any greater than the differences between, say, certain dialects in New England and Alabama.

It's not surprising that American and English grew apart, seeing as the Atlantic Ocean (or, as the English like to say, "the pond") divides the two groups of speakers. Just as a species that divides itself into two geographic regions might eventually evolve into distinct species, no longer breeding and mixing genes with each other, it stands to reason that two groups of speakers of the same language who no longer speak to each other would diverge in their languages. It's also not surprising, for the same reason, to see some fairly large differences across regions within the United States; its early population was far-flung, making it easy for the language to develop different "gene-pools."

You'd expect then, that as technology made travel and communication across regions much easier, and as people began to move around more from one region to another, that you'd see these differences becoming diluted. Linguistic gene pools should intermix. But recently, when a group of linguists undertook the first comprehensive study of dialects in North America, they were startled to find exactly the opposite: that the dialectal differences across regions in North America are growing, not shrinking.

Vowels on the Move

This pulling apart of American dialects is a puzzle. For Bill Labov, the founder of modern sociolinguistics (the field that deals with social aspects of language), it raises some fundamental questions about the nature of language change. In a time when geographic barriers between regions are melting away, why would dialects cluster by region? What's acting as a wall between the dialects, keeping them from blending together?

To get to the heart of these questions, Labov decided to focus his attention on one particular linguistic change that's occurring in the northern regions of the United States clustering around the Great Lakes. This dialect region is called the Inland North, and runs from just west of Albany, NY on the eastern edge, includes Milwaukee in the west, looping down to St. Louis, and traces a line to the south of Chicago, Toledo, and Cleveland. Thirty-four million speakers in this region are in the midst of a modern-day rearrangement of their vowel system. This rearrangement, called the Northern Cities Shift, is the result of a chain reaction of vowel changes. The whole thing looks a bit like vowels playing a game of musical chairs.

First, the vowel in the word *cat* started to be pronounced a bit higher and towards the front of the mouth, and with a touch of gliding. To the ears of outsiders it sounds a bit like "kee-at."

This left a gap where the *cat* vowel used to be. To fill the gap, the vowel in the words *cot* and *father* slid into this space, so that *cot* started to sound like *cat* used to.

The "o" sound in *boss* and *caught* was originally different for Northern Inland speakers from the "o" in *cot*—it was pronounced a bit higher in the mouth, so that *cot* and *caught* had different vowels. After the *cot* vowel shifted towards the former *cat* vowel space, the *caught* vowel sounded like the former *cot*.

All this seems to have de-stabilized the "e" sound in *desk* and *head*, shifting *desk* towards *dusk* and *head* towards how *had* would have been pronounced originally before any of the vowels started to move. Given that the *dusk* vowel was now feeling crowded by *desk*, it shifted into the space left behind by *boss* and *caught*, so now, *cut* sounded a lot like *caught* used to.

Finally, the vowel in *bit* shifted towards the space left empty by *desk* and *bet*, so that it now sounded more like the former *bet*.

Got all that? (If you want to actually hear these vowels, try visiting Labov's generously detailed web page.) It sounds complicated, but it's actually a classic example of a chained sound change within a language's vowel system, where one change triggers a cascade of other changes. These types of shifts are seen fairly regularly by linguists who study language change (though less often on this grand scale). For example, the Northern Cities Shift is similar in kind to the Great Vowel Shift that occurred in the move from Middle English to Modern English between 1400 and 1600. Our writing system shows many remnants of the pre-Vowel Shift pronunciations. For example, *like* and *wide* used to be pronounced like *leek* and *weed*, and *our* would have rhymed with modern-day *poor*. Once these vowel spaces were vacated, we got Modern English *beet* from its Middle English version which sounded like the way we say *bait*, and Modern *moon* from Middle *moan*, with *teach* also shifting from the vowel in modern *cat* (for those not involved in the Northern Cities Shift!) to its current pronunciation. These spaces were filled in to get Modern *oak* from what used to sound like the vowel in *caught*, and modern *name* from the vowel we now have in *father*. Finally we capped things off with a move to get *son* from a vowel that resembled the one in *book*, and with certain diphthongs becoming simple vowels—for example, the word *said* used to be pronounced as *say* with a "d" sound tacked on.

So, the Northern Cities Shift looks like an organic, typical language change in terms of the patterns that are involved in the change. These kinds of chain shifts are often triggered by one unstable vowel, which then causes everything else to slide around until the system reaches equilibrium. And Labov thinks he can identify the trigger of the Northern Cities Shift well enough. The first change to the pronunciation of the vowel in *can* and *that* occurred during the building of the Erie canal in the early 1800s when speakers of different dialects and different pronunciations of that vowel mingled together. Some of these dialects pronounced a "raised" version of the vowel in front of some consonants, but not others (for example, some English dialects still raise the vowel in front of *can*, as in "kee-an," but not *cat*). This kind of mingling often gets resolved with some sort of unconscious agreement to adopt one simpler pattern—in this case, the vowel got raised no matter what consonant followed it, setting in motion the chain reaction.

The real puzzle is, why has the change persisted and continued in only one dialect? It's not unusual for linguists to find an instability within the language that flips back and forth for a while, with some speakers using the old form, some using the new, but then converging on one form, sometimes erasing the original change. Or, the new change spreads more generally throughout the language to become the new norm. So why is it that the Northern Cities change got entrenched, shifting fairly uniformly throughout a region of 88 thousand square miles and 34 million speakers, only to stop cold south of Cleveland and west of Milwaukee? That an international border creates a natural boundary separating Canadians from the northern edge of this region is understandable (*those* folks are known for their odd pronunciation of *out* and *house* as a result of their own vowel shift). But why do people in Cleveland sound a whole lot like people in Syracuse and Milwaukee, but a whole lot *unlike* their fellow Ohioans in Columbus, a short distance away?

The Northern Cities Shift is an intriguing puzzle in part because it forces linguists to confront some of the ways in which language evolution seems to be quite different from the evolution of biological species. Once a genetic mutation occurs in an animal, whether it will be maintained (and amplified) depends on whether the mutation is one that helps it to survive and reproduce. But what maintains and amplifies a linguistic mutation? In what way does it *enhance* the linguistic system as a whole? It's hard to see how the change leads to any improvements. And in particular, it's hard to see what the Northern Cities Shift accomplishes. Every now and then, language changes happen because they make certain words easier to pronounce—but if anything, the newer Northern vowels actually take slightly *more* energy to produce. And sometimes changes make it easier for hearers to understand speakers. But that doesn't seem to be happening here either. In fact, to the extent that speakers within the dialect have to interact with speakers outside of the dialect, the shift results in confusion. I remember having trouble with this when I first moved to Rochester from outside the dialect region. A new local friend remarked that what she really appreciated about her husband was that he was "a salad guy." While I was puzzling out why she was so excited about his dietary habits, she clarified: "You know, you can really count on him."

I'm not the only one with vowel problems. Labov describes the following situation, reconstructed from an incident reported in the *Philadelphia Inquirer*:

Gas station manager:	It looks like a bomb on my bathroom floor.
Dispatcher:	I'm going to get somebody (that somebody included the fire department).
Manager:	The fire department?
Dispatcher:	Well yes, that's standard procedure on a bomb call.
Manager:	Oh no, ma'am, I wouldn't be anywhere near a bomb. I said I have a bum on the bathroom floor.

(8 firefighters, 3 sheriff's deputies & the York Co. emergency preparedness director showed up at the gas station to escort the homeless transient out.)

And the following example shows the perils of cross-border shopping in Canada, where Americans commonly misunderstand their northern neighbors' shifty vowels:

Ruth (from Connecticut): [looking at bed frame] What supports the mattress?
Canadian Saleswoman: There's a rack underneath.
Ruth: A rock?
Saleswoman: No, a rack.

By Labov's estimate, about a quarter of all misunderstandings are due to dialect differences, many of them because of sound changes in progress.

A controlled experiment shows just how much confusion can ensue as a result of shifty vowels. Labov had speakers from each of three different dialect regions—Chicago, Philadelphia, and Birmingham—read aloud a list of monosyllabic words beginning with a "k" sound and ending in a "d" sound. Inserting all possible vowels into this frame resulted in a list of common real words (*kid, cad, could,* etc.), as well as a couple of brand names or nonwords (*Ked, kide, koid*). For the study, Labov chose speakers whose vowels were quite far along in terms of the ongoing shifts in these regions. He recorded them as they carefully read this list of words, and then played the recordings to listeners in each of these regions, so that each listener heard a speaker from his own regions as well as two others. Listeners were given the same list of words and nonwords that the speakers read from, and had to match up the spoken sounds with the items on the list, having been warned ahead of time that the speakers might come from a different dialect group. This allowed Labov to measure how comprehensible each of the vowels was to listeners from local and nonlocal regions.

Not surprisingly, listeners could identify the vowels of local speakers more easily than those of nonlocals. For example, Philadelphia speakers were understood 89% of the time by fellow Philadelphians, but only 64% of the time by Birmingham listeners, with some vowels scoring as low as 6% accuracy when they came from a different dialect. But what was surprising was just how badly listeners did on some of the vowels even when the speakers and listeners came from the same region. For example, Birmingham listeners heard the vowel in "*Ked*" as "*kid*" the vast majority of the time. This means that even within a dialect region, where listeners are exposed to the shifting vowels on a regular basis, more conservative speakers in the region have trouble pegging the vowels of less conservative speakers. And this is happening even when the speaker is articulating carefully while reading a list of words that are being recorded. This is no small matter, since these differences in vowel sounds are responsible for distinguishing one word from another. So, the rapid vowel shifts are creating quite a lot of potential for misunderstanding, even within a single geographic region.

Of course, in normal language situations, there's a lot of information in the context that might help listeners identify words. Labov's research team took recordings of spontaneous speech by less conservative speakers from Birmingham, Chicago, and Philadelphia. They then played back either isolated words, phrases, or whole sentences containing these words to listeners, again in each of the three regions. Comprehension of isolated words was abysmal, hovering between 18 and 24% accuracy. Context helped quite a bit, but still was not enough to resolve the sound difficulties. When hearing "*senior citizens living on one block*" uttered by a Chicago speaker, 33% of Chicago listeners—people from the same region as the speaker—*still* heard "*block*" as "*black*." Apparently, this fact was lost on Apple when the company chose the name for its new tablet computer in 2010. Best not to order either an iPod or an iPad over the phone if you're from Chicago, or are calling a store located there.

It's hard, then, to see how these regional vowel shifts could be said to improve the language. In fact, language change of any kind is usually seen as an ominous slide towards linguistic degeneration and maybe even moral turpitude (though English speakers *did* eventually make their peace with the Great Vowel Shift). As Labov notes, "Some older citizens welcome the new music and dances, the new electronic devices and computers. But no one has ever been heard to say, '*It's wonderful the way young people talk today. It's so much better than the way we talked when I was a kid.*' "

You are What You Speak

If a particular language change fails to make pronunciation easier, and it actually makes it harder for people to understand each other, what in the world drives the change forward? Shouldn't it simply die out as a very un-useful mutation?

It may well come down to the fact that people adopt certain vowels for much the same reason that they buy expensive and not very functional products—to broadcast a personal identity.

The first linguistic study to pinpoint how personal identity can be related to pronunciation was in fact Bill Labov's Master's thesis, now considered one of the founding works of modern sociolinguistics. While tagging along with a filmmaker buddy to the island of Martha's Vineyard in Massachusetts, Labov noticed that many of the islanders had a funny way of saying words like *rice* and *sight*—they pronounced them higher in the mouth, not quite *roice* and *soight*, but somewhat in that direction. But locals varied quite a bit in terms of how they pronounced their vowels, so Labov set about taking painstaking recordings of people from all over the island, and running them through detailed acoustic analyses. What he found was that the raised "ay" sound was more concentrated in some groups than in others. It was also more common among 30–60-year-olds than among the elders of the community, so it appeared to be a thriving part of the dialect. Eventually, a profile of the typical "ay" raiser emerged.

It was especially prevalent in the fishing community of Chilmark, and within that community, fishermen raised their vowels more than others did. Many of these fishermen, who hung on to a fading way of life and set of traditions, felt strongly tied to their glorious whaling history. They looked askance at the "summer people" and newcomers that traipsed around the island as if they owned it. Labov had the idea that the vowels were somehow associated with a sense of local pride in island culture and heritage, and a way of reacting against the increasing influence of the outside world. When he asked people directly about how proud they felt of their local heritage, and how resentful they were of summer visitors like himself, he found that people who most valued the fading local way of life also raised their vowels the most. High-schoolers who planned to come back to the island after going to college raised their vowels more than those who thought they would build a life away from the island. What was really interesting is that most residents of Martha's Vineyard actually weren't consciously aware that they produced different vowels than the mainlanders. They knew their accent was different from the mainland accent, and they could point out some ways in which the two differed, but they didn't seem to be aware of this particular vowel distinction. Nevertheless, they subconsciously used their vowels as a subtle badge of identity.

Labov's work was considered groundbreaking because this was the first time that a linguistic variable had been linked to an *attitude*, and not just to a demographic group defined by region, age, or social class. So, people living side by side might pronounce their vowels differently depending on how strongly they resisted the invading mainland culture. This was an example of a language change that was driven by ideology.

When you think about it, the group of people with elevated Martha's Vineyard vowels bears a striking resemblance to the Travis Heights community in Austin that Bill Bishop writes about: both are friendly, cohesive groups with strong ideals and more than a hint of resentment of outsiders. A motivation to draw boundaries between "us" and "them" creates fertile soil for the growth of dialects, and maybe even the germination of new ones.

It's not much of a stretch to see how linguistic markers of solidarity and identity could emerge in a community like the Martha's Vineyard "ay" raisers. This was a small group with plenty of daily face-to-face interaction. If you resonated with those who held on to their traditional independence, you'd be more likely to hang out with them. You'd hear their vowels more often, and you might subconsciously try to act and sound like them (I bet you'd buy the same kinds of products too).

But can ideological sound changes spread throughout a much larger area, and among people who don't even know each other, let alone interact directly with each other? Could an *attitude* be linked with a vast change like the Northern Cities Shift?

Bill Labov thinks maybe it could. He's traced the population of what is now the Inland North back to its origins, and found some interesting facts. In trying to account for why the vowel shift extends as far west as Milwaukee, but drops off just south of Toledo, he notes that there were two very distinct settlement streams moving from East to West in the 1800s. One was the migration of people from New England westward along the Erie canal as it was being built. The other was the flow of people from Pennsylvania south into the Appalachian region, and then west to southern Ohio, Indiana, Illinois, and Iowa. The boundary between these two migration streams happens to line up with the southern boundary of the Inland North dialect boundary. So the two populations seem to have dispersed from two distinct groups. Settlers from the Pennsylvania stream even had different methods for building log cabins than the New England settlers.

The patterns of migration were quite different too. The New Englanders moved west *en masse*, with entire communities remaining intact and packing up and moving together. But the Pennsylvania settlers tended to move as individuals or as single families, leaving their neighborhoods behind. This might help explain why there's so much cohesion in the dialect of the Inland North—migration by community would have helped preserve the traditions and identity of the group as a whole. Further south, cities have developed their own distinct accents—you could easily tell a Pittsburgher from a Philadelphian, for example—as the settlers shed their old identities to build new ones away from their traditional communities.

But what cultural identity could have persisted long after the westward movement of the original Pennsylvania and New England settlers, linking together people through swaths of time and space? After all, the two groups had plenty of contact with each other since very soon after the earliest settlements, and plenty of opportunity for their dialects to bleed together.

Yes, but the two groups often didn't seem eye to eye. When they did mix, you get the feeling there weren't many group hugs going around. Labov quotes Midland historian Richard L. Power, who as late as 1953 can't help but express his antagonism towards northern culture in his account of the early interactions between the neighboring groups:

> [T]hese [northern] newcomers not only displayed a disgusting predilection for self-improvement schemes but were also fond of pointing out their virtues to those who took life at a less feverish pace . . . It was the Yankees who were described as yearning to constitute a social and cultural elite that would sponsor and support higher education, literary societies, and lecture courses, and follow their inclination to regulate the morals of the whole society.

Northern Yankees' views of their southern neighbors were just as complimentary—they thought of them as "lean, lank, lazy creatures, burrowing in a
hut, and rioting in whiskey, dirt and ignorance." Not hard to see why the
Midlanders would think: O-kaay. You can *keep* yer stinkin' vowels!

Not surprisingly, the two groups didn't cozy up to each other's politics either.
The northerners held the view that government was there to help people achieve
good and morally virtuous lives—it represented communal values, and was
justified in intervening in private lives if it served community goals. The settlers
to the south had a much more individualistic point of view, and felt that
government shouldn't meddle in people's private affairs and choices. The two
groups stood on different sides of the fence when it came to the issue of the
abolition of slavery. Given that the Republican Party at that time was most
closely aligned with liberal northern values, this was the favored party of the
Inland North.

This political opposition has persisted until today. Labov notes that although
the Republican Party was founded in 1854 on the main issue of opposition to
slavery, the platforms of the Democratic and Republican parties reversed in the
1960s when it came to civil rights for African Americans. Since Kennedy, it's been
the Democratic Party that has championed equal rights for blacks. At this time, the
northern vote flipped over to the Democrats, showing that this population voted
according to values rather than party loyalty. When Labov looked at the relationship between voting patterns by county over the last three presidential
elections and how much the speakers in each county shifted their vowels, he
found a tight correlation between the two. And the states that participated in the
vowel shift also tended to have resisted the death penalty.

Do vowel-shifters *sound* more liberal to modern ears? Yes, at least to some
extent. Labov had students in Bloomington, Indiana listen to a vowel-shifting
speaker from Detroit and a non-vowel-shifter from Indianapolis. The students
rated both speakers as equal in likely intelligence, education, and trustworthiness.
They also didn't think they would have different attitudes about abortion (both
speakers were female). But they did think the Detroit speaker was more likely to be
in favor of affirmative action and gun control.

We can't really tell from these data whether shifted northern vowels are a direct
marker of liberal political ideology, in the same way that raised "ay" was a marker
of valuing the traditional Martha's Vineyard way of life. We'd need to look at not
just regional correlations with political views, but individual ones as well, just as
Labov did on Martha's Vineyard. Without finer-grained data, we don't know
whether northern vowels are most extreme for those with the most liberal values. It
could be that the relationship is less direct, with the vowels signaling allegiance to
local norms—of which a specific set of political leanings is one.

In the same way, we also don't know whether hearers are detecting a style of
speech that directly signals something about political attitudes. They could just be
inferring the likely attitudes of the speaker because they can identify where she's

222   Sold on Language

from, and they happen to know that Detroit tends to vote Democrat. In either case, however, the local accent is one more useful piece of information that can help identify people as belonging to a certain population with a characteristic set of values and attitudes.

Back in corporate America, McDonald's has recognized the power of language in creating a sense of special group membership. In 2009, the company chomped through some market research numbers, and found that New Englanders tended to prefer a fairly light blend of coffee. It made sense to serve coffee that catered to local taste—and to tie the coffee in with the local identity. McDonald's created the following commercial, designed to befuddle a dark-roast-guzzling Seattle coffee snob:

A young man in a plaid shirt walks up to his friend at a boat dock, bearing two cups of take-out coffee. "*Nice, McDonald's.*" says his friend. Plaid Guy pulls the coffee out of reach and proceeds to administer a quiz that his friend must pass before earning the beverage. He fires off a series of questions that come straight out of a "You know you're a New Englander when . . ." survey—all in a thick New England accent.

> "*Blizzard of . . .?*" (pronounced "blizzuhd")
>   "*'78.*"
> "*Newyorkachusetts.*"
>   "*Connecticut.*"
> "*Drinking fountain.*"
>   "*Bubbler.*" (pronounced "bubblah")
> "*Whadda they ask for at a packy?*"
>   "*ID.*"
> "*Sprinkles or jimmies?*"
>   "*Aw, jimmies.*"
> "*Five inches of snow.*"
>   "*A dusting.*"
> "*Manhattan chowder.*" (pronounced "chowdah")
>   "*Never heard of it.*"

Plaid Guy, apparently satisfied that his buddy has proven himself worthy of the coffee, hands it over. Only a red-blooded local would know about the blizzard of 1978 that unloaded two feet of snow on the area and killed dozens, that "Newyorkachusetts" is a term for the state of mixed baseball loyalties that divides the region into New York Yankees fans to the south and Boston Red Sox fans to the North, that a "packy" or "package store" is a shop that sells liquor and cigarettes, and that jimmies are the little candy sprinkles you put on your ice cream. Not to mention that the only kind of clam chowder you'd ever consider eating is the creamy New England variety—the tomato-based "Manhattan clam chowder" being beneath contempt.

A voice-over tells us, "*True* New Englanders take pride in their heritage—and their coffee. So McDonalds had Newman's Own create a new exclusive blend that you can only get here." The shirt, the vowels, the dropped "r" sounds, the quirky lexicon and the special coffee are all signs that you belong to the club.

Do You Speak *Prestige*?

Scientists and scholars get to enjoy a decent amount of respect. Most of the time, new scientific discoveries and ideas are happily consumed by an interested and appreciative public. (As in: Huh. North American dialects are getting *less* similar to each other, rather than converging. Who knew?) But every now and then, science comes up with a conclusion that some people just spit right out of their mouths. When that happens, it seems that no amount of empirical evidence or logical reasoning can persuade true disbelievers. Take evolution: to some, the idea that humans and chimpanzees have a common ancestor, and that both evolved from much less complex life forms just *feels* so wrong that there's simply no swallowing it. Scientists can twist themselves into knots explaining and presenting data and bullying with the sheer numbers of their consensus—and *still* might well run into *med students* who cheerfully learn the techniques of medicine, all while proclaiming disbelief in evolution.

Well, there must be something deeply threatening about the idea of change and evolution—especially as applied to humans—because what scientists have learned about how *languages* evolve meets with similar resistance. With language, just about everyone can stomach the idea that current English evolved from earlier versions that sounded very different. It's not that unpalatable to think that modern English "mutated" from earlier forms. What's hard to handle is the naturalness of *future* change. Can you make peace with a future English in which nouns have been promiscuously verbed, in which dose young kids are speakin English like dis, in which everybody loves their mother and nobody takes no guff from their kids, and in which *virtually* really does mean *truly* (and not *as if truly*) and *literally* means *as if literally* (and not *truly literally*)? It seems especially hard not to see these encroaching changes as evidence of lazy speech, sloppy thinking, and the death of logic. Hardest of all is letting go of the unscientific idea that there is a "right" versus a "wrong" way to use language.

The difference between "right" and "wrong" English boils down to a socio-political accident of history, nothing more. If African Americans in North America, or Scots in Britain, had become the dominant economic and political groups, "Black English" or a Scotch dialect would sound impeccable to everyone. A child speaking in BBC English would be chastised for sloppy language (and of course, *broadcasters* wouldn't be caught dead in the dialect). It feels mind-bending to visualize scenarios like this, because for us, education and success are enmeshed with certain dialects and not others. But it's not because these prestige dialects are intrinsically more subtle, or clear, or precise. It's because we've created certain associations between linguistic patterns and personal attributes. Here's an analogy: think of everything that's evoked by the word *apple*—the crisp freshness, the firm, spherical shape, the juiciness, the rosy healthiness of it. And yet, it's an accident of the universe that you happen to understand enough English so that the sounds in the word *apple* light up all these memories and sensations. For French speakers, the word *pomme* does the trick just as well. It would be a stretch to say that *apple* is inherently more apple-y than *pomme*, but your brain certainly treats them differently if you know English but not French. It simply can't disconnect the word from its learned associations. It's the same with dialects.

To knock today's prestige dialects off their pedestals, it helps to realize that they are really foul perversions of yesterday's prestige dialects. Or at least that's what *former* speakers of prestige would have you think. In his book *Word on the Street*, linguist John McWhorter points out that until the 1600s, *you* was only used to refer to two or more people. To address one person, you would say *thou* or *thee*, so unless you were a polygamist, you'd never say *I love you* to whoever you were married to. When things started to shift, and people began using *you* in the singular form, speakers of "correct" English got pretty riled up at this *obviously* illogical usage. McWhorter treats us to the rant of one English scholar:

> *Is he not a Novice and unmannerly, and an Ideot and a Fool, that speaks You to one, which is not to be spoken to a Singular, but to many? O Vulgar Professors and Teachers, that speak Plural, when they should Singular.*

The same scholar living today would probably spill some bile all over speakers who use *youse* or *y'all*—but *these* speakers are simply reverting *back* to the pre-1600s distinction between singular and plural second person. All of which makes it tricky to figure out which is the more "logical" usage. It's kind of like keeping track of "correct" hemlines.

Using double negatives is another symptom of not thinking straight: you're supposed to know that saying "I never loved no one" *really* means that you haven't had a single love-free moment. Well, explain it to the French. The folks over at the *Académie Française* are fairly uppity about correct language usage, and their noses get out of joint when they hear people using a *single* negative, when everyone knows it's proper to have two. Dropping the second negative is uncouth, and even orphans should be taught to say "Je **n**'ai **pas** de parents" and not "J'ai **pas** de parents."

Once you start comparing the gold standard for today's preferred English dialect to the prestige forms in other languages or other eras, it becomes impossible to justify absolute standards on their own merits of clarity or logic. It becomes apparent that like hemlines, the standard dialect reflects current practices and fashions, and one grammarian's sterling language is another one's tainted slang. Mind you, it's certainly possible to use *any* dialect—whether prestige or nonstandard—unclearly or illogically. I don't mean to claim that there's no difference between gorgeously virtuosic or fumblingly inarticulate uses of English. But it's not a matter of which dialect you use; it's what you do with it that counts.

Sounds of language as well as grammatical structures, can be exalted or stigmatized. To many speakers of English, a full-on twanging, lilting Southern dialect just does not sound as suave or as brainy as the posh English that comes out of the mouth of movie spy James Bond. Here are some entries from a Southern American English pronunciation guide affectionately compiled by linguist Robert Beard, who happens to be a native of North Carolina:

Agonna: *v. aux.* Future tense auxiliary, as in 'Ahm agonna gichew ifn yew don't quit bothern my dawg!'

Bard: *v.* Past tense of *borry*, as in 'My brother bard my pickup truck in never brung it back.'

Dissermember: *v.* Antonym of *member*, to forget: 'I planned to stop for a mess of butterbeans but I plum dissermembered.'

Retard: *v.* Past tense of *retar*. To have stopped working due to age 'Paw retard when he hit 95.'

Gubmint: *n.* A bureaucratic institution. Usage: 'Them gubmint boys shore is ignert.'

Ice: *n.* A bad word we can't define here, so we'll just give an example: How do you ketch a polar bar? Well, fust you digs a hole in the ice. Then you sprankle peas awl round it. Now, when the polar bar stops to take a pea, you kicks him in the ice hole.

The Geico car insurance company got playful with Southern stereotypes in its ad featuring a talking ditzy female *pothole* who slathers on a thick Southern drawl after blowing the tire of a car that's just driven over her: "Oh nooo! Yer tar's all flat 'n junk. Did ah do thay-ut? Here, let me git mah cilluler out 'n call yer wraicker. Aw, Sheewt. Ah got no phone. 'Cuz ahm a pothole?" The accent stands out even more starkly once you hear the buttoned-down voice-over of the company spokesman, uttering in bland, neutral, standard American English: "Accidents are bad. But Geico's good. Emergency Road Service."

But dialect stereotypes are fickle. Today's prestige accent could be tomorrow's local yokel talk and accents that people now work hard to shed may well be emulated in the future. Bill Labov documented this when he studied the relationship between speech and social class in New York City English. New York was first settled by a group of people who, like most of their English countryfolk, dropped the "r" sound after vowels, so that a word like *park* would be pronounced without the "r" sound. Until about World War II, the "r-less" variety of English was the prestige accent in the United States, and broadcasters and actors would learn to drop those "r"s—and sound just like Franklin Roosevelt. But after the war, Britain's reputation as a world power was sadly battered, and very abruptly, the preferred sound in America gave way to the "r-ful" kind that was spoken in most of North America. Much of the South, which had previously dropped its "r"s, now acquired them, and Labov found that even in New York, where the accent persisted, it became stigmatized. When people were conscious of their speech, or were trying to project a high-class image, the "r" sound was carefully articulated.

Labov tested this out in the field. He approached sales clerks at three department stores: the upscale Saks Fifth Avenue, the respectable Macy's, and the discount store S. Klein. He asked the clerks for directions to a particular department that he knew was located on the fourth floor, and listened for the presence of "r"s. Pretending not to hear the clerk's response, he asked again, with the goal of hearing what the clerks would say when they were conscious about producing careful, rather than causal, pronunciation. The fancier the store, the more "r"s showed up in the clerks' speech. And it was the Macy's staff that seemed most eager to "repair" their speech when first misunderstood, shifting from dropping their "r"s most of the time to producing it more often than not the second time. Nowadays, the "r-less" accent is even more closely associated with lower-class speech.

When people think of a neutral, unaccented variety of North American English, they typically think of the dialect that they most often hear on national news broadcasts. In fact, there is no "clean" or stripped accent—and over the years, North Americans have changed their views about the particular regional accent that best represents the continent as a whole. The Inland North used to have that privilege, before it got too radical with its Vowel Shift. Nowadays, the Midland region of the Midwest is the default dialect. But as economic clout gets concentrated in the Sun Belt, the "neutral" dialect shows signs of giving way to the Southern sounds. Southern accents are spreading more quickly throughout the United States than any other dialect. These days, that drawl is sounding decidedly less ditzy, and to many people, a Southern accent now evokes some of the more positive traits associated with the South, such as friendliness and personal warmth.

Geico clearly has a penchant for playing with nonstandard dialects. The talking pothole commercial ran as part of a series of "Talking Accident" ads, all of which feature animated objects with nonstandard dialects as the causes of accidents. In one, a tree branch with a Boston accent falls on a car's windshield; in another, an old car with a Brooklyn accent rear-ends another vehicle; and in yet another, a car backs into a steel pipe that has a Russian accent. *These* voices are funny. The disembodied voice in standard American English is the straight guy.

And even the well-loved Geico gecko who serves as the company mascot has undergone a dialect transplant: he started out with a classy BBC accent spoken by actor Kelsey Grammar. But Geico shifted away from this rather stuffy dialect, and eventually opted for a Cockney voice. Why the nonstandard dialect? The company was aiming for a "cheekier" more humorous effect, and it's hard to be funny when you're wearing such a straight-laced accent.

You Wouldn't Borrow Your Teacher's Clothes, So Why are You Wearing Her Vowels?

Of course, telling your twenty-something daughter to go ahead and feel free to sprinkle double negatives throughout her interview for that job as a law clerk would be about as responsible as advising her to show up in black lipstick, a leopard-print miniskirt, and fishnet stockings. People extract information from the dialect you slip on. But while they might *think* that the way you talk reflects how smart you are, or how much personal initiative you have, what they're often getting is a signal as to whether you're willing—and able—to fit in with a certain social group.

If you really want to study how language gets used as an accessory to create identity, it makes sense to spend some time in high school. That's exactly what linguist Penny Eckert did in the early 1980s, escaping her office on campus for the luxurious environment of Detroit area high schools in order to spend hundreds of hours talking to teenagers. Eckert describes how the social life of these teens was organized around two opposite poles of identity. On one side were the Jocks. This term didn't just refer to the sports players (who were called Sports Jocks). It grouped together all kids who were achievement-oriented, and bought into the notion that it was worth investing time and energy in the activities that were officially sanctioned and controlled by the school. These were the kids who attended school clubs, and ran for student council, often with the aim of padding their college applications. They socialized mostly with other kids at school. On the other side were the Burnouts, kids who saw high school as less about preparing them for their futures, and more as just time they had to put in before their real lives started. Their social lives centered around their local communities; many of them didn't expect to go to college, and if they did, they assumed it would be nearby. Since they didn't see themselves as competing at a national (let alone global) level, they saw less point in packing their schedules with official extra-curricular activities. Their networks were tightly local, and most of their meaningful socializing took place outside of school.

For these kids, the social categories encompassed all aspects of their lives. The two groups controlled different territories on the school grounds. Jocks congregated around school lockers, and in the cafeteria, while Burnouts took over the courtyard, which the Jocks took detours around. The two groups dressed differently and wore different make-up. And Eckert found that the leg-to-waist ratio of the kids' jeans correlated not only with the number of extra-curricular activities they were involved in, but also with the patterns of their vowels.

Remember that Detroit is smack in the midst of the Northern Cities Shift. In their schools, the Burnout kids were pulling the vowels to the most extreme positions as a way to broadcast their nonconformity with everything they associated with the standard, more "conservative" dialect. Shifting vowels was an act of rebellion. Now, clusters of Burnout kids didn't meet to coach each other on accents. The speech of the two groups split apart because kids unconsciously modeled their speech after people they admired. For the Jocks, this meant those who were successful within the adult establishment and for the Burnouts, it was those in their local social networks who most clearly advertised their decision not to play by those rules. It was basically an example of linguistic group polarization, even among people who were made to spend huge chunks of time at close quarters, exposed to each other's accents.

What Eckert found has been confirmed by a number of other studies: advances and innovation in local dialects are often driven by young people, often women, who resist conforming to many of the social norms around them. Over time, these rebellious acts of language can become incorporated into a broader sense of local identity and spread throughout a region, as is happening in the Northern Cities. Who knows what future shifts of economics and power may happen—the vowels of the 1980s Burnouts could well become the speech of future Jocks.

Detailed sociolinguistic studies like these show that there is an ongoing tension between prestige dialects and local ones. The task of choosing the right accent for a TV commercial or an automated voice system, or even a voice for a GPS navigation system can become quite complex. Do you go with a classy, smart-sounding prestige accent that inspires confidence and a sense of "having it together," or with a chummier local one? Studies like Eckert's show that there's more to prestige accents than meets the eye, and nonstandard dialects maybe have their own cachet.

Of course, many of the students in Eckert's study didn't fall neatly into either the Jock or Burnout categories. They referred to themselves as the In-Betweens, and had a foot in each world. This is true for many speakers of nonstandard dialects as well; they identify with more than one culture. To go along with this dual identity, they may easily control two dialects in the same way that people control two languages.

Have you ever been around bilingual family members where everyone speaks and understands both languages? Funny things can happen. They'll often slide in and out of their two languages, mixing them up in the middle of sentences. This seems really weird. Why in the world would anyone bother to switch languages mid-stream when the other person can understand both of them? Why not just stick with one language? Next time pay close attention. You might start to notice that there are subtle differences in what each language is used to express. In one family I know, family members tend to use English to explain abstract ideas and talk about what happened at work, but slip into the Czech they learned at home when they want to make jokes, tease each other, and express affection. These shifts, which linguists call code-switching, aren't deliberate. At one point, the mother and one of her daughters began shouting at each other in Czech in the presence of an English-only boyfriend. The boyfriend complained that they should use English so that everyone could understand. Mother and daughter turned around, insisting, "We *are* speaking English!" Apparently, fighting could only be done in Czech.

It's the same thing with dialects. Bi-dialectals tend to use the standard dialect when some formality or distance is called for. But when they want to play with their language, or be emotionally expressive, or show solidarity with their fellow nonstandard dialect-speakers, they shift away from the prestige forms.

John McWhorter points out that the reason many African Americans object to being portrayed as speakers of the nonstandard Black English dialect is that this tends to be an oversimplified caricature that doesn't capture the range of their linguistic versatility and control. Many blacks have mastered a subtle linguistic palette of standard and nonstandard forms, and code-switch with style and nuance. He describes how the actress Hattie McDaniel, who'd played the maid Mammy in *Gone with the Wind,* later managed to negotiate a clause in her contract for the radio sitcom Beulah that she would not have to speak in nonstandard dialect on the show. Hattie McDaniel was a perfect speaker of Black English, but as McWhorter writes:

> *What McDaniel used her clout to escape was having to utter entire paragraphs of socially implausible sentences like, 'I'se yo bestes' frien, Massa Tommy, an' when you goes off to de university don' you never forget who done take care of you and who it is can make de bes' peach cobbler dis side of de Mississippi' in the role of a suburban maid in a middle-class family.*

Controlling a nonstandard dialect gives its speakers some special tools for social expressiveness. It's a way of connecting with each other and drawing a circle of intimacy around a group that excludes outsiders. It's exactly the feeling that McDonald's was aiming for with its New England commercials.

But this intimate aspect of dialects makes them a very delicate thing to use in advertising. A dialect can be like a garish costume when used by an outsider or in the wrong context. Penny Eckert had the good sense to never lapse into Burnout talk when interviewing her subjects. If she had, they'd have dismissed her as a fake, and felt that she'd barged in where she wasn't invited.

Judging from some of the Internet reactions to the McDonald's New England commercials and its advertising aimed at Black and Latino communities, some people feel that the corporation has done just that. Reactions tend to be especially strong when nonstandard forms of grammar are used in an ad, more so than just the use of accent, which is probably less consciously perceived. For example, viewers seemed to hate a 2004 McDonald's ad in which a black woman stopped a flight attendant from taking away her chicken strips by saying "You better don't!"

Many posted comments that this was inappropriate and stereotyping. But it's interesting to see that, in walking the tightrope between using dialect to convey solidarity and appropriating someone else's language, commercials make their own attempts at something akin to code-switching. Nonstandard dialects appear in the mouths of fictional *characters*, and never in the mouth of the (entirely nonfictional) company itself, in the form of the disembodied voice-over. The Geico gecko can get away with a Cockney accent, and talking potholes and plaid-clad guys on boat docks can speak Southern or New Englandese. When the language "works" for consumers, it's because the ads are perceived as poking gentle fun at the stereotype, the way an insider might, rather than as mocking or socially invading a social group. But when the consumer is addressed by the very real company in the form of the voice-over, it's always in a standard dialect. The *company* itself can never pose as a buddy or a family member.

Who Do You Think You're Talking To?

Speakers of multiple dialects use different accents or different grammatical forms depending on who they're talking to. But even if you're limited to a single dialect, your language reflects the kind of relationship you have with your conversational partner. Ad copywriters are sensitive to this. For example, here's some text from a 1994 ad for Rolls Royce:

> *Among its refinements, one will discover the addition of a passenger side air bag, creating the safest Rolls Royce motor car ever. Equally notable is the most powerful engine of any Rolls Royce. And now, the assurance of free scheduled maintenance for three years and unlimited miles elevates an already rarefied experience. A milestone for those who have crafted it. And for those who attain it. Please call for the dealer nearest you.*

By contrast, in the same year, Toyota splashed the following quote from *4-Wheel & Off-Road* magazine at the top of its ad for the company's line of trucks: "Toyotas are darn near indestructible." The ad copy beneath it read:

> *The first thing you'll notice about tough Toyota Trucks like the 1994 4X2 Standard Bed DX probably isn't just how good they look, or the proven 2.4 liter engine. Not even the spacious cargo bed. It's that year in, year out, Toyotas have a habit of sticking round.*

> *We started selling trucks in America 30 years ago. And now over three million are still on the road. Still working hard. Still playing hard. And still satisfying owners...* *So if you're looking for another way to describe Toyota Trucks, try incomparable. Toyota Trucks. You just gotta love 'em.*

Lest you think that the copy in the Rolls Royce ad belongs to the bygone era of the mid-1990s, a look at the company's 2010 website suggests Rolls Royce is still using the same writers. The interior of the Rolls-Royce's Ghost sedan is described in the same hushed, resplendent language:

> *Inside, Ghost is refined and cosseting. Entering and exiting is both effortless and graceful – the low sill height means you step 'onto' rather than 'into' Ghost. The unique rear-hinged coach doors open to 83 degrees adding an extra sense of theatre for the rear passengers.*

> *Once inside, you are greeted by a simple yet contemporary interior with large expanses of soft full-grain leather, natural wood veneers and Blenheim wool carpets. The cashmere-blend roof lining adds to the sense of openness and space, enhanced by the optional Panorama sunroof.*

> *It's like being cocooned in your own convivial private sanctuary that leaves you relaxed and unruffled after the longest journey.*

When you have enough status to buy a Rolls Royce, you expect people to treat you—and *talk* to you—differently than they would a Toyota owner. The Toyota ad isn't written in any local dialect, but it has a completely different feel. Sentences are shorter. The text uses plenty of contractions like *you'll* and *you're* and *isn't*. The copywriters have ignored the pernickety advice of language style experts, and have begun sentences begin with a*nd*, and used *like* instead of *such as*. The ad uses basic common words like *working hard*, *good* and *tough*, and *started* instead of *began*. Colloquialisms like *darn near* and *have a habit of sticking around* and *you just gotta love 'em* are sprinkled throughout. A prospective Rolls Royce buyer might feel disrespected.

It's not that the Rolls Royce buyer goes around sounding like a luxury car ad. He might talk (or send emails) that sound just like the Toyota ad to his own drinking buddies. But he would expect a car salesman (or company) to show a bit more deference (note the "*please* call" in the 1994 Rolls Royce ad). Using Rolls Royce language is like breaking out the fine china. It would be pretentious to bring it out for a family barbecue, but an important client would feel slighted if you served dinner on paper plates. The Rolls ad's language sounds expensive. Actually, it *is* expensive. In terms of cognitive resources, it takes more brain power to pull out words like *cosseting* and *convivial* from your mental lexicon, to build complex sentences with multiple clauses, and to carefully enunciate all your words (none of this *you gotta love 'em* stuff). These formalities make up a certain linguistic style—or a *register*, as it's referred to by linguists—that is used when you're talking with someone of higher social status than you (or to someone you don't know, before you've fully nailed down which of you is of the higher status). It implicitly sends the signal that you think they're worth the cognitive trouble of using more complex forms.

Much of what we think of as politeness comes down to linguistic signals that are given out by people lower on the status ladder than the person they're talking to. Using a more formal register is part of it. Another big part of being "polite" is beating around the bush and talking indirectly, especially when you're trying to get the other person to do something or provide some information. If you feel entitled to make that demand, go ahead and use a direct form. But if you're trying to signal that you're making a request or suggesting an action to which you have no divine right, it might be best to wrap some shiny linguistic paper around it. For example, if you're trying to extract Jane's phone number from a mutual acquaintance, here are some of your linguistic options:

> *Gimme Jane's number.*
> *Please give me Jane's phone number.*
> *Could you please give me Jane's telephone number?*
> *Do you know Jane's telephone number?*
> *Would you happen to know Jane's telephone number?*
> *I don't suppose you'd happen to know Jane's telephone number.*
> *I would really appreciate having Jane's telephone number.*
> *I would really like to call Jane, but I unfortunately, I don't have her telephone number.*

Notice that not only do you add more linguistic *stuff* as you go up the politeness scale, but that it really does serve the function of wrapping paper: it's not just decorative, but manages to artfully "hide" the fact that you're making a request. In the last example, the request for information is so cleverly disguised that you leave the other person completely free to pretend they hadn't noticed it was a request at all. If they do pass on Jane's number, it can all be done under the pretense that it was their idea to do so all along, and that you would never be so presumptuous as to ask them for that small favor.[6]

You may have noticed that it's generally the ads for the more downscale products that tend to use language like: *Act now! Go visit your dealer! Order yours today! Don't miss this great opportunity!* This kind of language boldly uses verbs in their imperative form, as issuing a command. And companies that use imperatives in their taglines are usually not aiming to sound like your butler (Apple: *Think Different.* Ford: *Drive One.* Wal-Mart: *Save Money. Live Better*). But using imperative linguistic forms seems a bit forward for the really upmarket ads. So, what to do in the part of the ad where you're trying to get the consumer to call a

---

[6] Indeed, the general rule of thumb is that for maximal politeness, speakers should use indirect forms that disguise the request, hearers should act as if the speaker had done something other than make a request—all the while complying with it. For example, if someone says "I don't suppose you'd happen to know Jane's telephone number," you wouldn't just tell them what it is. You would first say: "Actually, I do know." As if they'd asked about the state of your *knowledge*.

specific toll-free number or visit a website? Toyota can just come out and say "call (222-555-4545), or visit ourwebsite.com." But this would be inappropriate for the ads in *Fortune* magazine. Fortunately, there are several solutions to this sticky social dilemma:

1. Use the magic word:
   Please call for the dealer nearest you. (in the above ad for Rolls Royce)

2. Get downright obsequious:
   May we help you develop your plan? Visit ourwebsite.com *or call 222-555-4545.* (ad for Cessna aircraft, touting its various private ownership plans, in *Fortune* magazine)

3. Entirely leave off the pesky imperative verb:
   *For private appointments: 222-555-4545.*ourwebsite.com. (ad for Ralph Lauren Stirrup Watch, in *Forbes*)

4. The harsh effect of the imperative verb can also be softened by burying it in the middle of the sentence, where it's hanging onto the edges of your attentional spotlight rather than smack in the middle of it. Notice that the entreaty in the Unum ad sounds subtly more polite than the one from Christmas Seals:
   To learn more about the Simply Unum Solution, call your broker, Unum representative or visit ourwebsite.com. (ad for the Unum Group, in *Fortune* magazine)
   *Go to*ourwebsite.com*to learn more.* (ad for Christmas Seals by the American Lung Association, in *Fortune* magazine)

By the way, note the extreme courtesy in the Cessna ad above, aimed at company executives. It's a tad different from another ad by Cessna in which the company recruited Cessna *pilots* to help transport athletes to the 2010 Special Olympics. In the ad targeting the pilots, there's no "may we help you," not even a "please" slapped onto the "call 222-555-4545." But the pilots at least warranted enough deference to get the writers to slide the imperative further downstream and away from the jarring position at the front of the sentence: "For more information, or to register, visit ourwebsite.com or call 222-555-4545."

If you're speaking to your betters, you also probably want to be a touch delicate about pointing out when they have spinach stuck between their teeth, toilet paper dragging behind their shoe, or some cosmetic inadequacy that needs to be addressed with the right shampoo or wrinkle cream. You might, for instance, suggest that they use your product to "maintain a smooth complexion" rather than improve their currently crappy one. In one department store, I found two brands of shampoo with somewhat different labeling. One identified itself as being "for thick hair full of body" and the other as being "for fine limp hair." Despite their identical syntactic forms, I'm guessing that the first shampoo wasn't offering to solve your thick hair problem, and the second wasn't promising to deliver fine limp hair. And I suspect *you* can guess which one was more expensive. By a lot.

If you're shopping for make-up, you can expect to shell out about two to four times as much for Estée Lauder products as you would for Cover Girl cosmetics. At Estée Lauder, your well-toned pocketbook will buy you (in addition to a French brand name) flattering phrases like these, culled from the company's website:

> *Reveal your beautiful skin today*
> *. . . if you want to protect your skin so you can look younger longer*
> *Bring back vibrancy*
> *Resist the look of aging* (since you've managed to keep it at bay so far).

And when one really must mention the customer's shortcomings, it's done in a somewhat circumspect manner: "to dramatically reduce the look of lines and wrinkles." Cover Girl, on the other hand is a bit more blunt and graphic, letting you know that one of its products will help you deal with "even severe dark circles." (Gee, do they really look *that* bad? Only a friend would tell you so.) And at Cover Girl, not only do you have the "look" of dark circles and wrinkles—you actually *have* them too. Instead of promising to "reveal" your flawless beauty, Cover Girl tells it like it is and admits its products are there to "conceal dark circles" and "cover imperfections and under-eye circles." But notice that not even Cover Girl uses the language of presupposition to tell you that its products will "conceal *your* dark circles." That'd be hitting it just a bit too close to home.

Both companies post videos giving you helpful tips on applying their make-up. Cover Girl introduces you to a pretty-but-not-too-beautiful make-up artist who addresses you, the viewer, directly and refers to the older client she is making up in the video by her first name. The video is peppered with friendly conversational language like "okay," "awesome" and "gonna." At Estée Lauder, the client is addressed by a faceless voice-over while the make-up artist—whose face is never shown—does her work silently. The language is scripted, formal, and impeccably pronounced. There is a respectful distance from the client.

But politeness is a funny thing. Using more formal language between equals can be just as insulting as using overly intimate and informal language to a social superior. More formal registers communicate a distance, a certain barrier between the speaker and hearer. If you talk to your friend the way you would to the CEO of your company, it can feel like a rejection of the relationship you have. Your friend, rebuffed, may say "Hey. It's *me* you're talking to."

Recently, when Toyota decided to market its workhorse Corolla sedan by giving it a touch more prestige, it was in a bind. It couldn't use Rolls Royce copy with a straight face anymore than your drinking pal could. Toyota's solution? Mimic the style and load on the gilded images while firmly inserting tongue in cheek:

A quiet place to revel in your entitlement
The day you purchase the 2009 Corolla is the day you'll start living the dream. Being the grand fromage in high society is indeed a lot to think about, hence the tranquil interior is the perfect place to contemplate your domination of the latest cotillion. This crowning achievement is the result of an acoustic noise-reducing front windshield designed to help keep clamor and peons out and thoughts of grandeur in.

Speaking Truth to Power

The language of status gets even more complicated. Using it implies not just that you're aware that you're addressing someone higher on the pecking order; it also shows that you know that *they* are aware of it, and that they appreciate your acknowledging it. If this whole discussion about status and social superiority makes you squirm uncomfortably, Rolls Royce language may be lost on you, even if you can easily afford one. In fact, it may even subtly offend you, because it seems to suggest you're the kind of person who enjoys lording it over others. (And hence the irony in the Corolla ad.)

Ads for similar products and services communicate quite different relationships and attitudes about status. Have a look at the following pair of ads, each offering retirement planning advice, and showing an exquisite sensitivity to status language. One of them shows a photo of a couple of grinning middle-aged men paddling in a raft. Some statistics printed beside the photo make it clear who's being targeted.

Men who will become vice presidents this year: 13 442
Who will retire before age 60: 940
And reconnect with their younger brother: 83
While drifting down the Amazon: 1

The body of the ad, while not as opulent as the Rolls Royce copy, has the proper formality of someone who knows his place:

By developing a deeper understanding of who you are and where you want to go, your advisor can create a long-term plan to make your goals a reality. With a unique culture of independence, your Raymond James advisor has the complete freedom to offer unbiased financial advice. It's all focused on creating a personalized financial plan to fit your idea of retirement, no matter when you want that journey to begin.
(ad for Raymond James & Associates, in *Fortune* magazine)

Reading this ad, you don't get the sense that your financial advisor will start the meeting off by swapping raunchy jokes with you. But based on the following ad, you might expect a slightly more egalitarian interaction with your advisor.

> *Ready for whatever the economy throws at you? Now is a good time to know THE PRINCIPAL. So you need to be ready with the right financial solutions. With The Principal, you have a wide range of investment options—from mutual funds and annuities to CDs and more. Along with easy-to-use financial tools to help you figure out your best game plan.*
> (ad for The Principal Financial Group, in *Fortune* magazine)

This ad might resonate with you if you'd rather your financial advisor didn't act like your servant, and in fact, the text later on makes it clear that he won't: "And since we're one of the nation's retirement leaders, you'll be more comfortable knowing you have a strong, dependable partner."

I've noticed that in magazines like *Fortune* or *Forbes*, ads that appear to target executives and financial officers tend to use a more formal register than those that target higher-ups who make technical decisions. Ads for technically oriented services tend to use pretty relaxed prose, and even naked imperatives. I suspect that when it comes to feelings about hierarchy and status, there's a different culture among technically trained hotshots than ones who have come out of business schools. I somehow get the feeling that a journalist might talk in different ways to, say, Bill Gates and Warren Buffet (and since Buffet had pledged to give 85% of his fortune to the Gates Foundation, it makes you wonder what language Bill Gates will use to thank him).

Individuals and subcultures may fall back on social norms that provide some guidance as to how overtly differences in status should be acknowledged. This is true of entire nations as well, though people within any given country will vary a great deal. Sometimes, cultural norms about status language can have deadly consequences.

In his book *Outliers*, Malcolm Gladwell explores why the airline Korean Air kept dropping its planes. Between 1988 and 1998, Korean Air had a crash rate seventeen times that of the U.S.-based United Airlines. Things got so bad that the U.S. Army (not known for being wussy) wouldn't allow its personnel to fly with the airline. Canadian officials warned that if things continued, they would bar the airline from flying over or landing in Canada.

One of the airline's biggest problems, it turned out, was status language. Psychologists who study differences across cultures have identified several important dimensions that vary across culture, and one of these is the dimension of power distance. People from high power distance cultures expect there to be a wide gap between the society's elite and its subordinates. People are expected to behave in ways that show their awareness of their particular place in the power hierarchy. But low power distance countries (like Sweden, New Zealand, and Canada) tend to bristle at these distinctions. They're not as likely to put up with big differences in pay or treatment between the CEO of a company and its lowest-paid employees. And even those low on the totem pole expect that they should have a voice and be listened to.

When psychologists looked closely at international pilots, they found that Korean pilots ranked second in terms of power distance, just behind Brazil.[7] This matters, because, as we've seen, the language of status dictates that you speak to your superiors indirectly. Remember the "politeness" ladder involved in asking for Jane's phone number? Well, suppose you're an inferior co-pilot speaking to your pilot, who outranks you. It's become apparent to you that unless the pilot changes course immediately, the plane he's about to land will miss the runway. Problem is, your socially superior pilot seems oblivious to this—maybe he's been up too late, and the lousy weather has him stressed out and exhausted. Consulting your communicative menu, you have the following options, climbing from the bottom of the politeness hierarchy to the top:

Turn 30 degrees right.
I think we need to deviate right about now.
Let's go around the weather.
Which direction would you like to deviate?
I think it would be wise to turn left or right.
That return at 25 miles looks mean.

Sound familiar? You'll notice that by far the most efficient form of communication, in sheer economic terms, is the brief direct command—the rudest option. As you go up the ladder, there are more linguistic units to process, and the intent of the speaker becomes more and more opaque. This means that the *most* polite forms are also those that take the most brain power to decode.

When communication scientists Ute Fischer and Judith Orasanu looked at how co-pilots and pilots would communicate with each other, they found that pilots tended to issue commands, while co-pilots used the most polite hinting strategies more often than the less deferential more direct ones, even in high-risk situations. This might explain the bizarre statistic that more plane crashes happen when the *pilot* is flying than when the less experienced co-pilot is at the helm. The pilot has no compunctions about efficiently barking orders at his first officer when something goes wrong.

Dipping into black box data to retrieve the interactions between pilots and co-pilots can reveal the tragic consequences of too much politeness. For example, on August 5, 1997, Korean Air flight 801 crashed while the pilot was attempting to

---

[7] Brazil is the country that inspired the word *Brazilification*, which has been used in journalistic circles to refer to a widening gap between rich and poor. As in: *The past few decades have seen the growing Brazilification of North America, as incomes between the top and bottom earners have pulled apart.*

execute a visual landing during terrible weather. The co-pilot chose to express his concern about the pilot's landing strategy by offering up the comment: "The weather radar has helped us a lot." Admittedly, this is more polite than "Turn the weather radar on or you'll crash the plane." But the point was lost on the stressed-out pilot. He said, distractedly, "Yes, they are very useful." Moments later, the plane slammed into the side of a hill.

Would You Let Your Computer Talk to You Like That?

As the future bears down on us, communicative interactions with machines will make up a bigger and bigger part of our lives. These days, our car navigation systems tell us where to go, computers make our airline bookings for us, help us with our banking, and take our shopping orders over the phone. And designers of voice generation and speech recognition systems promise that within a few years, we won't have to type, or push buttons—we'll just chat with our machines. All of which raises the question of *how* they will talk to us.

Stanford University communications expert Clifford Nass studies the intimate relationships between humans and computers and spends a lot of time thinking about how people resonate to aspects of voice, computer voices included. He's found that we human beings are so profoundly social that, given the slightest excuse, we can't help treating machines like fellow humans. Very basic cues—like the mere use of language—get us behaving as if we were talking with a real person. People (and not just Canadian people) will *apologize* to an automated voice system. And they apply the full force of their unconscious stereotypes to computer voices. You know how women often complain that if they make a suggestion at a board meeting, it will be ignored, but as soon as a man says the same thing, everyone thinks it's a fantastic idea? Well, they're not imagining it. And Nass found that computers too are the victims of gender stereotyping; people judge male com-puter-generated voices to be more credible than female ones—unless they are discussing sewing, or women's rights.

It's not that the people Nass tested didn't realize they were hearing machines talking. There's no doubt that they did. But humans are "voice-activated" creatures, and the social stereotypes we've learned to associate with vocal cues automatically kick in. The effect is kind of like the stubborn Mueller-Lyre illusion in which the two lines *look* to be of different lengths even though they're identical. When you're looking at them, you're not fooled for one second that you're seeing anything but a two-dimensional drawing. But this certainty isn't enough to change the way your visual system interprets the visual cues, based on its experience with *three*-dimensional space. It's the same thing with a computer-generated voice. Your auditory system automatically endows the voice with a full, three-dimen-sional human identity.

As with our human companions, we tend to want to hang out with computers that are just like us. Nass has found that people trust a computer more when it talks in the same accent as they do. In one study, American subjects interacted with a computer-generated voice that provided information about travel to Sweden. You might think that someone who talks like a Swede would know more about that country's tourist attractions. But in fact, the subjects were somewhat more leery of the machine with the Swedish accent than the American one.

Not only that, but people are drawn to computers with similar *personalities*. With better living through speech synthesis, people will be able to surround themselves with like-minded neighbors in their virtual neighborhoods as well as in their physical ones. In case you're wondering how to alter a computer's personality, Nass will tell you that it's a trivial matter of tweaking a few speech parameters. To create an extroverted computer voice, you simply dial up the volume, pitch, and speech rate, and increase the pitch range (the difference between the highest and lowest pitches). More contemplative computer voices speak more slowly, quietly, and using a lower-pitched more monotone voice. Apparently, it's so easy to recognize and produce the voice characteristics linked with personality, that in theory, an automated voice system might be programmed to match the user's level of gregariousness after a few minutes of interaction. Nass warns, though, that it's a bit off-putting if the shy, bookish voice that answered your call suddenly morphs into Miss Congeniality. A better strategy might be for the original voice to "pass on" the caller ("I'm going to turn you over to Pamela now"), once the user's personality has been typed.

If people take care not to insult computer voices and actually apologize to them for their own rude behavior, it only stands to reason that they expect the machine to reciprocate by respecting social niceties as well. This creates an enormously complex problem for computer voice designers. How deferential should the computer be?

Here again, culture matters. When BMW first rolled out its in-car navigation system to its German customers, it was a disaster that ended up in a product recall. The system worked beautifully; it was able to accurately pinpoint the car's location, and had an extensive databank that contained information about almost any street address. There was a little glitch that turned out to be a huge problem for the mostly male drivers of BMW vehicles: the navigation system was female. The German drivers simply could not trust directions given by a woman. The relationship with the driver was all wrong.

BMW bowed to this rather chauvinistic objection, and the company recruited Clifford Nass to help design its new navigation voice. Nass approached the problem as a complex issue of *casting* the right voice. First the company had to decide *who* should be in the imaginary passenger seat with the driver. Then, Nass would create a voice to match that persona. One option was to make the system sound like a German engineer. Since the voice interface also provided mechanical warnings ("Your wiper fluid is low") as well as safety information ("There is a pedestrian crossing 0.5 miles ahead"), this loud and authoritative persona might give the computer voice some credibility that the female one apparently lacked. But this voice character was deemed *too* competent—it might intimidate the driver and make him feel inadequate. A submissive chauffeur voice was ruled out, because BMW drivers don't want to feel that someone else is in charge of their car—*they* want to feel in control of the machine. A friendly "sidekick" personality was dismissed on grounds that it didn't exude *enough* competence. What was really needed was someone who accepts that the driver is in control, but is knowledgeable and able to help if needed. Ahhh, a *co-pilot*. The final product was a voice that was fairly deep in pitch with a tight pitch range (suggesting controlled emotion), medium in volume (confident but not alarming), used fairly terse language, and issued statements rather than commands (as a pilot would) or questions (as a chauffeur would). Luckily, BMW was able to avoid the kinds of co-pilot catastrophes that dogged Korean Air. The fact that German culture is quite nonhierarchical freed up the BMW co-pilot voice from having to dispense information in the form of veiled hints.

Back to Babel

The twentieth century should have been the century that unified humanity. The first audio transmission by radio took place in 1900. In 1920, Bell Labs first transmitted moving images on a television screen by cable. In 1936, the Olympic Games in Munich were broadcast on TV for the first time. TV commercial broadcasting—and TV commercials—burst onto the American public in 1941, a couple of years after the BBC broadcast the first sci-fi show based on a play by Karel Capek in which the word *robot* was used for the first time. The first televised U.S. presidential debate between Nixon and Kennedy took place in 1960. Since then, some of the most historic moments in the world were captured on film and broadcast around the world on TV: Martin Luther King Jr.'s "I Have a Dream" speech and JFK's assassination in 1963, Neil Armstrong's landing on the moon in 1969, the breaking down of the Berlin Wall in 1989, Nelson Mandela's release from prison in 1990, and the terrorist attacks on New York City on September 11, 2001. Since the dawn of television, people have devoted or sacrificed more and more of their waking hours watching TV, and by 2008, the *average* number of hours in front of the screen was 151 per month.

In the biblical story of the tower of Babel, humans are punished for their arrogant attempt to build a tower that reaches heaven; the tower is destroyed, and humans find themselves all speaking different languages, and being unable to communicate with each other. But you'd expect that there'd be a reversal of the Babel story once humanity started erecting communication towers that sent the *same* language into millions of individual homes. You'd expect especially that differences across the regional dialects of a heavily broadcast language like English would give way to a uniform standard. The fact that it hasn't worked out that way is causing linguists to look at language in a new light. Language, it turns out, is not just a tool for communicating ideas and knowledge; it's also a tool for announcing what makes us different from our neighbors.

Nowadays, there's less and less "mass" in mass communication. Though people are watching more television, the number of viewers for any one program is getting smaller as TV networks breed like rabbits. In 1960, it was possible to reach 80% of American women with a spot aired simultaneously on NBC, CBS, and ABC. By 2004, according to a *Business Week* article, a company would have had to buy spots on a hundred channels to reach the same number of female eyeballs. Once-venerable national papers are gasping for breath while readers track blogs instead of front-page headlines. Technology, which once made it possible to reach millions, now makes it possible to reach those few that are deeply interested. And individuals have an unprecedented choice to settle into physical and virtual communities that reflect their own lifestyle, values, and attitudes.

As the media splinters into smaller and smaller segments, it's hard to imagine that the result will be anything but greater fragmentation of the social landscape. In marketing, the Holy Grail is "one-to-one marketing," in which a company will know enough about individual consumers to target them with messages that align with what they buy, where they eat, how they talk, and even how they think. Reams of data about consumers' Internet behavior—which websites they visit, how much time they spend there, and what they choose to buy—are collected to help companies predict which users will be most receptive to their messages. It's not just shopping behavior that's potentially useful to advertisers, but information from online surveys and quizzes about personality traits and attitudes, the political orientation of blogs that we read, and once we start *talking* to our computers, even the accent we produce.[8]

---

[8] A lot of current work in psychology focuses on individual differences in how people process information. For example, people vary quite a bit in terms of how likely they are to think deeply about the content of a message and evaluate it on its merits. This trait is captured by a standardized questionnaire called the "Need for Cognition" scale. It's been reliably found that people who have a high "Need for Cognition" are better able to distinguish between strong and weak persuasive arguments. People who score lower on this scale are more likely to think "peripherally" and rely on cues such as whether the person doing the persuading is an "expert." It's not hard to imagine that different messages could be crafted based on information gathered about a person's cognitive style on Internet personality quizzes.

Marketers might also like to know about individuals' specific patterns of associations, given that automatic associations have been shown to drive behavior. Since people might have very different sets of associations, the same "priming" stimulus could well lead to different behavior. Researchers Christian Wheeler and Jonah Berger have indeed found different priming effects for men versus women, and introverts versus extroverts, and suggest that marketers will need to accurately segment their audiences if they want to get the best results from nonconscious priming.

To hear the new "behavioral targeting" industry talk about it, all this is going to result in informative and less invasive advertising. The logic is this: If advertisers can reach consumers with ads that they'll *want* to read or hear, there's less need for the attention-grabbing tactics described in Chapter 3, and maybe even room for ads that are richer in information and rely less on merely making an impression. And possibly fewer ads hurled at the consumer. Having targeted ads online, after all, is not all that different from having a local shopkeeper, who knows you well enough to be able to suggest new products that might be of special interest to you.

Fair enough. But helpful suggestions are one thing. It would be quite another if your friendly shopkeeper started studying your speech patterns to mimic your accent, or began asking other shops what you bought there, or peered at the stack of library books you had with you to see what you were planning to read before going to bed, or called your pharmacist to find out what medications you were taking. Sure, his suggestions would be more "helpful" as a result, but you'd probably think of the whole thing as a bit on the creepy side. Advantages to the consumer have to be weighed alongside of their privacy preferences.

But privacy issues aside, this slicing and dicing of communication has some potential consequences that are worth thinking about. For people like Cass Sunstein, who worries about the effects of group polarization, the concern is that it makes it easier and easier for groups who hold very different opinions to be blissfully unaware of each other, and never have to engage with each other. Sunstein points out that there can be upsides to group polarization. It can inject a collection of individuals with the necessary passion to actually produce badly needed change—think of the civil-rights movement, for example. But Sunstein also argues that the dangers of group polarization can only be prevented in a society that allows for public spaces in which opposing viewpoints can be aired and debated. For example, Sunstein notes that the U.S. Supreme Court ruled that people are allowed to stand on a street corner or in a park and announce any opinion they might hold; their right to do this is enshrined by law. The reasoning behind this is that it's important for people of all opinions to be exposed to ideas that are not their own. So, setting aside public spaces where these kinds of encounters might happen dampens some of the worst risks of extremism within groups. It puts limits on the possibility of self-segregation.

But nowadays opportunities for self-segregation are almost boundless. Instead of going out to the street corner to buy the paper (the same paper read by most of your fellow city dwellers, containing "letters to the editor" from a cross-section of the public), and then reading the paper in the park, you're far more likely to get your news from your favorite personal news source online. If you lean politically to the right, chances are you're not spending too much time on left-wing news sites and blogs. Who needs that kind of assault on the blood pressure? When people become insular, it can create the conditions for unproductive and even dangerous polarization. But audience targeting requires segmented media outlets to reach its intended group. By driving the structure of media communications, the practice may inadvertently contribute to these unhealthy conditions.

Audience targeting is not just about where advertisers talk to you, but also how they talk to you. In recruiting visible (and audible) symbols of social group identity, they play a role in widening the gap among social groups. Those in the advertising industry object to charges like this. They point out that they wouldn't *be* using social markers like accent or stereotypical characters if people didn't already respond to them with pre-formed categories. That's certainly true. And here, advertisers are caught in a bind: bucking stereotypes makes advertising less effective, because as Clifford Nass and his colleagues have shown, people respond badly to any perceived incongruity. People are put off if the gender or accent of a voice goes against the grain of people's expectations. Imagine Warren Buffet with a working class Jersey accent for instance. But it's wishful thinking to believe that by using characteristics that mirror people's stereotypes, advertising is leaving no mark. That'd be like saying, let's take Pavlov's dogs, who've been taught to associate a ringing bell with dinner after, say, 10 bell-ringing episodes. Clearly, adding another 100 bell-ringing episodes isn't going to change anything, right? It may not make the dog drool more profusely, but it sure will make it harder for the dog to learn a new trick and associate dinner with the sound of a buzzer instead.

So, when BMW recalled its car because drivers couldn't abide the female voice navigation system, in one sense, it was just giving its customers what they wanted. Good companies are supposed to do this, and no one could fault BMW. But at another level, it seems a lost opportunity. Maybe, if BMW's "co-pilot" voice had been female, over time, drivers would have been better able to imagine women as competent holders of positions of authority. Maybe they would even interact more productively with that woman project manager at the office. Or promote a junior female colleague to "co-pilot" status.

What's more, the current climate of targeted marketing has the potential to not just reinforce social divisions, but also to create them. When companies like Subaru or Apple diligently do their market research, and gear all their design and advertising at defining the "Subaru driver" or "Mac user," each with their specific attitudes, consumption patterns, speech patterns, and ideology, new social categories are born. After all, what Mac owner, after watching those wonderfully entertaining ads of the cool, young, up-and-coming Mac squaring off against the conservative, dorkily dressed, insecure, buffoonish PC—well, how could he suppress the slightest judgmental smugness from leaking out in the direction of his PC-owning colleague?

8

The Politics of Choice

Against Democracy

Plato, revered by Western culture as one of its great thinkers, was not exactly a cheerleader for democracy. In the writings that make up Plato's *Republic*, he portrayed ordinary citizens as vulnerable to social fads, dazzled by tricks of persuasion, and entirely unequipped with the knowledge or wisdom to discern what's best for themselves, let alone what's good for society. As Plato saw it, it was dangerous to let the corruptible majority make the really important decisions. And you certainly couldn't leave the ruling to those who were born into wealth and privilege—their main motives were bound to revolve around preserving power for themselves. The only people really fit to govern were those who devoted their lives to contemplating truth and honing their ability to reason without bias. The logical conclusion: philosophers should be kings. They'd be reluctant to do it, of course, since it was knowledge, and not power that drove them (that is, if they were the right sort of philosopher in the first place). But they'd agree, knowing it was the only way to bring about a good and just society.

We're used to thinking of democracy as a fairly recent invention of humanity, the pinnacle of civilization's long evolution. But Plato's doubts weren't based on speculating about what democracy *might* be like in the abstract, if it ever came about. They came as a result of actually living in the democratic society of ancient Athens, which prided itself as serving as a model for all other societies. Democratic Athens, after all, was the exceptional society whose achievements came from unleashing the creative potential of individuals who were free to live their lives as they chose, liberated from mindless obedience to traditions or the decrees of a ruling elite. Plato for one, was not entirely enamored of the Athenian democracy experiment.

No doubt, Plato was traumatized by seeing democratic Athens murder his teacher Socrates (for voicing dissent, of all things). From a more modern vantage

Sold on Language: How Advertisers Talk to You and What This Says About You. By Julie Sedivy and Greg Carlson
© 2011 John Wiley & Sons Ltd.

point, some of the great atrocities of the twentieth century have been brought about by majority rule, either directly or indirectly: Hitler was elected by democratic vote, as was the Serbian leader Slobodan Milošević, and the Rwandan genocide was sparked when the Hutu majority was incited to violence against the Tutsi minority. For Plato, these examples wouldn't be historically unique aberrations of an otherwise virtuous political system. They'd be evidence of the fundamental wrong-headedness of democracy.

One of Plato's issues with democracy was that it takes the focus away from good leadership and puts the emphasis on skilled persuasion instead. Because persuasion is more concerned with appearance than with truth, a skilled persuader can sway minds towards a bad idea just as easily as towards a good one. And for that matter, the people who will be most convinced by flawed arguments coming out of the honeyed mouth of a smooth persuader are those whose knowledge is shaky in the first place. So it's in the interest of someone with a fundamentally weak proposal to target most heavily those who will be less likely to notice the problems with it.[1] In the end, the worry is that by making choice freely available to everyone, there's no way to tilt the balance in favor of good leadership over poor leadership.

Whether or not you have any reservations about unbridled democracy, though, you'd likely view what Plato proposed in its place as belonging more in the category of dystopian nightmare than that of just society. Here are some of the features of what Plato conceived of as the good society: The philosopher-king would have a heavy hand in censoring poetry and art, since these could easily distort people's desires and cause them to want things that weren't good for them. (You can imagine what Plato would say about modern forms of advertising.) Instead, people's desires would be shaped by a carefully controlled universal education system (designed by philosophers of course.) Family structure would be cast aside, as it causes people to feel irrational love for some children, with disregard for others. Instead, couples would be chosen by the leaders on the basis of their suitability as breeding partners, and all children would be raised jointly by society. Private property would be abolished. People would be assigned into occupations by their wise rulers, based on their innate talents. To make this sorting more palatable to them, they'd be told, in the form of a "noble lie," that there were actually three different species of human beings, each suited for different tasks, and that only the leaders could tell for sure what type of human each individual was.

---

[1] Joseph Goebbels (Hitler's Minister of Propaganda) was pretty blunt about all this: "There was no point in seeking to convert the intellectuals. For intellectuals would never be converted and would anyway always yield to the stronger, and this will always be 'the man in the street'. Arguments must therefore be crude, clear, and forcible, and appeal to emotions and instincts, not the intellect. Truth is unimportant and entirely subordinate to tactics and psychology."

In short, the work comes off as an assault on free speech, private property, freedom of expression, personal love, and an all-around condemnation of freedom of choice. Any takers?

It's a bit hard to warm to these ideas, to say the least. They bring to mind Aldous Huxley's *Brave New World*, or Pol Pot's horrific experiments in social engineering. In fact, they're so repugnant that modern admirers of Plato—struggling to reconcile such totalitarian notions with his brilliant contributions to the birthing of Western philosophy, science and logic—have suggested that his description of a just society in the *Republic* was intended metaphorically, or ironically, or was meant to lead the reader to the opposite conclusion.

The philosopher Karl Popper, one of the most ardent modern defenders of liberal democracy, saw this dodge as a blatant whitewashing of Plato. Pulling no punches, Popper declared Plato an enemy of the open and free society, lumping him together with Hegel and Marx as the ancestors of twentieth-century totalitarianism. His writings, according to Popper, should be dismissed as the insecurities of someone who had trouble coping with the challenges of a free, dynamic, pluralistic society, and who quite possibly harbored vain fantasies of becoming an all-powerful philosopher-king himself.

And yet. There's something in Plato's detailed and thoughtful analysis of human nature and the consequences of free choice that's, well . . . not crazy. Contemporary philosopher Martha Nussbaum points out that Plato's political proposals were not just a *manifesto*. They were conclusions to *arguments*— arguments that managed to accurately pinpoint some disturbing but true aspects of human nature. So, if these arguments are worth taking seriously, then as Nussbaum notes, "we are under heavy pressure to show to ourselves and to others why the repellant conclusions should not be drawn. That is why Plato has been over the centuries the best friend democracy could have had: for he challenges it to know, and to justify itself."

What Do We Really Want?

Modern democracies and free market economies are based on a fundamental disagreement with Plato: they are built on the idea that all people are capable of exercising reason, and that, given freedom of choice, they'll tend to make rational decisions in their own best interest. Unlike in Plato's ideal republic, for example, *we* build public schools not in order to control the desires of individuals, but to give them the tools they need to participate in their own governance. So the story goes. But if you stand on the heap of scientific findings about the study of the human mind—especially those that have been accumulating over the past couple of decades—it's not so easy to dispel Plato's worries. And people who earn their living thinking about government or the economy have started to take note.

In 2002, Daniel Kahneman was awarded the Nobel Prize in Economics. But Kahneman is no economist. He's a psychologist who's best known for studying decision-making that flies in the face of logic.[2] For example, Kahneman and his colleague Amos Tversky asked people to imagine that the United States was preparing for an outbreak of a deadly Asian disease, expected to kill 600 people. Their subjects had to choose between two alternative programs to combat the disease. In the first, Program A, it was estimated that 200 people would be saved. In Program B, it was estimated that there was a 1/3 probability that all 600 people would be saved, but a 2/3 probability that no people would be saved. Most people (72%) chose Program A over Program B (28%).

A second group of people was given a slightly different set of options for coping with the oncoming disaster. In Program C, it was estimated that 400 people would die. In Program D, it was estimated that there was a 1/3 probability that no one would die, but a 2/3 probability that 600 people would die.

If you look closely at all of these options, it's obvious that programs A and C are identical, as are programs B and D. They're just *worded* differently. So, people should choose C about as often as A, and D about as often as B. Right?

Wrong. Revealing that something other than cool reason is at play, Tversky and Kahneman found that only 22% chose program C (compared with 72% for Program A!) and 78% chose program D (instead of 28% for Program B). In other words, people's preferences for each of the programs were almost entirely flipped around, just by tinkering with the *language* of these options. Focusing attention on the number of people *saved* made the deciders more inclined to go with the conservative program in which the outcome was known, but focusing on the number of people who would *die* made them more willing to choose the risky option that had the potential to avoid any deaths at all, but that could also result in a greater loss of life.

By the way, expertise doesn't make people immune to these illogical shifts. When doctors were presented with similar medical scenarios, they too were susceptible to changes in the wording of alternative treatments. In a variant on the experiment, doctors were more likely to recommend an operation if they were told that after five years, 90 out of 100 people who have the operation are still alive than if they're told that 10 out of a 100 are dead.

Kahneman and Tversky's work kicked the feet out from under some common assumptions by economists about how people make (rational) decisions. It also launched the beginning of the new field of behavioral economics, which zeroed in on some of the biases and shortcuts that people use when making decisions, focusing on replacing assumptions about the rational choices people make with the empirical study of how they *actually* make choices. Since the early work of

---

[2] Kahneman was given the Nobel Prize for work he did beginning in the late 1970s with his colleague Amos Tversky. It's generally assumed that, had Tversky been alive in 2002, he would have shared the Nobel with Kahneman.

Kahneman and Tversky, here are a few other things that have been documented about the presumably rational citizen.

People rarely think like economists do about the value of money. For example, if you're shopping for a calculator and see one in the store for $15, but learn that a store across town is selling the same thing for $10, do you make the extra drive to get the cheaper one? Many people would. But they'd be much less inclined to make the schlep to save $5 on a gadget that cost $125. How come? Isn't five bucks worth five bucks in either case?

And how much are you willing to pay for a nice bottle of wine? Wait, before you decide, first think about the last two digits of your social security number (or your license plate, or your telephone number). If your digits happen to be fairly high (say 89), you're likely to offer more cash than someone whose last two digits are much lower (say 24). One study found that by getting people to write down this completely irrelevant number, they could be lured into bidding as much as 120% more for items if their last two digits fell on the high side. Findings like these throw a harsh and unflattering light on traditional economic theories with their assumptions that the inherent value of a product drives what people are willing to pay for it. And shopkeepers are well aware of these biases—the high-priced items in a store are often there as a decoy, to inflate what people are willing to pay for the other, more frequently selling items.

Humans are also notoriously lousy when it comes to judging risk. They rush out to buy insurance against earthquakes shortly after seeing one in the news, but are blasé about it a couple of years later. The *risk* of an earthquake hasn't changed (in fact, in many cases, the risk of an earthquake goes up the longer it's been since the last one in the region), but the vividness of their memory has. Having a vivid memory of a terrible event makes people more eager to vote for tough-on-crime legislation (even if their memories come mostly from watching crime shows on TV) or more willing to give up civil liberties in order to fight terrorism. No one gets worked up about tough-on-sunburn legislation, though. A bad sunburn rarely makes the news.

Not only do people rely on flawed thinking when making choices, their "choices" often reflect an outright absence of decision-making. For example, one study showed that 12% of Germans agreed to donate their vital organs after their death. *Ninety-nine* percent of Austrians did. It's *possible* that Austrians are enormously more altruistic than their German neighbors when it comes to their recyclable body parts. But doubtful. More likely, the difference has to do with the fact that in Germany, you have to sign a document in order to give consent that your organs be used for transplant. In Austria, your consent is presumed, and you have to sign a document to revoke it. Now, you might not like the idea of the state *presuming* it's OK to remove your liver in the event you die. What if you just forgot to register your objection, but actually feel strongly that you'd prefer your body left intact? Well, the state of Illinois began a program in which you *have* to state whether you're willing to be an organ donor when you got to renew your driver's license. You're neither presumed to give consent nor presumed to withhold it, but you're not given the option to just ignore the issue either way. In Illinois, the donor rate is 60%, quite a bit higher than the national average of 38%.

People act similarly when it comes to enrolling in a pension plan. They generally just go with whatever is specified as the default at the time they start their jobs—they're usually thinking about too many other things at the time to give much thought as to how they're going to allocate their investments. But then they simply forget about it, often costing themselves tens of thousands of dollars, if not more. It's not what they *intend* to do. It just happens.

Time and time again, people's long-term goals and intentions come crashing down in the face of immediate decisions. The whole habit of announcing New Year's Resolutions (and the inevitable failure to achieve them) shows the tension between what people "want" and how they actually behave on the spur of the moment. Throw in some subtle cues about social norms, add a dash of mindless shortcut thinking, sprinkle in some of the infamous bias for short-term pleasure over long-term gain, and you have a recipe for a pursuit of happiness that constantly short-circuits itself.

In fact, it's doubtful if we can even *think* about happiness competently. Psychologists who study that slippery state of mind conclude that we're pretty crummy at gauging what will actually make us happy. We tend to falsely believe that we'll feel the same longings and desires tomorrow as we do right now, we overestimate the importance of relatively trivial things on our happiness, and fail to consider our inborn ability to adapt—whether to bad things like debilitating accidents or good things like winning a lottery or owning a new pair of designer shoes. As a result, we spend too much time worrying about things that may not be as bad as we think, and too much time chasing things that end up feeling kind of hollow after all. If America's founding fathers had known all this, maybe they wouldn't have bothered to enshrine the pursuit of happiness in the nation's Declaration of Independence.

Academic journals these days are stuffed with new findings of our tendencies to make decisions using shallow and error-prone thinking. Add these to the broader collection of results showing the mackerel-minded and unconscious ways in which we absorb information or take in persuasive messages, and it becomes hard to just brush aside Plato's somewhat dim view that most of us are ill-equipped to govern ourselves. We may have to face up to the fact that the founders of our political and economic systems, in thrall with Enlightenment Age ideas about the power of individual choice and the reasoning power of all human beings, overshot the extent to which these choices can bring about the good society.

Democracy in the Age of the Mackerel Mind

In light of all this, it's really interesting to go back and read the writings of Edward Bernays, that enterprising young nephew of Sigmund Freud. This master persuader took very seriously his uncle's view that, like a floating iceberg, most of the mind's action is submerged from consciousness. Bernays had no idealistic illusions about the rationality of the average consumer or citizen. In his 1928 book *Propaganda*, he wrote:

> *Men are rarely aware of the real reasons which motivate their actions. A man may believe that he buys a motor car because, after careful study of the technical features of all makes on the market, he has concluded that this is the best. He is almost certainly fooling himself. He bought it, perhaps, because a friend whose financial acumen he respects bought one last week; or because his neighbors believed he was not able to afford a car of that class; or because its colors are those of his college fraternity.*

Throughout his writings, Bernays seems to share some of Plato's opinion about the gullibility of the masses. There's no effort to flatter the public. For example:

> *Universal literacy was supposed to educate the common man to control his environment. Once he could read and write he would have a mind fit to rule. So ran the democratic doctrine. But instead of a mind, universal literacy has given him rubber stamps, rubber stamps inked with advertising slogans, with editorials, with published scientific data, with the trivialities of tabloids and the platitudes of history, but quite innocent of original thought. Each man's rubber stamps are the duplicates of millions of others, so that when those millions are exposed to the same stimuli, all receive identical imprints.*

For some reason, Bernays is not overly bothered by this. Unlike Plato, he certainly doesn't see it as a reason to reject democracy. But his view of democracy is probably a touch different from what the founding fathers had in mind:

> *The conscious and intelligent manipulation of the organized habits and opinions of the masses is an important element in democratic society. Those who manipulate this unseen mechanism of society constitute an invisible government which is the true ruling power of our country.*
>
> *We are governed, our minds are molded, our tastes formed, our ideas suggested, largely by men we have never heard of. This is a logical result of the way in which our democratic society is organized. Vast numbers of human beings must cooperate in this manner if they are to live together as a smoothly functioning society.*

A democracy in which individuals were full, engaged participants in political discourse was fine for the type of political activity that took place in the late 1700s, says Bernays. In that era, people got together in small towns and villages to hammer out the rules of their society. But the method doesn't scale up. In a much larger and more complex society, there's no way government could sort through all kinds of independent opinions, and there's no way individual citizens could manage to know enough about the relevant issues. So, to avoid sliding into complete chaos, according to Bernays, "ours must be a leadership democracy administered by the intelligent minority who know how to regiment and guide the masses."

It might occur to you to wonder: why choose Bernays's brand of democracy over Plato's rule by the philosopher-kings? After all, if individual choice boils down to being a rubber stamp, why bother with the pretense? If you're going to be ruled by an "intelligent minority" anyway, why not just go ahead and give the power to those whose job it is to reason, rather than those whose job it is to persuade?

Maybe the *semblance* of choice really does matter, by giving some legitimacy to the ruling class, and averting regular bloody revolutions and tribal jockeying for power. But Bernays saw another advantage to ruling-by-persuasion: there are some basic limits on what the population will accept, and these have to be respected by those who aspire to mold the mass mind. For example, any marketing campaign worth its consulting fees will do a pile of research to figure out how receptive the public might be to a type of product or a particular message. A subsequent ad campaign may skillfully push certain buttons, but it first has to find out what the buttons are.

Perhaps this is where Plato's blueprint for the ideal society misfires so badly. Plato saw no reason to pander to people's norms and beliefs about what they want. After all, the philosopher would surely be plugged into higher truths, and know what was best for them. And to Plato's credit, among his less attractive ideas are some that seem pretty good, especially when seen with the advantage of a modern set of lenses. For instance, Plato argued that women, and not just men, should be educated, with society reaping the benefit of their full talents. In his time, this may well have seemed as crazy as the idea of government-legislated mating. But most of us today would have to agree that a society in which women participate is better than one in which they don't. And remember too, that Abraham Lincoln's vision of a slave-free America was seen as an affront to democratic principles by the Southern states. So there's some merit to the notion that there are standards for a good society that go beyond people's habits of the time.

But taking into account public receptiveness forces leaders to acknowledge that there's a price to pay for imposing rules that run against the grain of social norms. Plato may well have been right that in principle, societies would function better without the messy passions of romantic love or complicated familial attachments. But simply overriding these passions ignores what people *are*, in all their irrational, emotional glory or deficiency. It doesn't take into account what they're able to tolerate based on their cultural—or, for that matter, biological—programming. Because effective persuasion hinges on some measure of sensitivity to the public, a Bernays-style democracy manages to avoid imposing rules that couldn't be maintained without the use of force.

The Big Business of Political Persuasion

According to Bernays, the skilled politician should make use of the same persuasive tools that companies use to sell soap, cigarettes, or cars—including the sophisticated use of market data, peer pressure, color schemes, and dramatic public events such as his staging of the smoking feminist debutantes with their "torches of freedom." In *Propaganda*, Bernays takes politicians to task for neglecting to sharpen their tools of influence, lamenting that, although politics had come up with some terrific propaganda techniques during World War I (which were then copied by the business community), by 1928 it lagged badly behind the business world in honing its persuasive methods.

It's not surprising that persuasion innovation has been led by business. Since the Roaring Twenties, advertising expenditures in the United States have kept pace with the Gross Domestic Product, reaching a quarter trillion dollars by the turn of this century. This gargantuan sum makes even the most swollen political campaign budget seem measly by comparison, and its raw economic heft pretty much guarantees that the evolution of advertising, marketing, and public relations is going to be tuned to the survival of the fittest in the commercial world. The vast majority of persuasive messages are designed to meet the pressures and needs of companies who aim to convince you to part with some chunk of your paycheck on their behalf.

These messages have changed over time, in response to new pressures and new technologies. When the marketplace became crowded with scores of similar products that mostly did what they were supposed to do, companies focused less on selling the product, and more on selling you a *relationship* with the product, and a means of announcing your own identity. When faced with your narrow attentional spotlight, companies developed ways to create an impression in the sidelines of your awareness. And they've used new ways to find out intricate details about you, and craft messages made especially for you, announcing products made especially for you—to share with others just like you. Your typical ad agency doesn't put much of a premium on consumer deliberation, nor does it assume you are invested in balancing your desires and interests against the desires or needs of anyone else.

If you see democracy as Bernays did, as simply a means to rubber-stamp decisions made by the intelligent minority, then it makes perfect sense to import all the new techniques you can from the business world. But who chooses the intelligent minority? Obviously, we do. If we're relying on minds that are "innocent of original thought" then political races boil down to contests for those best able to shape the collective rubber-stamp mind. But then we run into

Plato's objection. How can we be sure that those who are most skilled at persuasion are best fit to govern?[3]

Not everyone agrees that political persuasion should take all its cues from business. Some take seriously the notion of the marketplace of ideas, in which the best arguments are likely to prevail through competitive jostling. For example, two-time presidential hopeful Adlai Stevenson famously objected to the commercialization of politics when he stated: "the idea that you can merchandise candidates for high office like breakfast cereal—that you can gather votes like box tops—is . . . the ultimate indignity to the democratic process." He lost both of his races.

Recent history has tended to reward political campaigns that draw on talents from the business sphere. In 1964, the Lyndon B. Johnson camp looked for a helping hand from the famous advertising firm Doyle Dane Bernbach (DDB)—the folks who invented Volkswagen's "Think small" campaign, and Avis' "We try harder" pitch. In the depths of the Cold War, Johnson was trying to position himself as a cool-headed alternative to Barry Goldwater, playing off some remarks Goldwater had made about exploring the possibility of using nuclear weapons in Vietnam. DDB came up with the stunningly innovative—and controversial— "Daisy" ad.

The one-minute TV spot opens with a close-up of a freckle-faced four-year-old girl standing in a field, plucking petals from a daisy and childishly counting, "one, two, three, four, five, seven, six, six, eight, nine, nine." Her innocent moment is interrupted by the sound of man's voice booming over a loudspeaker. He is counting down: "ten, nine, eight, seven, six, five, four, three, two, one." The camera zooms in on the little girl's face until we see the black of her large pupil—she seems to be looking at something that caught her attention. There is the sound of a massive explosion, and a mushroom cloud fills the screen. Over this image of destruction, LBJ's voice urgently intones: "These are the stakes—to make a world in which all of God's children can live, or go into the dark. We must either love each

---

[3] You don't need to look beyond the Father of Spin himself to see that mastery of persuasion doesn't necessarily guarantee the best results for the greater good. In the 1950s, Bernays lent his services to the United Fruit Company, a U.S.-based company that grew bananas for export in Central America. In Guatemala, the UFC was able to control enormous tracts of land with the help of a pliable and possibly corrupt government. In 1954, Jacob Arbenz was elected by a full 65% of the popular vote on a platform of agricultural reform, promising to reduce the amount of land that was used for export crops in favor of growing crops for the malnourished Guatemalan population. Bernays launched a public relations blitz, disseminating "reports" to the press and to the U.S. Congress in which Arbenz was portrayed as a communist eager to establish ties with the Kremlin and the UFC as devoted to putting down communist uprisings. (Apparently, Bernays's well-known liberal views and disagreements with the UFC over the company's labor policies didn't keep him from lobbying on the company's behalf.) With public opinion on his side, the Eisenhower administration sent CIA-backed forces to topple the Arbenz government in a military coup. Needless to say, the coup led to fairly tense relations between the U.S. and several Central American countries for some time.

other, or we must die." The screen fades to black, and an announcer's voice concludes: "Vote for President Johnson on November 3rd. The stakes are too high for you to stay home."

Created a full two decades before Apple's riveting "1984" commercial, this ad shares many of its elements. As the viewer, you are instantly yanked into a compelling fictional world. Emotions are buzzing from the first few seconds, and they shift dramatically as you follow an entire plot that is compressed into 60 seconds; in "1984," a youthful hero smashes the forces that keep a world locked down in bleak slavery, while in "Daisy," evil and hate triumph, and innocence and hope explode to pieces. In both commercials, you don't know what the message is about until the very end of the spot. Imagine seeing "Daisy" for the first time having no idea that it was a political ad (and you wouldn't, since it was unlike any political ad you'd ever seen). You've already *experienced* the horror of the story before you've had the opportunity to activate any preconceived notions about Lyndon Johnson, or to raise a cynical screen to filter a one-sided political message. Both "1984" and "Daisy" make allusions to texts with deep cultural resonance, tapping into a whole network of knowledge and associations you have related to Orwell's dystopian novel and the Bible. And both commercials rely on you, the viewer, to make the link to an unseen, unmentioned evil force—IBM and Barry Goldwater—that must be stopped. The villain is never mentioned. It's you who connects the dots, who puts in the meaning between the words, and who shares (at least psychologically) some of the responsibility for making the accusation.

Like "1984," the "Daisy" ad aired only once. Interestingly, it was inserted in a commercial break of the biblical epic *David and Bathsheba*, reaching 50 million viewers. It detonated enough controversy to be aired on news broadcasts another three times (at no cost to LBJ's campaign). It immediately put Barry Goldwater on the defensive, which only served to focus attention on the issue of whether his finger should be anywhere near "the button." And it changed the expectations for what political advertising could and should look like.

Bill Moyers, who served as Johnson's advisor and approved the "Daisy" ad, later suffered pangs of regret at having portrayed Goldwater as a warmonger, when it was Johnson who escalated the Vietnam War upon re-election. And, in an interview with *The Washington Post* 20 years later, he voiced doubts about the techniques the campaign had used: "We advanced the technology and the power far beyond what is desirable for political dialogue. We didn't foresee the implications of serious messages in such an abbreviated form. Our use of the commercial was regrettable. The Frankenstein we helped to build is loose in the world."

But the ad was effective. A week after it aired, a poll showed that 53% of women, and 45% of men believed that Goldwater would drag the country into a war. Goldwater lost badly to Johnson, winning only six states to Johnson's forty-four.

Politicians have continued to borrow heavily from business. Bernays would have approved of Bill Clinton's re-election strategy, when he brought in strategist

Dick Morris to help him win a second term in a political climate that was increasingly hostile to Democrats. Morris' advice? To think like a businessman:

> I said that I felt the most important thing for him to do was to bring into the political system the same consumer rules philosophy that the business community has. I think politics needs to be as responsive to the whims and the desires of the marketplace as business is, and needs to be as sensitive to the bottom line—profits or votes—as a business is . . . So that instead of feeling that you can stay in one place and you can manipulate the voters, you need to learn what they want, and move yourself to accommodate it.

To help Clinton accommodate himself to the voter marketplace, Morris brought pollster Mark Penn on board to help him slice the electorate into segments—and identify the most important slivers.

Penn did for Bill Clinton, Round 2, what he'd done for the phone company AT&T. He used "lifestyle" polling (similar to the VALS survey) to turn an undifferentiated clump of potential voters or customers into sets of distinct groups, each with their particular attitudes, habits, and likelihood of defecting to the competition. At AT&T, Penn argued that the company had been foolishly creating advertising messages that would appeal to their longtime customers, who weren't likely to de-camp to other pastures under any circumstances. Why bother pitching to *them*? Penn showed them smaller groups of "swing" consumers—for example, immigrants who tended to make international calls to the motherland. Acting on his advice, AT&T developed special lures and advertising for just those customers whose loyalties were more fickle.

Arguing that what's good for the commercial goose is good for the political gander, Penn nailed down Clinton's swing voters. In fact, they were divided into two distinct groups, nicknamed Swing 1 and Swing 2. Clinton needed to win over 60% of Swing 1, a group of mostly women with families, who tended to be fiscally conservative, but more socially liberal. To these suburban moms, Clinton promised goodies like the V-chip, designed to allow parents to screen the TV programs their kids could tune into. He also needed 30% of Swing 2, who were largely male, and who resonated with policies like welfare reform. To these voters, Clinton presented a much more culturally conservative face. It turned out that both groups of swing voters wanted to hear about policy details, and cared less about "big picture" politics, so Clinton talked the talk they wanted to hear. Nuts and bolts, no "big ideas" or vision statements.

Penn's calculations held true, and Clinton won a second term. Since then, advances in marketing have become ever more quickly folded into political campaigns and messaging. Political messages became routinely "dial-tested"; Republican advisor Frank Luntz perfected the technique of measuring voters' (and consumers') moment-by-moment reactions to messages by having them turn a dial towards "like" or "dislike" as they listened to a speech or ad pitch. This makes it possible to pinpoint specific words and phrases that alienate or excite. Bush's 2004 campaign ramped up niche marketing techniques, and Obama's 2008 run turbo-charged them with the expert use of social media marketing. Politics has become so entwined with commercial messaging that *Advertising Age* voted Obama Marketer of the Year by a wide margin (with Apple mopping up in second place and the iconic Nike straggling behind at a mere fourth).

All this is reflected in the way we talk about politics. We've become increasingly comfortable marrying the language of politics with talk of commercial branding. Out of curiosity, I tracked the number of times the phrase "Republican brand" appeared in news articles since 1950. It hovers around a dozen or so uses for each decade through to the 1980s, begins to rise to 32 in the 1990s, and then explodes to 1570 between 2000 and 2009. (The phrase "Democratic brand" shows the same pattern, but lands at a more muted 259 uses from 2000–2009.)

Bernays might have cheered. But not everyone is overjoyed with these developments. Robert Reich, Clinton's Secretary of Labor (who resigned almost immediately following his 1996 re-election), publicly expressed the view that by pandering to niche groups, Clinton had sacrificed a mandate in exchange for another four years in office. He had this to say about Clinton's tactics:

Fundamentally here we have two different views of human nature and of democracy. You have the view that people are irrational, that they are bundles of unconscious emotion. That comes directly out of Freud. And businesses are very able to respond to that, that's what they have honed their skills doing, that's what marketing is really all about. What are the symbols, the images, the music, the words that will appeal to these unconscious feelings? Politics must be more than that. Politics and leadership are about engaging the public in a rational discussion and deliberation about what is best, and treating people with respect in terms of their rational abilities to debate what is best. If it's not that, if it is Freudian, if it is basically a matter of appealing to the same basic unconscious feelings that business appeals to, than why not let business do it? Business can do it better, business knows how to do it, business after all is in the business of responding to those feelings.

In 2002, Reich himself ran for public office as governor of Massachusetts. Mark Penn wasn't invited to the campaign race. Reich lost.

It's All in How You Say It

Long before any Nobel prizes were given out to psychologists who revealed the limits of rationality in decision-making, Edward Bernays understood that simply laying your best facts on the table would never win you a persuasion contest. What mattered was making the right imprints on people's minds. He would have found a kindred spirit in Frank Luntz, a well-known pollster and political messaging consultant. Luntz sounds like he's channeling Bernays when he preaches that in matters of persuasion, whether it's a political campaign, or a corporate branding effort, or talking your way out of a speeding ticket, *it's not what you say, it's what people hear* that counts. And Luntz has discovered that different words for the same thing are heard, well, differently.

Luntz runs a consulting company called The Word Doctors, whose website promises that "if you need to build support for legislation, we'll find the right words. If you need to kill a bad bill, we'll show you how." For example, let's say you're trying to get people on board with your plan to cut back on government health spending. Never say that you're going to deny benefits. Instead say that you will not give benefits. *Deny* sounds like a door being slammed in the face of a citizen who was merely trying to claim what was rightfully hers. *Not give* sounds like you're declining to put money in the palm of someone waiting for a handout.

Of course, if a patient actually shows up at the hospital, the outcome for all concerned is exactly the same regardless of whether the government decides to deny her benefits or not give them to her. But most people will look more kindly on a policy that proposes to do the latter than one that suggests the former.

In his exercises in wordsmithing, Luntz taps into the same phenomenon that drives the Asian disease decision. Remember how people had wildly different reactions to the hypothetical health programs depending on whether they were framed in terms of how many people would be saved rather than how many people would die? Framing effects of this sort are pretty easy to find. People will think a product is healthier if it's described as 75% fat free than as having 25% fat. A government program that will result in 95% employment meets with stronger approval than one that will result in 5% unemployment. All this is pretty baffling if you assume that people make decisions based on facts in the world, and that language is basically just a way to describe certain facts. How can language that presents the same facts lead to such different reactions?

As we've seen, though, language does much more than just march an auditioning set of facts across our mental stage. It can throw a spotlight onto some facts, and sweep others into the dim corners of the stage. It can move some facts away from the foreground where all the action is and weave them into the taken-for-granted background stage set. And when different words for the same facts are used, pulling these words from our memories pulls out different sets of memories, and different links to other words and ideas. These resonating memories and links throw very different colors onto the same facts, just as stage lights can make the same scene look cheerful, or sinister, or bleak. In other words, it's not what's on the stage, but what people see that counts, and language plays a big part in creating the overall effect. Persuaders who understand this, and who've mastered the necessary artistry, have a clear advantage over those who don't. After all, everyone's speaking to the sort of minds that are susceptible to being nudged to pay more for a bottle of wine simply by thinking of a really big social security number.

Frank Luntz's admirers and detractors are in agreement that he is uniquely skilled at the art of shaping public perception. In his book *Words that Work*, Luntz makes dozens of suggestions for casting aside less effective words and phrases in favor of ones that evoke just the right impressions (in both senses of the word, given his conservative orientation). Here are a few of them:

Never Say:	Instead Say:
private health care	free market health care
tax cuts	tax relief
drilling for oil	exploring for energy
foreign trade	international trade
undocumented workers	illegal immigrants
wiretapping	electronic intercepts
estate tax	death tax

It's easier to get people into a state of happy anticipation about "tax relief," for example, than about "tax cuts." "Tax cuts" has an aggressive edge to it, and perhaps brings to mind some of the programs that may be cut along with the tax revenue. And, as Luntz points out, people are skeptical of "tax cuts" because lower taxes have all too often been promised in the past, with little in the way of noticeable results for the taxpayers. "Tax relief" is much softer, more sympathetic. It *presupposes* that taxpayers have been burdened with too many taxes, and that they will feel so much better once their onerous load is lifted.

Luntz is probably most famous for pushing the phrase "death tax" as a replacement for the "estate tax." Both phrases refer to the same inheritance tax, paid out of the estate of someone who has died and passed on his assets to his heirs. When the Republican Party wanted to repeal the tax, they began referring to it as the "death tax" rather than by its previous name. Not hard to see why. *Death* is an ugly word, and it's hard to be pro-death *anything*. And throwing *death* and *taxes* together in the same phrase activates a sense of inevitability—as in: "nothing is certain but death and taxes." In fact, Luntz suggested that in order to kill the tax, Republicans would do well to really heighten this association with a message such as: *"Benjamin Franklin, perhaps the wisest of our founding fathers, said there were two certainties in life: death and taxes. But I do not believe that even Franklin could have foreseen that today, both would occur at the same time."*

But the tax was only inevitable if you happened to be among the wealthiest 2% of the population or so. The other 98% could count on being safely buried without a detour to the Internal Revenue Service. Luntz has taken a fair bit of heat for the rebranding of this tax. Critics objected that the associations triggered by *death tax* were misleading and too emotionally loaded, that they served to obscure certain facts. To which Luntz responded by saying that *estate tax* is not a neutral term either—it "conjures up images of rolling green hills and vast real estate holdings, of

J.R. Ewing and Donald Trump rubbing their hands together and cackling like corporate villains."

At least in public, Luntz is not willing to go quite as far as Bernays in saying that his life's work is all about creating a particular imprint for the rubber-stamp mind of the public. Rather, his how-to-persuade manual is drizzled with statements that his goal is to identify the simplest, clearest, most effective, and most *accurate* means of communication. But Luntz clearly uses his polling data and dial-testing methods, which measure on-the-spot gut reactions, to zero in on language that best persuades, rather than language that best lights up the facts. When his testing methods reveal a wide gap between people's responses to two different ways of saying the same thing, his recommendation is always to go with the one that is most persuasive, not to investigate which one creates the most accurate impression. A 20-point spread in attitudes towards the same policy expressed in different ways opens up linguistic opportunities that should be seized upon.

But the sorts of framing effects that Luntz makes a business of exploiting are viewed with some worry by people who believe that voters' decisions should be about more than rubber-stamping the most persuasive messages. Since decisions have consequences in the *real* world, and not just in our gut reactions to them, a competent decision-maker should have a pretty clear sense of the relevant real world facts and outcomes. So it's troublesome when people express different opinions about denying benefits versus not giving them—when these phrases actually *do* refer to the same facts. And the economic consequences of preserving or repealing a specific tax are the same regardless of what it's called.

In fact, while Luntz's communications strategy may have helped sway public opinion in favor of killing the death tax, many of those who ended up supporting its demise had opinions about the tax that looked anything but rational. Political scientist Larry Bartels wanted to get a clearer sense of how people were thinking about this tax, especially in light of the fact that incomes between the most and least wealthy Americans have been pulling apart for decades—a gap that would likely increase with the death of the death tax. To get some insights, he sifted through the results of the 2002 National Election Survey, in which people were asked about their thoughts on economic inequality and various tax-related policies. Overall, 70% of the population was in favor of repealing the death/estate tax. Now, given that the tax only applied to the wealthiest Americans, you might expect that those who wanted to get rid of it either figured they had a shot at making it into the ranks of the wealthiest 2%, or felt that the wealthiest deserved the tax break, or perhaps thought generally that the government should reduce its scope. But Bartels' analysis of the survey data led to some mystifying results:

> [A]mong people with family incomes of less than $50 000 (about half the sample), 66% favored repeal. Among people who want to spend more money on federal government programs, 68% favored repeal. Among people who said that the difference in incomes between rich people and poor people has increased in the past

20 years and that that is a bad thing, 66% favored repeal. Among those who said that government policy is a 'very important' or 'somewhat important' cause of economic inequality, 67% favored repeal. Among those who said that the rich are asked to pay too little in federal income taxes, 68% favored repeal. And finally, among those with family incomes of less than $50 000 who want more spending on government programs and said income inequality has increased and said that is a bad thing and said that government policy contributes to income inequality and said that rich people pay less than they should in federal income taxes—the 11% of the sample with the strongest conceivable set of reasons to support the estate tax— 66% favored repeal.

Digging deeper into the data, Bartels found that the biggest predictor of people's desire to get rid of the tax was whether they *themselves* felt overly burdened by their tax bill—despite the fact that the vast majority of them would never have to pay the death tax they were so eager to abolish. And they seemed generally confused about who was likely to be affected by the tax—49% of people said that it applied to "most families," and 69% believed that "it might affect YOU someday."

These data would sober up anyone genuinely concerned with choosing language that best allowed voters to understand the tax. In the face of the survey data, you'd be hard-pressed to argue for *death tax*, with its associations of inevitability, over *estate tax*. In fact, bringing to mind the likes of Donald Trump might actually do some work in correcting people's *mis*perceptions that the tax affected the majority of ordinary Americans.

Metaphorically Speaking

Like the tax code and many other finer points of policy, science is complex, and filled with important facts. Organizing and remembering new knowledge can take some concerted effort. For example, at some point in your life, you likely took a biology class in which you studied the inner workings of cells. You may have memorized a list of cell parts and their functions:

nucleus: determines what proteins will be made and controls all activity in the cell
plasma membrane: regulates what enters and leaves the cell
cytoplasm: location of most of the cell's activity
ribosomes: build proteins
endoplasmic reticulum: where ribosomes do their work
lysosomes: responsible for breaking down and absorbing materials taken in by the cell
cytoskeleton: maintains cell shape
mitochondria: transform one form of energy into another.

If you were lucky, you had a teacher who made the job easier. If she told you to think of a cell as a factory, you might have been encouraged to think of the cell parts like this:

nucleus = CEO
plasma membrane = shipping/receiving department
cytoplasm = factory floor
ribosomes = assembly line workers
endoplasmic reticulum = assembly line
lysosomes = maintenance crew
cytoskeleton = walls, floors, ceiling, support beams
mitochondria = power plant.

Having a familiar framework that you could easily visualize and remember probably made it a lot easier to understand and remember how a cell works. And chances are, if you learned to think of a cell as a factory, even if you've forgotten the scientific terms for all the parts, the core idea of a cell as a complex system of coordinated activity has stayed with you. Being able to map the unfamiliar new material onto a vivid knowledge structure you already had in place made the new knowledge much less vulnerable to being dislodged and flushed out. It also made the lesson a lot less dull, making it more likely you'd pay attention in the first place. For all these reasons, the best teachers routinely make heavy use of metaphors in teaching new abstract concepts—good metaphors can motivate and guide learning in powerful ways.

For these same reasons, politicians also make use of concrete, vivid metaphors to guide the thoughts of voters and leave them with a lasting impression. On most days, the average citizen may be tempted to stifle a yawn at the words "foreign policy," and likely doesn't feel qualified to understand the intricate chess moves made by his government on the international plane. But during the Cold War, numerous leaders—beginning with Dwight Eisenhower—managed to communicate their ideas about the potential spread of communism by describing it metaphorically as a domino effect. As a metaphor, the idea of a domino effect does a lot of work in organizing how people might think about communism. First of all, you immediately think of countries that adopt communist rule as "fallen," as failed or collapsed states. And if you've ever tried to stop a set of falling dominoes in motion, you'll know that to keep them standing, it's best to keep that first one from ever tipping over. So at a foreign policy level, you can't afford to ignore the "tipping" of one country without risking some enormous consequences. The metaphor also creates the impression that countries sharing borders are the ones that will be most likely to be "tipped" next. All of these notions suggest fairly specific approaches to foreign policy, and indeed, the concept of a domino effect was used to justify American intervention in Vietnam in the 1960s and in Latin America in the 1980s.

But while metaphors can be very useful in understanding complex ideas, there's the danger that they can also box in how you think about an issue. In science, seemingly useful metaphors sometimes prevent scientists from asking questions that are incompatible with their metaphorical way of thinking about the problem. A limiting metaphor might cause scientists to spend too much time following what turn out to be scientific dead ends, and neglecting other ideas that are suppressed by the dominant metaphor. Some cognitive scientists, for instance, feel that progress in their field has been slowed down by the constraints imposed by the metaphor of the human mind as a computer. In science and politics both, it's always healthy to take a step back and ask what other metaphors might be used instead.

For instance, leave aside for a moment images of toppling dominoes. Instead, imagine communism as an earthquake tremor causing buildings (countries) to shake. The same tremor might flatten shoddily built structures, but leave sturdy ones standing. Foreign policy could look quite different now. You might focus on figuring out which buildings are weakest, and shoring them up. You'd be less concerned about stopping the triggering event (you can't stop plate tectonics), and much more concerned with addressing the conditions internal to vulnerable countries. And you wouldn't assume that countries would turn to communist rule simply because their immediate neighbors have.

Both metaphors provide a vivid way for thinking about the causes and effects of communism and ways to deal with it (and notice that both still suggest that communism is destructive and *should* be stopped). But they line up differently with the facts in the world, which is why it makes sense to think outside the metaphorical box and imagine different ways of structuring the world.

Metaphors are as useful as they are because they compress an enormous amount of information into a small and vivid linguistic space. In politics, they not only act as ways of organizing complex ideas and policies, but often suggest an appropriate attitude towards them. It's no accident that charged historical periods spawn huge quantities of metaphors. Just think, for example, of the **cold war**, when the **iron curtain** separated West from East, with both sides caught up in an **arms race** that **escalated** and threatened to bring about a **nuclear winter**, leading some to protest in favor of a **nuclear arms freeze**. Moscow set up **puppet states** in countries like Poland, Hungary, and East Germany in which all media were **organs of the state**. When one of these **satellite countries**—Czechoslovakia—asserted its independence during the **Prague Spring**, Moscow invaded, claiming it was acting on its own version of the **domino theory** of capitalism. Eventually, a **revolutionary wave** swept throughout the Soviet bloc, leading to the **collapse** of communism, and the **thawing** of relations between East and West.

Ever wonder how *our* Cold War metaphors differ from Soviet metaphors from the same era? The idea of what counted as a failed state was certainly reversed. I'm told that Soviet messaging focused on the idea of **building Communism**, and references to the West were riddled with the language of **rot** and **decay**, painting a picture of Western nations as **corrupt, dying** societies.

Part of the power of metaphor comes from the fact that it provides a way of grounding an abstract domain of ideas in a much more concrete set of physical experiences. Because metaphors turn on memories of experiences, they can also play a role in triggering not just a specific set of *thoughts*, but also a specific set of *feelings*—steering voters to a certain emotional response to a proposed policy. This aspect of metaphor is like turning on the colored stage lights. Using metaphor can have the effect of switching from a flat white light aimed at the stage to one that bathes the scene in melancholy blue. It makes you care.

Political scientist Todd Hartman demonstrated how metaphors matter by applying them to the rather arcane policy issue of network neutrality. The issue affects how information is priced and transmitted over the Internet, and became important in response to lobbying efforts by broadband service providers to be allowed to charge a premium for transmitting certain data at high speeds. Those opposed to the lobbying efforts argued that tiered pricing would violate the "neutrality" principle of the Internet—in other words, the principle that the Internet was originally created with the intent of treating all data equally. To see whether metaphors could move people more than straight, unembellished language, Hartman had some volunteers in his study read this accurate, but somewhat dry statement:

> *Congressman Alan Davidson, who specializes in technology issues, supports Network Neutrality legislation. He recently told reporters: 'Telecoms want to charge fees on the Internet to connect content providers to their customers. Network Neutrality would prevent this from happening. It would ensure that we don't have a system where some companies have access to fast services, while the rest are left with slower connections.'*

Others got a version that was built around the metaphor of the Internet as the information superhighway:

> *Congressman Alan Davidson, who specializes in technology issues, supports Network Neutrality legislation. He recently told reporters: 'Telecoms want to set up toll booths on the Internet to stand between content providers and their customers. Network Neutrality would prevent this from happening. It would ensure that we don't have a system where some companies have access to an express lane, while the rest are stuck waiting in line at the toll booth.'*

The first message communicates pretty much the same policy content as the second metaphor-filled message. But it treats the issue as an *abstract* policy matter. Most people likely feel they don't have enough of a framework within which to evaluate the consequences of the proposed fee structure. The emotional impact of the language is pretty bland: sometimes fees for service are good, or at least necessary; sometimes they're bad. The message itself gives no particular reason to think one way or the other about them. But the second message brings the whole thing into the domain of personal experiences that everyone can relate to. Voters' experiences with toll booths aren't abstract—they're very concrete, and *very* annoying. And by alluding to the idea of the Internet as an information superhighway, with its images of speed, modernity, and dynamic movement, the message draws into the foreground people's feelings about the transformational potential of unfettered access to the Internet. Who could possibly be in favor of informational gridlock?

Not surprisingly, the persuasive effects of the two messages were dramatically different. People who read the dry version that was stripped of metaphor were no more supportive of network neutrality afterwards than another group who'd read neither of the messages—both of these groups were about 44% in favor of network neutrality. So, the persuasive work of the plain language was approximately zilch. But among the group who'd read the message laced with metaphor, the level of support for network neutrality soared to 61%. And generally, Hartman found that the impact of metaphor was strongest on volunteers who were less politically knowledgeable than those who were more savvy.

So it's no surprise that when politicians want to change policy, they often start by changing the metaphors. In 2009, the Obama administration announced it would no longer talk about the "war on drugs". A military metaphor for dealing with drug problems in society activates thoughts like these: *there are organized opponents (and maybe states) that should be defeated; force will solve the problem; resources should be put into military or police enforcement; casualties—possibly among civilians—will occur; a sense of honor or patriotism is at stake; one side or the other will eventually "win".* For Obama's new head of National Drug Control Policy, Gil Kerlikowske, the language was a problem. Calling the war metaphor a "bellicose analogy," he stated, "regardless of how you try to explain to people that it's 'war on drugs' or 'war on a product,' people see a war as a war on them. We're not at war with people in this country." Kerlikowske suggested the issue should be framed as one of public health. Using a metaphor such as "curing the drug disease" brings different thoughts to the surface: *the afflicted are ill, not enemies; addicts should be treated, not punished; knowledge will help solve the problem; resources should go into research and treatment; the problem may be "contagious"; everyone wins if we get rid of the problem.*

But once one metaphor is firmly lodged in people's minds it can be impossible to replace it with another. For example, in the fall of 2008, when U.S. presidential candidate John McCain addressed the unpopular $700 million "bailout package" that was passed in response to the financial collapse that year, he objected to the use of that metaphor: "*The first thing I'd do is say, let's not call it a bailout, let's call it a rescue because it is a rescue. It's a rescue of Main Street America. We haven't convinced people that this is a rescue effort, not just for Wall Street, but for Main Street*

America." Rescues bring to mind acts of God and brave heroics. But despite a concerted attempt by McCain and the White House to shift the language, the b-word stuck. As Steve Liesman, senior economics reporter for CNBC put it: *"You rescue the unwitting victims of a boat accident. You bail out an experienced captain who sailed knowingly into a storm . . . Wall Street, which should have known better, is getting bailed out."*

The Futility of Denial

After the "Daisy" spot appeared, Barry Goldwater's campaign team went ballistic, and condemned the ad as a dirty and libelous attempt to whip the public into a frenzy of misplaced fear. Republican National Committee Chairman Dean Burch complained that it implied that Lyndon Johnson "is a careful man and Senator Goldwater may somehow cause some sort of atomic conflict because he is a perfectly reckless person." He condemned the ad as "the most violent political lie that be told."

This response was just what the Democrats had hoped for. In an elated letter to Johnson, Bill Moyers wrote of Burch's response: "Well, that's exactly what we wanted to imply. *And we also hoped someone around Goldwater would say it, not us.* They did. Yesterday was spent in trying to show that Goldwater *isn't* reckless." Moyers understood that the Republicans had done Johnson a favor by spelling out the message of the ad, allowing the Democrats to keep some distance between themselves and the implied claim. He also understood that the enraged denials served to keep voters focused on the claim about Goldwater's nuclear irresponsibility. Mission accomplished.

Some of the most striking memories of presidential guilt come firmly attached to images of angry denial by the accused. Nixon's "I'm not a crook" and Clinton's "I did not have sexual relations with that woman" are permanently tattooed on the public mind, and they sharpen rather than soften any sense of outrage at the presidential guilt. But denials often work against politicians even when the allegations are completely untrue. Inevitably, they bring the allegations into the mental spotlight, and somehow, these seem to be more brightly lit than the denial of the charges.

Several studies point to the depressing fact that merely bringing to mind the question of a person's guilt can contaminate people's opinions of him. In one of these, subjects rated fictitious political candidates after reading various newspaper headlines that had allegedly been written about them. Some of these reported incriminating findings—"*Bob Talbert Linked with Mafia.*" Others were completely neutral—"*George Armstrong Arrives in City.*" But others either raised a question about some potentially damaging information—"*Is Karen Downing Associated with Fraudulent Charity?*" or even exonerated a candidate—"*Andrew Winters not Connected to Bank Embezzlement.*" Not surprisingly, people had the most negative opinions about the candidates when the headlines promised a report of the evidence of guilt. But readers also looked askance at the candidates when the headlines merely posed a question about their guilt, or even when they *cleared* the candidate of wrongdoing. This contamination effect even happened when the headlines supposedly appeared in a paper like the *National Enquirer*, which the subjects themselves rated as not very credible. (The only thing that seemed to lessen the damaging impact of the innuendo was to focus the subjects on possible motives the writer of the headline might have had. When subjects felt that the writers might have been trying to dodge charges of libel by insinuating rather than directly claiming some dirty dealings, innuendo lost its power.)

If you ever get a phone call asking for your opinions on a political poll, it's worth paying close attention to the questions. In 2000, when George W. Bush was competing against John McCain for the Republican nomination, many people in South Carolina received calls from a "poll" which included the following question: "*Would you be more likely or less likely to vote for John McCain for president if you knew he had fathered an illegitimate black child?*" The question had no basis in truth—in fact McCain and his wife had legally adopted a dark-skinned Bangladeshi girl. But it planted a seed in voters' minds that easily spread and was part of an aggressive negative campaign against McCain. Despite easily winning the New Hampshire primary, McCain lost to Bush by a wide margin in South Carolina. Tactics like these have been called "push polls"—they masquerade as polls, but their real function is to influence voters, not gather information from them.

And again, the science suggests that these tricks are effective. Persuasion researchers Gavan Fitzsimons and Baba Shiv turned their attention to the effects of hypothetical questions just like the one in the push poll that targeted McCain. They found their subjects' opinions of a candidate were battered just as badly by a negative hypothetical question as by an incriminating factual news story. To see just how broad the effects of hypothetical questions were, the scientists also looked at the effects of hypothetical *positive* questions, even ones that seemed unlikely to be true. In this version of the study, some subjects were asked to report how it would affect their eating habits if science were to discover that eating cake was not that bad for you after all (others were not asked this question). When all the subjects were later offered the choice of a fruit salad or chocolate cake as snack, those who'd answered the hypothetical question were more likely to choose the cake. But they had very little insight into what prompted them to make the choice. They understood that the information about the healthiness of sweets was hypothetical, and not necessarily true, and they claimed that their choice was not influenced in any way by the earlier part of the study that involved the hypothetical scenario. So the information seemed to be working much like the subliminal priming effects we saw in Chapter 2—it affected behavior by making some information more accessible in the mind, but not in a way that could be consciously evaluated as the source of influence.

Once a false rumor is out there, its effects can't easily be erased. In a way, denials are like asking voters to not think of a pink elephant. Often, all this does in people's minds is turn the elephant a hotter shade of pink. This may reflect a general fact about the psychology of trying to *cancel* thoughts. For example, in one study, scientists at the University of Western Ontario tried to train people to "just say no" to social stereotypes. Volunteers saw male or female names paired with words that either suggested strength or weakness. They were told to reject a stereotypical pairing (a woman's name paired with a "weak" word, or a man's name paired with a "strong" word) by pressing a button. This active rejection of stereotypes backfired—when the scientists later measured unconscious associations of their subjects, they found that the stereotype became more firmly embedded *after* the training. Trying to reject the stereotypical associations just made them stronger. But there was a different form of training that *did* work in weakening the effects of the stereotypes. Instead of rejecting a stereotypical pairing of names and words, some volunteers were told instead to *accept* a pairing that went against the stereotype—that is, they were told to press a button whenever they saw a woman's name paired with a "strong" word or a man's name paired with a "weak" word. The trick was to override the stereotypical associations with their opposites, not simply to reject the original associations.

One way to think about denial is that it's a bit like the "SOLD" stickers that get slapped onto bulky items that you buy at the store, but in this case, they're like "NOT" stickers that are affixed to thoughts. When you hear Nixon say "I am not a crook," what your mind does is compute the meaning of "I am a crook," and *then* it puts on the "NOT" sticker. If your mind is busy or distracted, it might forget to put the sticker on altogether. This notion is supported by an intriguing study concocted by psychologist Dan Gilbert and his colleagues. They created a scenario in which study volunteers read a crime report about a fictional character named Tom. The volunteers were told that some of the statements in the report were true, and some were false. It was easy to identify the false statements—these always appeared against a red background. All of the volunteers read five clearly false statements about Tom that presented him in a bad light. Half of the volunteers read another two damning and clearly false statements as well; but the other half saw the same two damaging statements on a black background, and therefore marked as clearly true. Both groups then had to answer a number of questions measuring their impressions of Tom. The researchers wanted to see how easily people could discount the effects of the obviously false statements.

When the volunteers were allowed to give their full attention to the crime report, they were able to take into account the falsity of two of the damaging statements— the group that saw these two statements against a red (false) background tended to like Tom better than those who saw them against the black (true) background. But things changed when their reading of the statements was interrupted by a separate task, or when they were asked to speed read the statements. Now this group's impression of Tom was just as poor as the group that had read only true derogatory statements about him. They'd computed the negative meanings of the statements, but had failed to discount them—the "NOT" sticker never got firmly attached—so the fictional Tom suffered the negative effects of the false smear campaign.

Gilbert's data suggests that rejecting a message is slower and more easily disrupted than computing the meaning of the message in the first place—basically a cognitive version of Mark Twain's famous quote that "a lie can travel halfway around the world while the truth is still putting on its shoes."

What's really interesting is that even when the "NOT" sticker gets attached to a message, and the message is rejected, it seems that over time, the sticker can peel off from the message. In the 1940s, Carl Hovland, one of the fathers of scientific persuasion research, noticed an interesting phenomenon: when he studied the attitudes of soldiers who watched war propaganda films, he noticed that some of them seemed to be unaffected by the propaganda a few days after seeing the film, but nine weeks later, the propaganda had taken hold. This finding, which Hovland called the "sleeper effect," was very surprising, because normally, the persuasive punch of a message is strongest shortly after the message is first seen, and then decreases gradually over time. Hovland discovered that the sleeper effect tended to happen under specific conditions, when the soldiers first reacted to the films by discounting their credibility. With time, that discounting somehow got detached from the memory of the propaganda message. Sleeper effects have been found for negative political ads too. Ads that are initially rejected as not credible (and even disliked) can become more persuasive over time, showing that it's not always within the power of voters to "just say no" to negative political campaigning.[4]

Bias, What Bias?

There's a tall stack of bad metaphors you could reach for if you wanted to pull out some wrong ideas about how the human mind processes information. Here's one of them: The mind is an impartial judge that carefully sifts through and evaluates all information in a thoughtful and deliberate manner. If this was an idea you entertained before reading this book, it probably evaporated somewhere in the middle of Chapter 2.

Here's another one: The mind is a soft lump of clay on which every passing bit of information leaves its imprint. Like many inaccurate metaphors, this has some

---

[4] Notice that this is a variant of the same phenomenon that was discussed in Chapter 6 in the context of fictional information. Even though information might be clearly understood as fiction at the time it's first encountered, over time, it gets absorbed into memories of real events. In both cases, what seems to be happening is that memory for the content is preserved, but memory about the source of the content becomes corrupted.

important elements of truth to it, many of which I've focused on in this book. It's certainly true that our minds are much more easily molded than we might have thought by information we're not even aware of, in ways we can't control. This belief drove Bernays's supremely successful persuasion campaigns, and to a large extent, has been validated by recent science. But there are a couple of things that Bernays wouldn't be able to account for when he wrote that "*each man's rubber stamps are the duplicates of millions of others, so that when those millions are exposed to the same stimuli, all receive identical imprints.*"

One of these is the interesting fact that two people can watch exactly the same presidential debate, for example, but have completely different ideas about who "won" once they click the TV set off. There's also the interesting fact of presidential approval ratings that can only be described as schizophrenic. Results of the 2004 National Election Studies showed that George W. Bush enjoyed an exuberant 90% approval rating—among Republican voters. His approval rating among Democrats was *less than 19%*. Sixty-six percent of Republicans *strongly* approved of Bush's performance, while 64% of Democrats strongly *dis*approved. Nor was Bush an anomaly. Although Bush's split between approval ratings by party affiliation was especially striking, to some extent, this seems to have been part of a growing historical trend. In 1972, the difference between Republican and Democrat approval ratings for Richard Nixon was 36 points. It was 42 points for Jimmy Carter in 1980, 52 points for Ronald Reagan in 1988, and 55 points for Bill Clinton in 1996. The 2004 spread between Republicans and Democrats for Bush was 71 points. And when it comes to the more recent Barack Obama, he's been labeled as Messiah and anti-Christ, and everything in between.

Clearly, not everyone is being persuaded in the same direction.

To some extent, of course, this growing polarization in presidential approval may have come about because Republicans and Democrats aren't reading the same newspapers, watching the same cable TV stations, visiting the same blogs, or talking to the same neighbors. But this itself is no accident—much of the time, people are *choosing* the information they will be exposed to. It's worth asking why this happens.

When it comes down to it, the explanation for why people seek out different sources of information is actually pretty similar to the one for why people who watch the *same* debate can come to very different conclusions. Even when the same information is put in front of people, they often make very different choices about what to pay attention to and how to process it. Back in Chapter 3, you read about how we all have a certain amount of control over where to aim our attentional spotlight—so that when we're focused on a tricky task, for instance, we can easily ignore gorillas sauntering through the visual landscape right in front of our eyes. This turns out to be an absolutely general truth about how we interact with the torrents of information out in the world; some things attract our very close scrutiny, while we suppress awareness of others. To a very large extent, the information we pay attention to is determined by the goals we have in place at the outset.

It would probably be more accurate to apply scare quotes in talking about how we "choose" to be selective in our attention to information based on our "goals." At this point, it might not surprise you to learn that such "goals" and "choices" can drive our information-seeking without the fringe benefits of conscious awareness and deliberate control. Remember the studies in Chapter 2 showing that people could be nudged towards the cognitive goal of deeply processing text rather than simply memorizing it—all via subliminal presentation of words like *judge*, *evaluate*, and *understand*? So our information-processing "goals" can be triggered by external suggestions we're not aware of. But they're also triggered by some hidden built-in tendencies that make all of us apt to seek out biased information.

It may seem perverse to suggest that people who suffer from depression "choose" to focus more on the negatives in life, but a number of studies suggest that this is exactly what happens, at least at an unconscious level. For example, when depressed people look at a computer screen that has pictures of happy and sad events, they tend to spend less time looking at the happy ones, and more time looking at the sad ones. Other states of mind can lead to this self-perpetuating bias—people who are in an anxious state of mind, for example, spend more time looking at images that depict some kind of threat or danger.

Odd as it may be, our minds appear to be wired to eagerly search for evidence that confirms the beliefs we happen to have about the world, even if this sometimes makes us miserable or outright wrong. For example, if you struggle with arthritis, you may have noticed that your pain gets worse when bad weather blows into town. Arthritis sufferers have been making this connection and reporting it to their doctors since the time of Hippocrates in 400 B.C. And through the rigorous wonders of modern science, we now know that the consistent medical evidence for this "phenomenon" approximates zero. How can this be? Can thousands of patients be wrong about their own experiences? Yes. Apparently, just entertaining the hypothesis that there's a connection between the weather and their pain makes people much more likely to notice and remember when the pain flares up on crummy days. If you believe that rainy days make you ache, pain on warm sunny days is just not that compelling. What's more, outside observers looking at hard data can be duped by the same belief as well: in one study, volunteers were falsely told that patients' arthritis generally got worse as a result of changes in air pressure. They were then shown graphs plotting both the pain levels of a patient and the air pressure over a period of days. The volunteers "saw" a relationship between the two even when there was none—showing just how easy it might be for a medical professional to jump to the wrong conclusions and recommendations. But take heart—after thousands of years, medical practice is finally catching on to the science. Patients were once advised by their doctors to move to warmer climates if they had a bad case of arthritis. Nowadays, doctors are trained to downplay the connection, no doubt disappointing condo developers throughout Florida and Arizona.[5]

This drive to confirm what we think we already know—think of it as *partisan* thinking—leaves its trace in just about every situation that psychologists have thought to look at. No one (including psychologists) seems to be immune from it. Obviously, the cure is for people to make sure they are exposed to balanced messages from all sides.

Or maybe not. In some cases, when people are confronted with evidence *against* their beliefs, this makes them really dig in their attitudinal heels and emerge even more gloriously convinced of their original position. They behave like a teenager whose parents are obviously wrong about everything before even opening their mouths, but whose idols seem to perspire the truth. They find ways to argue with the counterevidence, and manage to find all the possible flaws in the reasoning of their opponents, while eagerly and uncritically absorbing arguments for their own side.

Clearly, this level of bias is tempered by deeper knowledge and political sophistication. Or maybe not. When political scientists Charles Taber and Milton Lodge looked closely at biased information-processing, they found that people who were *more* knowledgeable politically were *less* likely to seek out distasteful political opinions, were more critical of them when they did read them, and actually became more convinced of their original opinions after being given the opportunity to read opinions from both sides. This happened even though, at the beginning of the study, all the volunteers were told to read the material in as evenhanded a way as possible, so that they would be able to fairly summarize the arguments for or against each issue. Volunteers who came into the study with less knowledge about politics showed less bias, and less hardening of their opinions. It's unlikely that the knowledge itself creates the bias. Taber and Lodge suggest that political knowledge is one marker of people's level of political engagement. The more passionate people are about politics, the more likely they are to hold opinions they are attached to and eager to defend. Unfortunately, a gain in political conviction may mean a loss in political objectivity. This seems to turn on its head the idea that it's a *good* thing to combat voter apathy and boost the general level of political engagement. What if getting people to care about politics also means getting them to be more biased and less open-minded?

Hang on, you might object. Being set in your thinking and weighing evidence unequally isn't necessarily irrational. Let's suppose you've arrived at your opinion by carefully sorting through many different arguments, and you've reached a reasonable and stable conclusion. Maybe you've also carefully evaluated the

---

[5] I confess to being one of those who believed my aches and pains got worse whenever the air pressure dropped, until being confronted with the hard evidence. Never mind the evidence—I *still* think I ache more when it rains.

credibility of various sources. Isn't it rational at that point to treat the arguments *unequally?* After all, giving equal weight to all arguments all the time would mean you'd be committed to giving full consideration to new arguments that were likely to be wrong. A dogma of total "balance," for instance, would mean you should give as much weight to arguments against evolution as you would those for it. But if you've really done your homework already, you know that an argument against evolution is far more likely to be wrong than right. Doesn't it make sense to waste as little cognitive capital on it as you can?

Excellent objection. There's no question that some ideas are simply less wrong than others, and giving equal treatment to bad and good ideas alike would lead to some flawed decisions—not to mention mental implosion. But when it comes to the human hunger for confirming evidence, it seems that there is much more going on than simply the reasonable pursuit of one idea that is more likely to be right than others. Often, it looks a lot less like cool reason, and a lot more like Freud's notion that people try to unconsciously repress thoughts that make them squirm. For Freud, this might mean repressing your aggression towards your father and your sexual longings for your mother. These days, psychologists argue that holding contradictory thoughts or feelings—that is, having a feeling of cognitive dissonance—is so uncomfortable that people try to subconsciously resolve the tension by getting rid of it in whatever way they can. Often this means denigrating some perfectly valid evidence.

Recently, psychologist Drew Westen has poked around in people's brains to see what gets stirred up when people are confronted with evidence that casts their favorite political candidates in an unflattering light (the study was carried out during the 2004 U.S. presidential election). For example, while lounging in a brain scanner, committed Democrats read the following statement about Democrat John Kerry:

> *During the 1996 campaign, Kerry told a* Boston Globe *reporter that the Social Security system should be overhauled. He said Congress should consider raising the retirement age and means testing benefits. 'I know it's going to be unpopular,' he said. 'But we have a generational responsibility to fix this problem.'*

They then read a statement that suggested some inconsistency on Kerry's part. In response, they had to judge whether they thought his actions contradicted his earlier words: "*This year, on Meet the Press, Kerry pledged that he will never tax or cut benefits to seniors or raise the age for eligibility for Social Security.*"

This statement was meant to collide with their good feelings about Kerry, and it did. When Kerry supporters were shown similar incriminating evidence pointing to the inconsistency of Republican George W. Bush, or of politically neutral people (actor Tom Hanks, writer William Styron), they had no trouble judging them accordingly. But they were less likely to say that Kerry contradicted himself (Republicans showed exactly the reverse, showing a willingness to forgive Bush).

What was especially interesting was what was happening in their brains during all this. Reading the evidence of contradictory behavior by their favorite candidate caused a lot of commotion in a part of the brain that registers emotional distress. The unflattering evidence seemed to whip up some negative emotion—which the study volunteers then resolved by denying that there *was* a contradiction. By comparison, the same brain region stayed pretty serene when people read about contradictions involving the *opposing* candidate or the politically neutral person—that is, when the contradiction didn't threaten the esteem they had for that person. The neural signature for distress didn't show up when the evidence wasn't on a collision course with people's own beliefs.

Just as interesting is what Westen and his colleagues *didn't* see when people read the damning evidence about the candidate they supported: the scans showed no surge of activity in the part of the brain that deals with conscious reasoning. In other words, when Democrats decided that Kerry wasn't contradicting himself, they probably didn't reach that conclusion by coolly working through logically possible scenarios and dispassionately coming up with a plausible hypothesis. As Westen put it, "they thought with their guts."

The link between emotional threat and bias can be seen in another way: creating an anxious state of mind can push people into a more biased style of information-gathering. In one study led by Howard Lavine, people were more likely to avoid opposing points of view if they were first made to write down thoughts about their own death and mortality. But Lavine found that not everyone became more biased after wallowing in these morbid thoughts. Thinking about death had a dispro-portionate effect on people who scored high on the scale of *Right Wing Author-itarianism*. The *RWA* is a scale that's used by psychologists and political scientists to capture what seems to be a stable collection of personality traits and ideological leanings. People who score high on the scale tend to be willing to submit to established authority figures, have a general aggressiveness towards those who fall outside of accepted social categories, and put a high premium on tradition and social norms.[6] In Lavine's study, when thoughts of mortality weren't activated, these folks behaved no differently from others who scored much lower on the scale. But when jolted in a threatening way, they became a lot less eager to seek out other viewpoints. One way to think about these results is that the combination of personal traits and a stressful situation pushed some people beyond their capacity to cope with the internal conflicts they would face by reading viewpoints that contradicted their own. So they chose to avoid them.

---

[6] The connection between Right-Wing Authoritarianism and political orientation is complicated. In North America, high scores on the scale have tended to correlate with party affiliation as Republican (in the U.S.) or Conservative (in Canada), and especially with support for policies such as capital punishment, and opposition to gay marriage and abortion. But many conservatives are not author-itarian, nor are all authoritarians conservative or "right-wing" in the political sense—for example, in the Soviet Union, authoritarianism was linked mostly with left-wing ideology.

In a historical context, you can begin to see why unstable social and political situations so readily give rise to extremism and the death of reason. A defeated Germany after World War I, the turmoil of post-communist Yugoslavia, an Afghanistan that spent decades fending off foreign invasion—in all of these cases, a swirling set of anxieties might have blocked the ability of people to engage in the finer points of deliberation and civil debate of opposing viewpoints.

And more recently in the United States, given the steady diet of fear in the post-9/11 world, generously blended with angst over a spectacular economic nosedive, it probably shouldn't come as a surprise that lately, American politics have been more dysfunctionally partisan than they've been in long time. Stressful conditions create just the right environment in which irrational beliefs persist in the face of perfectly good evidence. It's not hard to find examples of this—whether it's the conviction that Barack Obama was not born on United States soil, despite copious documentation to the contrary, or the sticky belief that Saddam Hussein was responsible for the 9/11 terrorist attacks.

A group of researchers led by Monica Prasad actually took a close look at why so many people continued to believe there was a link between Saddam Hussein and the 2001 terrorist acts, even though the White House itself eventually declared there was no evidence for this. The tenacity of this false belief was fairly worrisome, as the 2004 presidential elections focused very heavily on foreign policy issues involving Iraq—which would mean that many voters were badly mistaken about critical issues relating to the campaign.

Prasad and her colleagues sent a survey to strongly Republican precincts and found that 76% of people who sent back the survey agreed that Saddam Hussein was at least partly responsible for the attacks. Not surprisingly, Republicans were much more likely to believe this than Democrats. The researchers then met with everyone who fell prey to the false belief, and confronted them with newspaper clippings about the findings of a commission that reported there was no evidence of a link between Saddam Hussein and the attacks, and an article that quoted George W. Bush as saying "*This administration never said that the 9/11 attacks were orchestrated between Saddam and Al-Qaeda.*"

Some of these people, when shown the articles, said that they'd made a mistake in filling out the survey—they'd gotten Iraq mixed up with Afghanistan in their minds at the time, but were aware there was no link between Saddam and Al-Qaeda. But most of them truly did hold the belief that there was a connection between the two. When challenged with the facts, they dealt with it in a number of ways.

Some completely ignored the evidence, and never even acknowledged having seen it, even though the interviewer was holding the newspaper clips right in front of their eyes and describing their contents. Some of them admitted to seeing the evidence, but just refused to talk about it (*"I'm gonna pass on this one for now"*). Many of them just changed the subject to focus on other good reasons for invading Iraq. Some maintained that they were entitled to their opinions despite the facts. For example, one person said, "*Well, I bet they say that the Commission didn't have any proof of it but I guess we still can have our opinions and feel that way even though they say that.*" And some reasoned backwards: they argued that because America was in a war with Iraq, there had to be a good reason for it, therefore Saddam Hussein must have been involved in the 9/11 attacks—*despite having been shown the article that quoted Bush as denying there was any connection between the two.*

The number of people out of 49 who revised their belief about the link between 9/11 and Saddam when presented with the facts? One.

Winning the Hearts, Minds, and Biases of Voters

From a strategic standpoint, it's obvious that it's in the interest of political candidates and parties—at least in the short term—to promote as much bias as possible in their favor. Persuading voters anew every time with fresh detailed arguments for every policy is hopelessly inefficient. In fact, as the Democrats flailed at the ballot box throughout much of the past few decades, commentators from both sides of the political fence were in the habit of criticizing the party's messaging on grounds that it was dry, unemotional, overly intellectual, and relied on voters to be motivated enough to follow the twists and turns of intricate policy debates. As the story goes, the Democrats floundered in part because they insisted on communicating to the head instead of at the gut.

Here's an example of one such communication blunder: When Democrat Michael Dukakis was asked whether he would oppose the death penalty for someone who raped and killed his wife, he answered:

I think you know that I've opposed the death penalty during all my life. I don't see any evidence that it's a deterrent, and I think there are better and more effective ways to deal with violent crime.

This was a disastrous answer. But why? After all, Dukakis answered the question with some reasonable justification for his position. But that's exactly the problem. He addressed the issue *as if all that mattered* was addressing the issue. What he missed was that every question was also an opportunity to create an impression that would guide how all *subsequent* answers to questions got interpreted.

Drew Westen (who advises Democrats on communications strategy when he's not peering at political brains in scanners) wrote:

What the average listener heard was his answer to three very different questions: 'Are you a man?' 'Do you have a heart?' and 'Are we similar enough that I could trust you to represent me and my values as president?' For most Americans, the answer to all three questions was no.

What should he have done instead? Linguist Geoff Nunberg, who remarked that by answering the way he did, Dukakis "branded himself a bloodless technocrat," suggested a more muscular response in the vein of Democrat Mario Cuomo, who defended *his* opposition to the death penalty as follows:

> *Because it's wrong, because it's dumb, because it's counterproductive, because it's an instruction in violence, because it won't make my daughter safe. It won't make my mother safe. It never has.*

When pressed as to whether he would kill a man who'd molested his daughter if he caught him, Cuomo answered:

> *I don't know ... and I don't want to know. But the point is, God forbid I should make laws that are only as good as me! ... I want something much, much better than Mario Cuomo.*

Cuomo responded to the *issue* by using an argument that was identical to Dukakis'. But by using emotional, direct, and forceful language, he also answered "yes" to the other three questions. And it was his response to these three questions that shaped voters' biases in a way that would color any future message from him.

Placing bias at the center of a political communication strategy is the smart thing to do for candidates who want to win. But notice it runs in exactly the opposite direction of how we normally think about deliberative democracy. In theory, democracy is supposed to work kind of like jury duty: You're supposed to scrutinize the evidence thoroughly, putting aside your own emotions, personal experiences, and gut reactions, and withhold judgment until you've heard the full panoply of arguments from both sides. Only *then* are you supposed to start the process of evaluating it. But taking this approach seriously almost guarantees political suicide.[7] Hence the political expediency of using language that packs as strong, as personal, and as immediate a response as possible in favor of your message and against your opponent.

At its most benevolent, bias can give us a handy way to structure and understand new and complex information. And it can also be used to deflate some of the most obnoxious aspects of political campaigns. For example, hard as it is to undo the damage of negative attacks *after* the fact, bias can be used defensively to create a barrier that makes the attacks less likely to penetrate voters' minds in the first place. Given, for instance, that one analysis of the Bush and Kerry 2004 campaigns found

---

[7] In *practice*, jury duty probably works a bit more like politics. Trial lawyers are not just being superstitious when they sternly advise their clients how to dress, how to hold their heads, and how to speak. And juries have been shown to be susceptible to many of the same biases and cognitive errors that turn up elsewhere—including making up their minds fairly early on and being reluctant to override those early impressions, and having a hard time disregarding incriminating evidence or insinuations that slip into the trial against the rules of evidence.

that about 80% of all "news releases" on their campaign websites contained an attack on the opposition, this seems like a good thing—especially when you consider evidence that negative campaigning plays a role in turning voters apathetic and more likely to stay home on Election Day.

Obama's 2008 campaign used bias in this way to great advantage (to defuse both legitimate criticism and dirty politics). When he ran against Hillary Clinton for the Democratic nomination, his campaign responded to negative messages from the Clinton camp—mostly focusing on his inexperience—by making the following statement:

> *Iowans have found that Senator Clinton is running the most negative campaign of any candidate.*[8] *These attacks take attention away from solving people's problems and exact a real cost on our political process.*

The Obama team then reinforced the idea of "costs" in a creative and literal-minded way: An online fundraising campaign called itself "*The Costs of Negativity*" and solicited money from supporters in order to prove that when opponents "*attack Barack Obama it will literally make our campaign stronger.*" The campaign also launched a website called "*Hillary Attacks*" which actually *tracked* negative comments from the opposition. Voters were advised to "*be vigilant and notify us immediately of any attacks from Senator Clinton or her supporters as soon as you see them so we can respond with the truth swiftly and forcefully.*"

The notification was beside the point—Obama's campaign was surely well aware of any negative remarks. The purpose of the website was to vaccinate the minds of voters against negative comments aimed at Obama. It did this by injecting voters with the expectation that attacks by Clinton were groundless, and to be taken as evidence of her deficiencies as a leader. With these antibodies swimming through voters' brains, Obama didn't actually have to do much to neutralize the negative attacks—he could count on voters doing that themselves.

Lovemarks and Hatemarks in Political Branding

Kevin Roberts of Saatchi & Saatchi believes that great brands are "Lovemarks" capable of stoking in consumers' hearts a "loyalty beyond all reason." He raises brands like Apple on a pedestal as Lovemark icons. These days, what many Lovemark brands seem to do is give you an image in the mirror you can really fall in love with. Take those famous Mac versus PC commercials. Mac is attractive, hip, smart, and supremely comfortable in his own skin. PC is frumpy, bumbling, insecure, and catty. The hidden question to viewers is: Are *you* a Mac or a PC? Be

---

[8] Note the use of the presuppositional language here. Part of the message here is that Clinton's running the most negative campaign of all is not up for debate.

careful what computer you buy—it says something about who you are. (And so does your car, your ringtone, and the kind of mustard you use.)

Given how fully we now breathe in the air of identity marketing, it's a small step to think about political brands in the same way. At some level, voting can become like buying a Mac—loyalty and passion aren't ignited when people deliberate over a set of product features or a collection of policies. But both of these can easily be fired up when the brand allows you to express who you are.

If you think back to the Mac versus PC ads, it becomes apparent that the ads do more than just get warm emotional juices oozing at the thought of a Mac. They also spark disdain for the competition. In American politics, the closest counterpart to the bumbling, inadequate PC is the scorned caricature of a hyper-educated, wealthy, out-of-touch elite, the kind of figure that says to many Americans, "I'm not like you."

Given that just about all political leaders are wealthy and hyper-educated, it can be a hard image to shed—one that Republicans have generally sloughed off with more ease than Democrats over the past few decades. Look up "liberal elite" on Wikipedia, and you'll find a detailed entry. There's no Wikipedia listing for "conservative elite". What's striking is just how enmeshed the stereotype has become with consumer identity symbols. During the 2004 Kerry campaign, CNN reporter Candy Crowley recounted an anecdote in which Kerry ordered green tea at a restaurant in Dubuque, Iowa. Apparently, the waitress stared at him for a moment before responding, "*We have Lipton's.*" According to Crowley, this revealed a fundamental problem with Kerry's candidacy: "*There were many green tea instances. There's a very large disconnect between the Washington politicians and most of America and how they live. Bush was able to bridge that gap, and Kerry was not.*"

In the same year, a TV commercial by the conservative Club for Growth featured a Middle America couple expressing their views about Democratic candidate Howard Dean. Here's what they tossed into the linguistic stewpot:

I think Howard Dean should take his tax-hiking, government-expanding, latte-drinking, sushi-eating, Volvo-driving, New York Times reading, body-piercing, Hollywood-loving, left-wing freak show back to Vermont, where it belongs.

In the 2008 campaign, the opponents and media alike pounced on an Obama "green tea" moment—or rather, a green leaf incident in which Obama referred to the price of arugula in the presence of a group of Iowan farmers. According to a *Newsweek* article, this was seized upon by the Republican camp as "*an opportunity to paint Obama as an out-of-touch elitist, a Harvard toff who nibbles daintily at designer salads, while the working man, worried about the layoffs at the plant, belts another shot.*"

And *Media Matters for America*, a website devoted to "correcting conservative misinformation," countered allegations that Obama appealed more to the upscale "wine-track crowd" than the "beer-track crowd" by documenting copious examples of Obama's public acts of beer-drinking.

Numerous liberal commentators have argued that conservatives invented this branding exercise as a way to inflate the "out-of-touch liberal elite" stereotype. It may well be true that the caricature was most skillfully cultivated by conservatives. But the general consumer climate of equating identity with the things we buy would certainly have offered up a fertile, well-tilled soil. In any case, talk by and about politicians is now thoroughly infused with these politico-product pairings. In 2008, *The Times* in the UK offered up a "consumer guide" for those having trouble distinguishing Obama's policies and Clinton's; Obama's supporters were described as "latte liberals" for whom *"Starbucks, with its $5 cups of coffee and fancy bakeries, is not just a consumer choice but a lifestyle. They not only have the money. They share the values . . . They live by all those little quotes on the side of Starbucks cups about community service and global warming."* Clinton's supporters, on the other hand, were branded as "Dunkin' Donut Democrats" who don't have the money to burn on *"multiple-hyphenated coffee drinks—double-top, no-foam, non-fat lattes and the like . . . For them caffeine choice doesn't correlate with their values but simply represents a means of keeping them going through their challenging day."*

Nor is the phenomenon limited to American politics—Australia has its own cadre of "chardonnay socialists." The language of groceries and beverages now flows freely through the international political bloodstream.

This kind of language is deeply irritating to some. Writer Paul Allor responded to the kerfuffle over the Obama arugula incident by insisting:

> No one makes election decisions based on food choices. And if someone did, you would probably want to pull them aside and ask them, politely but firmly, to either take their civic responsibility more seriously, or stay the Hell home next election day . . . We are an omnivorous nation. Regardless of geography, we fashion our own food choices . . . Most importantly, we don't expect our friends and neighbors—or our governors and presidents—to make the same choices we do. So God bless America, and pass me the tofu.

Obama seems to echo this sentiment in a passage in his book *The Audacity of Hope*. He writes about taking a road trip through Illinois with his legislative aide Dan Shomon, who comes across as a tad preoccupied with the symbology of clothing and culinary choices:

> Four times, he reminded me how to pack—just khakis and polo shirts, he said; no fancy linen trousers, or silk shirts. I assured him that I didn't own any linens or silks. On the drive down, we stopped at a TGI Friday's and I ordered a cheeseburger. When the waitress brought the food, I asked her if she had any Dijon mustard. Dan shook his head.

'He doesn't want Dijon,' he insisted, waving the waitress off. 'Here'—he shoved a yellow bottle of French's mustard in my direction—'here's some mustard right here.'
The waitress looked confused. 'We got Dijon if you want it,' she said.

Obama's account of the incident is a reverse re-write of the Kerry green tea anecdote offered by CNN's Candy Crowley. In Crowley's version, the waitress stares at Kerry after his ordering faux-pas, as if he'd just revealed he was from Mars—or the East Coast. In Obama's story, it's the political handler who sees a deep connection between Dijon and disconnection from The People. To the waitress, Dijon mustard is not an emblem of class-based cluelessness. She's baffled by Dan Shomon's antics. Obama, true to himself, orders whatever he wants, and she reads nothing into it. Sometimes, mustard is just mustard. God bless America.

But whether or not Obama himself believes that class identity symbols have no role to play in election politics, that's not how his presidential campaign went about things in 2008. If Dijon mustard could send the wrong signals, so could the *typeface* used on campaign posters. Rahaf Harfoush, a new media strategist for the Obama team, wrote why the campaign made a choice to switch away from using the Gill Sans typeface:

Under scrutiny, the typeface Gill Sans appeared elegant, sophisticated, and classic, but it also appeared stylistically formal, aloof, like a European black-tie affair . . . So we began exploring other possibilities . . . The top choice became Gotham . . . The face was inspired by the letters at the Port Authority Terminal in New York City; the type was 'attractive but unassuming,' and appeared blue collar, but could dress up well. It was the perfect choice. Perfectly American.

I have no idea whether different fonts set off neural fireworks that subconsciously light up mental scenes of Euro-elite parties or the hardworking heroes at the Port Authority Terminal in New York (interesting question, though). But when it comes to the politics of arugula, Paul Allor is probably too quick to dismiss the subtle impact of a sense of common identity. It would indeed be stupid to suggest that our beliefs about health care reform boil down to a shared fondness or disdain for certain leafy greens. And I doubt that you will find any voters who would justify their ballot behavior by talking about what a candidate had for dinner last night. What you *will* find, though, are people who say about their candidate, "I feel that he's trustworthy. He seems to know what he's talking about." These are the kinds of positive biases that encourage us to give someone the benefit of the doubt on an issue we're not that sure about. When we instinctively feel that someone is like us, it's easier to grant that bias. A sense of affinity can play in these margins. How big the margins are, of course, depends in part on how deep our knowledge and scrutiny of the issues are.

But there's too much evidence from human behavior—in the lab and otherwise—to discount the fact that we're built to be sensitive to shared traits and preferences. Who among us hasn't experienced that extra jolt of attraction to someone who—oh joy!—happens to share our love for a certain obscure Bulgarian psychedelic funk musician or for fried-egg-and-nutella-and-peanut-butter sandwiches? On the negative side, writer Ayn Rand famously judged admiration of Beethoven's music (which she loathed) to be a moral failing. And in the animated film "Wallace and Gromit," we know that Wallace's relationship with Wendolene (which to date has survived near death at the hands of her psychopathic murderous robotic dog) is doomed when the cheese-addicted Wallace learns that Wendolene "can't abide the stuff."

The affinity-seeking surely gets amplified in a consumer culture where mustard often is *not* just mustard. Marketers know perfectly well it's not just a matter of naked taste preferences, or they could never effectively target the stuff at specific zip codes. And implicitly, we are likely to make certain inferences about Dijon-eaters as well. Consumer behavior, more than ever, gives us a way to sort people into categories. Nowadays, we've turned verb phrases like *getting a Mac* and *owning a Passat* into noun phrases like *Mac person* and *Passat people*. If politics has coined its own noun phrases as a means to divide and conquer the electorate, well then, it's trekking in some well-trod commercial footsteps.

Talking the Talk

Using mustard as a code for social identity may be a recent phenomenon. But using language to accomplish the same thing is probably written into our DNA. Remember the Martha's Vineyard residents who—unconsciously—signaled their attitudes towards the intruding mainlanders by virtue of how they pronounced their vowels? And the experiments showing that people are more trusting of voices that sound like their own—even when they know these voices come from a computer? Facts like these point to some deep wiring in our minds for connecting language and identity.

We seem to be living in a political era where prestige is its own stigma. Drew Westen (the psychologist who studied the brains of rationalizing partisans) made this point by lambasting a TV ad created by the 2004 Kerry campaign as being "tone-deaf." The offending ad actually used the word *privilege* and made references to Kerry's Massachusetts ties and Yale education. Westen noted that the only time George W. Bush spoke publicly about *his* Yale degree was at a commencement ceremony when he reminded his audience that he'd been a C-student (assuring the less-than-stellar students in the crowd that "you too can become President"). So it stands to reason that political candidates would be somewhat eager to slip out of any kind of language that makes it clear just how much prestige has accumulated on their persons.

Fortunately for them, the English language has a few features that do the trick more handily than guzzling beer in public. One of these is the habit of "dropping *g*'s"—for instance saying *dropping* as *droppin'*.[9] To many people, the "*g*" dropping sounds lazy and possibly uneducated, or at the very least, informal. Not the kind of thing you'd expect to hear spoken by newscasters on the BBC or on the CBC or even ABC. In a 2006 study by linguist Bill Labov, listeners scored speakers as less professional-sounding when they dropped their g's than when they didn't—even if they only dropped them 10% of the time.

But "*g*"-dropping is no newfangled degradation of the English language like saying "nucular" or "She was like, Oh my God." It's been around since Early English in medieval times, when the *dropped* form was the default, and various sound changes turned some endings into the now more tony versions. The two have competed ever since, and *ing* eventually became the standard prestige form. Some historians believe that teachers as far back as the early seventeenth century were slapping their pupils' wrists for their uncouth use of *in'*. Throughout just about all varieties of current English, from Australia to the United Kingdom to North America, the dropped version is considered to be the lower-class form.

Although a few people consistently use only one or the other form, for the most part, folks don't divide up neatly into *in'* users and *ing* users—just like most people can enjoy a classy Pinot Noir and a cold Bud on different occasions. The greatest variation is actually found in the speech of those at the middle to lower end of the socioeconomic ladder, possibly because they so often negotiate between identities. At the very highest and very lowest ends of the scale, people tend to stick to either the prestige or the nonstandard form. Like most nonstandard pronunciations, *in'* is used most in casual speech, and less in prepared speeches or when people are reading. Men pepper their speech with it more than women, and it's used more often when people are talking to someone they're on cozy terms with than when they're talking to a stranger. Even the topic of conversation can make a difference. In the course of a single conversation, people often seamlessly slide in and out of the prestige and nonstandard forms.

This has nothing to do with being confused about how to pronounce words. When people do this, they're instinctively and skillfully making use of a very subtle aspect of language. Just like words are attached to memories of their uses, accents and language varieties come attached to certain cultural and social memories as well. (For instance, bilingual speakers have been shown to behave more or less altruistically depending on which of their two languages they happen to be hearing.) So by using *in'* rather than *ing*, speakers can trigger associations for their hearers of the situations in which these forms are typically used, and of the people that typically use them. The general effect is to add some extra seasoning to

[9] Actually, it's not quite right to say that the "*g*" is dropped. You never really pronounce a *g* consonant in the "*ing*" suffix, you just make a nasal sound in the back of your mouth, rather than one in which your tongue tip touches the ridge behind your teeth.

the content of their words—*in'* for a brawnier, friendlier and more relaxed flavor, and *ing* for a more refined or aloof one.

So it's interesting that, for all the fuss made in the media about Barack Obama's arugula-nibbling, wine-sipping ways, he turns out to be a virtuoso at sliding between *in'* and *ing*. For example, if you listen to the dignified "A More Perfect Union" speech he gave during his campaign on race relations after the controversy over his pastor's inflammatory remarks, you'll hear nary a stray *in'* throughout. A sampling of his speech during televised bipartisan discussions on health care reform turned up a 31% rate of *in'* versus *ing*. And in a prepared speech delivered to his supporters in October 2009, he used the nonstandard *in'* 48% of the time.

Like many people who code-switch between the prestige and anti-elite endings, a closer analysis of Obama's speech to his "Organizing for America" supporters shows that the shifts between the two are anything but random. They're closely tied to the content that's being delivered. For example, in addressing his supporters, he summarizes his administration's accomplishments like this:

> We passed a law that will prevent our children from being targeted by big tobacco companies ... We've begun to put in place a new national policy aimed at both increasing fuel economy and reducing greenhouse gas pollution for all new trucks and cars ...
>   That's in the first nine months. The fact is, we've already had one of the most productive first years of any administration in decades.

That's language seasoned with Dijon mustard. But in the next sentence, when he thanks his supporters, he breaks out the French's yellow mustard:

> That's because of you. That's because of the work you did. That's what **knockin'** on doors and **makin'** phone calls was all about.

There's a similar contrast in the health care talks. When he outlines details of policy, the language wears the authority of *ing* endings. But it puts on blue jeans when the focus is on ordinary people who will be affected by the policy. For instance, in responding to the suggestion of a Republican colleague who's argued in favor of private health accounts, Obama responds:

> Would you feel the same way if you were **makin'** forty thousand dollars. Because it is very important for us, when you say to listen, to listen to that farmer Tom mentioned in Iowa, to listen to the folks that we get letters from. Because the truth of the matter is, they're not premiers of anyplace, they're not sultans from wherever. They don't fly in to the Mayo and suddenly decide they're gonna spend a couple million dollars on the absolute best health care. They're folks who are left out. The vast majority of ... the people we're **talkin'** about, they work. Every day. Some of 'em work two jobs. But if they're **workin'** for a small business, they can't get health care.

Especially revealing is a passage from the "Organizing for America" speech. There's a segment in the speech that contains mostly the *in'* forms. But three prestige endings sneak in—and they happen to be just when there's a shift in focus from Obama and his supporters to an unnamed opposition:

> *We understand exactly who and what got us into this mess. Now, we don't mind* **cleanin'** *it up. I'm* **grabbin'** *my mop and my broom and we're* **scrubbin'** *the floor and* **tryin'** *to neaten things up, but don't just stand there and say, 'You're not* **holding** *the mop right.' Don't just stand there and say 'You're not* **moppin** *fast enough.' Don't accuse me of* **having** *a socialist mop. Instead of* **standing** *on the sidelines, why don't you grab a mop.*

As symbols of social identity, these are pretty organic. Unlike photo ops of bowling, beer-drinking, or Philly steak-eating, they're harder to stage. They're probably not marked up by speech-writers, and it's unlikely they show up on the teleprompter. If they did, the speech-writers would have to be an impressively accomplished bunch of linguists to arrange them in the nuanced way in which they turn up in Obama's speech—and in a way that mirrors the natural code-switching by people who are in the habit of doing that sort of thing. It's *possible* that Obama has learned to control this style of speech self-consciously, much as actors might. But it would probably be quite a feat to maintain it in the heat of debates over health care reform, unless he happened to already be a native code-switcher.

The impact of such linguistic gestures on the hearer comes from cognitive machinery that has evolved to automatically suck information out of a speaker's speech about what social tribe he belongs to. Unlike the endless media obsessions over what gets ordered in restaurants, these subtle shifts of pronunciation rarely make the news. And yet linguists know from many studies that people regularly use them as a means to claim membership in social groups, and to signal their social attitudes.

Like Obama's typeface, his language appears working class, but dresses up well, and accomplishes things that no font is likely to ever be able to do.

The Power of Choice

This whole journey into persuasion began in Chapter 1 by considering how having a choice opens the door to persuasion, and hence to persuaders. As choices proliferate, so do persuasive messages. One common way we deal with this proliferation of messages is to try and ignore most of the messages, and for those we do attend to, we mostly don't think about them very deeply, shuttling them off to our peripheral thinking instead. This in turn makes the persuasive messages aimed at our peripheral thinking the most successful among them. And it turns out to be surprising how many of our decisions are based on this portion of our minds.

However, unlike Edward Bernays, who shrugged off the idealistic notions of Enlightenment Age philosophers, most of us are at least somewhat attached to the idea of ourselves as people who put some stock in thoughtful discussion and rational deliberation. If you're one of these people, this book may have irked you at times, with its suggestions that you buy ketchup because of how it's named. Or that the shape of a politician's vowels influences how much you trust his foreign policy. Just how stupid do I think you and your fellow humans are?

But here's the thing: paradoxically, our intelligence wouldn't get very far without all the layers of automatic and unconscious thinking that I've claimed can be so persuasive. It forms the underground foundation for our towering human intellect. For instance, all the cross-wiring of words in our memories means that there is continual information leak from any given word, so that we can—seemingly irrationally—feel very differently about two words for the same thing. But without this cross-wiring, we almost certainly couldn't pack tens of thousands of words into our memory bin. The same design feature that makes us vulnerable to linguistic spin also gives us the vocabulary to craft a constitution.

This is where the recent stack of science demonstrating the power of the unconscious goes far beyond Freud's original observations. For Freud, many of our drives and motivations get pushed down into our unconscious minds because they conflict with our civilized sense of our selves. As the story goes, you don't *know* that secret sexual fantasies lurk beneath the veneer of your socially acceptable behavior, because knowing this would be too upsetting. But much of the new unconsciousness that's coming to light is of a different nature. Not knowing our own minds isn't just a product of our attempts to manage the thorny complexities of our emotional lives. It's part of the very nature of our muscular intelligence—an intelligence that's evolved to efficiently negotiate its way through mindboggling volumes of complex information. The vast majority of what we know and how we think hums along below the surface of our awareness, and forms the basis of the knowledge that we *can* consciously manipulate.

The fly in the ointment is that at times, all this efficient, automatic machinery can get in the way of really seeing a situation as it is. Think back to the visual illusion in which lines of identical length were made to look different just by virtue of having arrow ends that point in or out. Your visual system has adapted to process information in a way that works for most situations, allowing you to interpret the probable length of lines that appear in the foreground versus the background. And, since such judgments are a part of perceiving most scenes, you do this without having to consciously think it through: Every. Single. Time. The same visual system happens not to do so well with two-dimensional lines that have arrow ends pointing in or out. Suddenly, your conscious mind can't seem to tell your unconscious mind what to do. Much of the way we deal with language and with everyday decisions that we make has some elements of this conflict to it.

What's clear is that scientific understanding about how our minds work has progressed and changed since the times in which our economic and political institutions were forged. It's not surprising that thinkers in the eighteenth century were mainly impressed with the ability of all people to engage in rational thought. This was a time when the benefits of education were beginning to be offered to people who had historically been shut out. It quickly became apparent that ignorance among the lower classes was more a matter of opportunity than intelligence. It's also not surprising that the same thinkers were blissfully unaware of the many ways in which our minds make choices less consciously. After all, it's the conscious aspects of our reasoning that we're *aware* of when we think about how we think. Philosophers in the eighteenth century were convinced of people's inherent rationality for pretty much the same reason you might be convinced of your own—it's the part of your mind that's *accessible* to you. A fuller discovery of the depths of our unconscious basins of thought had to wait for twentieth and twenty-first century scientific techniques.

We are just now beginning to appreciate the extent of the collision between our conscious and unconscious minds, and their implications.

The real question now is what we do with that understanding. If our minds aren't built the way people thought they were back when they invented systems of democracy and the free market, what then?

One possible move is to submit to the sweetness of cognitive-dissonance management, and simply deny that our choices all too often lead down the path of irrationality. Tempting. But let's explore a few other options for a moment.

Another possible move is to say that Plato was right after all—that the notion of democracy rests on wishful thinking, and that the governance of a country can't be left to the mindless gut-level decision-making of a people who aren't in the driver's seat of their own minds. But Plato's solution of philosopher as king suffers from a critical flaw: it's only as good as the philosopher's understanding of human nature itself. This is bad news when you consider that the clearest conclusion to have come out of the science of the mind is how much of the mind remains hidden. Plato also badly underestimated a philosopher-king's ability to apply what he knows about human nature to himself. One of the most common forms of biased thinking, for example, is the belief that everyone is biased—except you! And even Nobel prize-winning scientists, trained in the techniques of bias-avoidance, have been seduced by truly irrational beliefs.

Yet another move is to stop worrying and buy wholeheartedly into the ideas of gifted persuaders such as Edward Bernays and Frank Luntz. If you line up on this side of the room, then democracy boils down to a technical contest of influence-shaping in which the field advantage goes to whoever has the consultants with the best words, the best polling techniques, and the most cutting-edge expertise. Then you cross your fingers and hope that the competitive arena guarantees that nothing *too* crazy happens.

But there are other things that can be done with a clear-headed view of human choice-making. One of them is to use this new understanding as a way to actually shape the choices we make. Happily, not all situations in which our less unconscious minds lead us into a dead-end turn out to be like the visual illusion. Much of the time, our conscious minds *do* talk back to our automatic pilots. Want to know how to neutralize all those priming effects in which people walk slowly if they read words associated with growing old, or behave rudely if they unscramble sent sentences containing aggressive language? Tell them about the effect just before you try it out on them. Like a card trick, its magic evaporates as soon as people know how it works. And the Asian disease problem? If people are told to treat the question as a problem in *statistics*, the framing effect goes up in smoke. And there are dozens of studies that document ways in which people come to rely less on *truthiness* in a situation—for example, a gut feeling that the source of a message can be trusted—and more on whether the argument itself is on solid ground. We may have to wrestle for control of our own attentional spotlight sometimes, but it's not totally outside of our power to take charge of where it's aimed. Understanding exactly how this works might help us figure out exactly how best to structure certain situations where we're targets for persuasion.

We might also have to account for the fact that other unconscious biases are less easily burst. For example, deeply embedded racial prejudices that have been learned by social osmosis don't seem to burn up like vampires just because a mental window opens up to let daylight in. Discussions of some issues might need to recognize this possibility and adjust for it. And that blasted confirmation bias can be a hard one to shake. (It's raining? Pass me two aspirin.)

Right now, new scientific knowledge about the hidden workings of our minds is striding a few steps ahead of understanding how we can control this hidden part of ourselves. With luck, newer knowledge about the internal landscape will provide some guidance as to how to maneuver our way through the mindlessness traps, and where the real sinkholes are. Where we run up against true limits in the ability of our conscious selves to take control (analogous to the line length illusion), we may need to have some tough conversations about how to structure our society to avoid truly crummy decisions. In these cases, the talks might need to be about whether we can live with sacrificing the *impression* of individual choice if it means better choices as a society. All of these questions are now beginning to wind their way into deliberations about public policy.

For example, behavioral economists Cass Sunstein and Richard Thaler have written about their notion of *libertarian paternalism*. The idea is to protect people from some of their own worst mistakes by taking into account what we now know about typical human biases and shortcomings of thought. This is done by setting decision defaults in such a way that the outcome will likely be a good one for people who choose fairly mindlessly. But at the same time, a full range of choices is available to those who are motivated to think through all the possibilities—or who are hell-bent on making choices that aren't necessarily in their best interest. In a sense, they're proposing the public policy equivalent of what supermarkets do when they place certain items at eye level on the store shelves. The goal is to identify certain "good" choices and place these at people's cognitive "eye level"—everyone is still free to stoop or reach for any of the other choices. So, for Sunstein and Thaler, public policy becomes in part an issue of choice architecture.

What's clear is that the prospects of us really exercising the full power of choice are thin unless we really start to pay attention to the ways in which our own minds work. If persuaders so often talk to our mackerel minds, it's because they are so often rewarded for doing so. There will probably be plenty of times when we'll be perfectly happy letting the less conscious part of ourselves take the wheel and make the decisions. But for those times when it becomes really important that the sober judges within us take charge, we'll need to make some changes in how we listen to persuaders, how we let them talk to us.

Do our big brains have what it takes? Do we have the capacity to not only choose, but to choose *how* we choose?

That remains to be seen.

Sources

Note: All the websites listed below were accessed on August 19, 2010.

Chapter 1

1. **Trillion dollar advertising business.** U.S. Advertising Expenditures Declined 1.6 Percent in First Half 2008. *TNS Media Intelligence Reports*, September 24, 2008: http://www.tns-mi.com/news/09242008.htm
2. **Calvin Coolidge addresses the American Association of Advertising Agencies.** The full speech, delivered October 27, 1926, can be found on *The Presidency Project*: http://www.presidency.ucsb.edu/ws/index.php?pid=412
3. **Mr. Medvedev's "persuasive" message to Olympic trainers.** Medvedev calls for resignation of Olympic officials. *The Telegraph*, March 1, 2010: http://www.telegraph.co.uk/news/worldnews/europe/russia/7348764/Medvedev-calls-for-resignation-of-Olympic-officials.html
4. **The choices in Barry Schwartz's neighborhood store.** B. Schwartz (2004) *The Paradox of Choice: Why More is Less*. New York: HarperCollins.
5. **Alvin Toffler's predictions of overchoice.** A. Toffler (1970) *Future Shock*. New York: Bantam Books.
6. **Jam-buyers are paralyzed by too much choice.** S. Iyengar & M. Lepper (2000) When choice is demotivating: Can one desire too much of a good thing? *Journal of Personality and Social Psychology*, 79, 995–1006.
7. **Polls show growing sense of loss of control.** L. Harris (1987) *Inside America*. New York: Random House.
8. **"Earth exit statement" by Heaven's Gate members.** The statement by "Glnody" and other members can be found on the Heaven's Gate website: http://www.heavensgate.com/
9. **Persuasion methods in cults.** Social psychologists Anthony Pratkanis and Elliot Aronson have a concise, readable discussion titled, "How to become a cult leader," which can be found in their book: A. Pratkanis & E. Aronson

Sold on Language: How Advertisers Talk to You and What This Says About You. By Julie Sedivy and Greg Carlson
© 2011 John Wiley & Sons Ltd.

(2001) *Age of Propaganda. The Everyday Use and Abuse of Persuasion.* New York: Henry Holt and Co.

10. **Mother acquitted of murder due to "mind control" defense.** Jury acquits Robidoux of murdering baby. *The Boston Globe,* February 4, 2004.

11. **Oxytocin-sniffers become more trusting.** M. Kosfeld, M. Heinrichs, P. Zak, U. Fischbacher & E. Fehr (2005) Oxytocin increases trust in humans. *Nature,* 435, 673–676. The commentary by neuroscientist Antonio Damasio: A. Damasio (2005) Brain trust. *Nature,* 435, 571–572.

12. **Boorstin on the limits of democracy.** D.J. Boorstin (1974) The rhetoric of democracy. In: *Democracy and its Discontents: Reflections on Everyday America.* New York: Random House.

Chapter 2

1. **Edward Bernays and "torches of freedom".** The description of the work Bernays did for Lucky Strikes, and the wording of the "feminist" telegram is taken from his memoir: E. Bernays (1965) *Biography of an Idea: Memoirs of Public Relations Counsel Edward L. Bernays.* New York: Simon & Schuster.

   There are several fascinating portraits of Edward Bernays and his work. Among these are: L. Tye (2002) *The Father of Spin: Edward L. Bernays and the Birth of Public Relations.* New York: Henry Holt and Co.; Adam Curtis (2002) *Century of the Self.* BBC documentary, released on DVD in 2009.

2. **Brain science does a Pepsi/Coke taste test.** S. McClure, J. Li, D. Tomlin, *et al.* (2004) Neural correlates of behavioral preference for culturally familiar drinks. *Neuron,* 44, 379–387.

3. **"Lovemarks", not brands.** K. Roberts (2006) *The Lovemarks Effect: Winning in the Consumer Revolution.* New York: Powerhouse Books.

4. **Implicit Association Test.** The IAT was first reported in a scientific journal in the following article: A. Greenwald, D. McGhee & J. Schwartz (1998) Measuring individual differences in implicit cognition: The implicit association test. *Journal of Personality and Social Psychology,* 74, 1464–1480.

   To try the implicit association test online, or to read countless papers on the IAT that have since been published, visit: https://implicit.harvard.edu/implicit/

   Malcolm Gladwell relates his personal experience with the IAT in: M. Gladwell (2005) *Blink.* New York: Little, Brown and Company.

   For a discussion of the validity of the IAT in predicting behavior: A. Greenwald, T.A. Poehlman, E. Uhlmann, & M. Banaji (2009) Understanding and using the Implicit Association Test: III. Meta-analysis of predictive validity. *Journal of Personality and Social Psychology,* 97, 17–41.

   A report of the German experiment of jurors' decisions and implicit attitudes: A. Florack, M. Scarabis & H. Bless (2001). Der Einfluß wahrgenommener Bedrohung auf die Nutzung automatischer Assoziationen bei der Personenbeurteilung. *Zeitschrift für Sozialpsychologie*, 32, 249–259.

5. **Visual illusions depend on the visual environment in which you grow up.** M. Segall, D. Campbell & M. Herskovits (1966) *The Influence of Culture on Visual Perception*. New York: Bobbs-Merrill Company.

6. **Infants learn which sound contrasts to "ignore."** P. Eimas, J. Miller & P. Jusczyk (1987) Infant speech perception and the acquisition of language. In: S. Harnad (Ed.), *Categorical Perception: The Groundwork of Cognition*. Cambridge: Cambridge University Press.

7. **Experimental evidence of lexical linkages in the mind.** The groundbreaking article on semantic priming is: D.E. Meyer & R.W. Schvaneveldt (1971) Facilitation in recognizing pairs of words: Evidence of a dependence upon retrieval operations. *Journal of Experimental Psychology*, 90, 227–234.

Semantic priming reveals access of multiple meanings of ambiguous words: D. Swinney (1979) Lexical access during sentence comprehension: (Re) consideration of context effects. *Journal of Verbal Learning and Verbal Behavior*, 18, 645–659.

Evidence from eye movements for the activation of related words: P. Allopenna, J. Magnuson & M. Tanenhaus (1998) Tracking the time course of spoken word recognition: evidence for continuous mapping models. *Journal of Memory and Language*, 38, 419–439; E. Yee & J. Sedivy (2006) Eye movements reveal transient semantic activation during spoken word recognition. *Journal of Experimental Psychology: Learning, Memory and Cognition*, 32(1), 1–14; J. Myung, S. Blumstein & J. Sedivy (2006) Playing on the Typewriter, Typing on the Piano: Manipulation Knowledge of Objects. *Cognition*, 98, 224–243.

8. **The pejorative use the word "liberal".** G. Nunberg (2006) Trashing the L-word. In: *Talking Right: How Conservatives Turned Liberalism into a Tax-Raising, Latte-Drinking, Sushi-Eating, Volvo-Driving, New York Times-Reading, Body-Piercing, Hollywood-Loving, Left-Wing Freak Show.* New York: Public Affairs Books.

9. **Ocean tides and laundry detergent.** R. Nisbett & T. Wilson (1977) Telling more than we can know: Verbal reports on mental processes. *Psychological Review*, 84, 231–259.

10. **Coinage of new words.** Merriam-Webster's Open Dictionary collects samples of new word usages. Anyone can submit a new entry. Words listed there are not official dictionary entries in the sense that they haven't been attested by dictionary experts to have spread throughout the language enough to be considered to be part of the general English lexicon. However, browsing through the Open Dictionary can reveal some interesting insights about wordplay and the sounds that come to mind when people try to invent new words: http://www3.merriam-webster.com/opendictionary/

11. **The bouba/kiki effect.** W. Köhler (1929) *Gestalt Psychology.* New York: Liveright; V. Ramachandran & E. Hubbard (2001) Synaesthesia: A window into perception, thought and language. *Journal of Consciousness Studies,* 8, 3–34; D. Maurer, T. Pathman & C. Mondloch (2006) The shape of boubas: Sound-shape correspondences in toddlers and adults. *Developmental Science,* 9, 316–322.

12. **Sound symbolism.** E. Sapir (1929) A study of phonetic symbolism. *Journal of Experimental Psychology,* 12, 225–239; J. Ohala (1984) An ethological perspective on common cross-language utilization of F0 of voice. *Phonetica,* 41, 1–16.

13. **Sound symbolism in brand names.** R. Klink (2000) Creating brand names with meaning: the use of sound symbolism. *Marketing Letters,* 11, 5–20.

14. **Sound symbolism in poetry.** C. Bök (2001) *Eunoia.* Toronto: Coach House Books.

15. **"Comfort scores" of politicians' names.** G. Smith (1998) The political impact of name sounds. *Communication Monographs,* 65,154–172.

16. **How male and female names sound.** K. Cassidy, M. Kelly & L. Sharoni (1999) Inferring gender from name phonology. *Journal of Experimental Psychology: General,* 128, 362–381.

17. **The story of Edsel.** P. Carlson (2007) The Flop Heard Round the World. Washington Post, September 4, 2007: http://www.washingtonpost.com/wp-dyn/content/article/2007/09/03/AR2007090301419_pf.html

18. **Trademark infringement of the BlackBerry name.** RIM sues LG over phone names. *The Globe and Mail,* November 8, 2007: http://www. theglobeandmail.com/news/technology/article796635.ece

19. **McDonald's rebrands McJobs.** The flip side of a McJob. *BBC News Magazine,* June 8, 2006: http://news.bbc.co.uk/2/hi/uk_news/magazine/ 5052020.stm

20. **Google faces genericide.** Google calls in "language police." BBC News Online, June 20, 2003: http://news.bbc.co.uk/2/hi/uk_news/3006486.stm
   2009 Word of the Year is "tweet"; Word of the Decade is "google." American Dialect Society, January 8, 2010: http://www.americandialect .org/index.php/amerdial/2009_word_of_the_year_is_tweet_word_of_the_ decade_is_google/

21. **Unconscious priming of behavior through words and images.** J. Bargh, M. Chen & L. Burrows (1996) Automaticity of social behavior: Direct effects of trait construct and stereotype activation on action. *Journal of Personality and Social Psychology,* 71, 230–244; A. Dijksterhuis, J. Bargh & J. Mideima (2000) Of men and mackerels: Attention, subjective experience, and automatic social behavior. In: H. Bless & J. Forgas (Eds.), *The Message Within: The Role of Subjective Experience in Social Cognition and Behavior.* Philadelphia: Psychology Press; J. Bargh & T. Chartrand (1999) The unbearable automaticity of being. *American Psychologist,* 54, 462–479.

22. **Subliminal priming of Lipton Ice.** J. Karremans, W. Stroebe & J. Claus (2006) Beyond Vicary's fantasies: The impact of subliminal priming and brand choice. *Journal of Experimental Social Psychology*, 42, 792–798.
23. **Republicans run subliminal RATS ad.** J. Egan (2000) RATS ad: Subliminal conspiracy? BBC News Online, September 13, 2000: http://news.bbc.co.uk/2/hi/in_depth/americas/2000/us_elections/election_news/923335.stm
24. **Testing the RATS ad.** J. Weinberger & D. Westen (2008) RATS, we should have used Clinton: Subliminal priming in political campaigns. *Political Psychology*, 29, 631–651.
25. **On the new unconsciousness research and free will:** J. Baer, J. Kaufman, & R. Baumeister (Eds.) (2008) *Are we free? The psychology of free will.* New York: Oxford University Press.
26. **Subliminally primed to "think different."** G. Fitzsimons, T. Chartrand & G. Fitzsimons (2008) Automatic effects of brand exposure on motivated behavior: How Apple makes you "Think Different." *Journal of Consumer Research*, 35, 21–35.

Chapter 3

1. **Keith Rayner on the perceptual span during reading.** K. Rayner (1975) The perceptual span and peripheral cues in reading. *Cognitive Psychology*, 7, 65–81; K. Rayner, A.D. Well & A. Pollatsek (1980) Asymmetry of the effective visual field in reading. *Perception & Psychophysics*, 27, 537–544; K. Rayner, A.D. Well, A. Pollatsek & J. Bertera (1982) The availability of useful information to the right of fixation in reading. *Perception & Psychophysics*, 31, 537–550.
2. **Perceptual studies on inattentional and change blindness.** The gorilla study: D. Simons & C. Chabris (1999) Gorillas in our midst: sustained inattentional blindness for dynamic events. *Perception*, 28, 1059–1074.

    Trading places behind the door study: D. Simons & D. Levin (1998) Failure to detect changes to people during a real-world interaction. *Psychonomic Bulletin & Review*, 5, 644–649.

    You can see some of the person-switching videos from the studies on change blindness and try the invisible gorilla experiment out on your friends and family by visiting Daniel Simons' website: http://viscog.beckman.illinois.edu/djs_lab/demos.html
3. **Eye-catching ads in unusual places.** An intriguing collection of unusual ads can be found at: J. Pisani. Eye-catching ads. *Business Week*, August 1, 2006. A slide show is available: http://www.businessweek.com/images/ss/06/07/weird_ads/index_01.htm
4. **Pop-up ads and the battle for attention.** P. Zhang (2006) Pop-up animations: Impacts and implications for website design and online advertising. In: D. Galletta & P. Zhang (Eds.), *Human–Computer Interaction and*

Management Information Systems: Applications. Advances in Management Information Systems, Vol. 5. New York: M.E. Sharpe; J. Dodd & R. Stevens (2004) The efficacy of pop-ups and the resulting effects on brands. White paper produced for Bunnyfoot Universality.

5. **Studying eye movements to visually incongruous scenes:** G. Loftus & N. Mackworth (1978) Cognitive determinants of fixation location during picture viewing. *Journal of Experimental Psychology: Human Perception and Performance*, 4, 565–572.

6. **Amusing ambiguities in headlines.** Many examples are documented on the following website, where you can also find links to books and other material on ambiguity and wordplay: http://www.fun-with-words.com/ambiguous_headlines.html

7. **How the mind deals with linguistic ambiguity.** M. Tanenhaus & J. Sedivy (1999) Ambiguity. In: R.A. Wilson & F.C. Keil (Eds.), *The MIT Encyclopedia of the Cognitive Sciences*, pp. 14–15; Michael Tanenhaus & John Trueswell (1995) Sentence comprehension. In: J. Miller & P. Eimas (Eds.), *Handbook of Cognition and Perception*. New York: Academic Press.

8. **The pleasures of puzzle-solving in ads.** B. Phillips (2000) The impact of verbal anchoring on consumer response to image ads. *Journal of Advertising*, 1, 15–24.

9. **Attention and the structure of sentences.** R. Tomlin (1997) Mapping conceptual representations into linguistic representations: the role of attention in grammar. In: J. Nuyts & E. Pederson (Eds.), *Language and conceptualization*, pp. 162–189. Cambridge: Cambridge University Press; L. Gleitman, D. January, R. Nappa & J. Trueswell (2007) On the give and take between event apprehension and utterance formulation. *Journal of Memory and Language*, 57, 544–569.

10. **Stephen Colbert on "truthiness".** *The Colbert Report*, October 17, 2005.
    To see the original episode, visit: http://www.colbertnation.com/the-colbert-report-videos/24039/october-17-2005/the-word---truthiness

11. **"Packaging" truthiness in advertising.** A nice discussion of various peripheral cues in advertising can be found in: A. Pratkanis & E. Aronson (2001) Packages. In: *Age of Propaganda: The everyday use and abuse of persuasion*, Chapter 17. New York: W.H. Freeman.

12. **Responding "mindlessly" to requests:** E. Langer, A. Blank & B. Chanowitz (1978) The mindlessness of ostensibly thoughtful action: The role of "placebic" information in interpersonal interaction. *Journal of Personality and Social Psychology*, 36, 635–642.

13. **Peripheral versus central thinking.** R.E. Petty & J.T. Cacioppo (1986) *Communication and Persuasion: Central and Peripheral Routes to Attitude Change.* New York: Springer-Verlag; R.E. Petty, J.T. Cacioppo, A. Strathman & J. Priester. (2005) To think or not to think? Exploring two routes to persuasion. In: T.C. Brock & M.C. Green (Eds.), *Persuasion: Psychological insights and perspectives.* Thousand Oaks, CA: Sage Publications.

14. **Persuasiveness of celebrity endorsements under high and low involvement.** R.E. Petty, J.T. Cacioppo & D. Schumann (1983) Central and peripheral routes to advertising effectiveness: The moderating role of involvement. *Journal of Consumer Research,* 10, 135–146.
15. **Distraction and persuasion.** R.E. Petty, G. Wells & T. Brock (1976) Distraction can enhance or reduce yielding to propaganda: Thought disruption versus effort justification. *Journal of Personality and Social Psychology,* 34, 874–884; T. Reichert, S. Hechler & S. Jackson (2001) The effects of sexual social marketing appeals on cognitive processing and persuasion. *Journal of Advertising,* 1, 13–27.
16. **Time compression and peripheral thinking.** D. Moore, D. Hausknecht & K. Thamodaran (1986) Time compression, response opportunity and persuasion. *Journal of Consumer Research,* 13, 85–99.
17. **Happy mood and peripheral thinking.** L. Worth & D. Mackie (1987) Cognitive mediation of positive affect in persuasion. *Social Cognition,* 5, 76–94; D. Kuykendall & J.P. Keating (1990) Mood and persuasion: Evidence for the differential influence of positive and negative states. *Psychology and Marketing,* 7, 1–9.

Chapter 4

1. **Dick Morris on selling Bill Clinton for President.** D. Morris (1997) *Behind the Oval Office: Selling the Presidency in the Nineties.* New York: Random House.
2. **Presuppositions and false memories for simulated traffic accidents.** E. Loftus & G. Zanni (1975) Eyewitness testimony: The influence of the wording of a question. *Bulletin of the Psychonomic Society,* 5, 86–88; E. Loftus, D. Miller, & H. Burns (1978) Semantic integration of verbal information into a visual memory. *Journal of Experimental Psychology: Human Learning and Memory,* 4, 19–31; K. Fiedler & E. Walthier (1996) Do you *really* know what you have seen? Intrusion errors and presupposition effects on constructive memory. *Journal of Experimental Social Psychology,* 32, 484–511.
3. **The Paul Ingram story.** L. Wright (1995) *Remembering Satan: A Tragic Case of Recovered Memory.* New York: Vintage Books.
4. **Planting false childhood memories.** E. Loftus & J. Pickrell (1995) The formation of false memories. *Psychiatric Annals,* 25, 720–725; C. Laney, E. Morris, D. Bernstein, B. Wakefield & E. Loftus (2008) Asparagus, a love story: Healthier eating could be just a false memory away. *Experimental Psychology,* 55, 291–300.
5. **Mis-remembering Bugs Bunny at Disneyland.** L. Braun-LaTour, M. LaTour, J. Pickrell & E. Loftus (2004) How and when advertising can influence memory for consumer experience. *Journal of Advertising,* 33, 7–25.
6. **Solomon Asch's conformity experiments.** S. Asch (1955) Opinions and social pressure. *Scientific American,* 193, 31–35.

7. **Social contagion in Viennese subway suicides.** G. Sonneck, E. Etzersdorfer & S. Nagel-Kuess (1994) Imitative suicide on the Viennese subway. *Social Science & Medicine*, 38, 453–457.

8. **Contagion of happiness and depression within social networks.** N. Christakis & J. Fowler (2009) *Connected: The Surprising Power of Our Social Networks and How They Shape Our Lives*. New York: Little, Brown and Company.

9. **Social norms and theft in the Petrified Forest.** R. Cialdini (2003) Crafting normative messages to protect the environment. *Current Directions in Psychological Science*, 4, 105–109.

10. **Using conformity to increase tax compliance.** S. Coleman (1996) *The Minnesota Tax Compliance Experiment: State Tax Results*. Minnesota Department of Revenue. The detailed report can be downloaded from: http://mpra.ub.uni-muenchen.de/5820/1/MPRA_paper_5820.pdf

11. **How telling kids to "just say no" to drugs and alcohol can backfire.** S. Donaldson, J. Graham, A. Piccinin & W. Hansen (1995) Resistance-skills training and onset of alcohol use: Evidence for beneficial and potentially harmful effects in public schools and private Catholic schools. *Health Psychology*, 14, 291–300.

12. **Implying social norms of condom use.** A. Stuart & H. Blanton (2003) The effects of message framing on behavioral prevalence assumptions. *European Journal of Social Psychology*, 33, 93–102.

13. **Thinking carefully about majority and minority opinions.** R. Martin & M. Hewstone (2003) Majority versus minority influence: When, not whether, source status instigates heuristics or systematic processing. *European Journal of Social Psychology*, 33, 313–330.

14. **Conformity in decline since the 1950s.** R. Bond & P. Smith (1996) Culture and conformity: A meta-analysis of studies using Asch's (1952b, 1956) line judgment task. *Psychological Bulletin*, 119, 111–137.

15. **Looking at a punk rocker makes people more independent-minded.** L. Pendry & R. Carrick (2001) Doing what the mob do: Priming effects on conformity. *European Journal of Social Psychology*, 31, 83–92.

Chapter 5

1. **Clinton's testimony before the grand jury.** August 17, 1998; released September 21, 1998. Transcript by the Office of the Independent Counsel; the full transcript can be found on *Jurist*: http://jurist.law.pitt.edu/transcr.htm

2. **Downing on reading between the lines.** M. Downing (2000) *Taking Control of Your Life*. Twenty-First Century Communications. Dr. Downing's book is intended as a self-help book for emotional health, and not as a theory of language. The excerpt in Chapter 5 is for expository purposes.

3. **Paul Grice on speakers' meanings versus the meanings of words.** H.P. Grice (1975) Logic and conversation. In: P. Cole & J. Morgan (Eds.), *Syntax and Semantics, Vol. 3, Speech Acts.* New York: Academic Press.

4. **Letter home from schizophrenic son.** P. McKenna & M. Tomasina (2008) *Schizophrenic Speech: Making Sense of Bathroots and Ponds that Fall in Doorways.* Cambridge: Cambridge University Press. The letter itself is taken from the writings and case studies of the Swiss psychiatrist Eugen Bleuler, a contemporary of Sigmund Freud, who originally coined the word *schizophrenia.*

5. **Do dogs and chimps understand pointing?** B. Hare, M. Brown, C. Williamson & M. Tomasello (2002) The domestication of social cognition in dogs. *Science,* 298, 1634–1636; U. Liszkowski, M. Schäfer, M. Carpenter & M. Tomasello (2009) Prelinguistic infants, but not chimpanzees, communicate about absent entities. *Psychological Science,* 20, 654–660.

6. **Kids imitate intentional, not accidental behavior.** M. Carpenter, N. Akhtar & M. Tomasello (1998) Fourteen to 18-month-olds differentially imitate intentional and accidental actions. *Infant Behavior and Development,* 21, 315–330; M. Carpenter (2006) Instrumental, social, and shared goals and intentions in imitation. In: S.J. Rogers & J. Williams (Eds.), *Imitation and the development of the social mind: Lessons from typical development and autism.* New York: Guilford.

7. **How children learn the meanings of words.** P. Bloom (2002) Mindreading, communication and the learning of names for things. *Mind & Language,* 17, 37–54.

8. **Babies learn by figuring out intention.** D. Baldwin (2000) Interpersonal understanding fuels knowledge acquisition. *Current Directions in Psychological Science,* 9, 40–45.

9. **Deceptive implications.** A number of case studies are discussed in detail in: I. Preston (1994) *The Tangled Web They Weave: Truth, Falsity & Advertisers.* Madison, WI: University of Wisconsin Press.

10. **Laws governing deceptive advertising.** In the United States, deceptive advertisers can be prosecuted by the Federal Trade Commission, whose policy statement on deception in advertising can be found here: http://www.ftc.gov/bcp/policystmt/ad-decept.htm

11. **Indirectness and the social taboo of social class.** P. Messaris (1997) *Visual Persuasion: The Role of Images in Advertising.* Thousand Oaks, CA: Sage Publications.

Chapter 6

1. **Arruda bans present participle.** C. Caminada (2007) Brasilia Governor Bans Verb Form, Citing Inefficiency. *Bloomberg News,* October 2, 2007: http://www.freerepublic.com/focus/f-news/1905561/posts

2. **British local councils ban Latin.** C. Hastings (2008) Councils ban "elitist" and "discriminatory" Latin phrases. *The Telegraph*, November 1, 2008: http://www.telegraph.co.uk/news/uknews/3362150/Councils-ban-elitist-and-discriminatory-Latin-phrases.html

3. **Performatives.** J.L. Austin (1962) *How to Do Things With Words.* Cambridge: Harvard University Press.

4. **Uncle Sam is looking at you.** P. Messaris (1997) *Visual Persuasion.* Thousand Oaks, CA: Sage Publications.

5. **Post-*Avatar* depression.** J. Piazza (2010) Audiences experience "Avatar" blues. CNN, January 11, 2010: http://www.cnn.com/2010/SHOWBIZ/Movies/01/11/avatar.movie.blues/index.html

6. **Seeing agency in moving shapes.** F. Heider & M. Simmel (1944) An experimental study of apparent behavior. *American Journal of Psychology*, 57, 243–259; P. Bloom & C. Veres (1999) The perceived intentionality of groups. *Cognition*, 71, B1–B9.

7. **Speaker roles.** Erving Goffman (1981) *Forms of Talk.* Philadelphia: University of Pennsylvania Press.

8. **"I'm a Mac."** You can watch the Mac versus PC TV spots here: http://www.apple.com/getamac/ads/

9. **Orson Scott Card on the rules of interstellar travel in science fiction.** S. Card (1990) *How to Write Science Fiction and Fantasy.* Cincinnati, OH: Writer's Digest Books.

10. **Rasputin and the Empress.** Details at: http://www.imdb.com/title/tt0023374/

11. **Federal Trade Commission guidelines for using endorsements and testimonials.** Revised guidelines—including rules for bloggers—can be found at: http://www.ftc.gov/os/2009/10/091005revisedendorsement guides.pdf

12. **The Easter Bunny is a salesman.** Federal Trade Commission decisions, Vol. 114 (January– December 1991). The Easter Bunny case can be found on p. 403 at: http://www.ftc.gov/os/decisions/docs/vol114/FTC_VOLUME_DECISION_114_(_JANUARY_-_DECEMBER_1991)PAGES_367-485.pdf

13. **Intrusions from fiction into fact.** R. Gerrig & D. Prentice (1991) The representation of fictional information. *Psychological Science*, 2, 336–340.

14. **Memory blurs fiction and reality.** M. Appel & T. Richter (2007) Persuasive effects of fictional narratives increase over time. *Media Psychology*, 10, 113–134.

Chapter 7

1. **Mass marketing is dead.** Anthony Bianco (2004) The vanishing mass market. *Business Week*, July 12, 2004.

2. **Daniel Boorstin on advertising as folk culture.** D. Boorstin (1974) The rhetoric of democracy. In: *Democracy and its Discontents: Reflections on Everyday America.* New York: Random House.

3. **The Values, Attitudes and Lifestyles survey.** A. Mitchell (1983) *The Nine American Lifestyles: Who We Are and Where We're Going.* New York: Macmillan.

    You can learn about the updated VALS survey at the VALS website by Strategic Business Insights (formerly Stanford Research International): http://www.strategicbusinessinsights.com/vals/

4. **Clustering of the "creative class."** R. Florida (2003) *The Rise of the Creative Class: And How It's Transforming Work, Leisure, Community and Everyday Life.* New York: Basic Books; R. Florida (2008) *Who's Your City? How the Creative Economy is Making Where to Live the Most Important Decision of Your Life.* New York: Basic Books.

5. **Clustering by Personality Type.** P.J. Rentfrow, S. Gosling & J. Potter (2008) A theory of the emergence, persistence and expression of geographic variation in psychological characteristics. *Perspectives on Psychological Science*, 3, 339–369.

6. **Like-minded political sorting.** B. Bishop (2008) *The big sort: Why the clustering of like-minded America is tearing us apart.* Boston: Houghton-Mifflin.

7. **Group polarization among the like-minded.** Polarization of mock juries: D. Myers & M. Kaplan (1976) Group-induced polarization in simulated juries. *Journal of Personality & Social Psychology*, 2, 63–66. Polarization of French citizens: S. Moscovici & M. Zavalloni (1969) The group as a polarizer of attitudes. *Journal of Personality & Social Psychology*, 12, 125–35. Polarization of racial attitudes: D. Myers & G. Bishop (1970) Discussion effects on racial attitudes. *Science*, 169, 778–779. Polarization of judges on federal court of appeals: C. Sunstein, D. Schkade, L. Ellman & A. Sawicki (2006) *Are Judges Political? An Empirical Analysis of the Federal Judiciary.* Washington DC: Brookings Institution Press.

8. **Zip-code marketing.** M. Weiss (2000) *The Clustered World: How We Live, What We Buy, and What It All Means About Who We Are.* Boston: Little, Brown and Company.

    There is a wealth of information about cluster markets on the Nielsen-Claritas "My Best Segments" website: http://www.claritas.com/MyBestSegments/Default.jsp

9. **Mark Twain on American versus English.** The full text of Twain's essay "Concerning the American Language" can be found on *The Literature Network*: http://www.online-literature.com/twain/3276/

10. **Language change and the "correctness" of language.** For highly readable discussions of the natural evolution of language over time, see: "The tower of Babel" and "Language mavens" in: S. Pinker (1994) *The Language Instinct.* New York: William Morrow and Company; J. McWhorter (2001) *Word on the Street:*

Debunking the Myth of a "Pure" Standard English. New York: Basic Books; R. MacNeil & W. Cran (2005) *Do You Speak American?* New York: Mariner Books.

11. **Diverging dialects in North America.** W. Labov, S. Ash & C. Boberg (2006) *The Atlas of North American English: Phonetics, phonology and sound change.* Berlin: Mouton/de Gruyter.

12. **The Great Vowel Shift.** A detailed discussion and analysis, including correlations with political attitudes, can be found in: W. Labov (forthcoming). *Principles of Language Change, Volume 3: Cognitive and Cultural Factors.* Advance drafts of chapters can be found on Dr. Labov's website: http://www.ling.upenn.edu/~wlabov/#Language%20change

13. **Accents and local identity on Martha's Vineyard.** W. Labov (1972) *Sociolinguistic Patterns.* Philadelphia: University of Pennsylvania Press.

14. **Robert Beard's delightful glossary of Southern American English.** http://www.alphadictionary.com/articles/southernese.html

15. **Language and social status in New York City.** W. Labov (2006) *The Social Stratification of English in New York City.* Cambridge: Cambridge University Press.

16. **Shifting vowels among high school students.** P. Eckert (2000) *Linguistic Variation as Social Practice.* Oxford: Blackwell.

17. **Code-switching between dialects.** J. McWhorter (2001) *Word on the Street: Debunking the Myth of a "Pure" Standard English.* New York: Basic Books.

18. **Indirect requests and politeness.** E. Francik & H. Clark (1985) How to make requests that remove obstacles to compliance. *Journal of Memory and Language*, 24, 560–568. H. Clark & D. Schunk (1980) Polite responses to polite requests. *Cognition*, 8, 111–143.

19. **Lethal politeness among Korean Air co-pilots.** M. Gladwell (2006) *Outliers.* Boston: Little, Brown and Company.

20. **Voice cues in computer-generated speech.** C. Nass (2005) *Wired for Speech: How Voice Activates and Advances the Human–Computer Relationship.* Cambridge, MA: MIT Press.

21. **Benefits and dangers of group polarization.** C. Sunstein (2009) *Going to Extremes: How Like Minds Unite and Divide.* Oxford: Oxford University Press.

Chapter 8

1. **Karl Popper slams Plato.** K. Popper (1971) *The Open Society and Its Enemies: The Spell of Plato.* Princeton, NJ: Princeton University Press.

2. **Martha Nussbaum on Plato's contribution to democracy.** M. Nussbaum (1998) *Plato's Republic: The Good Society and the Deformation of Desire.* Library of Congress: Bradley lecture series publication.

3. **Effects of linguistic framing and the Asian disease dilemma.** A. Tversky & D. Kahneman (1981) The framing of decisions and the psychology of choice. *Science*, 211, 453–458.

4. **High social security numbers inflate bids on consumer items.** D. Ariely, G. Loewenstein & D. Prelec (2003) "Coherent arbitrariness": Stable demand curves without stable preferences. *The Quarterly Journal of Economics*, 118, 73–105.

5. **Insurance-buying spikes after natural disasters.** P. Slovic, H. Kunreuther & G. White (1974) Decision processes, rationality and adjustment to natural hazards. In: G. White (Ed.), *Natural Hazards, Local, National and Global*. New York: Oxford University Press.

6. **Presumed consent and organ donation.** E. Johnson & D. Goldstein (2003) Do defaults save lives? *Science*, 302, 1338–39; R. Thaler & C. Sunstein (2008) How to increase organ donations. In: *Nudge: Improving Decisions about Health, Wealth and Happiness*. New York: Penguin.

7. **Flawed thinking about happiness.** D. Gilbert (2006) *Stumbling on Happiness*. New York: Knopf.

8. **Edward Bernays on persuasion in democracy.** E. Bernays (1928) *Propaganda*. Reprinted in 2005. Brooklyn, NY: Ig Publishing.

9. **Bernays' role in the Guatemalan coup.** M. Myers (1995) The United Fruit Company in Central America: History of a public relations failure. *7th Marketing History Conference Proceedings*, 7, 251–258.

10. **The "Daisy" ad during the Johnson 1964 campaign.** A detailed history of the creation of this iconic ad can be found at: http://conelrad.com/daisy/index.php

11. **Dick Morris on his advice to Bill Clinton.** Excerpt from an interview in: A. Curtis (2002) *Century of the Self*. BBC documentary, released on DVD in 2009.

12. **Mark Penn's micromarketing during the Clinton 1996 campaign.** J. Bennett (2000) The guru of small things. *The New York Times*, June 18, 2000.

13. **Robert Reich on business versus politics.** Excerpt from an interview in: A. Curtis (2002) *Century of the Self*. BBC documentary, released on DVD in 2009.

14. **Frank Luntz gives lessons in wordsmithing.** F. Luntz (2006) *Words that Work: It's Not What You Say, It's What People Hear*. New York: Hyperion.

15. **Do Americans understand the death tax?** L. Bartels (2005) Homer gets a tax cut: Inequality and public policy in the American mind. *Perspectives on Politics*, 3, 15–31.

16. **Metaphors and policy.** T. Hartman (2010) Metaphor matters: The persuasive appeal of policy metaphors. Appalachian State University: http://www.appstate.edu/~hartmantk/research.html

17. **"War on drugs" metaphor.** G. Fields (2009) White House czar calls for end to "war on drugs." *Wall Street Journal*, May 14, 2009: http://online.wsj.com/article/SB124225891527617397.html

18. **"Bailout" versus "rescue."** B. Stelter (2008) President Bush calls it a "rescue," but others are sticking with "bailout." *The New York Times*, September 29, 2008: http://www.nytimes.com/2008/09/29/business/media/29rescue.html

A. Barr (2008) McCain: Change name from "bailout" to "rescue." *Politico*, September 30, 2008: http://www.politico.com/news/stories/0908/14117.html

19. **The damning effects of innuendo.** D. Wegner, R. Wenzlaff, R. Kerker & A. Beattie (1981) Incrimination through innuendo: Can media questions become public answers? *Journal of Personality & Social Psychology*, 40, 822–832.

20. **The push poll targeted at McCain 2000.** R. Davis (2004) The anatomy of a smear campaign. *The Boston Globe*, March 21, 2004: http://www.boston.com/news/globe/editorial_opinion/oped/articles/2004/03/21/the_anatomy_of_a_smear_campaign/

21. **The persuasive power of hypothetical questions.** G. Fitzsimons & B. Shiv (2001) Nonconscious and contaminative effects of hypothetical questions on subsequent decision-making. *Journal of Consumer Research*, 28, 224–238.

22. **Rejecting a stereotype strengthens it.** B. Gawronski, R. Deutsch, S. Mbir-kou, B. Seibt & F. Strack (2008) When "Just say no" is not enough: Affirmation versus negation training and the reduction of automatic stereotype activation. *Journal of Experimental Social Psychology*, 44, 370–377.

23. **Believe first, disbelieve later.** D. Gilbert, R. Tafarodi & P. Malone (1992) You can't not believe everything you read. *Journal of Personality & Social Psychology*, 65, 221–233.

24. **Noncredible propaganda gets more credible over time.** C. Hovland, A. Lumsdaine & F. Sheffield (1949) *Experiments on Mass Communication: Studies in Social Psychology in World War II, Vol. 3*. Princeton, NJ: Princeton University Press; R. Lariscy & S. Tinkham (1999) The sleeper effect and negative political advertising. *Journal of Advertising*, 28, 13–30.

25. **Increasing polarization of presidential approval ratings.** A. Abramowitz & W. Stone (2004) The Bush effect: Polarization, turnout and activism in the 2004 presidential election. *Presidential Studies Quarterly*, 36, 141–154.

26. **Arthritis pain and the weather.** D. Redelmeier & A. Tversky (1996) On the belief that arthritis pain is related to the weather. *Proceedings of the National Academy of Sciences of the United States of America*, 93, 2895–2896.

27. **When hearing balanced arguments causes more polarization of attitudes.** C. Taber & M. Lodge (2006) Motivated skepticism in the evaluation of political beliefs. *American Journal of Political Science*, 50, 755–769.

28. **The brain's response to unpleasant contradiction.** D. Westen, P. Blagov, K. Harenski, C. Kilts & S. Hamann (2006) Neural bases of motivated reasoning: An fMRI study of emotional constraints on partisan political judgment in the 2004 U.S. presidential election. *Journal of Cognitive Neuroscience*, 18,

1947–1958; V. van Ween, M. Krug, J. Schooler & C. Carter (2009) Neural activity predicts attitude change in cognitive dissonance. *Nature Neuroscience*, 12, 1469–1473.

29. **Bias, threat and right-wing authoritarianism.** H. Lavine, M. Lodge & K. Freitas (2005) Threat, authoritarianism and selective exposure to information. *Political Psychology*, 26, 219–244.

30. **Rationalizing false beliefs about the Saddam–Al-Qaeda link.** M. Prasad, A. Perrin, K. Bezila, *et al.* (2009) "There must be a reason": Osama, Saddam and inferred justification. *Sociological Inquiry*, 79, 142–162.

31. **Michael Dukakis on the death penalty.** D. Westen (2007) *The Political Brain: The Role of Emotion in Deciding the Fate of the Nation.* New York: Public Affairs Books; G. Nunberg (2006) *Talking Right: How Conservatives Turned Liberalism into a Tax-Raising, Latte-Drinking, Sushi-Eating, Volvo-Driving, New York Times-Reading, Body-Piercing, Hollywood-Loving, Left-Wing Freak Show.* New York: Public Affairs Books.

32. **Negative campaigning by Bush and Kerry.** B. Souley & R. Wicks (2005) Tracking the 2004 presidential campaign websites: Similarities and differences. *American Behavioral Scientist*, 49, 535–547.

33. **Obama's inoculation program against negative campaigning.** R. Harfoush (2009) *Yes We Did: An Inside Look at How Social Media Built the Obama Brand.* Berkeley, CA: New Riders.

34. **The politics of food and lifestyle.** CNN's Crowley suggested Kerry's choice of green tea proves he is out of touch with "most of America." *Media Matters for America*, November 16, 2004: http://mediamatters.org/research/200411160005; P. Allor (2008) Food & Politics. *The Moody Kitchen*, November 4, 2008: http://moodykitchen.blogspot.com/2008/11/food-politics.html; E. Thomas, H. Bailey & R. Wolffe (2008) Only in America. *Newsweek*, May 5, 2008: http://www.newsweek.com/id/134398?tid=relatedcl; G. Nunberg (2006) *Talking Right: How Conservatives Turned Liberalism into a Tax-Raising, Latte-Drinking, Sushi-Eating, Volvo-Driving, New York Times-Reading, Body-Piercing, Hollywood-Loving, Left-Wing Freak Show.* New York: Public Affairs Books; B. Obama (2006) *The Audacity of Hope.* New York: Crown Publishers; R. Harfoush (2009) *Yes We Did: An Inside Look at How Social Media Built the Obama Brand.* Berkeley, CA: New Riders.

35. **The history of *ing* versus *in'*.** W. Labov (2001) *Principles of Language Change, Vol. 2: Social Factors.* Oxford: Blackwell.

36. **Obama's political speeches.** All the speeches quoted in the text were pulled from Barack Obama's YouTube Channel: http://www.youtube.com/user/barackobamadotcom?blend=1&ob=4

37. **Libertarian paternalism.** R. Thaler & C. Sunstein (2008) *Nudge: Improving Decisions About Health, Wealth and Happiness.* New York: Penguin.

Index

3D movies   168

accents
  in the Geico ads   226–7
  and identity   227–8
  see also dialect; pronunciation
accommodation   101
active sentences   81–2
ads (advertisements)
  ambiguous   77–80
  attentional hotspots in   82–4
  comparisons in   139
  goal of   4–5
  pop-ups   65–6
  presuppositions in   102–6
  reading between the lines   126–8
  slogans   196–7
  use of fiction   180–3
  see also commercials
advertising
  Coolidge's praise of   2–4
  deceptive   149–54
  expenditure   1–2, 253
  McDonaldization of   193–6
  media and techniques   10
  as the new folk culture   197–8
  overexposure to   59–61
  see also persuasion
affinity-seeking   281–2
African Americans
  McDonald's website for   194–5
  and nonstandard Black English
    dialect   229

unconscious bias against
    24–5
agency   169–70, 173–4, 179
Agreeableness personality trait   202, 203,
    205
Allor, Paul   280
alternative realities   168–9
Altoids mints ad   102–3
ambiguity
  in ads   77–80, 187–8
  and brand names   36–7
  garden path sentences   74–7
  in headlines   74
  and puns   71–3
"American language" essay, Mark
    Twain   212, 213
animal research study   121
animator role   171–4, 178
anti-drug campaigns   117–18, 119
Apple computers
  1984 commercial   154–5, 255
  and creativity   55–6
  Mac v PC ads   55–6, 181–2, 185–6, 188,
    278–9
  origins of brand name   45–6
  use of fiction   181–2
"apple", memories connected with
    word   35
Applewhite, Marshall   10–11
Arruda, Governor Jose Roberto   157, 159
arthritis-weather connection, fallacy
    of   271–2
Asch, Solomon   113–14, 122

Sold on Language: How Advertisers Talk to You and What This Says About You. By Julie Sedivy and Greg Carlson
© 2011 John Wiley & Sons Ltd.

Asian disease problem   248, 258, 288
Asians, McDonald's website for   195
Aspercreme ad   150–1
aspirated sounds   28–9
assertions in conversation   99–101
associations
    automatic   241
    stereotypical   268
assumptions   98–9
    about truthfulness   133–5
    challenging   114
    and comparisons in ads   139
AT&T, lifestyle polling   256
attention
    selective   61–4, 94, 271–2
    and the structure of sentences   80–4
    and visual incongruity   66–71
    and word learning   147
attitudes, unconscious   24–5
Audacity of Hope, The (Obama)   280–1
audience targeting   198, 242–3
Augustine, St.   146, 147, 155
author role   171–2, 174, 178–9
Avatar (3D movie)   168, 191
awareness
    of double meanings   74–5
    and inattentional blindness   63
Axe ads   176–7

Babel, tower of   240–1
Baggies sandwich bags   140–1
"bailout" metaphor   265–6
Baldwin, Dare   147, 155
Barber, Benjamin   48, 193
Bargh, John   49, 54, 55
Bartels, Larry   260–1
Beard, Robert   225
beauty industry   175–7
behavior priming   49–52, 288
behavioral economics   248–9
Behind the Oval Office (Morris)   97
beliefs
    about Al-Qaeda-Saddam link   275, 276
    drive to confirm   271–2
    and the fiction-reality barrier   183–4,
        185, 188–9

Berger, Jonah   241
Bernays, Edward   15–17, 94–5, 115,
        250–4, 255–6, 257, 270
bi-dialectals   229
bias
    in decision making   248–9
    link to emotional threat   274
    and political opinion   272
    unconscious   24–5, 288
    of voters   276–8
Big Five personality traits   202–6
Big Sort: Why the Clustering of Like-Minded
        America is Tearing Us Apart
        (Bishop)   206
bilingual speakers   228–9, 283
Birner, Betty   81
Bishop, Bill   206–7
BlackBerry   31, 46, 49
Blanton, Hart   118–19
blind taste test, Pepsi challenge   20–1
Blink (Gladwell)   24
Bloom, Paul   146–7
BMW, in-car navigation system   239–40
body language   92, 107–8
    pointing   144–5
Bök, Christian   41–2
Bond, Jonathan   94
Bond, Rod   121–2
Boorstin, Daniel   13, 197, 198
brain activity, reward center   20–1
branding   21
    brand naming   31–3
    importance of   18–24
    political   278–82
    using software   43–4
Brazilification   237
British Airways ad   77, 78
broadband charges, network neutrality
        legislation   264–5
Bugs Bunny, fake ad   111–12
Burch, Dean   266
Burnouts versus Jocks, accents of
        227–8
Bush, President George W.   267, 275,
        277–8, 282
    approval ratings   270

pronunciation of "nuclear"   213
  RATS ad   52, 53
business tactics and political
    persuasion   253–7

Cacioppo, John   89–90
Cameron, James   168, 191
Capek, Karel   240
Carpenter, Malinda   146
Cassidy, Kimberly   43
Castellanos, Alex   52
CBS, "egg-vertising" campaign   72, 77
celebrity endorsement of products
    90, 187
central vs. peripheral thinking   120–1
Chabris, Christopher   63
children
  actions influenced by ads   188
  imitation by   146
  impact of advertising on   5
  word learning   146–7
choice
  illusion of   10–14
  importance of   6–7
  problems of too much   7–10
  protection from mindless   288–9
Christaker, Nicholas   114–15
Cialdini, Robert   117
cigarette advertising   16, 115, 150–1
Clinton, Bill   42, 53
  and Monica Lewinsky   124, 152, 266
  re-election strategy   255–7
  use of presuppositions   97–8, 102, 106,
    113, 120
  and the word 'is'   124, 132–3
Clinton, Hillary   278, 280
cluster marketing   210–11
cognitive dissonance   273–4
Coke versus Pepsi experiments   20–1
Colbert, Stephen   86–7
Cold War metaphors   263–4
Colgate-Palmolive Baggies ad   140–1
Comcast ads   71–2, 77–8
comfort score   42–3
commercial branding and politics   256–7
commercials   64

first television   240
intonation in   84
time-compressed   91
using soap opera formula   181
see also ads (advertisements)
communication
  between copilots and pilots   236–8
  and language   158–9
  non-verbal   128–9
  search for relevance   135–8
communism, metaphors for   262, 263
company names   31
comparisons   139
computer-generated speech   238–40
conditioning, Pavlov's dogs   17–18, 243
condom-use ads   118–19
conformity   112–15, 121–2
Conscientiousness personality trait   202,
    203, 206
"conservative", hateful connotations   36
context and meaning   128, 130–1
contradictory behavior, brain response
    to   273–4
control, loss of with too much choice   9
conversation
  Grice's four commandments of   133
  responding to assertions in   99
  roles played by agents in   170–1
  rules of   164–5
Coolidge, President Calvin   2–4, 6, 17, 86,
    92, 94–5
copywriting   84–6
Cover Girl cosmetics   234
Creative Class   200
  link to Openness trait   206
  and location   200, 201
creativity, and the Apple brand   55–6
credibility versus truth   13–14
crime, false confessions   109–11
Crowley, Candy   281
cults, behavior of   10–12
cultural differences
  and relevance in messages   137–8
  status language   236–8
Cuomo, Mario   277
Cushing, Robert   206

Daisy ad 254–5
Damasio, Antonio 13
dating example 125
Davidson, Alan 264
Davis, Gray 53
Dean, Howard 279
death penalty, political speeches 276–7
death tax, irrational reasons for repeal
    of 260–1
deceptive advertising 149–54, 163
decision making, biases in 247–50
declarative sentences 160
definite descriptions 102–4, 105, 106
democracy
    Bernays' views 251–2
    Plato's arguments against 13, 245–7
Democrats 221, 280
    Bush's approval rating 270
    and contradictory behavior 273–4
    and the death penalty 276–7
    personality traits of 206–9
    subliminal priming 52–3
demographic groups, targeting of 198
demonstration of products 140–1
denial, futility of 266–9
depression 167, 204, 271
dialect
    bi-dialectals 229
    evolution of differences 212–14
    nonstandard 226–7, 228–30
    and personal identity 218–23
    and political views 222–3
    prestige 223–7
    vowel changes 214–18
dictionary entries 31–2, 35, 37–8, 45,
    48–9
Dijksterhuis, Ap 54
Disney theme park, fake ad 111–12
distraction, persuasion technique 90–1
documentaries, educational role of 4–5
Dodge ad 69
dogs, ability to read human cues 145
domino effect metaphor 262
double meanings 72–3
double negatives 224
Dove soap ads/campaigns 105, 175–7

Downing, Myron 125–6
Doyle Dane Bernbach (DDB) 254
Dukakis, Michael 276–7

Eckert, Penny 227–8, 229
Economist (Leader's Digest ad) 79
Edge razor experiment 90
Edsel, failure of 45
education, idea of advertising as 4
"egg-vertising" campaign, CBS 72, 77
Eisenhower, Dwight 262
election campaigns 52–4
Eli Lilly Pharmaceutical 142–3
Emerson, Ralph Wlado 114, 199
emotional threat and bias 274
emotions, manipulated by fiction 183
Emperor penguins example 4, 5
Estée Lauder cosmetics 234
Eunoia (Bok) 41–2
evolution of language 213–14, 223–4
Excedrin Migraine 147–8
experimental psychology 17–18
Extroversion 202, 203, 205, 206
ExxonMobil ad 106, 120
eye-tracking studies 32, 33
eyewitnesses, fallibility of
    memories 108–9

factives 104
facts, language used to describe 258,
    260
false beliefs, tenacity of 275
false information changing memory 109
false memories 109–12
Federal Trade Commission
    (FTC) 150–1, 187
feeling versus thinking 86–7
fiction
    and agency 169–72
    emotions triggered by 180–2, 183
    responsibility in 179–80
    rules for 184–5
    suspension of disbelief 182–3
    and truth in advertising 183–6
fiction, intrusion into reality 189–91
financial advisor ads 235–6

Finesse hair conditioner ad   154
first-person forms, ads using   165–6
Fischer, Ute   237
Fitzsimons, Gavan   267
Fitzsimons, Gráinne   55–6
Florida, Richard   200
folk culture, advertising as   197–8
Ford's "700% quieter" ad   138
Fowler, James   114–15
framing effects   258, 260, 288
Freud, Sigmund   15–16, 25–6, 54
Future Shock (Toffler)   8

"g" dropping   283–5
garden path sentences   74–80
Geico car insurance ads   225, 226–7, 230
gender equality, Plato's views   252
gender stereotyping, preference for male
     computer voices   238, 239–40
"genericide"   47–9
Gerrig, Richard   190
gestures, pointing   144–5
Gilbert, Dan   268–9
Gladwell, Malcolm   24, 236
glocalization, McDonald's meals   195
Goebbels, Joseph   246
Goffman, Erving   171
Gold Blend coffee commercial   181
Goldwater, Barry   254–5
Google   48–9
Gore, Al   52, 53
gorilla experiment   63, 65
grammar
     and presupposition   102, 105–6
     and sentence interpretation   75
"green tea" moments, political
     campaigns   279–80
Greenwald, Anthony   24
Grice, Paul   128, 129, 130–1,
     133, 143
group polarization   207–9, 242
Guatemalan military coup   254
Guerilla Advertising (Levinson)   85
guilt, presidential   266–7
guilty pleas, false confession   110
guilty verdicts, group polarization   207

happiness
     contagion within social
          networks   114–15
     decreasing with too much choice   8
     and framing of spoken messages   126
     and peripheral thinking   91–2
     pursuit of   250
Harfoush, Rahaf   281
Harris, Louis   9
Hartman, Todd   264
head nodding/shaking, persuasive effect
     of   92
headlines, ambiguity in   74
health promotion, use of cluster data   211
Heaven's Gate cult   10–11
"hereby", use of   161–3
Hewstone, Miles   121
Hispanics, McDonald's website for   195
hormones, oxytocin and trust   12–13
"hot spots" in sentences   80–4
Hovland, Carl   269
humor   69–80

identity
     and accent   218–20
     and choice of car   199
     and migration patterns   199–202
     and product purchase   8
     shedding of, cults   11
imitation by young children   146
imperative language   160, 232–3
implications   149, 151, 152–3
Implicit Associations Test (IAT)
     24–5
"inattentional blindness"   63
incongruity   66–71
indirectness in advertising   153–4
individualism   121–2
information overload   61–2, 87–8
information processing   61–4, 91–2
     and bias   271–2
Ingram, Paul, false confession of
     110–11
inheritance tax   259–60
innovation   200, 201, 209
instincts, orienting response   64–6

intentions   128–9
   ads masking   163–4
   and mindreading   144–7
   and speech acts   162–3
Internet data, network neutrality
      legislation   264–5
Internet pop-up ads   65–6
Internet search engines   48–9
interpretation
   of ambiguous sentences   74–7
   of meaning   123–8
interrogative sentences   160
"is", Clintonian meaning of   124, 132–3
iterative expressions   105, 106

James, Henry   84–5
Japanese SEGA ad   137–8
Jihad vs. McWorld (Barber)   48, 193
jingles   196–7
Jobs, Steve   45, 46
Johnson, Lyndon B.   254–5, 266
jokes   69–70, 74, 75, 202
jurors, shift to extreme viewpoint   207–9
jury duty and democracy   277

Kahneman, Daniel   248–9
Karremans, John   51
Kerlikowske, Gil   265
Kerry, John   273–4, 277–8, 279, 281, 282
Kirshenbaum, Richard   94
Klink, Richard   40–1
Korean Air crashes, status
      language   236–8
Kosfeld, Michael   12

Labov, Bill   214–21, 225–6, 283
Land Rover ad   71
Langer, Ellen   88
Language Instinct, The (Pinker)   49, 144
language-universal sound
      symbolism   38–40
Leader's Digest ad   79
leading questions   107–9
learning
   of new words   146–7
   pre-kindergarten   25–8

Leben, Will   46
legal and social sanctions,
      language   157–9
Levin, David   63
Levinson, Jay Conrad   85
Lewinsky, Monica   124, 132–3, 152
Lexicon Branding   46
"liberal", pejorative use of word   36
libertarian paternalism   288–9
Liesman, Steve   266
linguistic framing, effects of   258,
      260, 288
linguistic knowledge   28–30
linguistic styles (registers)   231–2,
      234, 236
Lipton Ice   51
Locke, John   146
Lodge, Milton   272
Loftus, Elizabeth   108–9, 110, 111, 112
Loftus, Geoffrey   66–7
logic and meaning   131–2
L'Oreal ad for mascara   86
Lovemark brands/icons   278–9
Lucky Strikes cigarettes   16, 115
Luntz, Frank   256–60
lying   132, 134–5

Macintosh computers
   first commercial for   154–5
   vs PC ads   55–6, 181–2, 185–6, 188,
      278–9
Mackworth, Norman   66–7
majority vs. minority influence   121–2,
      246
Marseilles soap ad   140
Martha's Vineyard, sociolinguistic
      study   218–19, 221
Martin, Robin   121
mass communication   240–1
Matrix car, Toyota ad campaign   70
"maybe", strengthening of possibility
      statements   141–2
McCain, John   265–6, 267
McClure, Samuel   20
McDaniel, Hattie   229
McDonaldization of Society (Ritzer)   193

McDonald's   193–6
  McJobs   48
  New England coffee ad   222–3, 229
  use of McLanguage   47–8
McWhorter, John   224
meaning
  children's inferences   147
  and context   129–31
  implied in ads   144, 149–51
  and logic   131–2
  systems for interpreting   128–9
memories
  associated with words   35–6
  false   109–12
  presuppositions altering   108–9
memorization vs. understanding   54–5
mental attention studies   62–4
mental lexicon   31–2, 35, 37
Mercedes-Benz ad   126, 128, 136–7
Merriam-Webster's Open
    Dictionary   37–8
messages, interpretation of   125–6
Messaris, Paul   153, 167
metaphors
  the cell as a factory   261–2
  and change of policy   265–6
  information processing   269–70
  limiting in science   263
  memory as a storehouse   108
  relating to communism   262, 263
Miedema, John   54
migration patterns
  and dialect shift   220
  and personality   199–206
Miller Beer versus Budweiser   175
mindless choices, protection from
    288–9
mindreading   144–9
misbehavior, inadvertently
    encouraging   117, 118
Mitchell, Arnold   198–9
money, irrational decisions about   249
mood and peripheral thinking   91–2
morphemes   48
Morris, Dick   97–8, 106, 256
Moyers, Bill   266

names
  influencing voting patterns   42–3
  male versus female   43–4
  of products   45–7
  see also branding
Nass, Clifford   238–40
navigation systems, German preference for
    male   239–40
"need for cognition" trait   90, 241
Nestlé's Gold Blend commercials   181
network neutrality   264–5
neural networks   43–4
Neuroticism personality trait   203
Nielsen Claritas, cluster markets   210
Nine American Lifestyles, The
    (Mitchell)   198
Noah, Timothy   36
noise see sound
nonpersuasion   6
nonstandard dialect   226–7, 228, 229–30,
    283–4
nonverbal communication   144–5
"normal" behavior   115–17, 118
"normal" declarative sentences   160–1
Northern Cities Shift   214–16, 228
nose-related words   37–8
novels, rules for reality   184–5, 186
nuclear weapons, "Daisy" ad   254–5
Nunberg, Geoff   36, 277
Nussbaum, Martha   247

Obama, President Barak
  bias in 2008 campaign   278
  Dijon mustard incident   280–1
  "g" dropping   284–5
  "liberal elite" criticism   279–80
  typeface on campaign posters   281
  "war on drugs" metaphor   265
obesity, spreading within social
    networks   114–15
Ogilvy, David   94
Ohala, John   39–40
one-to-one marketing   241
online banking ad, use of fiction   182–3
Openness personality trait   202, 203, 205,
    206

opinions, shift to extreme　207–8
optical illusions　26–7, 286
orange juice ads　132, 141
Orasanu, Judith　237
organ donation　249–50
orienting response　64–5, 69
Outliers (Gladwell)　236
oxytocin experiment　12

pain relief ads　143–4, 150–1
Paradox of Choice, The (Schartz)　7
Paramol ad　143–4
partisan thinking　272
passive sentences　81–2
Pavlov, Ivan　17–18, 243
PCs versus Mac ads　55–6, 181–2, 185–6,
　278–9
peer pressure　117–19, 121–2
Penn, Mark　256
Pepsi challenge　20–1
perceptual span　62–3
performative verbs　160–2
perfume advertising　19–20
peripheral thinking　88–92,
　120–1, 285
peripheral vision　62, 66, 71, 88
personality
　of computer voices　239
　regional variations in　200–6
persuasion
　and conflict of interest　4–7
　and democracy　13, 245–7
　factors influencing　89–92
　methods used by cults　10–12
　political　253–7
　and social contagion　115
　too much choice and loss of
　　control　9–10
Petrified Forest National Park,
　Arizona　117
Petty, Richard　89–90
photocopy study　88–9
Pinker, Steven　49, 144, 213
Plato　13, 245–7, 252, 287
poetry, sound symbolism in　41–2
pointing　144–5

politeness　49–50, 232, 234
　deadly implications of　237–8
political ideology and dialect　221–2
political knowledge, reducing bias　272
political persuasion, use of business
　tactics　253–7
political speeches　171–2
pop-up ads　65–6
Popper, Karl　247
Porsche 911 ad　112
"possible", meaning of word　131, 141–2
Power, Richard L.　220
power, status language　235–8
Prasad, Monica　275
Pratt Institute, use of cluster data　210–11
Prentice, Deborah　190
present participle　157–8
presidential approval ratings　270
presidential campaigns
　bias in　269–82
　and denial　266–9
　RATS ad　52–3
　and sound symbolism　42–3
　use of presuppositions in　97–8
prestige dialects　223–7, 228, 283
presuppositions　97–102
　in ads　102–6
　and central vs. peripheral
　　thinking　120–1
　and conformity　112–15
　defining normal　115–17
　false memories　109–12
　leading questions　107–9
　and social norms　117–19
priming
　of behavior　49–52
　methods of neutralizing　288
　semantic　33–5, 36–7
　sex differences in　241
　subliminal　50–4, 55–6
Principal Financial Group ad　236
principal role　171–2, 173–4, 177–9
product names　31, 83
　confusion arising from　147–8
　McDonald's　47–8
　subliminal advertising/priming　51–2

product purchase
  consumer control vs. advertiser's
    persuasive influence   9
  problem of too much choice   8–9
  reasons for   139–40
pronoun forms   165
pronunciation
  growth in dialect differences   214–18
  implicit knowledge of   28–31
  link to personal identity   218–24
  and social identity   282–5
Propaganda (Bernays)   251, 253
Prozac   142–3
psychographic groups   198–9
puns   71–4, 77–80
puzzle-solving ads   69–71, 79–80

questions, suggestive   107–9
quotation marks   178

"r" sound, dropping   225–6
Rasputin and the Empress (MGM
  film)   186, 189
rationality and irrationality   248–9, 257,
  272–3, 287
RATS advertisement   52–4
Raymond James financial advisor
  ad   235–6
Rayner, Keith   62
Reader's Digest (magazine)   79
reading
  between the lines   124–8
  and span of perception   62–3
reality
  and 3D movies   168
  and agency   169–70
  of fictional experiences   180–3
  and pretense   179–80
  truth and fiction-reality barrier   183–8
registers (linguistic styles)   231–2, 234,
  236
Reich, Robert   257
relevance
  and cultural differences   137–8
  search for   135–7
Rentfrow, Peter J.   202–3, 206

Republic (Plato)   245
Republicans   221
  Bush's approval rating   270
  persistent irrational beliefs   275–6
  personality traits   206–7
requests, responding mindlessly to   88–9
rescue metaphor   265–6
responsibility for speech acts   169–73
reward center of the brain   20–1
riddles   69–70, 139
Right Wing Authoritarianism (RWA)
  scale   274
*Rise of the Creative Class,
  The* (Florida)   200
risk, failure in judging   249
Ritzer, George   193
RJ Reynolds, Winston cigarette
  ads   150–1
Roberts, Kevin   21, 278
rock climbing ad   137
Rolls Royce ads   92–4, 230, 231
romance in commercials   181

Saatchi & Saatchi   21, 278
Saddam Hussein link to 9/11 attacks,
  belief in   275–6
safe sex promotion and social
  norms   118–19
Saint Augustine   146–7, 155
sarcasm and lying   134
schizophrenic man's letter   135
Schwartz, Barry   7, 8
second-person forms, ads using   165–6
SEGA video game company, TV
  ad   137–8
selective hearing and seeing   61–2
self-identity, and product choice   8
semantic priming   33–5, 36–7
sentences
  active versus passive   81–2
  attentional hot spots in   80–4
  declarative   160
  garden path   74–7
  interrogative   160
  with performative verbs   160–2
  using imperative verb   160, 232–3

shapes, words for describing   39
Shiv, Baba   267
Shomon, Dan   280–1
Simons, Daniel   63
"sleeper effect"   269
slogans for ads   196–7
Small World (Lodge)   183
Smith, Grant   42–3
Smith, Peter   121–2
Snuggle ad   177–8
soap operas   180–1
social class
    and dialect   225–6
    and "g" dropping   283–4
    and indirectness   153
social conformity   112–15
social identity *see* identity
social networks, inducing
    conformity   114–15
social norms   117–19
    and personality   205
social status   153, 231, 236–7
social stereotypes   91
society, fragmentation of
    209–11, 241
"some", meaning of   129–31
sound
    and acoustic frequency   40–2
    and meaning   37–40
    symbolism   38–9, 40–2
source memory, failure of   189–90
Southern accents   225, 226
speaker roles   171
    animator   171–4, 178
    author   171–2, 174, 178–9
    principal   171–2, 173–4, 177–9
speech acts   159–64
    action and reaction   164–9
    responsibility for principal   173–9
    speaker roles   169–72
Squier, Bob   97, 99, 102, 112–13
state verbs   104–5
status language   235–8
stereotypes   202, 225, 268, 280
Stevenson, Adlai   254
Stickley's furniture   99–100

stress
    and irrational beliefs   275–6
    and too much choice   8
Stuart, Anne   118–19
subliminal advertising   50–2, 55–6
subliminal priming   51–3
suicide imitation   114
Sunstein, Cass   208–9, 242, 288–9
SuperSize Me (documentary film)   194
surnames of presidents   42–3
survival instincts   64–6
symbolism
    associated with products   18–24
    sound   38–9, 40–2
syntactic structures   105–6

Taber, Charles   272
Take Control of Your Life (Downing)   125
Tanenhaus, Michael   32
tax compliance, using conformity to
    increase   117
tax cuts/relief   259
teenagers in Detroit, dialect study   227–8
television, origins of   240
temporal expressions   105
Thaler, Richard   288–9
Thompson Medical   150–1
thought prevention   89–92
Tide detergent, ads for   21–3, 127
Toffler, Alvin   8, 8–9
toll booth metaphor   264–5
Tomlin, Russell   82
Toyota ads   70, 152, 230, 231, 234–5
trademark laws   46, 47
traffic accident experiment   109
Tropicana orange juice ad   141
trust
    Mercedes-Benz ad   126–8, 136
    role of oxytocin   12–13
truth
    in conversation   133–5
    and deception in ads   149–51
    and fiction in advertising   183–8
    versus credibility   13–14
truthfulness, default assumption
    of   133–5

"truthiness"   86–9
Tversky, Amos   248–9
Twain, Mark   212–13, 269
typeface, Obama campaign posters   281

unaspirated sounds   28–9
Uncle Sam poster   167
the unconscious   15–16, 24–5
   and creativity   55–6
   and language   28–30
   power of   286
   role in memory   54–5
   subliminal priming   49–54
Unilever products   176–7

Values, Attitudes and Lifestyles survey
   (VALS)   198–9
Vicary, James   50, 51, 52
visual incongruity, attention
   grabbing   66–71
Visual Persuasion (Messaris)   167
visual system   26–7, 62, 286
voice generation, computer   238–40
Volvo ad   79
voting behavior   42–3
   link to vowel-shift   221
   and location   206–9

vowels   41–2
   regional shifts in   214–18

Ward, Gregory   81
"weasel words"   83, 84
Weinberger, Joel   52, 53
Weiss, Michael   210
Westen, Drew   52, 53, 273, 274, 276, 282
Wheeler, Christian   241
Winston cigarettes ad   150–1
Woods, Tiger   178, 187
Word on the Street (McWhorter)   224
word learning   146–7
word recognition   32–3
Word Spy website   48, 123–4
wordplay   71–4, 77–9
words
   linkages between   33–7
   meanings of   123–4
   memories associated with   35–6
   shaping behavior   49–52
Words that Work (Luntz)   259
WWRSD? (What Would the Rational
   Speaker Do?)   130, 133–8

Zhang, Ping   65
zip-code marketing   209–11